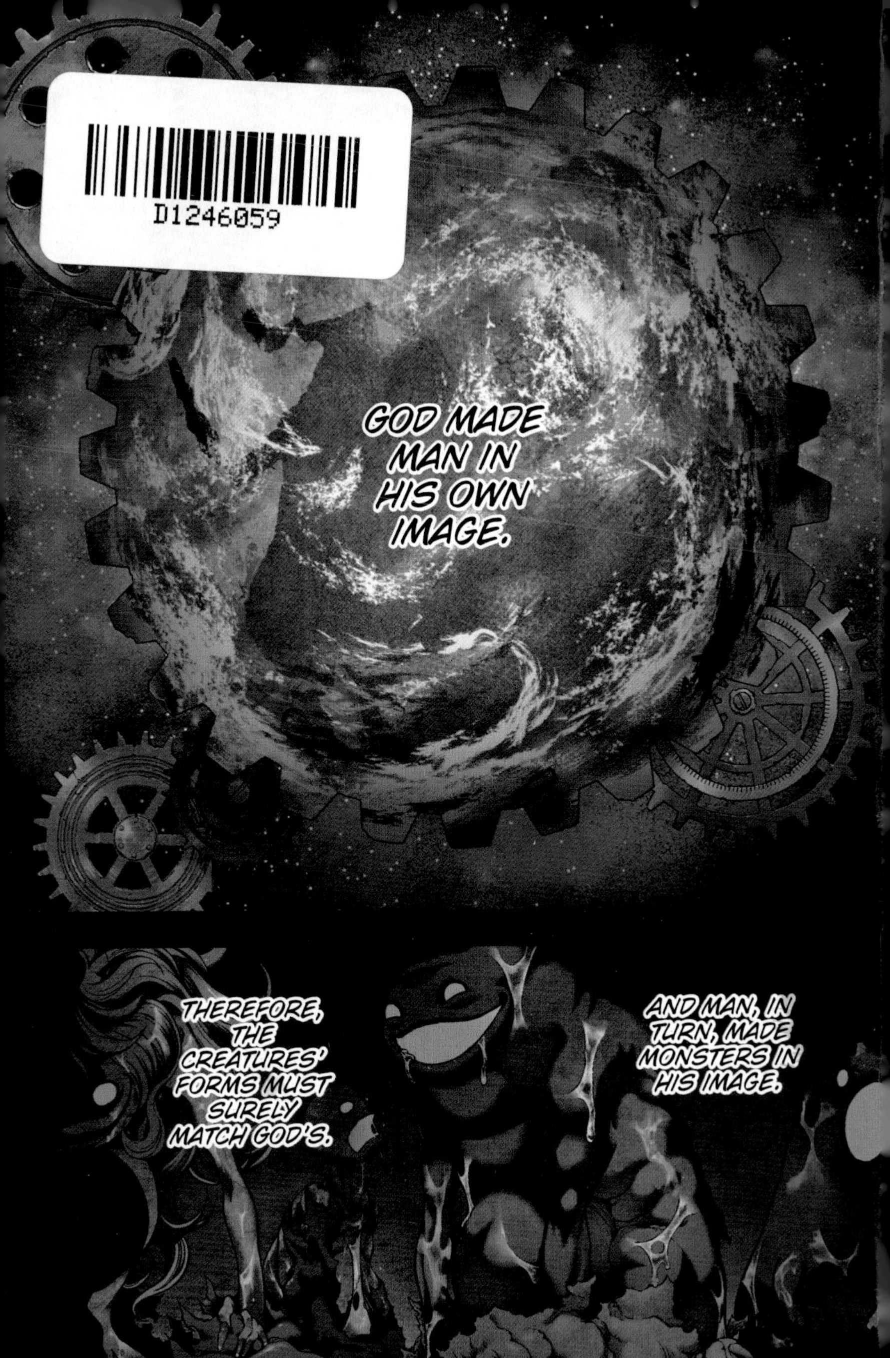
GOD MADE MAN IN HIS OWN IMAGE.
AND MAN, IN TURN, MADE MONSTERS IN HIS IMAGE.
THEREFORE, THE CREATURES' FORMS MUST SURELY MATCH GOD'S.

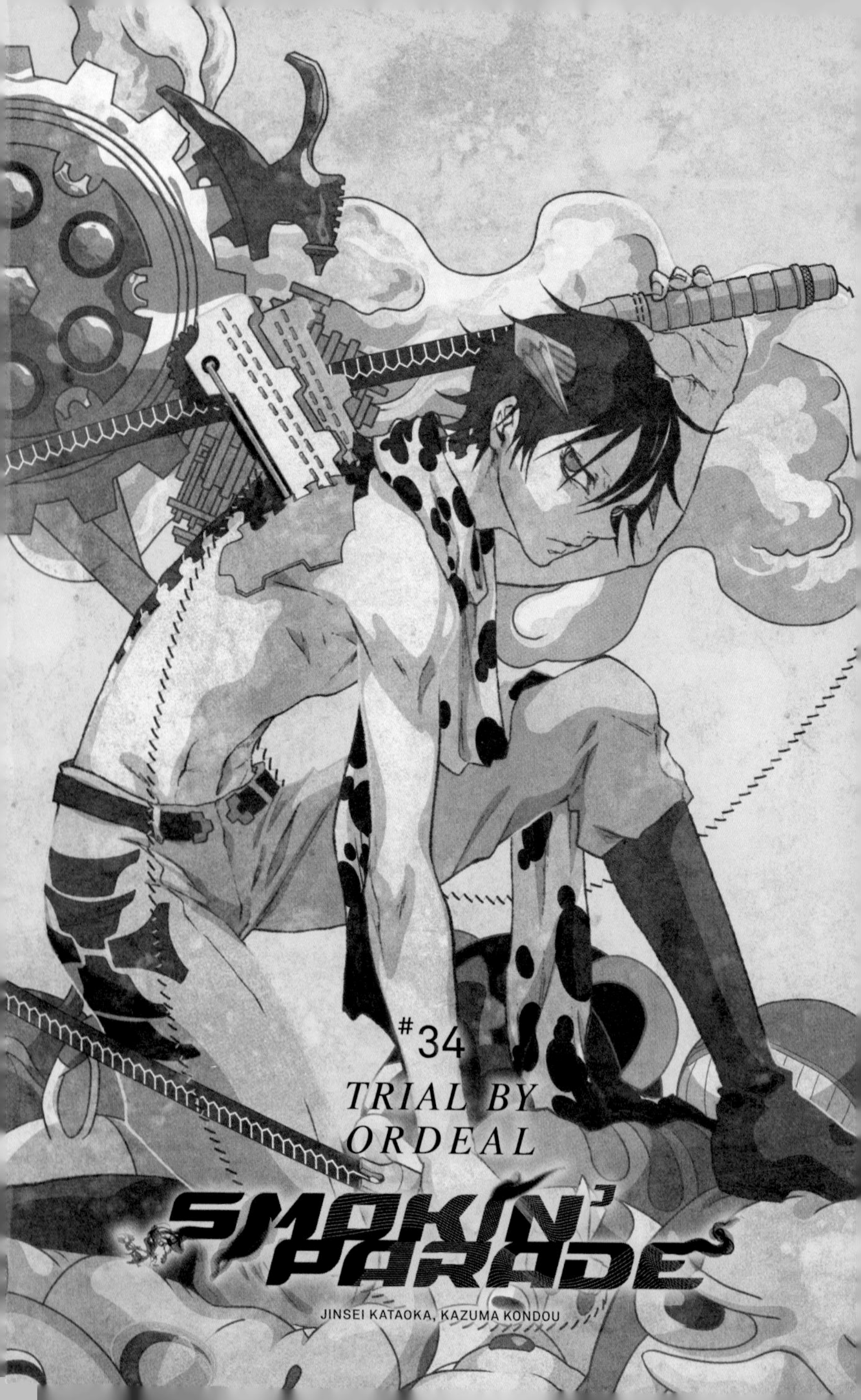
#34
TRIAL BY ORDEAL
SMOKIN' PARADE
JINSEI KATAOKA, KAZUMA KONDOU

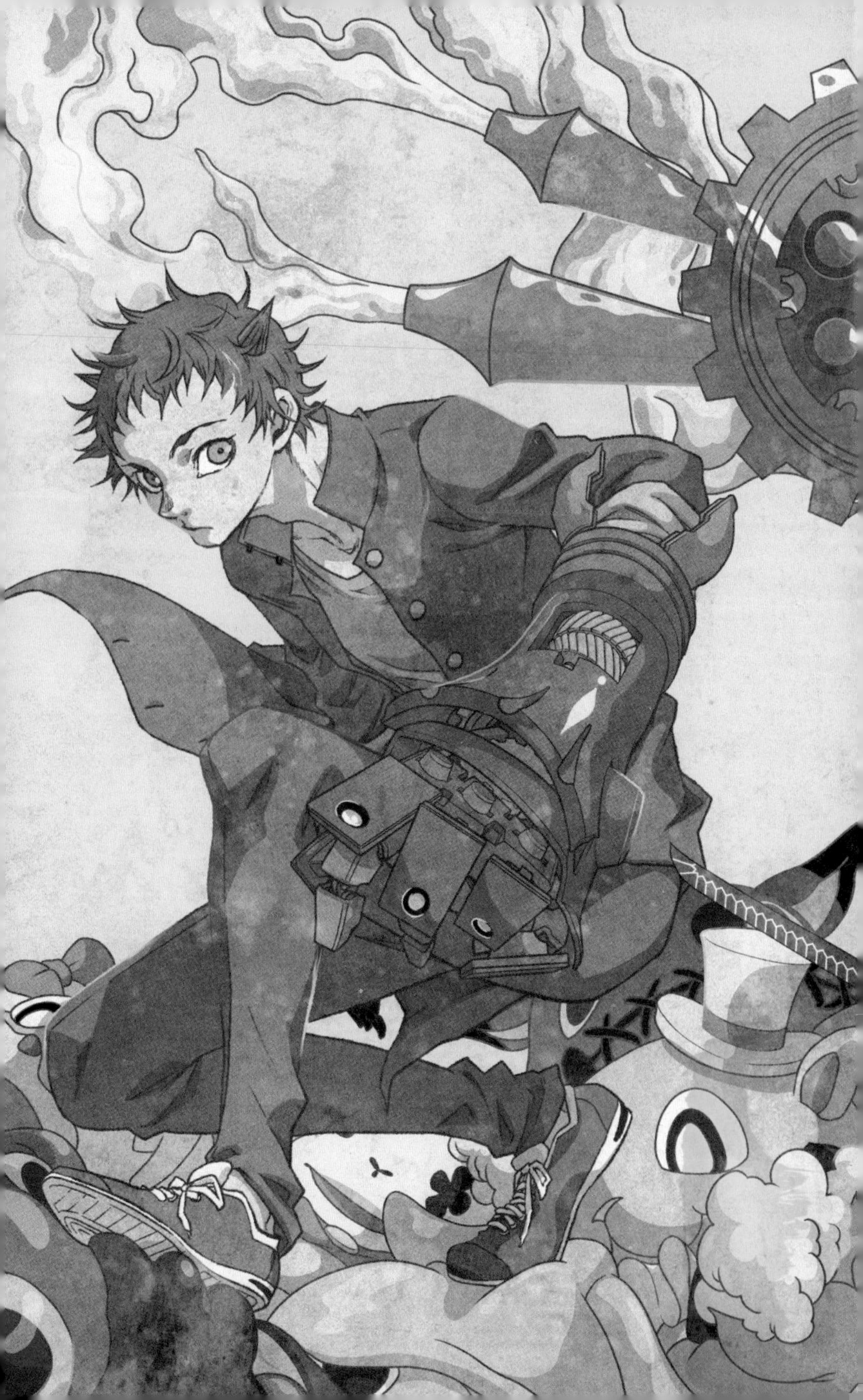

CONTENTS

SMOKIN' PARADE

CHARACTERS

AKUTA

A Jackalope who has taken a liking to Youkou because he sees himself in the kid. A heavy smoker with a sweet tooth.

YOUKOU KAKUJOU

A boy who lost both arms and his right leg when his younger sister turned into a Spider. He has replaced one missing arm with a Gear and joined the Jackalopes.

KOTOHARU

A member of the Jackalopes. He has an incredible amount of respect for Akuta and keeps a collection of items related to him.

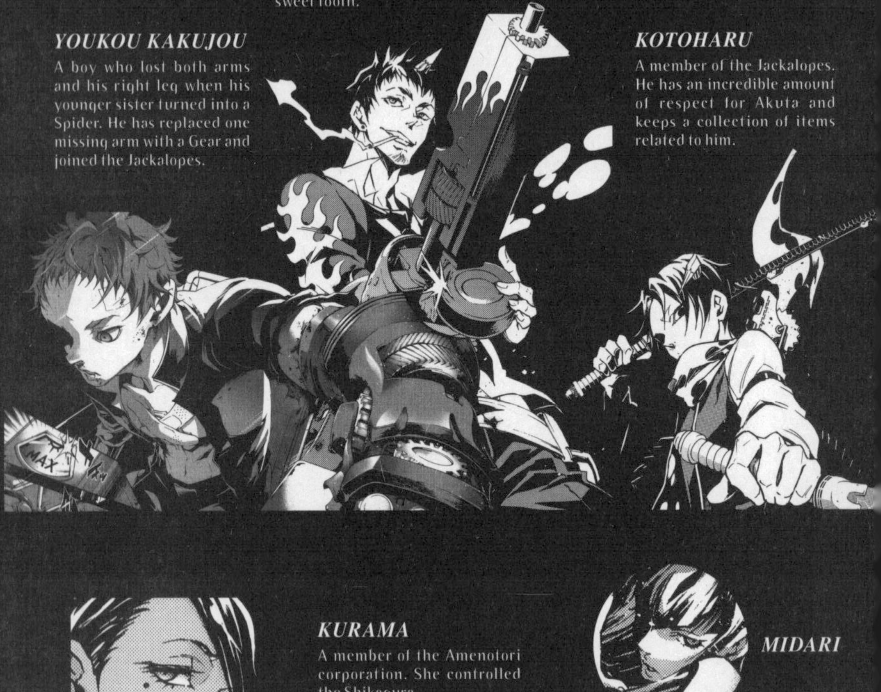
MAX

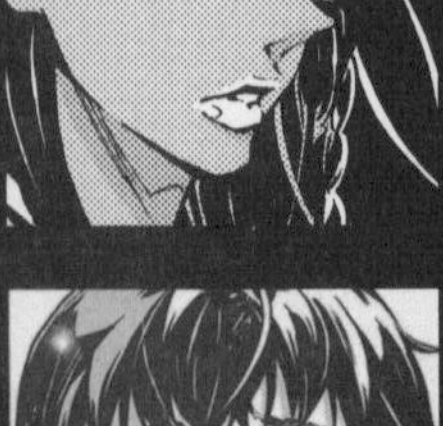

KURAMA

A member of the Amenotori corporation. She controlled the Shikagura.

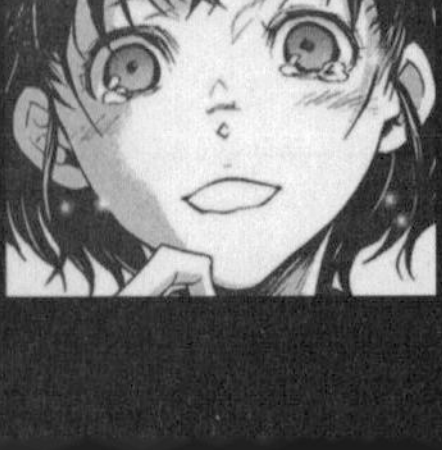

MIRAI KAKUJOU

Youkou's younger sister. She was believed to be dead, but instead she has turned into a Spider and is still living.

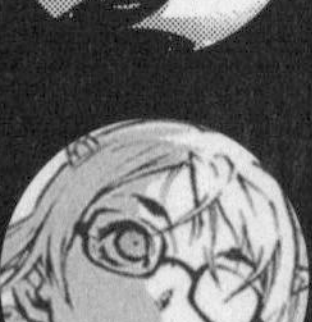

MIDARI

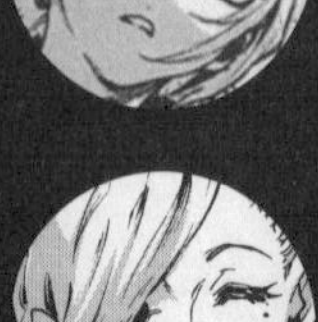

MATSUGO

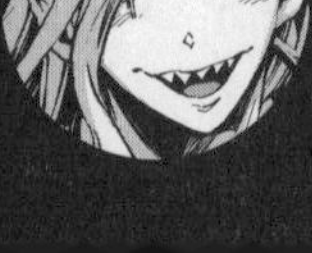

DOC

PORO
(PLOP)

〈HUH?
THANKS.〉

〈WHAT
IS THAT?〉

〈—YOU DROPPED
SOMETHING.〉

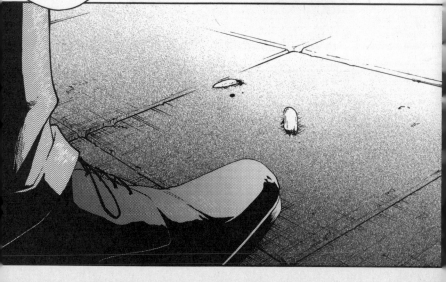

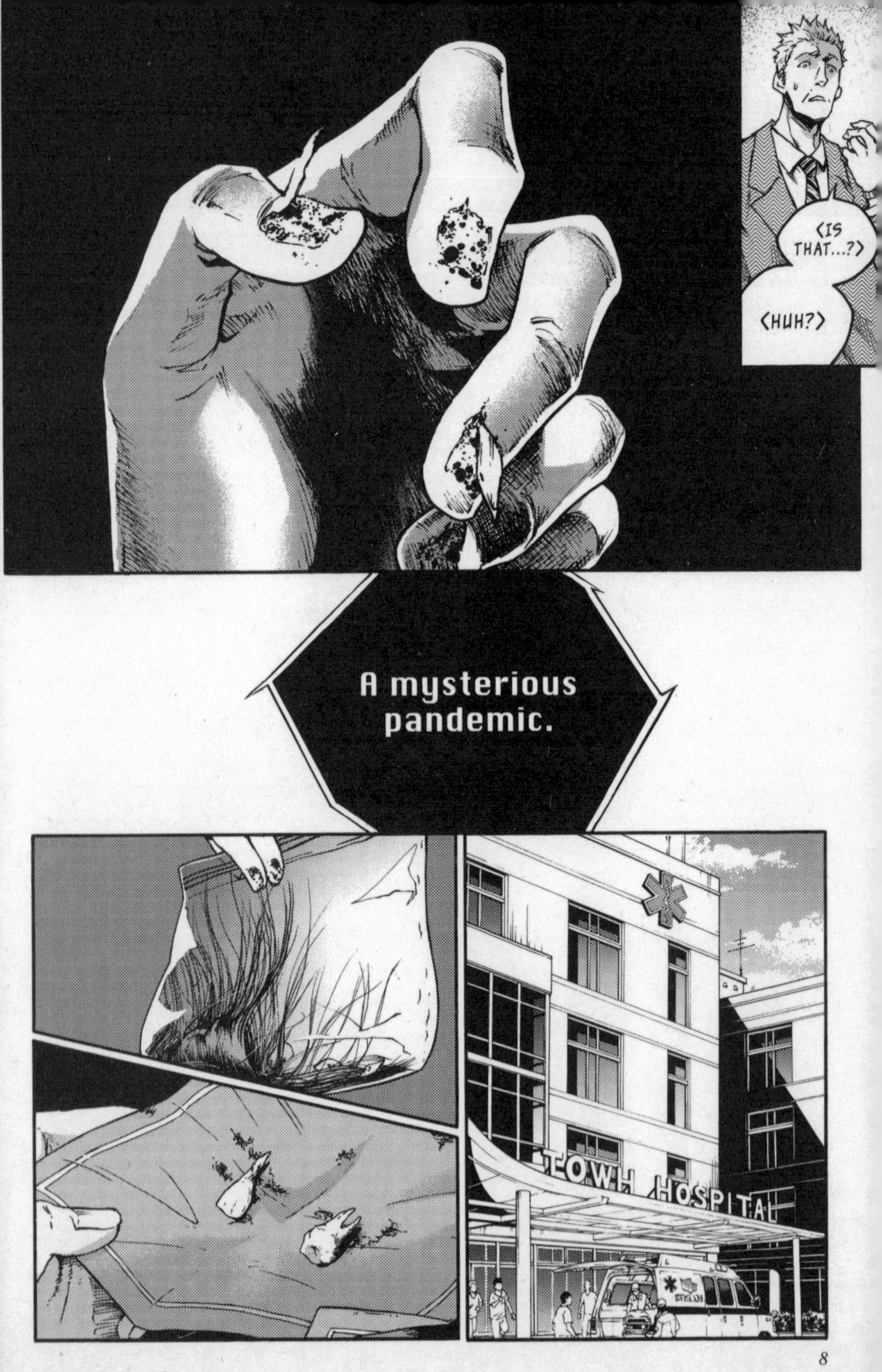
<IS THAT...?>
<HUH?>
A mysterious pandemic.
TOWN HOSPITAL

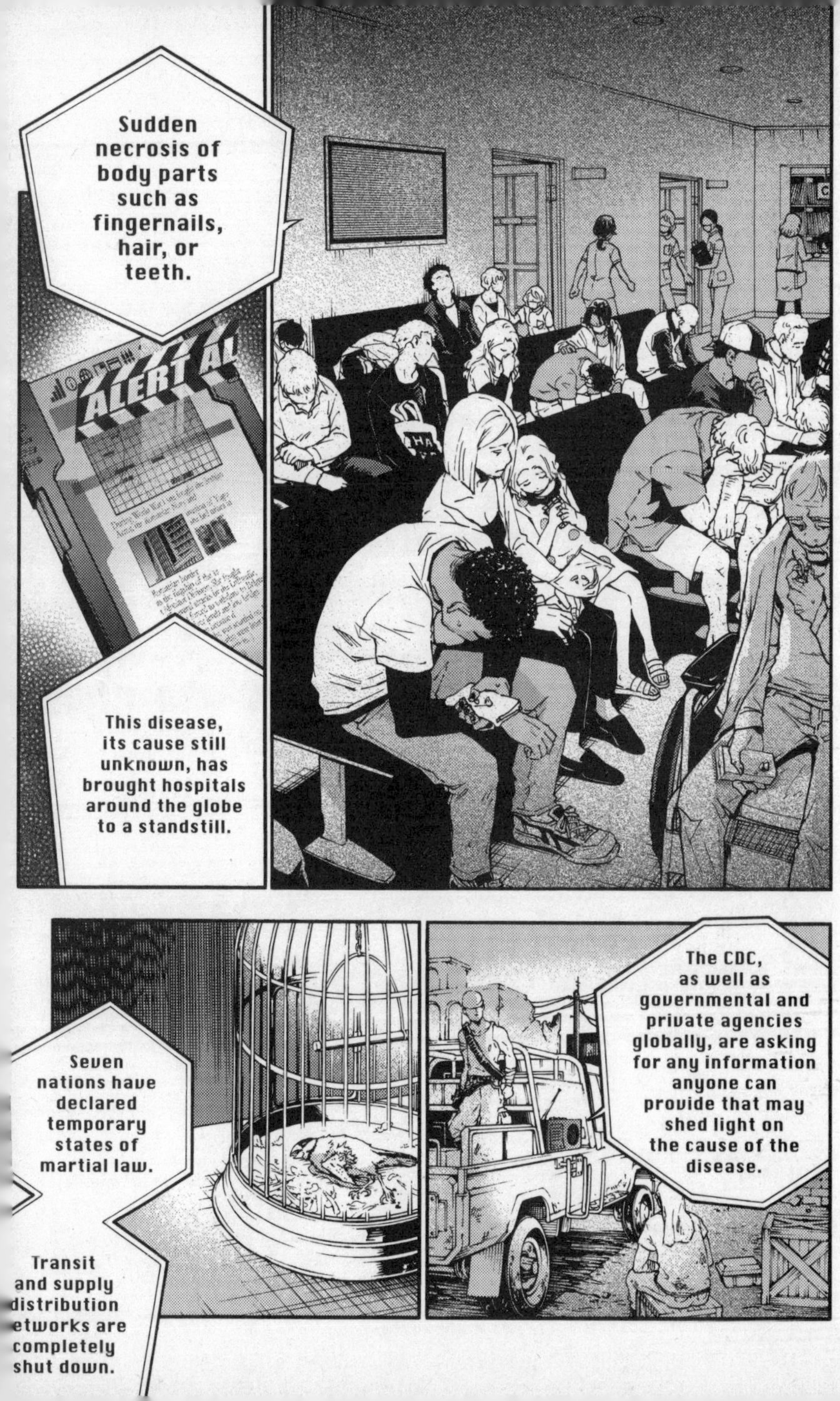
Sudden necrosis of body parts such as fingernails, hair, or teeth.
ALERT AL
This disease, its cause still unknown, has brought hospitals around the globe to a standstill.
The CDC, as well as governmental and private agencies globally, are asking for any information anyone can provide that may shed light on the cause of the disease.
Seven nations have declared temporary states of martial law.
Transit and supply distribution etworks are completely shut down.

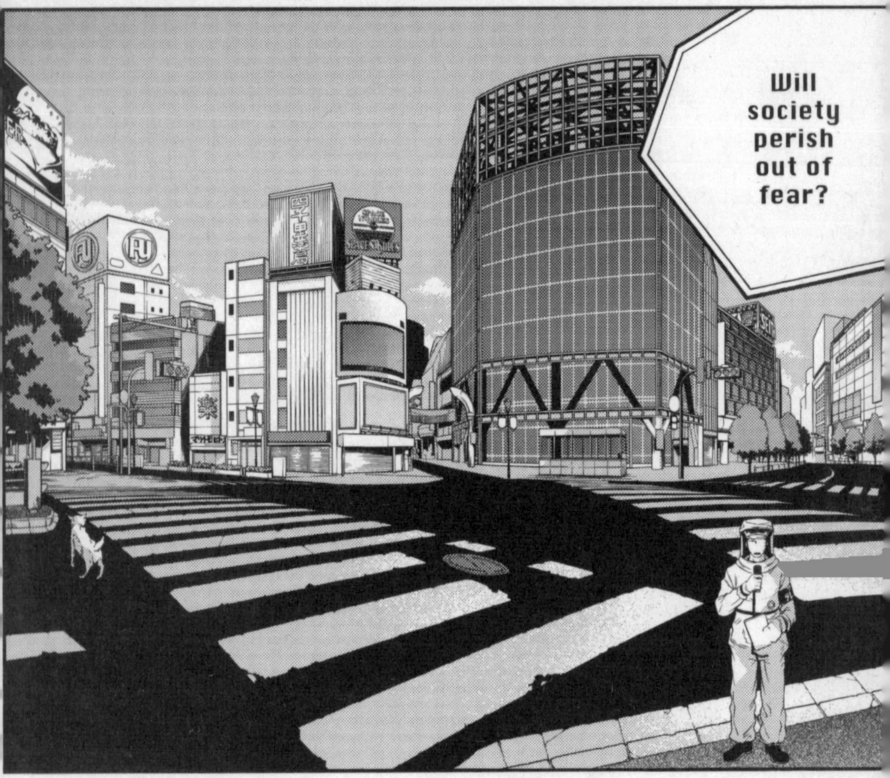
Will society perish out of fear?
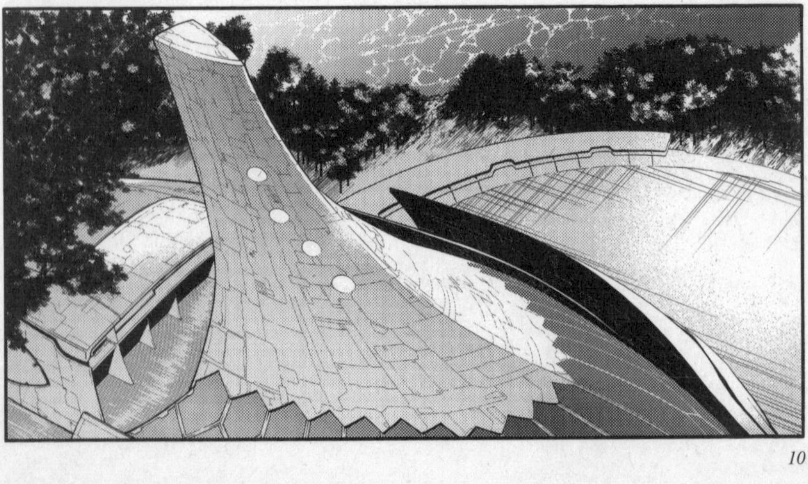

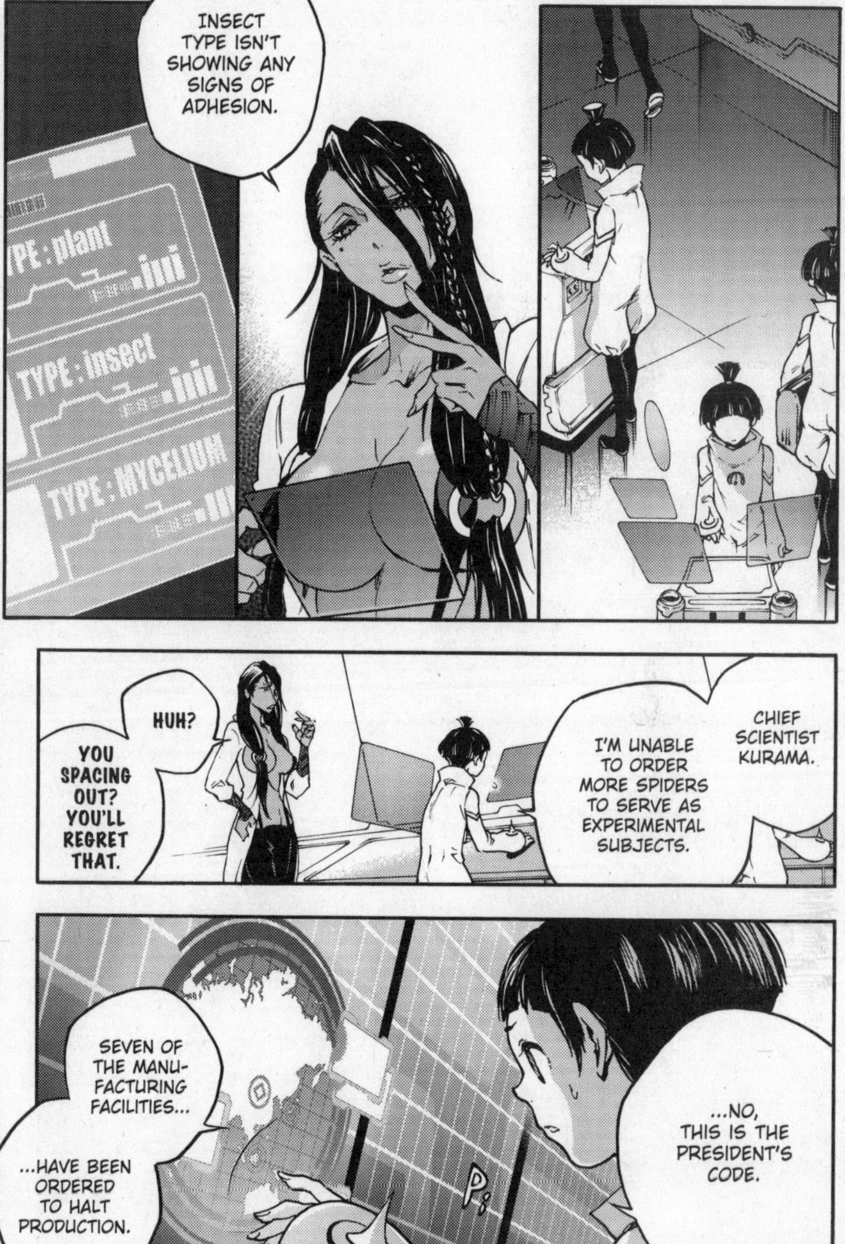
TYPE : plant
TYPE : insect
TYPE : MYCELIUM
INSECT TYPE ISN'T SHOWING ANY SIGNS OF ADHESION.
CHIEF SCIENTIST KURAMA.
I'M UNABLE TO ORDER MORE SPIDERS TO SERVE AS EXPERIMENTAL SUBJECTS.
HUH?
YOU SPACING OUT? YOU'LL REGRET THAT.
SEVEN OF THE MANU-FACTURING FACILITIES...
...HAVE BEEN ORDERED TO HALT PRODUCTION.
Pi
...NO, THIS IS THE PRESIDENT'S CODE.

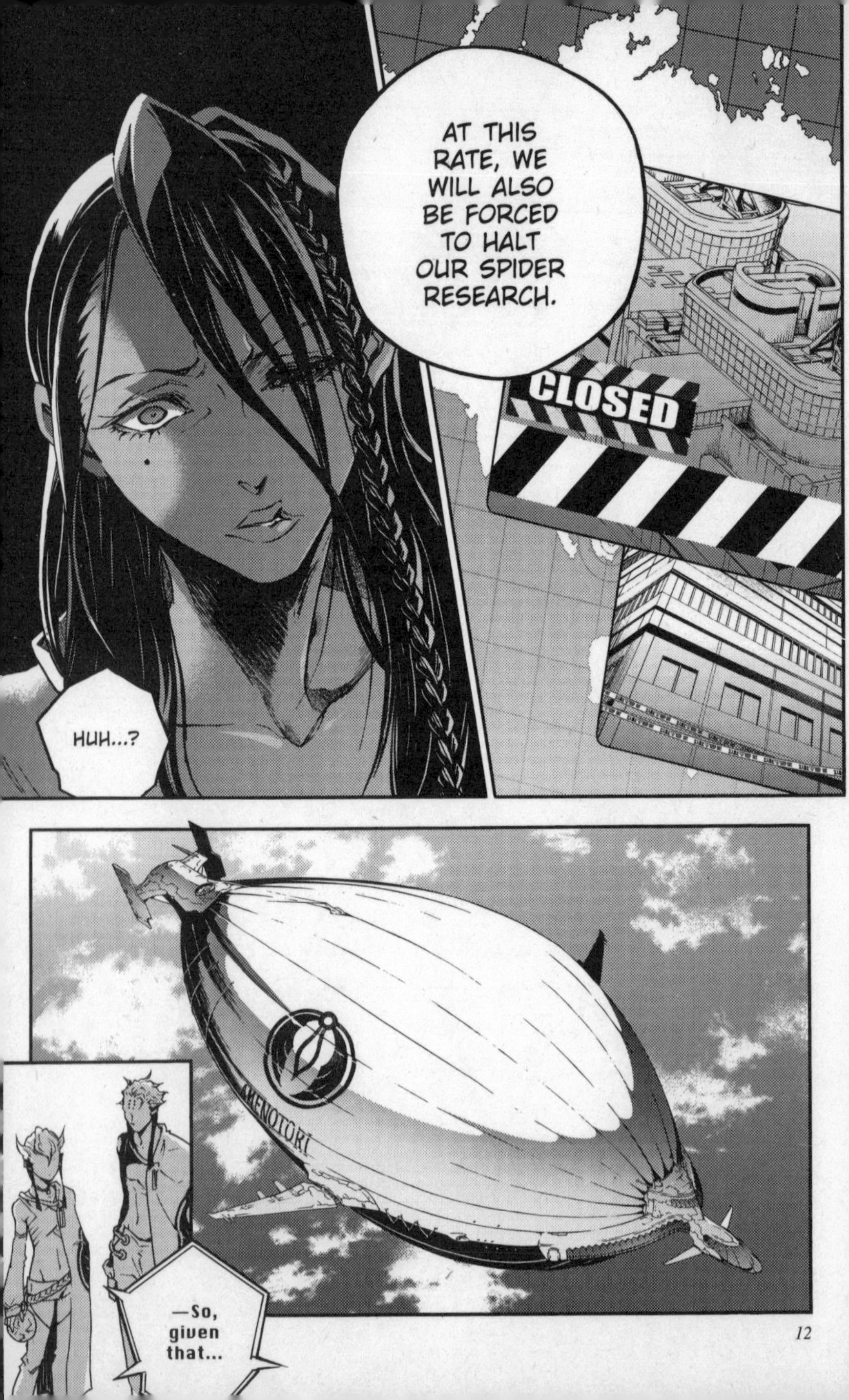
AT THIS RATE, WE WILL ALSO BE FORCED TO HALT OUR SPIDER RESEARCH.
CLOSED
HUH...?
AMENOTORI
—So, given that...

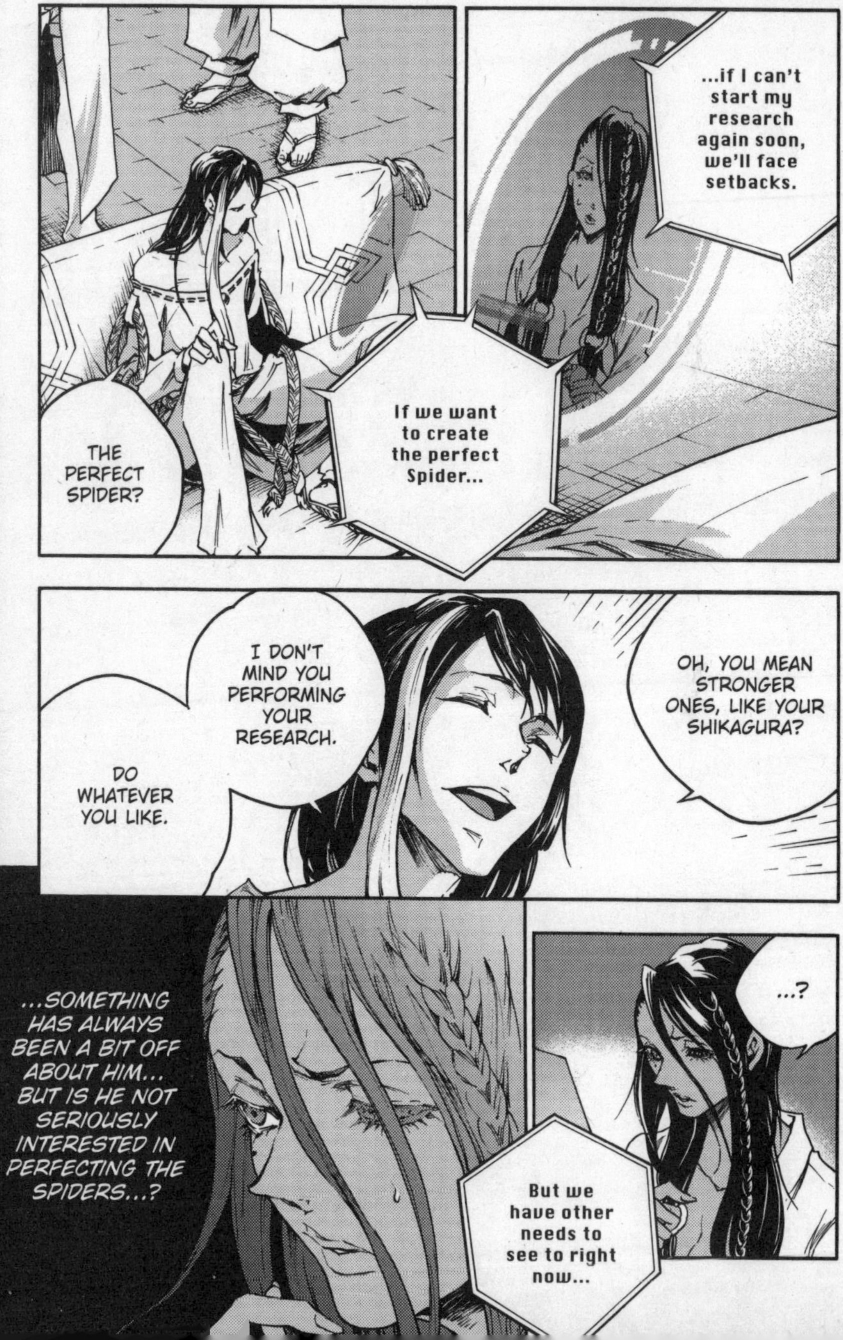
If we want to create the perfect Spider...
...if I can't start my research again soon, we'll face setbacks.
THE PERFECT SPIDER?
OH, YOU MEAN STRONGER ONES, LIKE YOUR SHIKAGURA?
I DON'T MIND YOU PERFORMING YOUR RESEARCH.
DO WHATEVER YOU LIKE.
...?
But we have other needs to see to right now...
...SOMETHING HAS ALWAYS BEEN A BIT OFF ABOUT HIM... BUT IS HE NOT SERIOUSLY INTERESTED IN PERFECTING THE SPIDERS...?

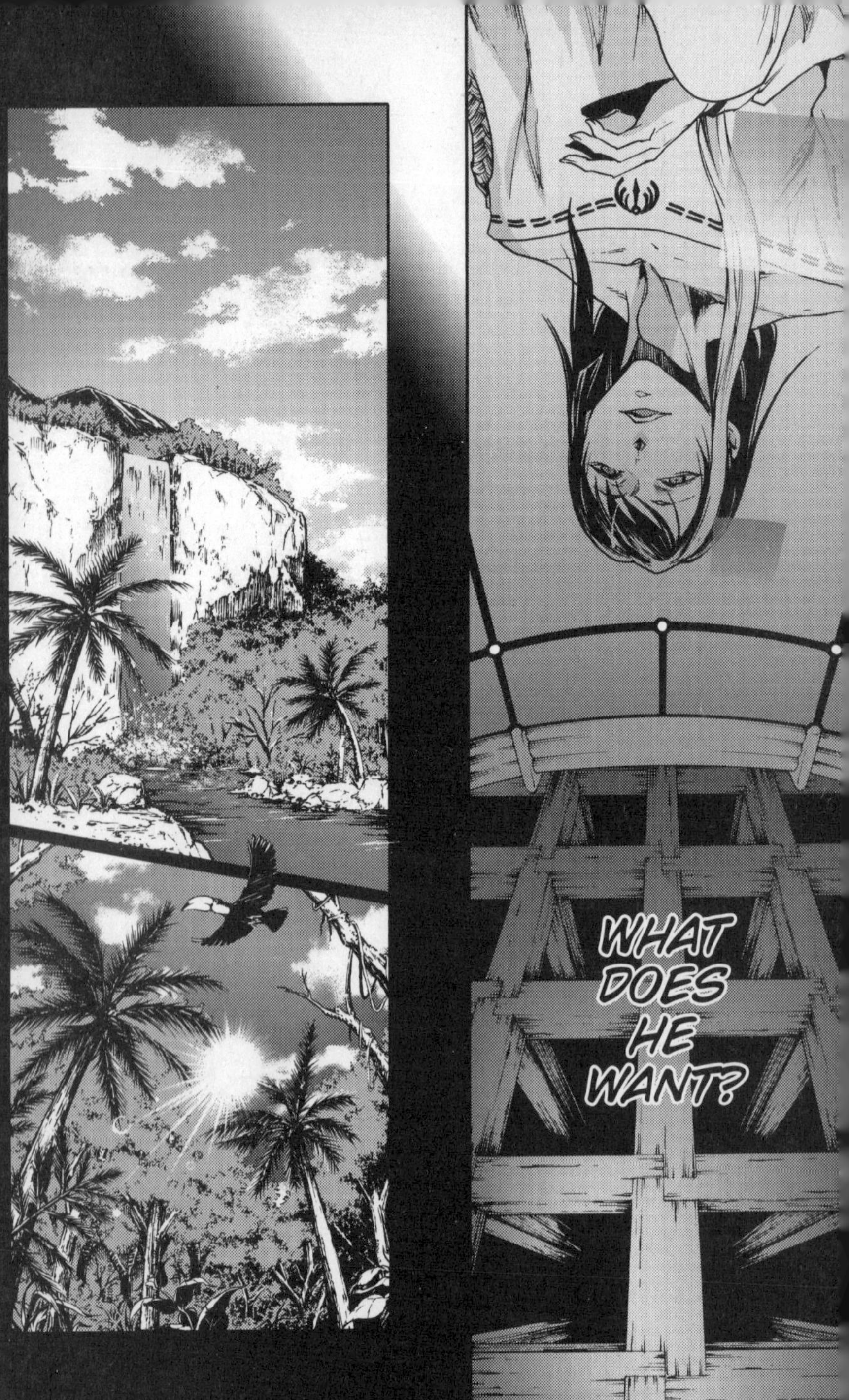
WHAT DOES HE WANT?

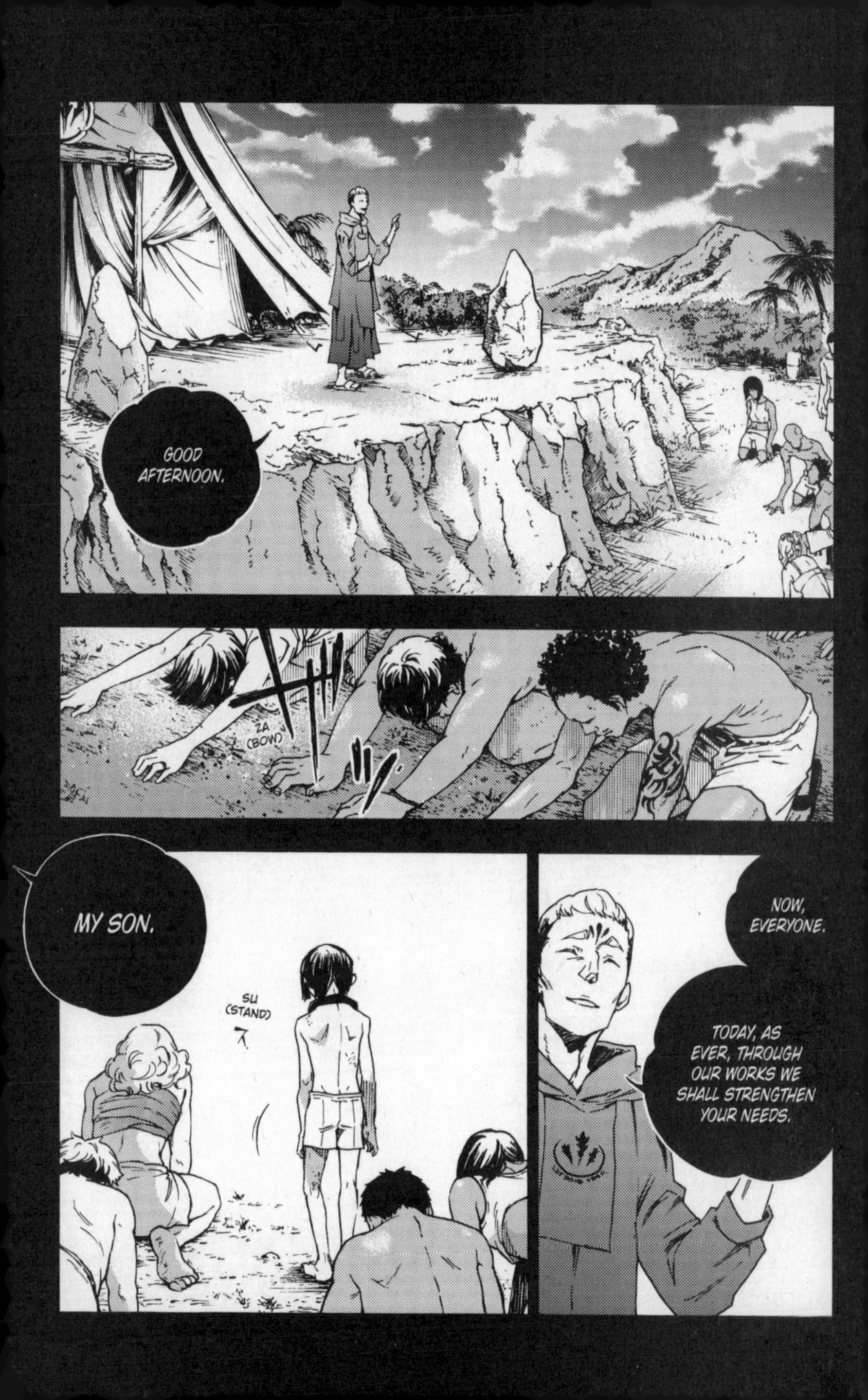
GOOD AFTERNOON.
ZA (BOW)
NOW, EVERYONE.
TODAY, AS EVER, THROUGH OUR WORKS WE SHALL STRENGTHEN YOUR NEEDS.
MY SON.
SU (STAND)

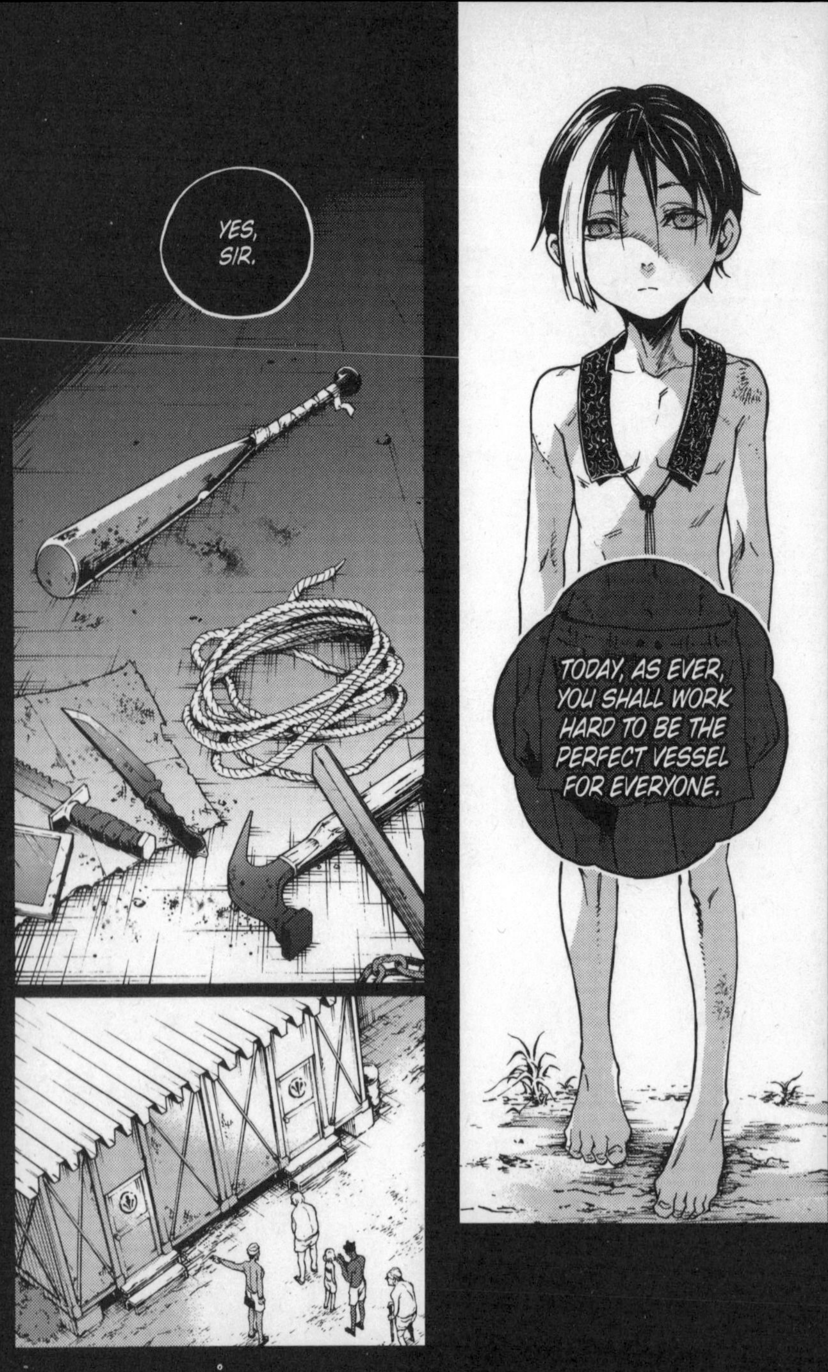
TODAY, AS EVER, YOU SHALL WORK HARD TO BE THE PERFECT VESSEL FOR EVERYONE.
YES, SIR.

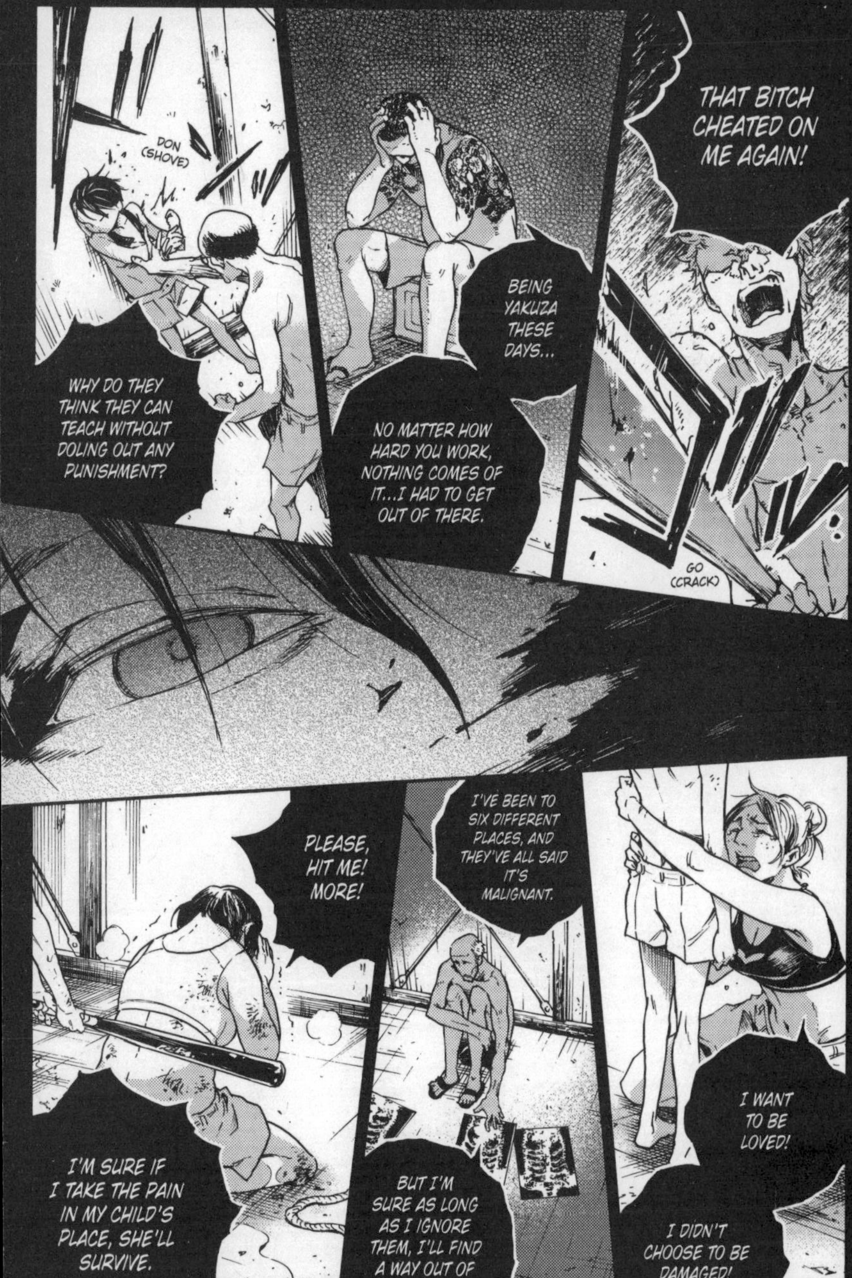
THAT BITCH CHEATED ON ME AGAIN!
GO (CRACK)
BEING YAKUZA THESE DAYS...
NO MATTER HOW HARD YOU WORK, NOTHING COMES OF IT...I HAD TO GET OUT OF THERE.
DON (SHOVE)
WHY DO THEY THINK THEY CAN TEACH WITHOUT DOLING OUT ANY PUNISHMENT?
I WANT TO BE LOVED!
I DIDN'T CHOOSE TO BE DAMAGED!
I'VE BEEN TO SIX DIFFERENT PLACES, AND THEY'VE ALL SAID IT'S MALIGNANT.
BUT I'M SURE AS LONG AS I IGNORE THEM, I'LL FIND A WAY OUT OF THIS.
PLEASE, HIT ME! MORE!
I'M SURE IF I TAKE THE PAIN IN MY CHILD'S PLACE, SHE'LL SURVIVE.

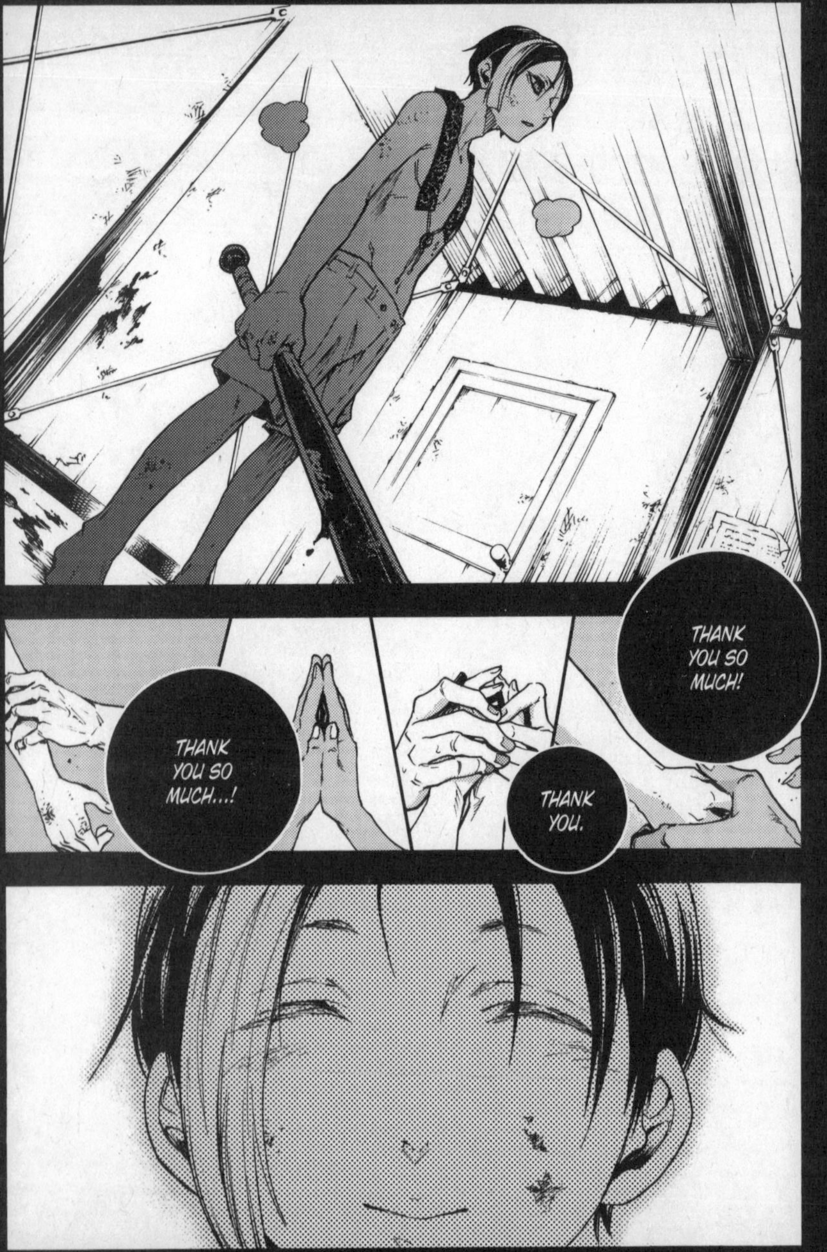
THANK YOU SO MUCH!
THANK YOU.
THANK YOU SO MUCH...!

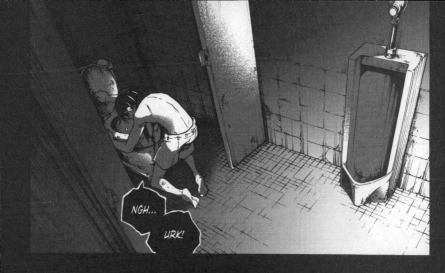

NGH...

URK!

IF GOD AND MAN SHARE THE SAME FORM...

...THEN GOD MUST HAVE WORKING EARS.

AND IF GOD HAS A WORKING BRAIN...

...THEN HOW DOES HE DEAL WITH THE CONSTANT BARRAGE OF DESIRES DRESSED UP AS PRAYER, 365 DAYS, 31,536,000 SECONDS...

...WITHOUT BREAKING?

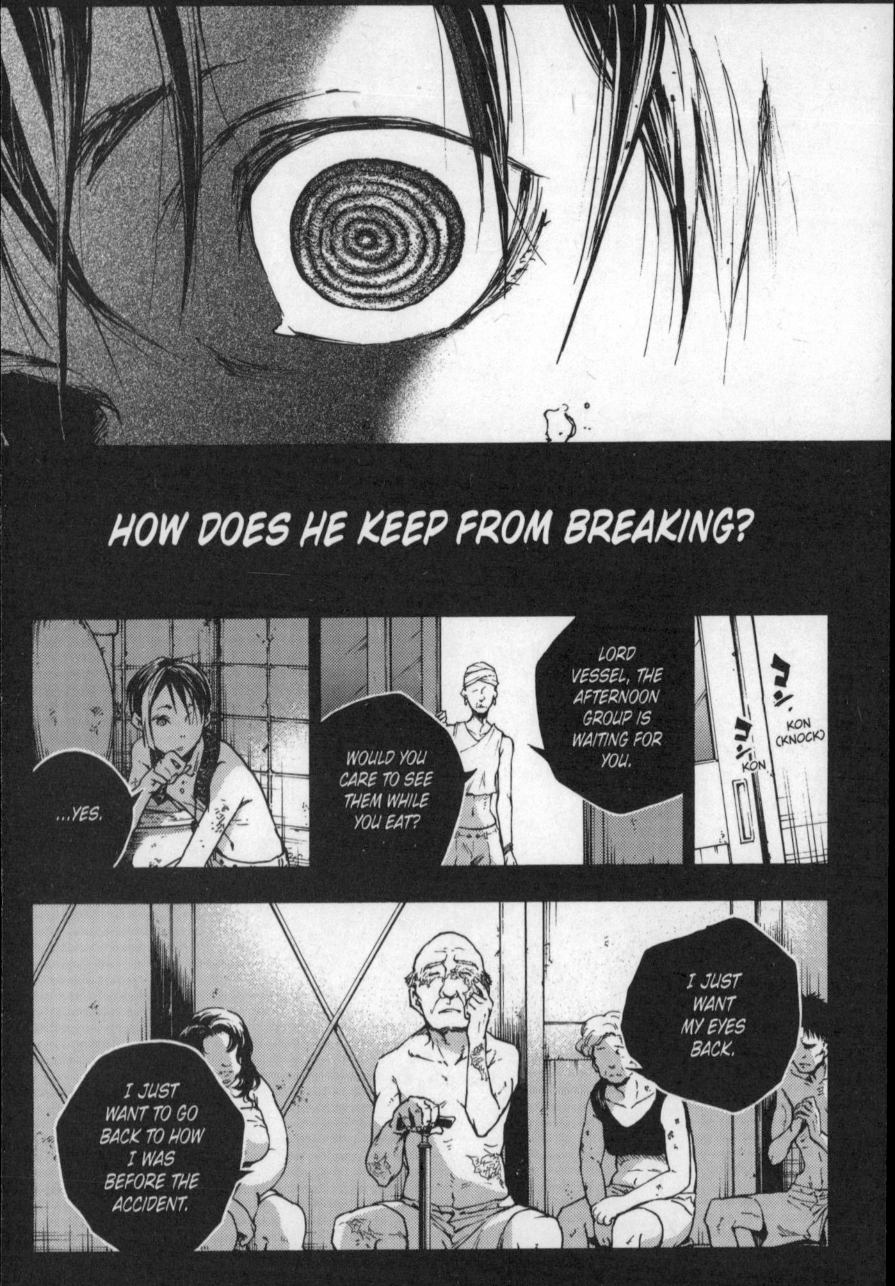
HOW DOES HE KEEP FROM BREAKING?
KON (KNOCK)
KON
LORD VESSEL, THE AFTERNOON GROUP IS WAITING FOR YOU.
WOULD YOU CARE TO SEE THEM WHILE YOU EAT?
...YES.
I JUST WANT MY EYES BACK.
I JUST WANT TO GO BACK TO HOW I WAS BEFORE THE ACCIDENT.

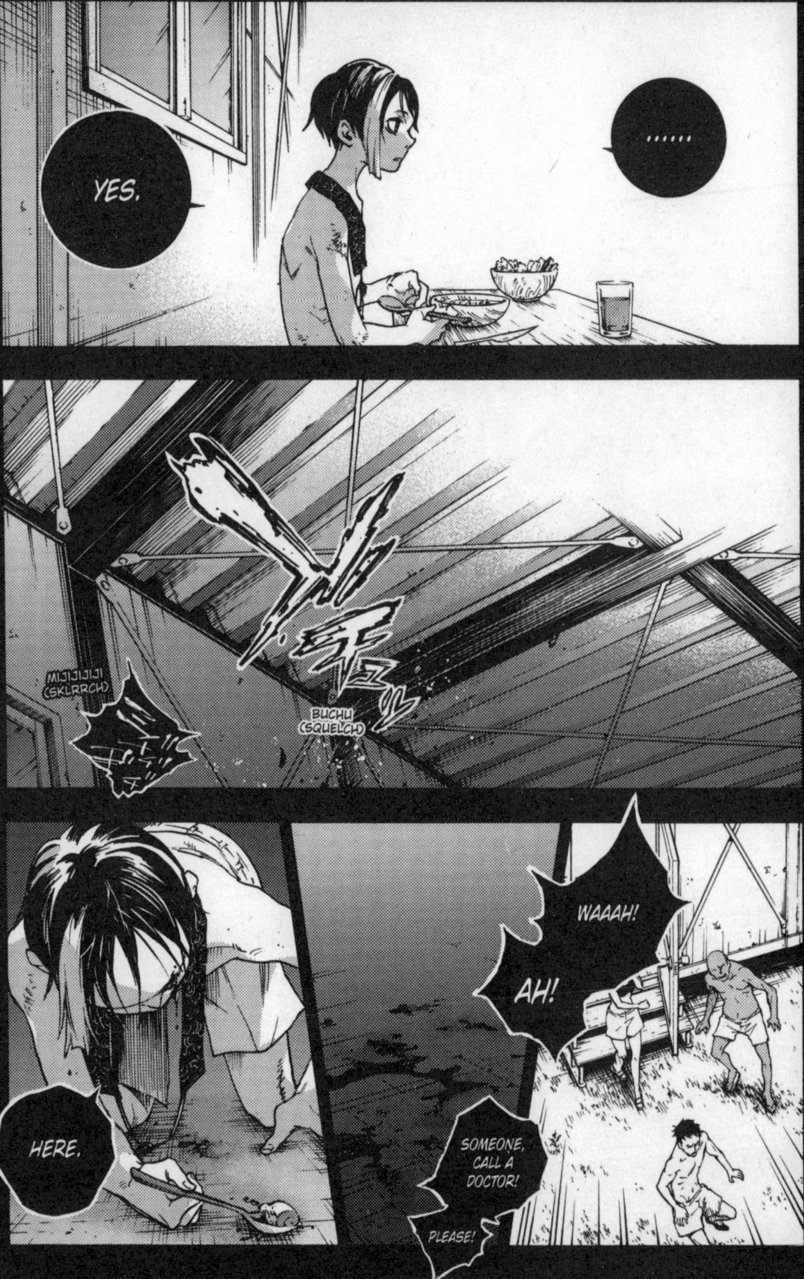
......
YES.
BUCHU (SQUELCH)
MIJIJIJI (SKLRRCH)
WAAAH!
AH!
SOMEONE, CALL A DOCTOR!
PLEASE!
HERE.

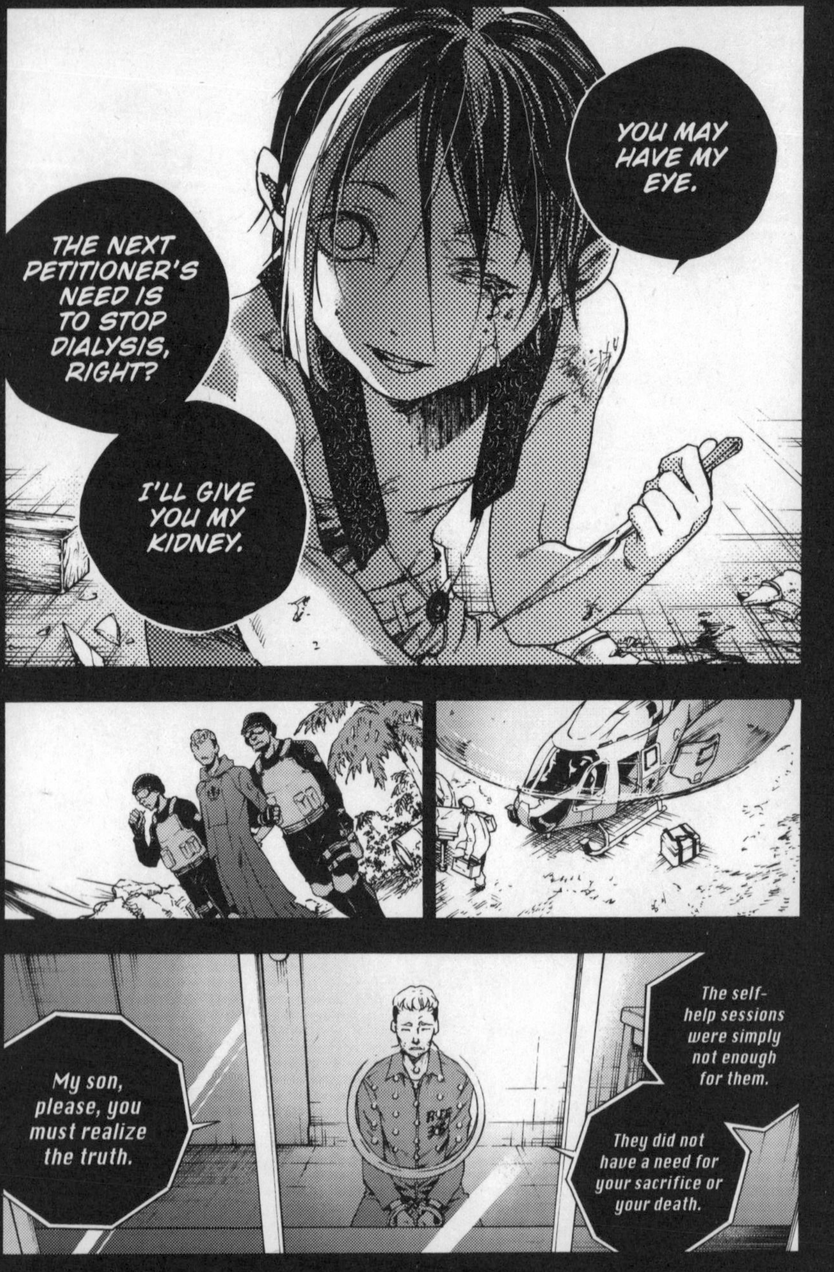
YOU MAY HAVE MY EYE.
THE NEXT PETITIONER'S NEED IS TO STOP DIALYSIS, RIGHT?
I'LL GIVE YOU MY KIDNEY.
The self-help sessions were simply not enough for them.
They did not have a need for your sacrifice or your death.
My son, please, you must realize the truth.

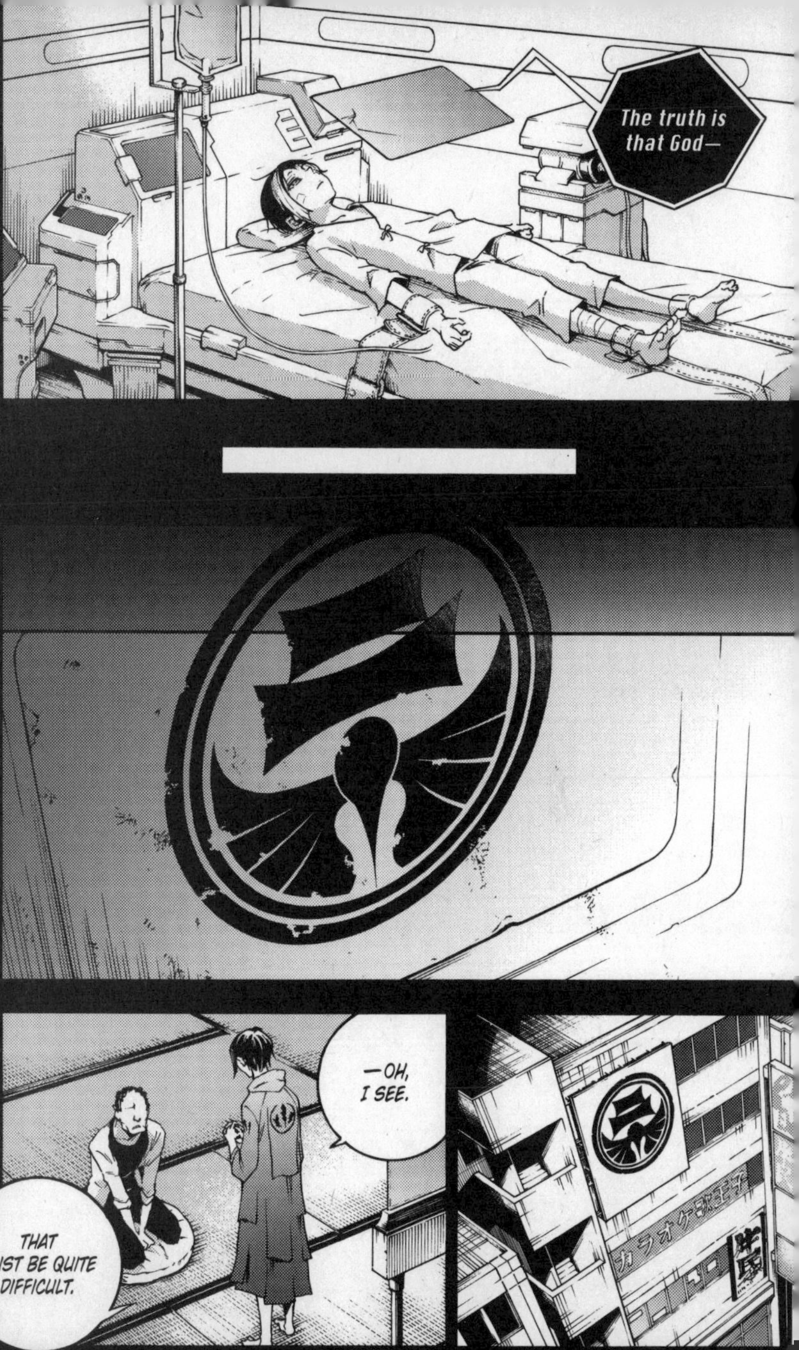
The truth is that God—
—OH, I SEE.
THAT MUST BE QUITE DIFFICULT.

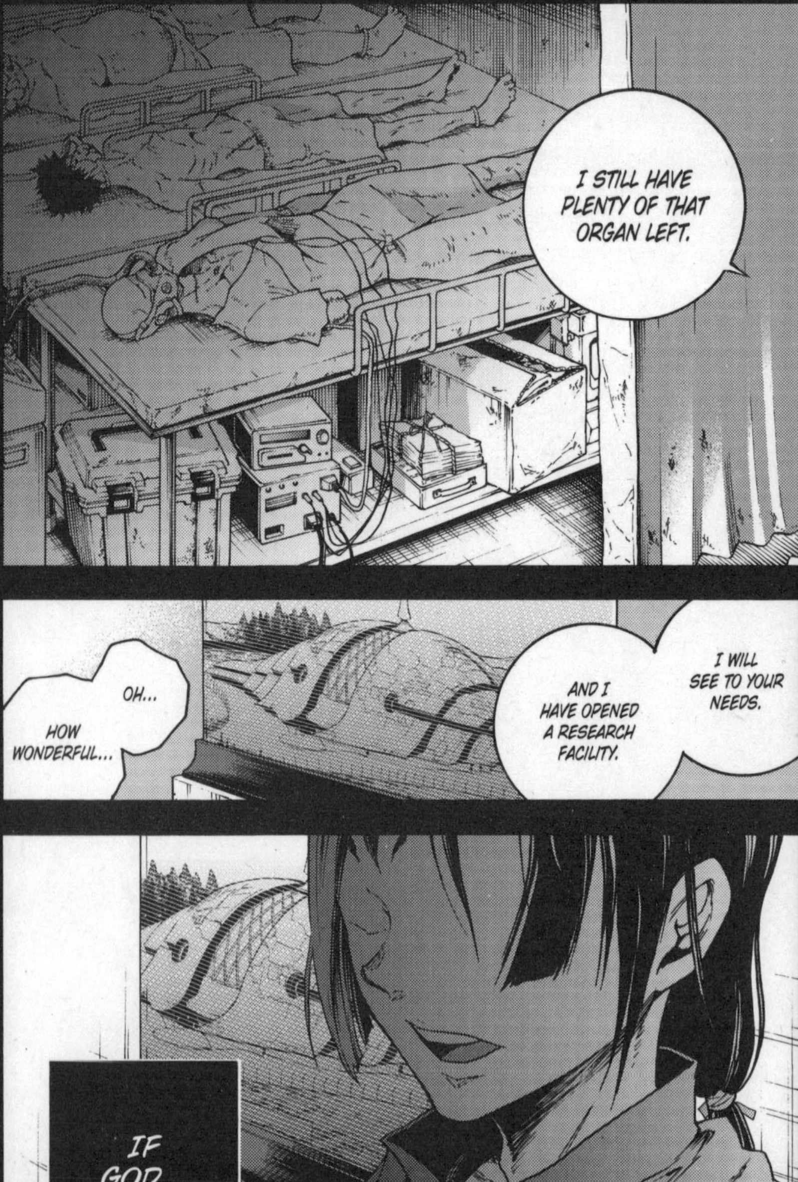
I STILL HAVE PLENTY OF THAT ORGAN LEFT.
I WILL SEE TO YOUR NEEDS.
AND I HAVE OPENED A RESEARCH FACILITY.
OH...
HOW WONDERFUL...
IF GOD...

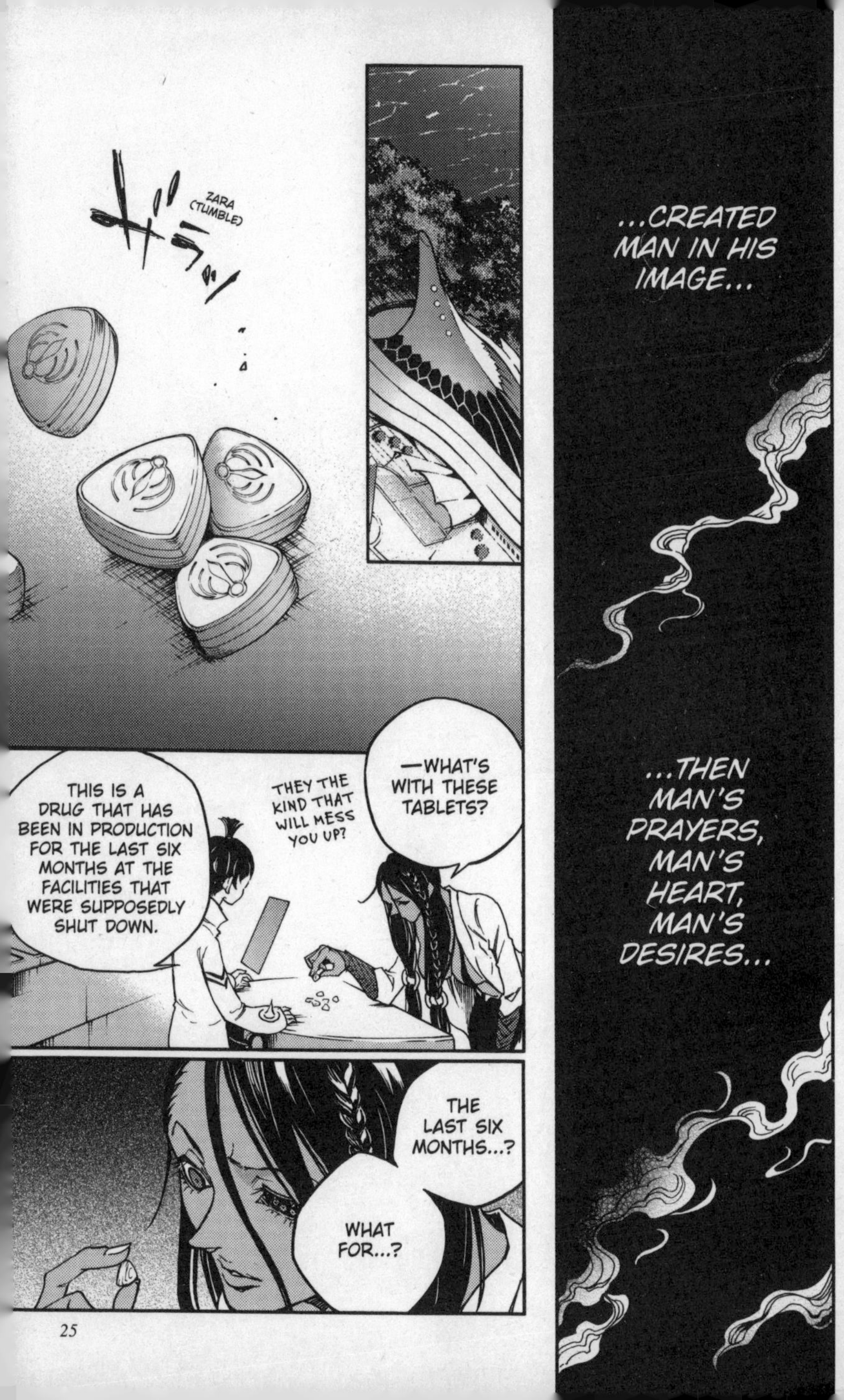
...CREATED MAN IN HIS IMAGE...
...THEN MAN'S PRAYERS, MAN'S HEART, MAN'S DESIRES...
ZARA (TUMBLE)
—WHAT'S WITH THESE TABLETS?
THEY THE KIND THAT WILL MESS YOU UP?
THIS IS A DRUG THAT HAS BEEN IN PRODUCTION FOR THE LAST SIX MONTHS AT THE FACILITIES THAT WERE SUPPOSEDLY SHUT DOWN.
THE LAST SIX MONTHS...?
WHAT FOR...?

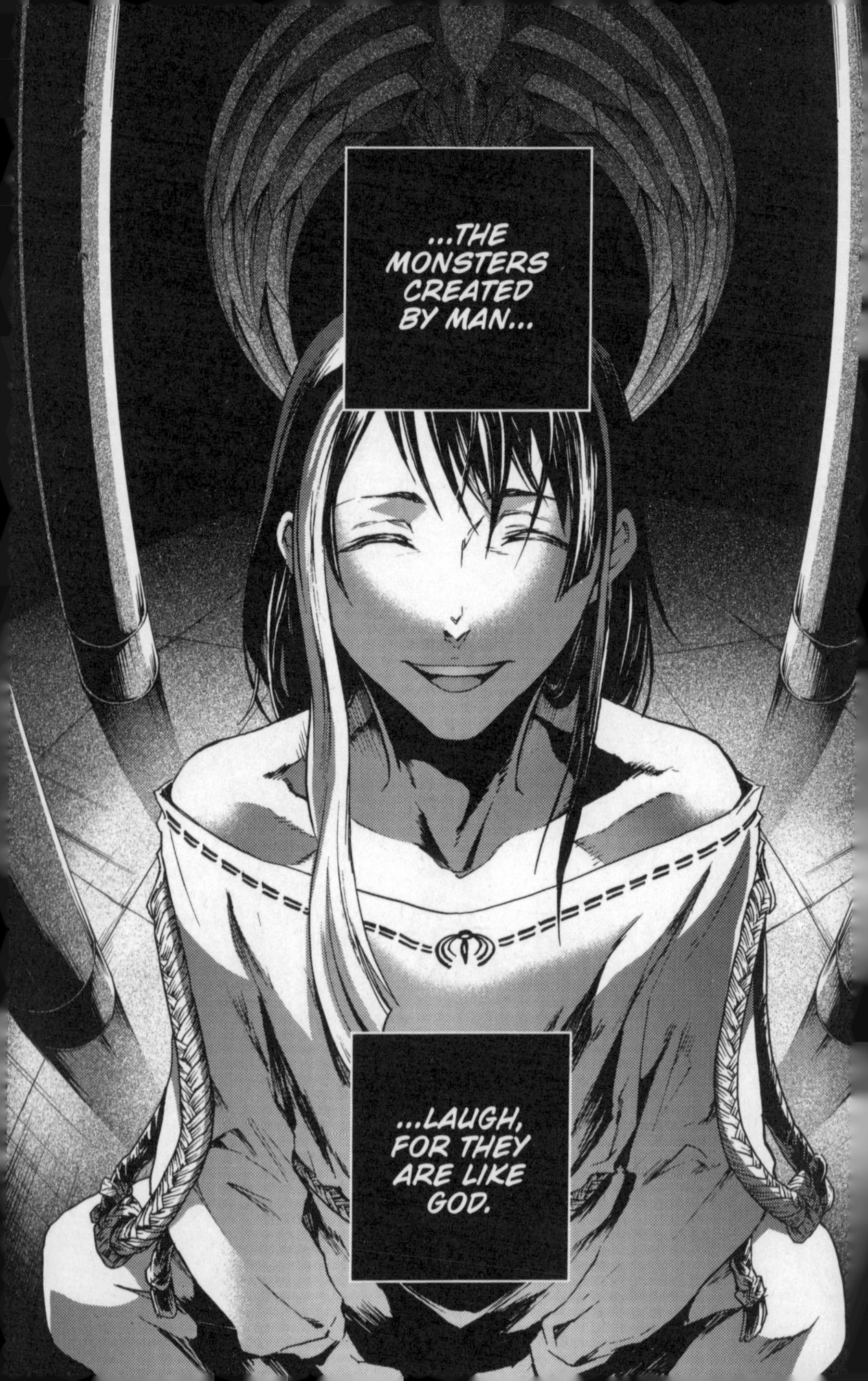
...THE MONSTERS CREATED BY MAN...
...LAUGH, FOR THEY ARE LIKE GOD.

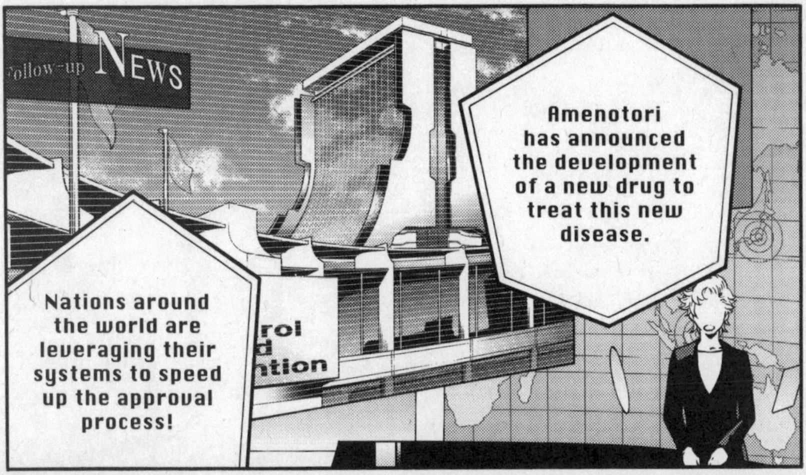
Follow-up NEWS
Amenotori has announced the development of a new drug to treat this new disease.
Nations around the world are leveraging their systems to speed up the approval process!
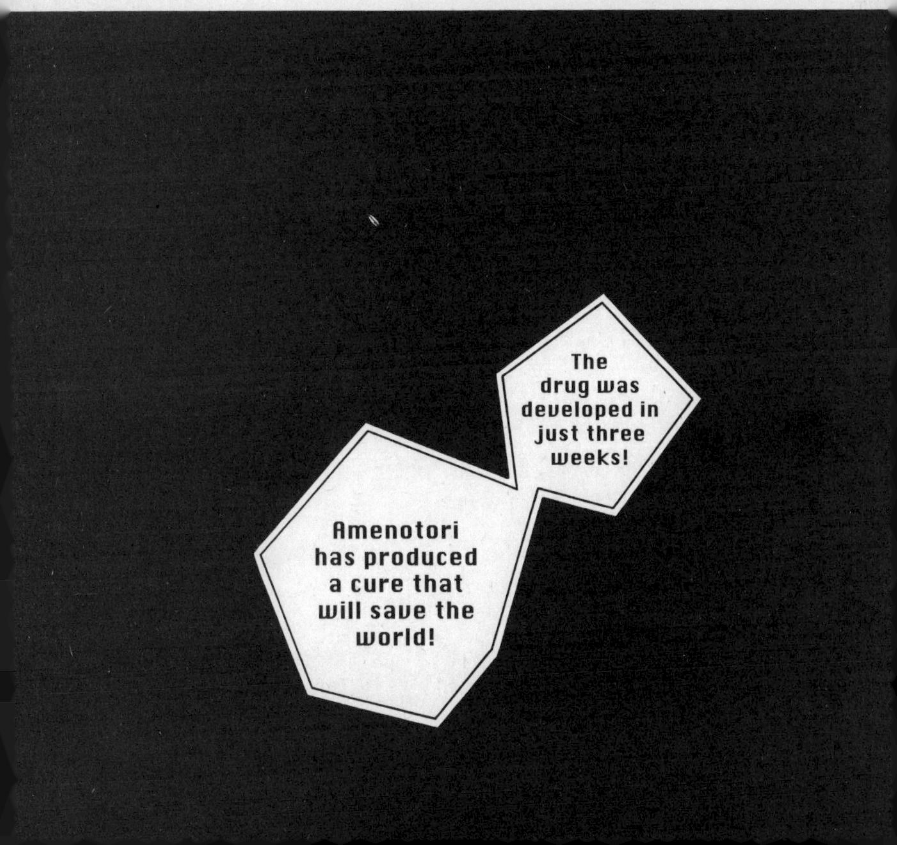
The drug was developed in just three weeks!
Amenotori has produced a cure that will save the world!

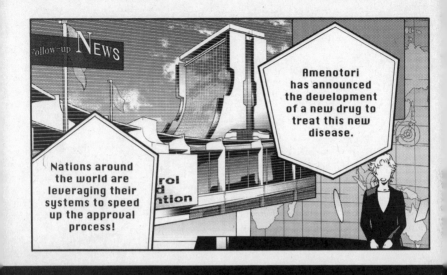

THE WORLD IS DEAD. THE PARADE WILL START.

JINSEI KATAOKA, KAZUMA KONDOU

SMOKING PARADE

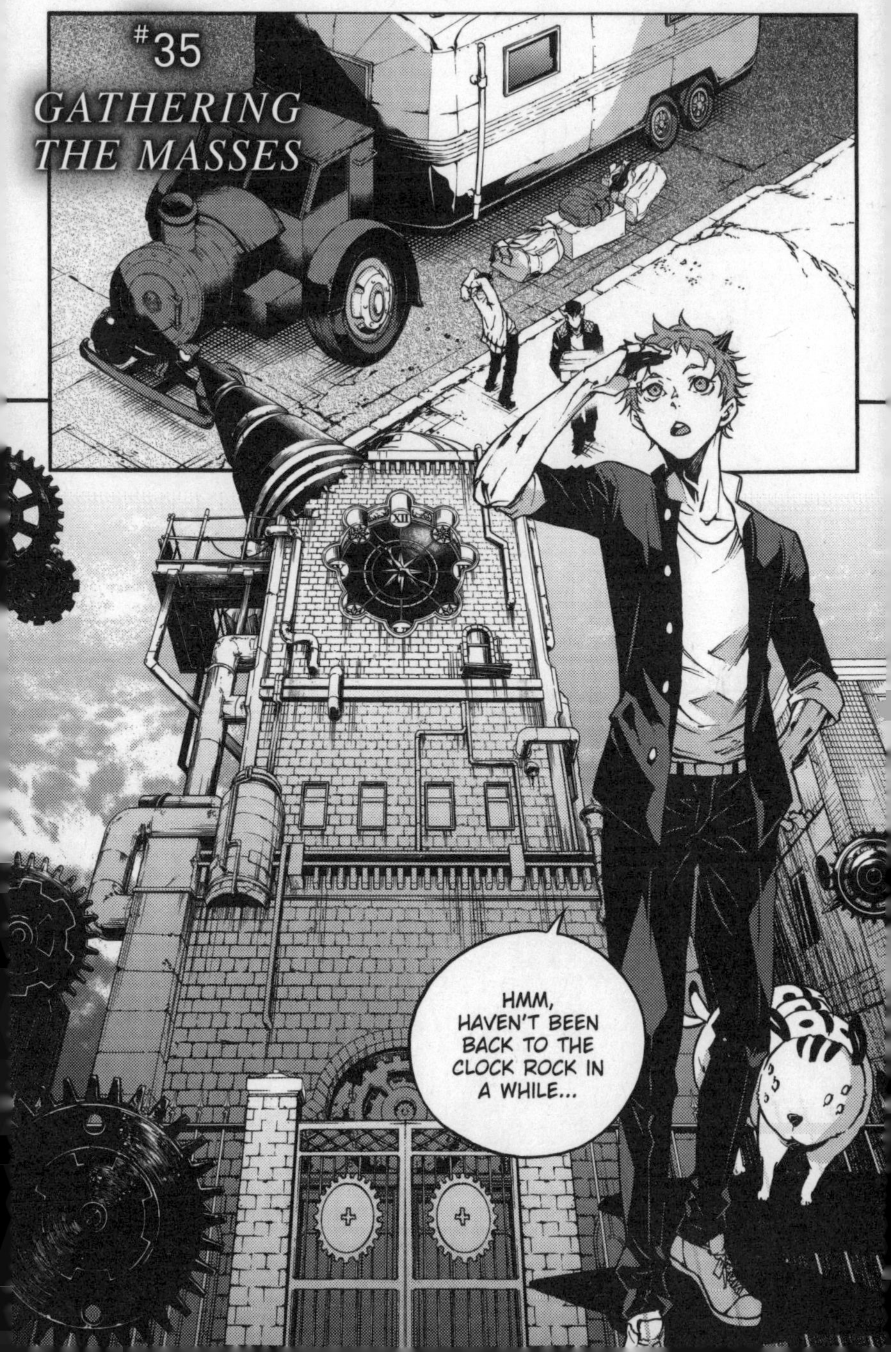
#35
GATHERING THE MASSES
HMM, HAVEN'T BEEN BACK TO THE CLOCK ROCK IN A WHILE...

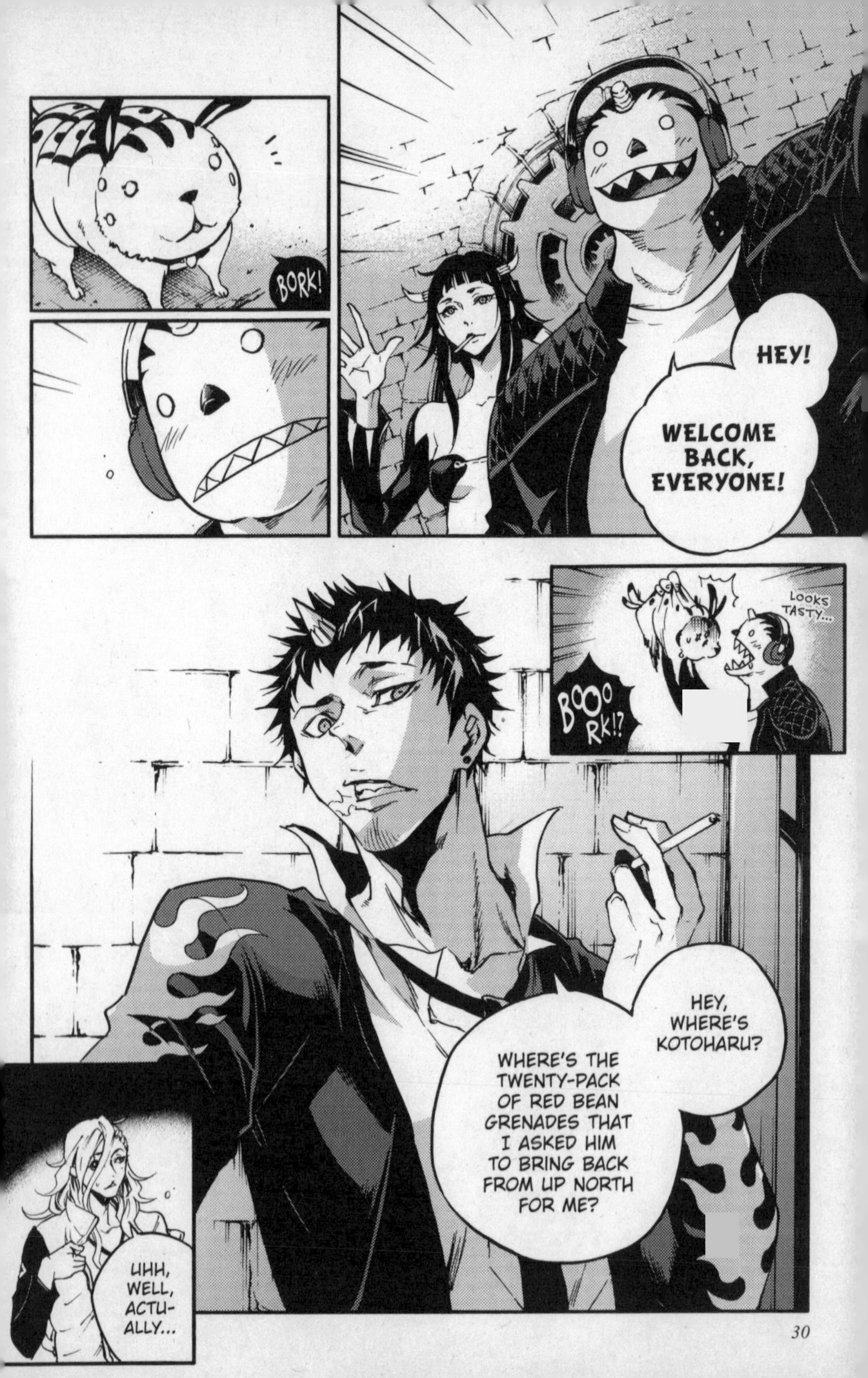
HEY!
WELCOME BACK, EVERYONE!
BORK!
LOOKS TASTY...
BOOORK!?
HEY, WHERE'S KOTOHARU?
WHERE'S THE TWENTY-PACK OF RED BEAN GRENADES THAT I ASKED HIM TO BRING BACK FROM UP NORTH FOR ME?
UHH, WELL, ACTU-ALLY...

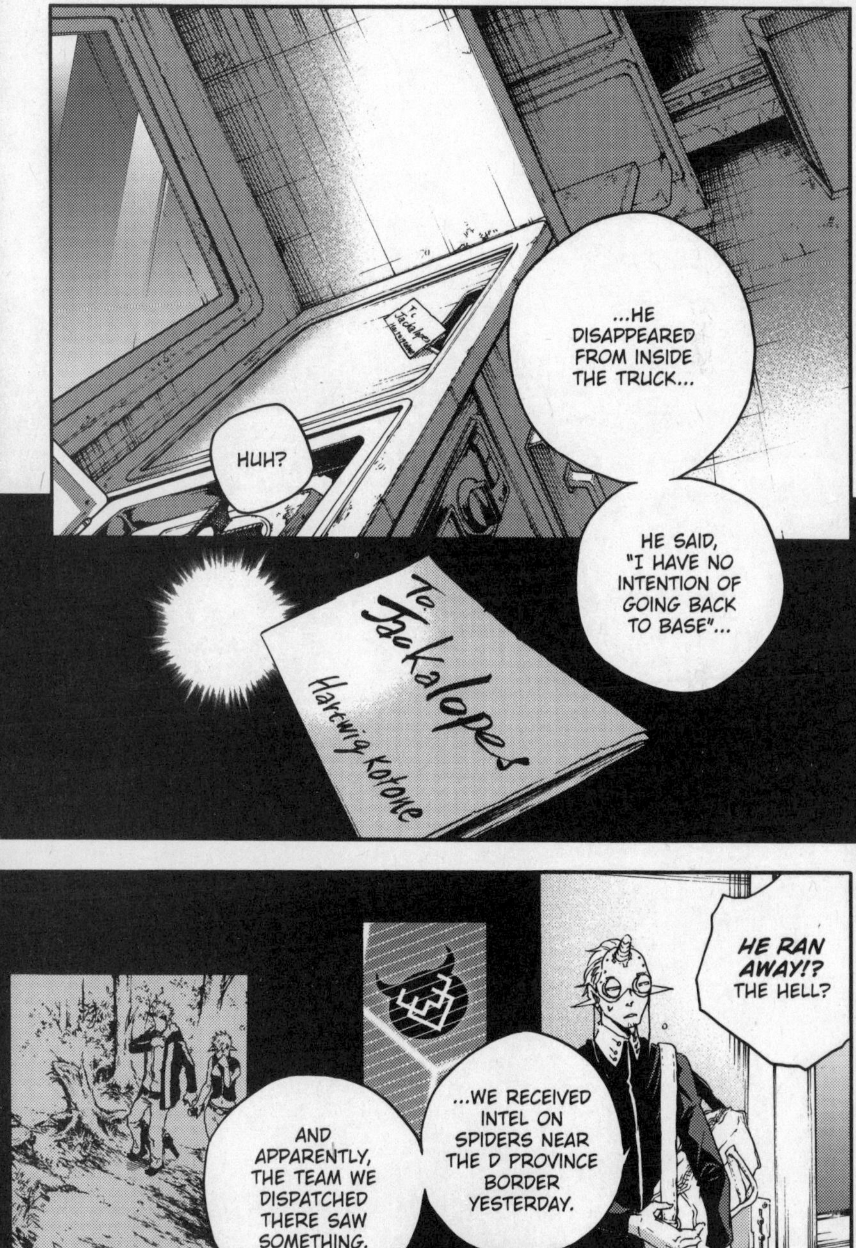
...HE DISAPPEARED FROM INSIDE THE TRUCK...
HUH?
HE SAID, "I HAVE NO INTENTION OF GOING BACK TO BASE"...
To. Jackalopes
Harewing Kotone
HE RAN AWAY!? THE HELL?
...WE RECEIVED INTEL ON SPIDERS NEAR THE D PROVINCE BORDER YESTERDAY.
AND APPARENTLY, THE TEAM WE DISPATCHED THERE SAW SOMETHING.

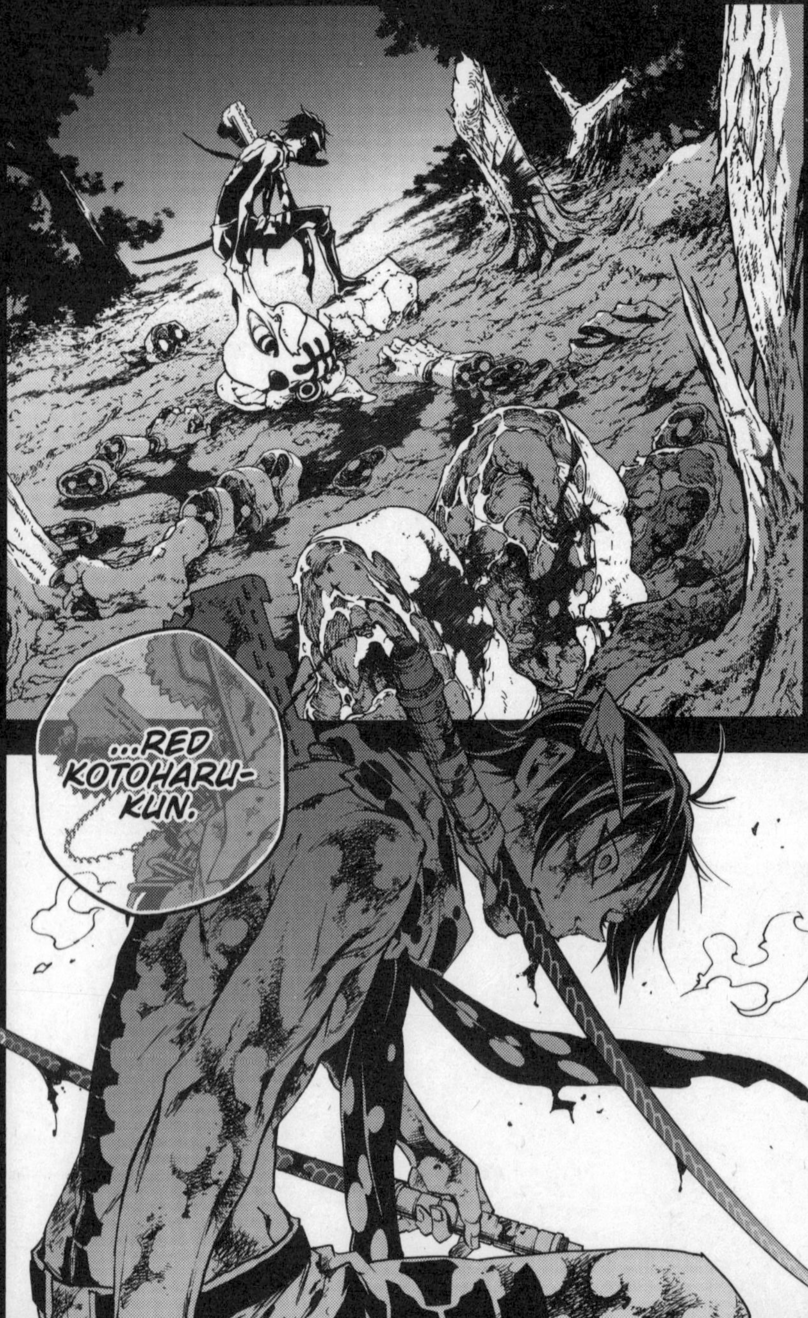
...RED KOTOHARU-KUN.

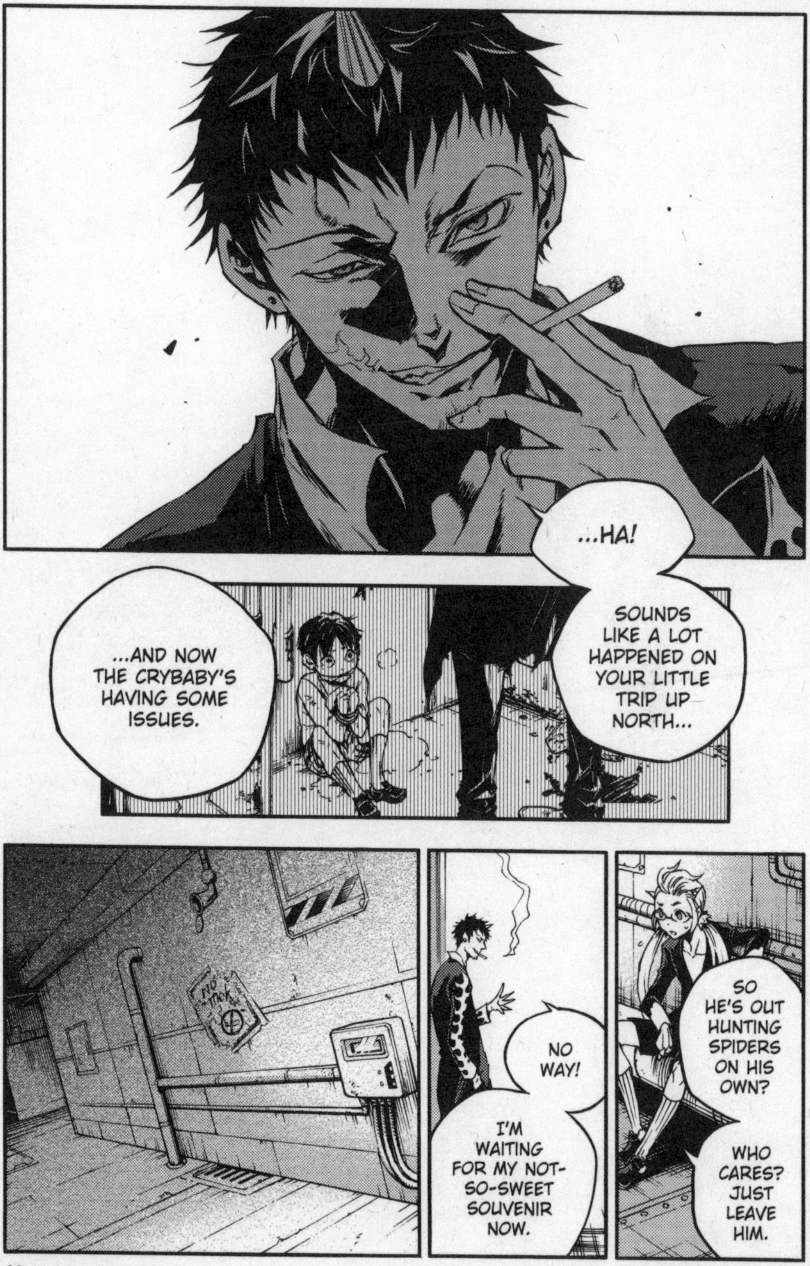
...HA!
SOUNDS LIKE A LOT HAPPENED ON YOUR LITTLE TRIP UP NORTH...
...AND NOW THE CRYBABY'S HAVING SOME ISSUES.
SO HE'S OUT HUNTING SPIDERS ON HIS OWN?
WHO CARES? JUST LEAVE HIM.
NO WAY!
I'M WAITING FOR MY NOT-SO-SWEET SOUVENIR NOW.

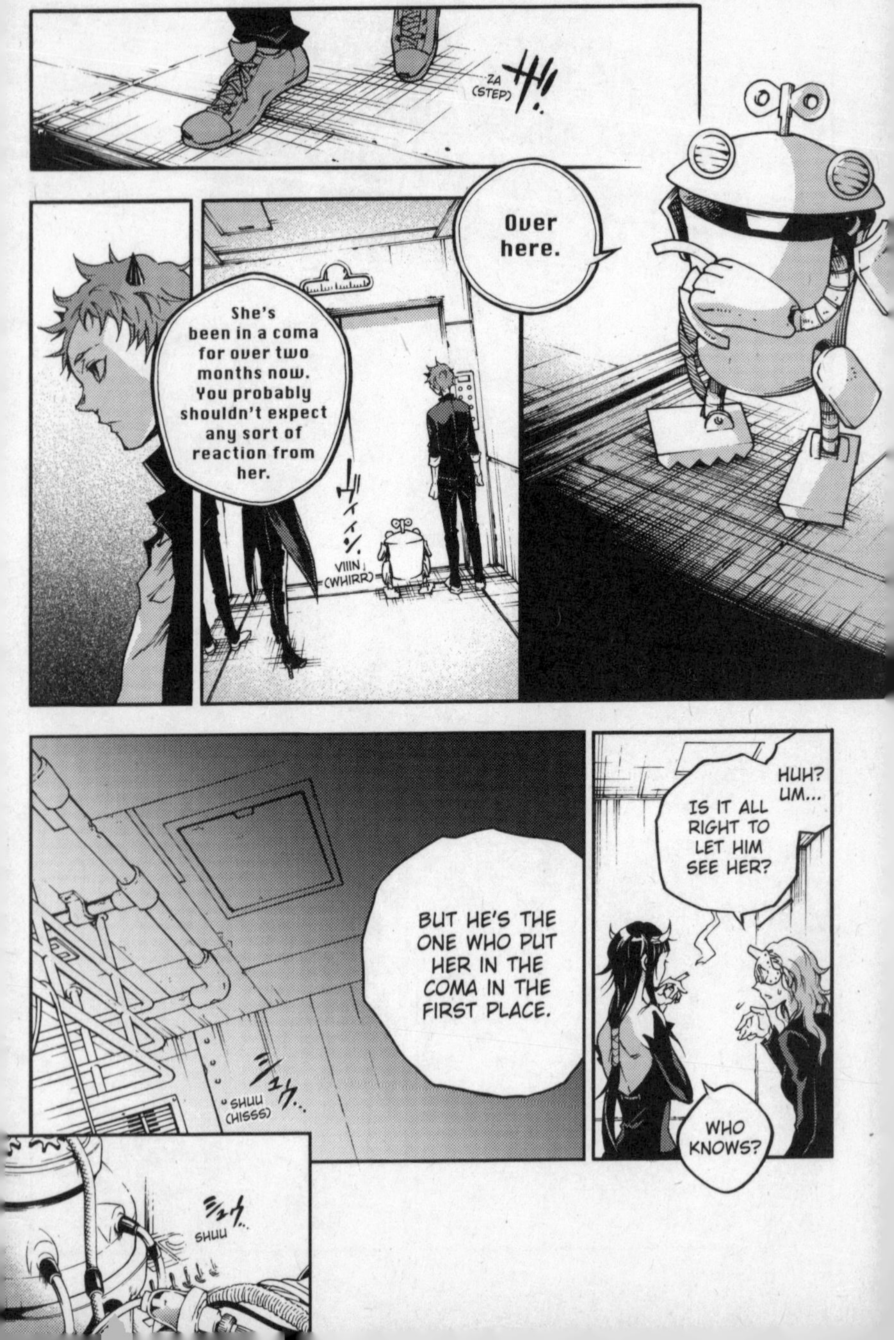
ZA (STEP)
Over here.
VIIIN (WHIRR)
She's been in a coma for over two months now. You probably shouldn't expect any sort of reaction from her.
HUH? UM...
IS IT ALL RIGHT TO LET HIM SEE HER?
WHO KNOWS?
BUT HE'S THE ONE WHO PUT HER IN THE COMA IN THE FIRST PLACE.
SHUU (HISSS)
SHUU

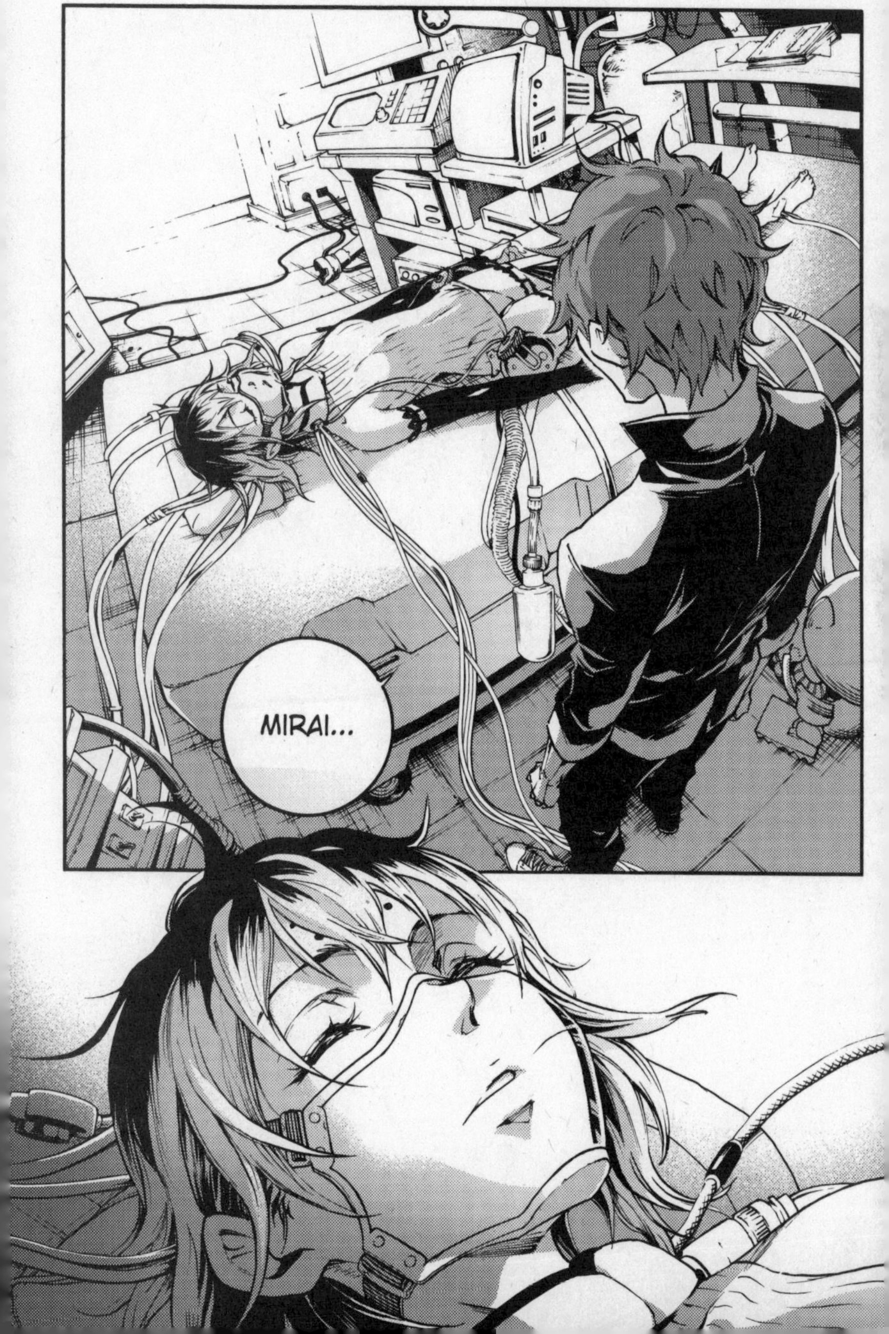
MIRAI...

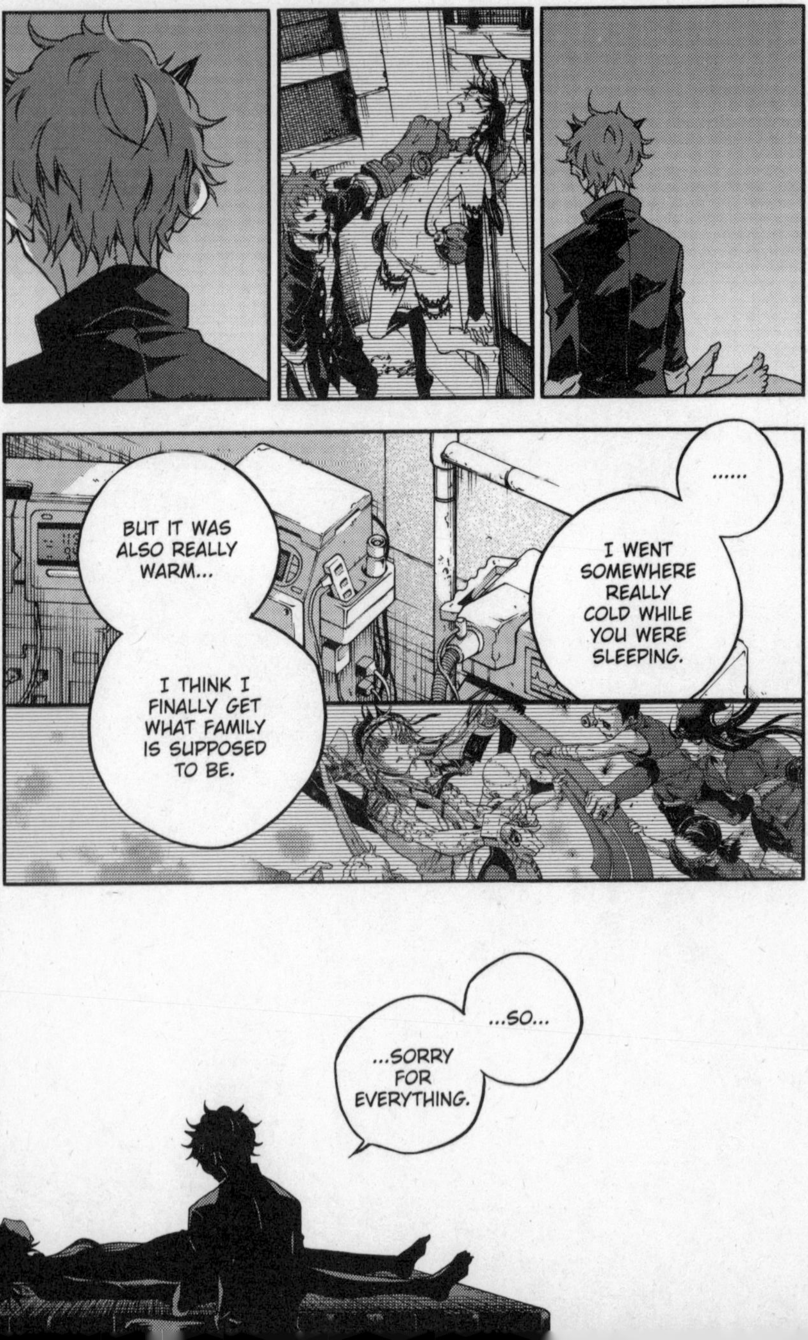
......
I WENT SOMEWHERE REALLY COLD WHILE YOU WERE SLEEPING.
BUT IT WAS ALSO REALLY WARM...
I THINK I FINALLY GET WHAT FAMILY IS SUPPOSED TO BE.
...SO...
...SORRY FOR EVERYTHING.

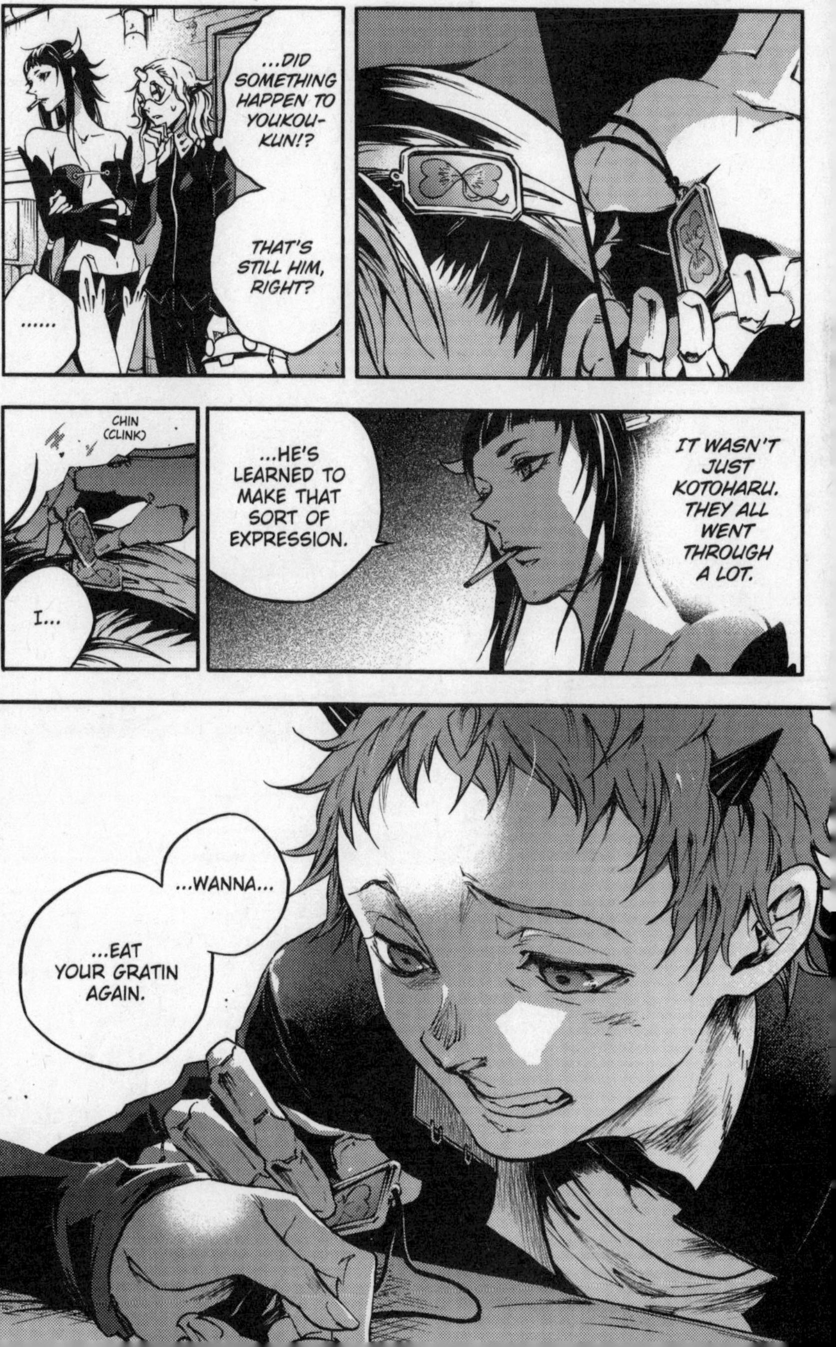
...DID SOMETHING HAPPEN TO YOUKOU-KUN!?
THAT'S STILL HIM, RIGHT?
......
IT WASN'T JUST KOTOHARU. THEY ALL WENT THROUGH A LOT.
...HE'S LEARNED TO MAKE THAT SORT OF EXPRESSION.
CHIN (CLINK)
I...
...WANNA...
...EAT YOUR GRATIN AGAIN.

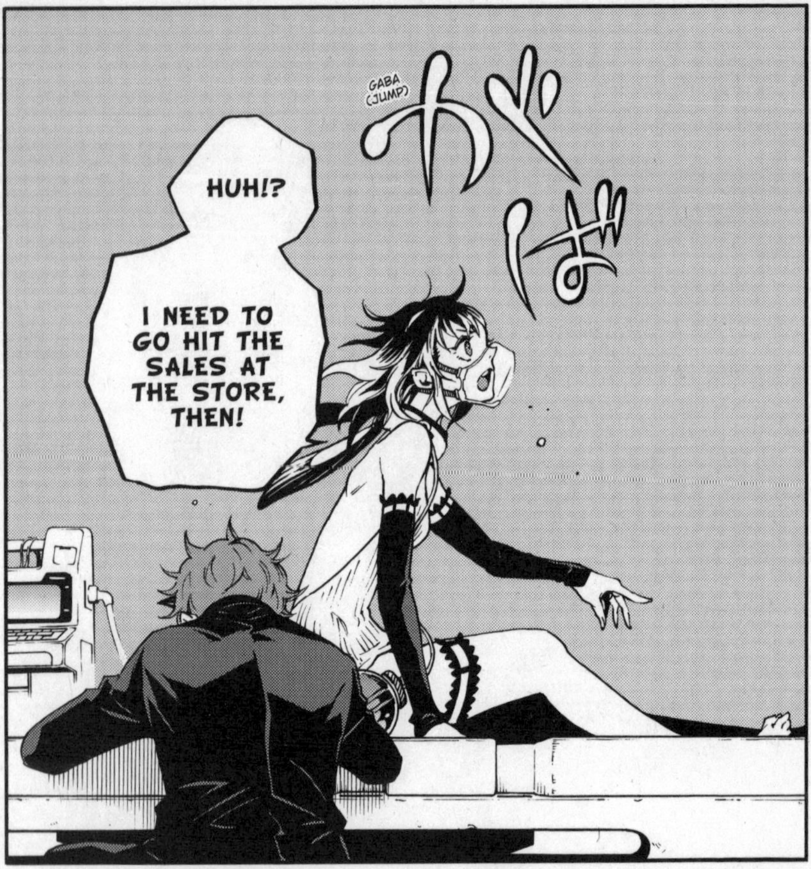
GABA (JUMP)
わば
HUH!?
I NEED TO GO HIT THE SALES AT THE STORE, THEN!
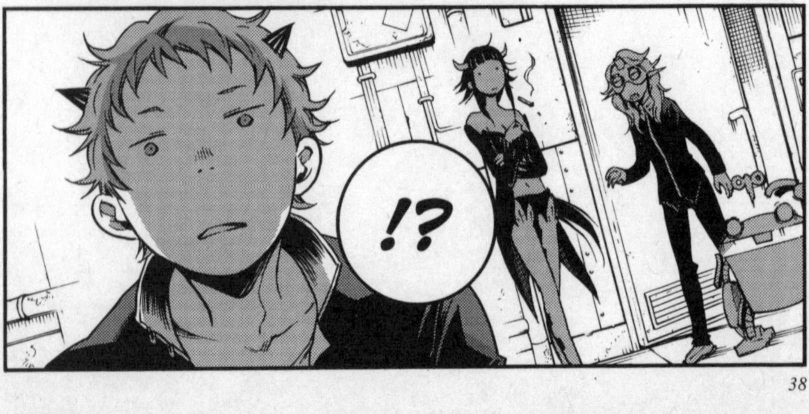
!?

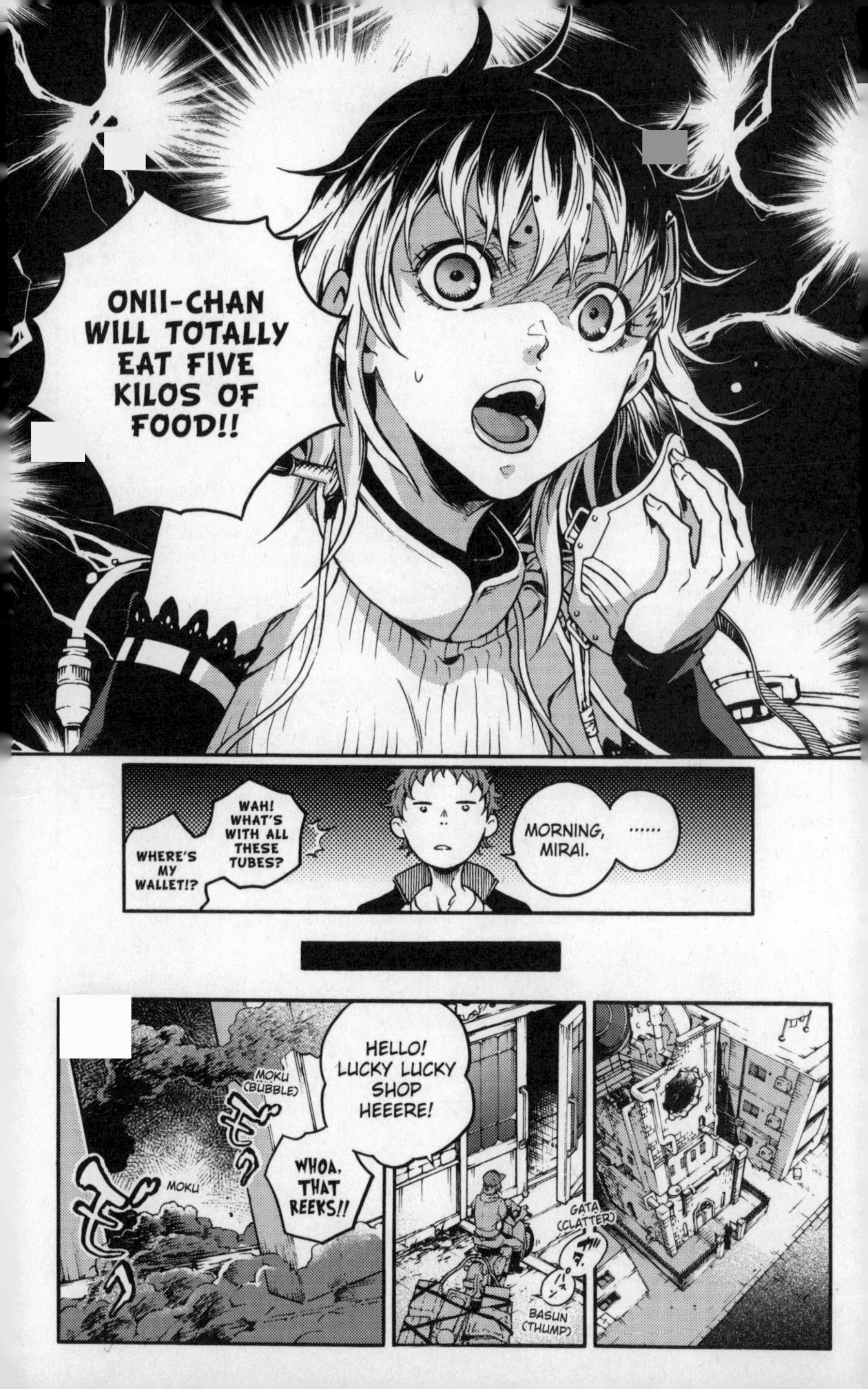
ONII-CHAN WILL TOTALLY EAT FIVE KILOS OF FOOD!!
......
MORNING, MIRAI.
WAH! WHAT'S WITH ALL THESE TUBES?
WHERE'S MY WALLET!?
[redacted]
GATA (CLATTER)
BASUN (THUMP)
HELLO! LUCKY LUCKY SHOP HEEERE!
WHOA, THAT REEKS!!
MOKU (BUBBLE)
MOKU

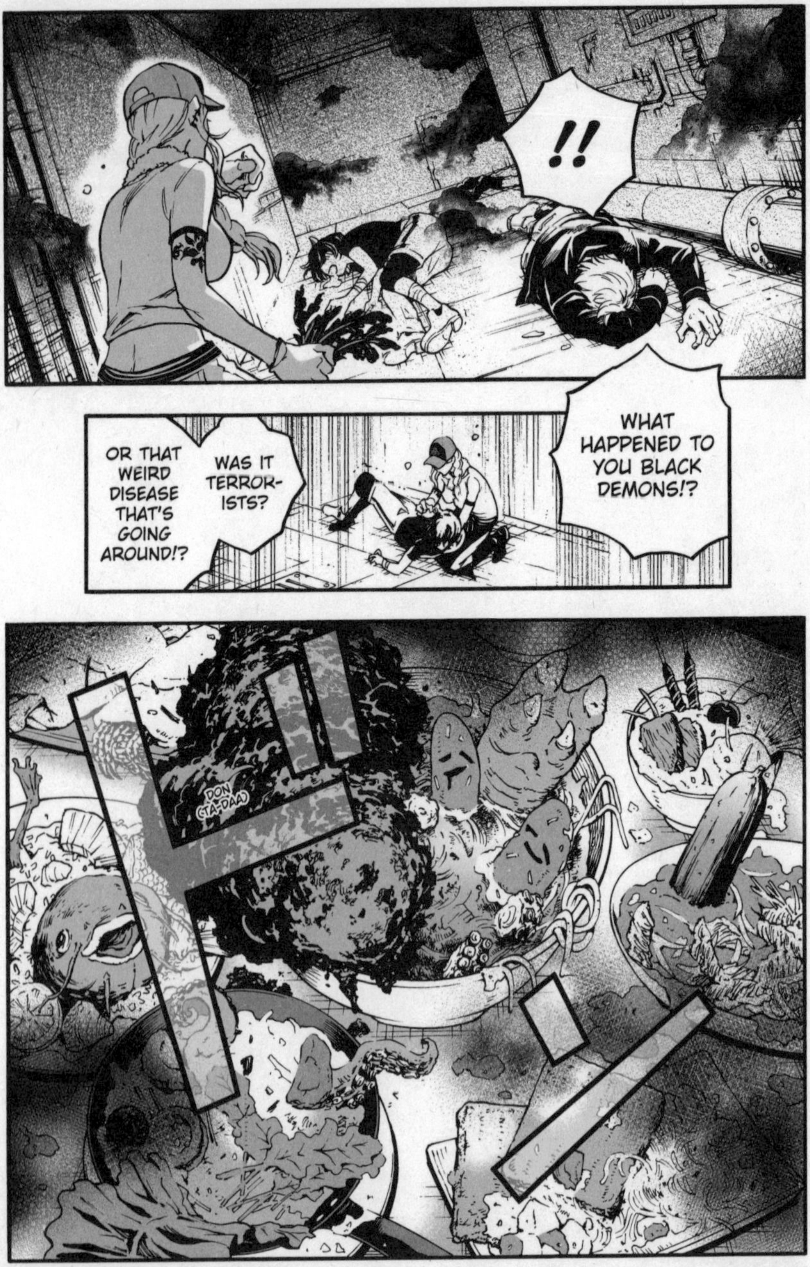
!!
WHAT HAPPENED TO YOU BLACK DEMONS!?
WAS IT TERROR-ISTS?
OR THAT WEIRD DISEASE THAT'S GOING AROUND!?
DON (TA-DAA)

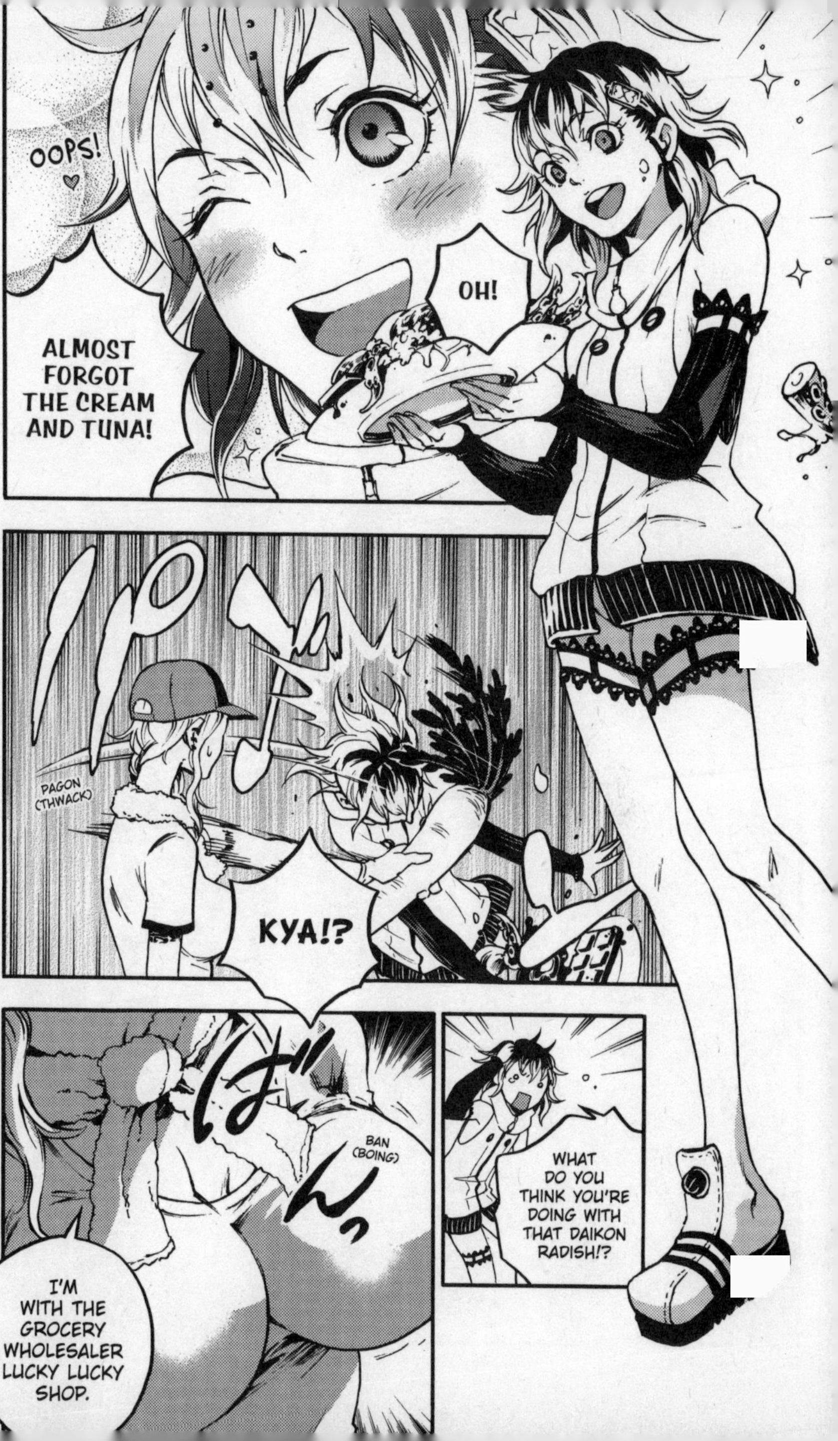
OH!
OOPS!
ALMOST FORGOT THE CREAM AND TUNA!
PAGON (THWACK)
KYA!?
WHAT DO YOU THINK YOU'RE DOING WITH THAT DAIKON RADISH!?
BAN (BOING)
I'M WITH THE GROCERY WHOLESALER LUCKY LUCKY SHOP.

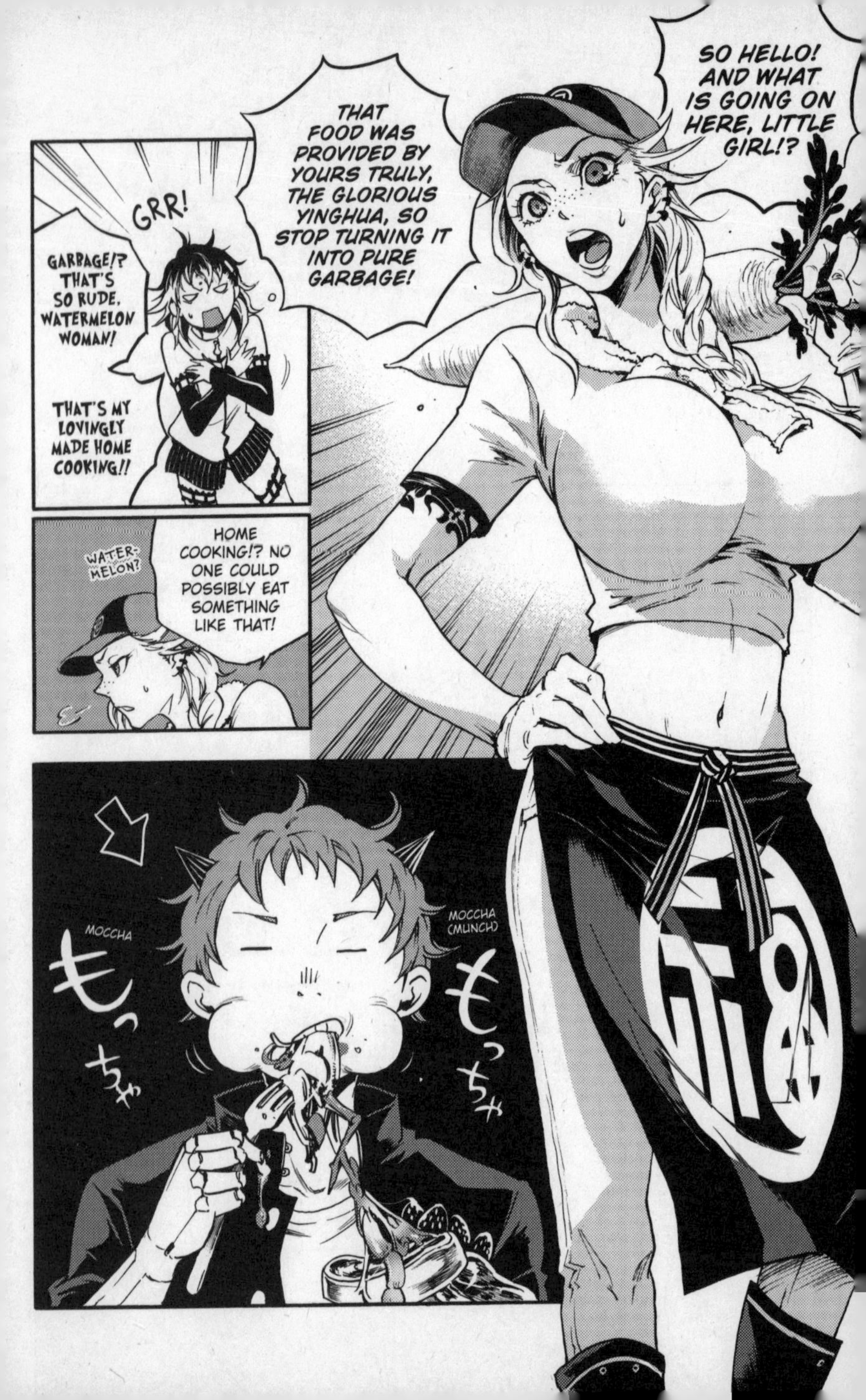
SO HELLO! AND WHAT IS GOING ON HERE, LITTLE GIRL!?
THAT FOOD WAS PROVIDED BY YOURS TRULY, THE GLORIOUS YINGHUA, SO STOP TURNING IT INTO PURE GARBAGE!
GRR!
GARBAGE!? THAT'S SO RUDE, WATERMELON WOMAN!
THAT'S MY LOVINGLY MADE HOME COOKING!!
HOME COOKING!? NO ONE COULD POSSIBLY EAT SOMETHING LIKE THAT!
WATER-MELON?
MOCCHA (MUNCH)
もっちゃ
MOCCHA
もっちゃ

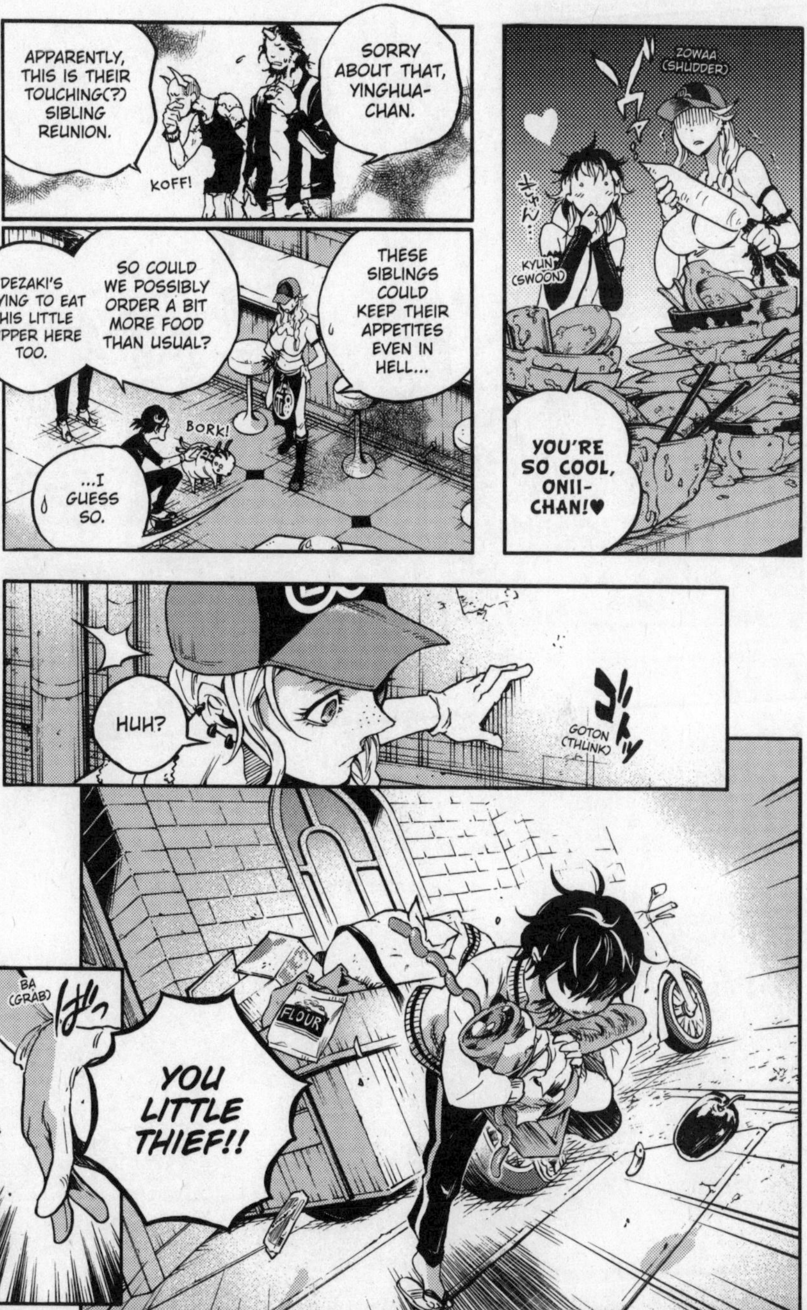
ZOWAA (SHUDDER)
KYUN (SWOON)
YOU'RE SO COOL, ONII-CHAN!♥
SORRY ABOUT THAT, YINGHUA-CHAN.
APPARENTLY, THIS IS THEIR TOUCHING(?) SIBLING REUNION.
KOFF!
THESE SIBLINGS COULD KEEP THEIR APPETITES EVEN IN HELL...
SO COULD WE POSSIBLY ORDER A BIT MORE FOOD THAN USUAL?
DEZAKI'S TRYING TO EAT THIS LITTLE PUPPER HERE TOO.
BORK!
...I GUESS SO.
GOTON (THÜNK)
HUH?
FLOUR
BA (GRAB)
YOU LITTLE THIEF!!

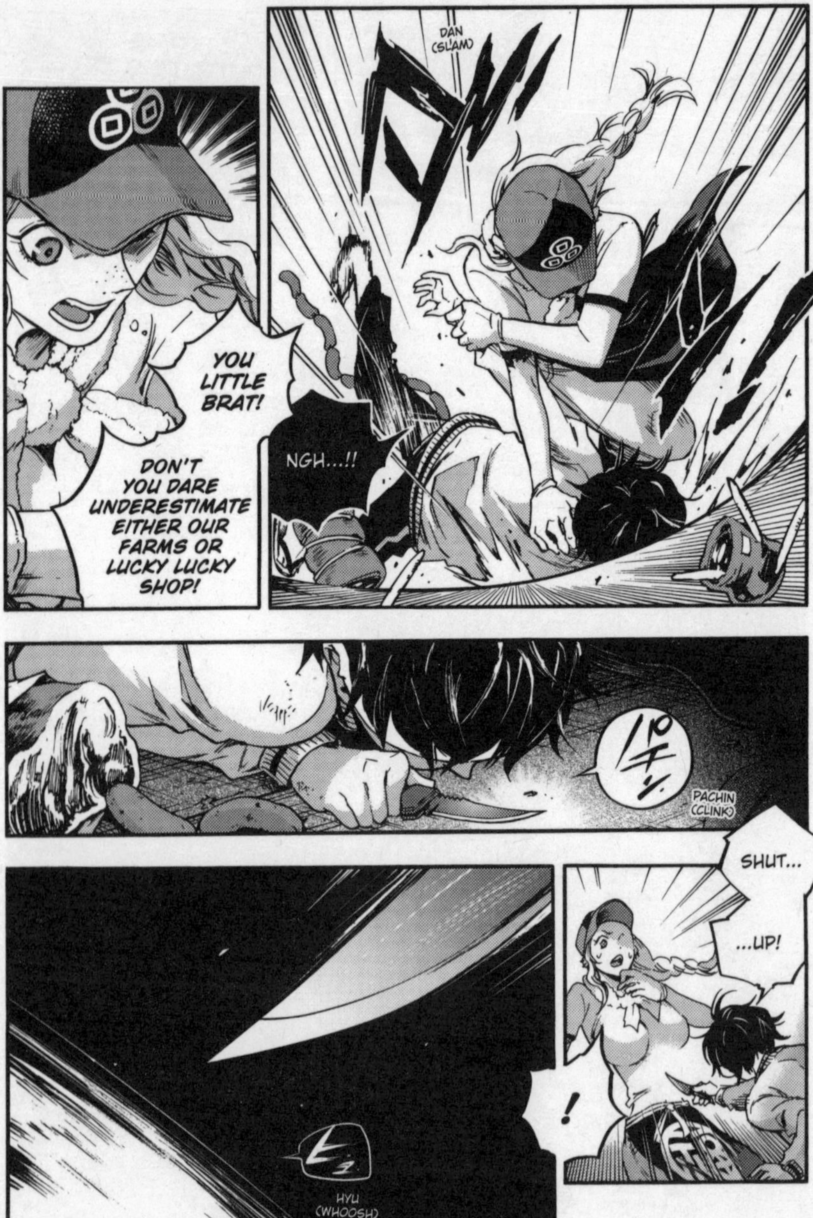
DAN (SLAM)
NGH...!!
YOU LITTLE BRAT!
DON'T YOU DARE UNDERESTIMATE EITHER OUR FARMS OR LUCKY LUCKY SHOP!
PACHIN (CLINK)
SHUT...
...UP!
!
HYU (WHOOSH)

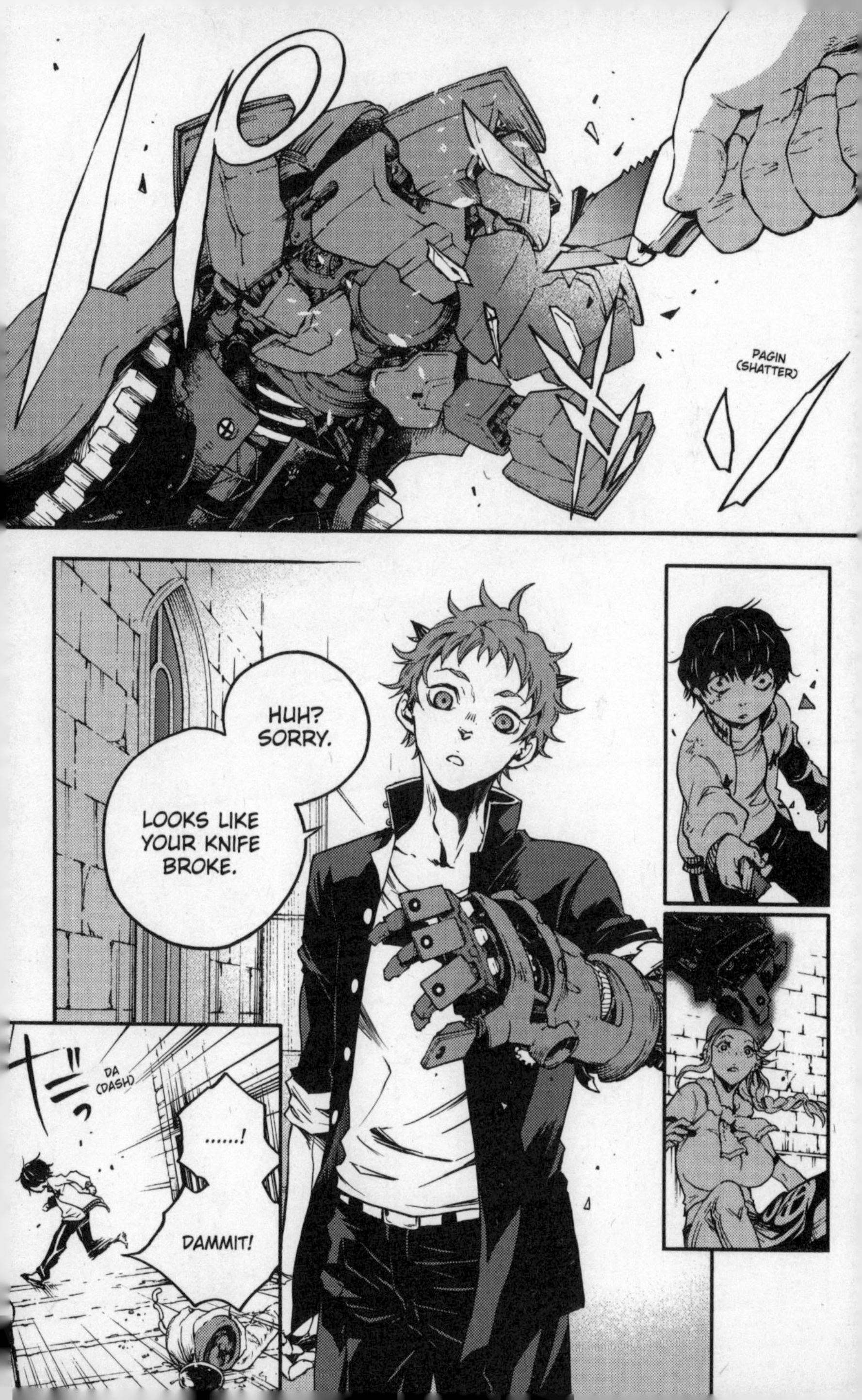
PAGIN
(SHATTER)
HUH? SORRY.
LOOKS LIKE YOUR KNIFE BROKE.
DA
(DASH)
......!
DAMMIT!

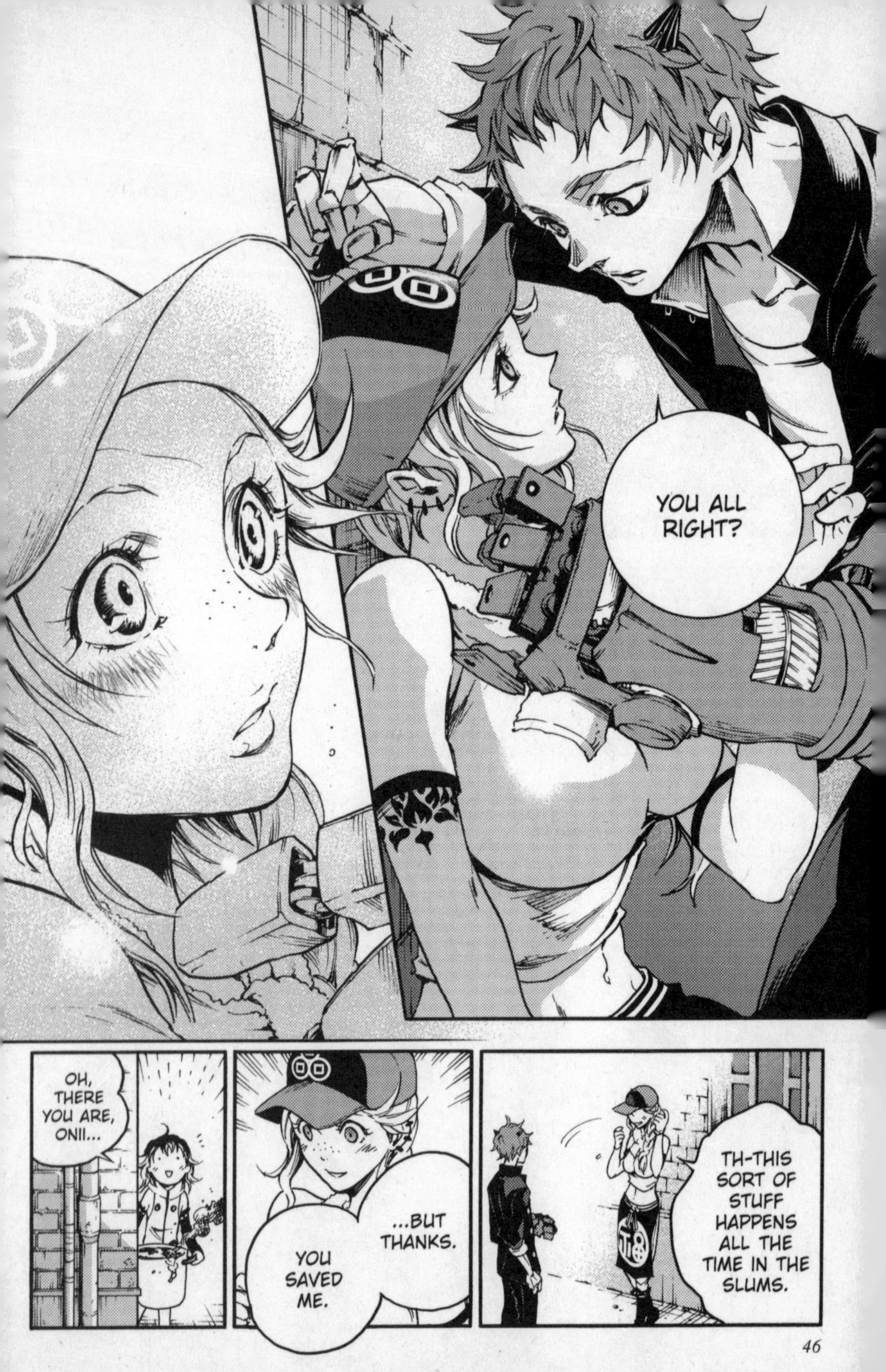
YOU ALL RIGHT?
TH-THIS SORT OF STUFF HAPPENS ALL THE TIME IN THE SLUMS.
...BUT THANKS.
YOU SAVED ME.
OH, THERE YOU ARE, ONII...

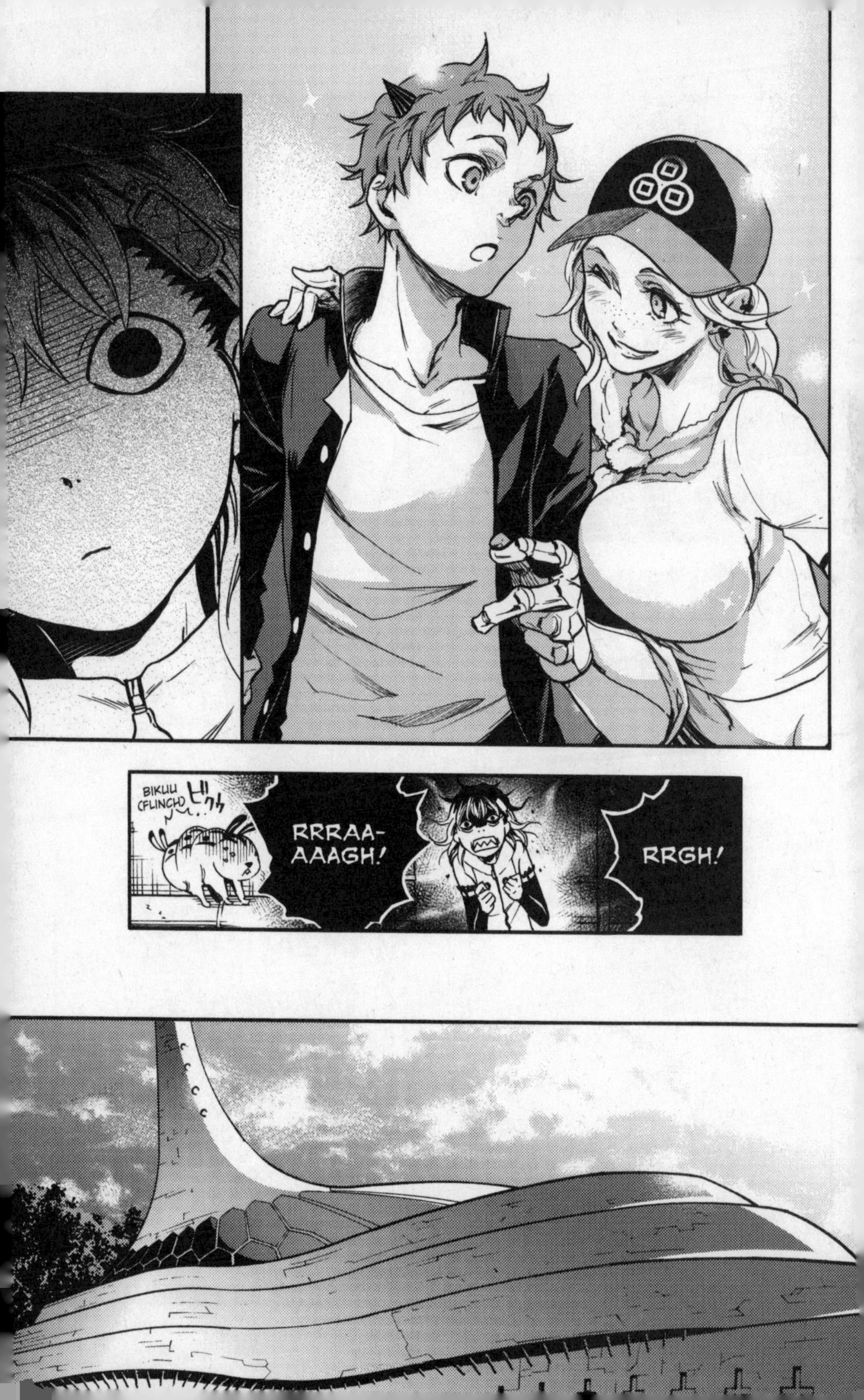
RRGH!
RRRAA-AAAGH!
BIKUU (FLINCH)
ビクッ

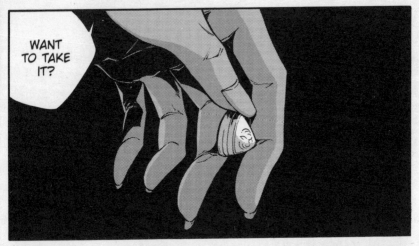

WANT TO TAKE IT?
NO.
IF I TAKE THE DRUG, WE WON'T BE ABLE TO GET CLINICAL DETAILS ON THE DISEASE.
THAT WOULD BE IRRATIONAL, CHIEF SCIENTIST KURAMA.
PLEASE WAIT. I WILL BE DEAD IN SEVEN HOURS.

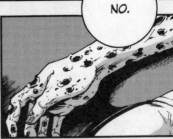

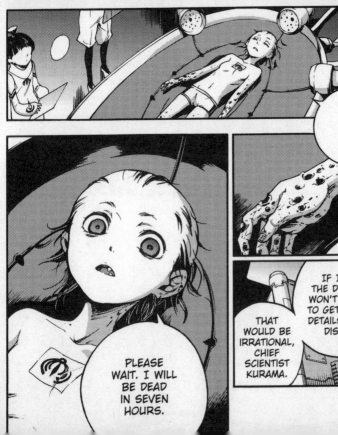

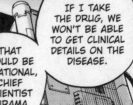

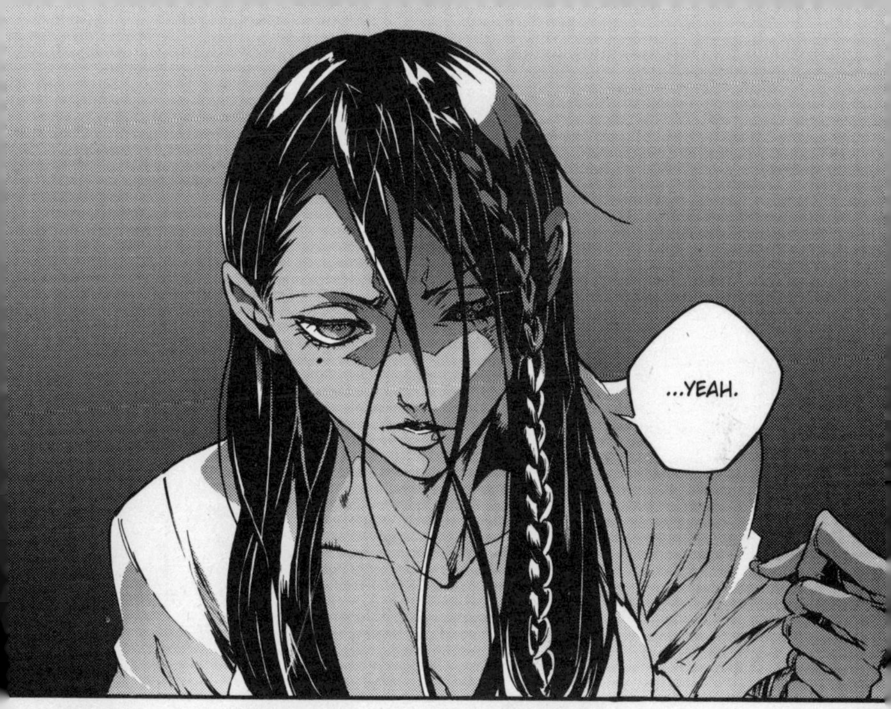
...YEAH.

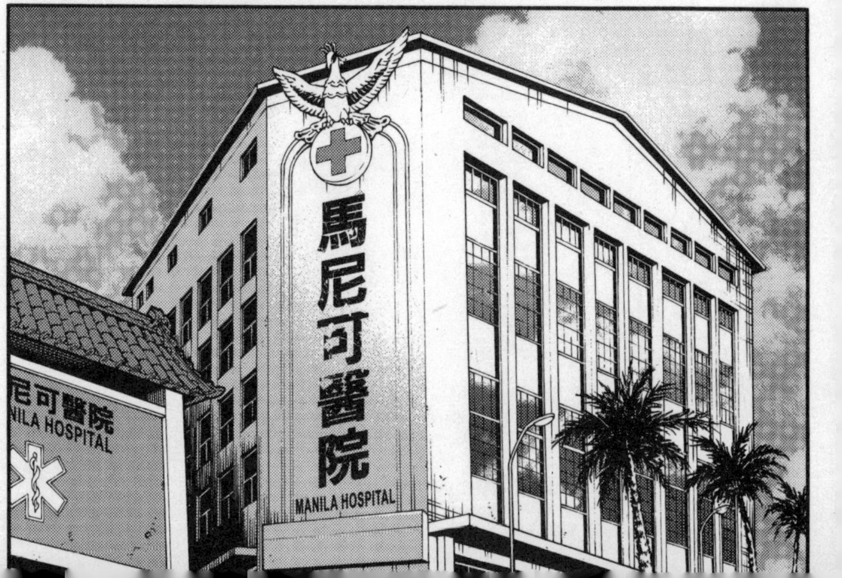
馬尼可醫院
MANILA HOSPITAL
尼可醫院
NILA HOSPITAL

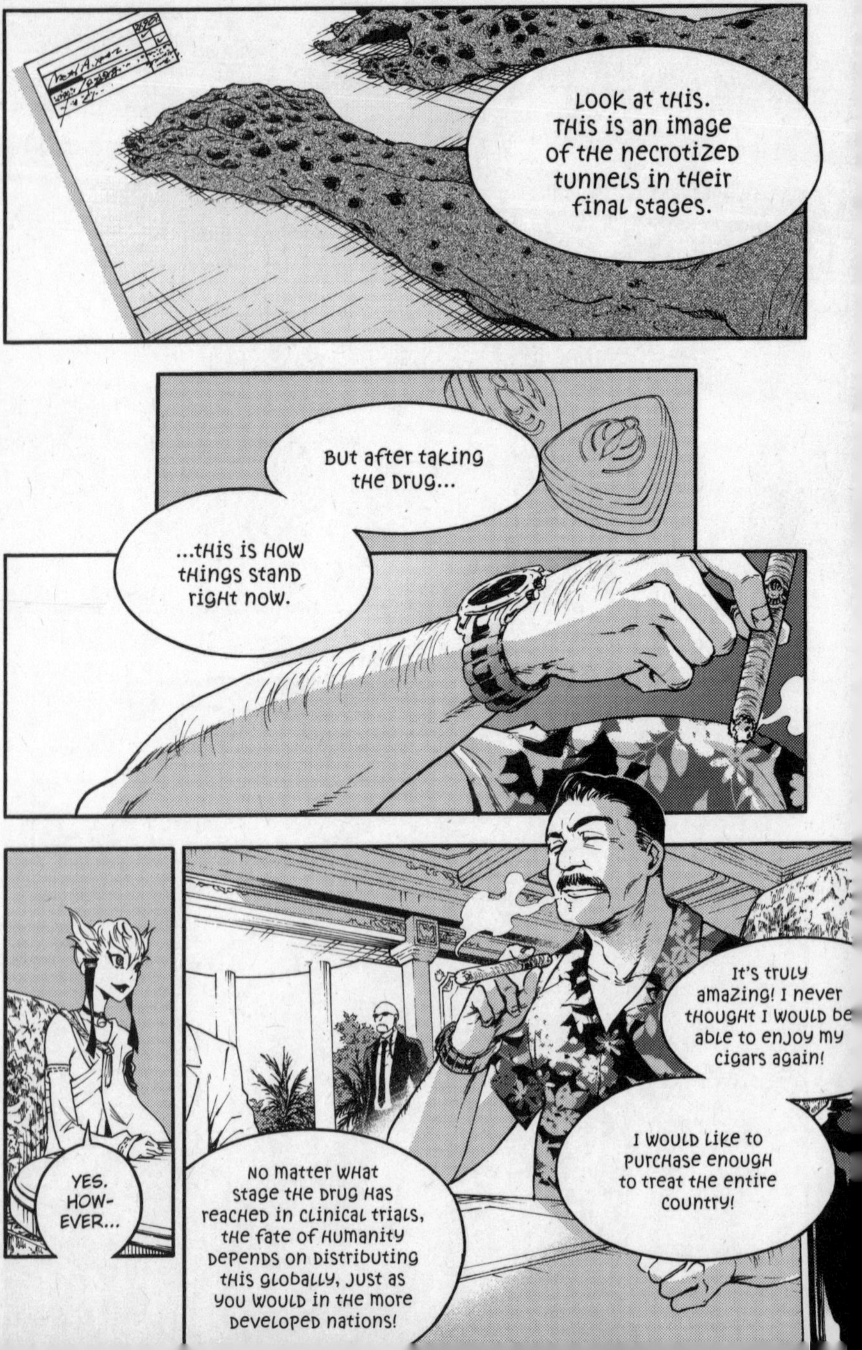

Look at this. This is an image of the necrotized tunnels in their final stages.
But after taking the drug...
...this is how things stand right now.
It's truly amazing! I never thought I would be able to enjoy my cigars again!
I would like to purchase enough to treat the entire country!
No matter what stage the drug has reached in clinical trials, the fate of humanity depends on distributing this globally, just as you would in the more developed nations!
Yes. How-ever...

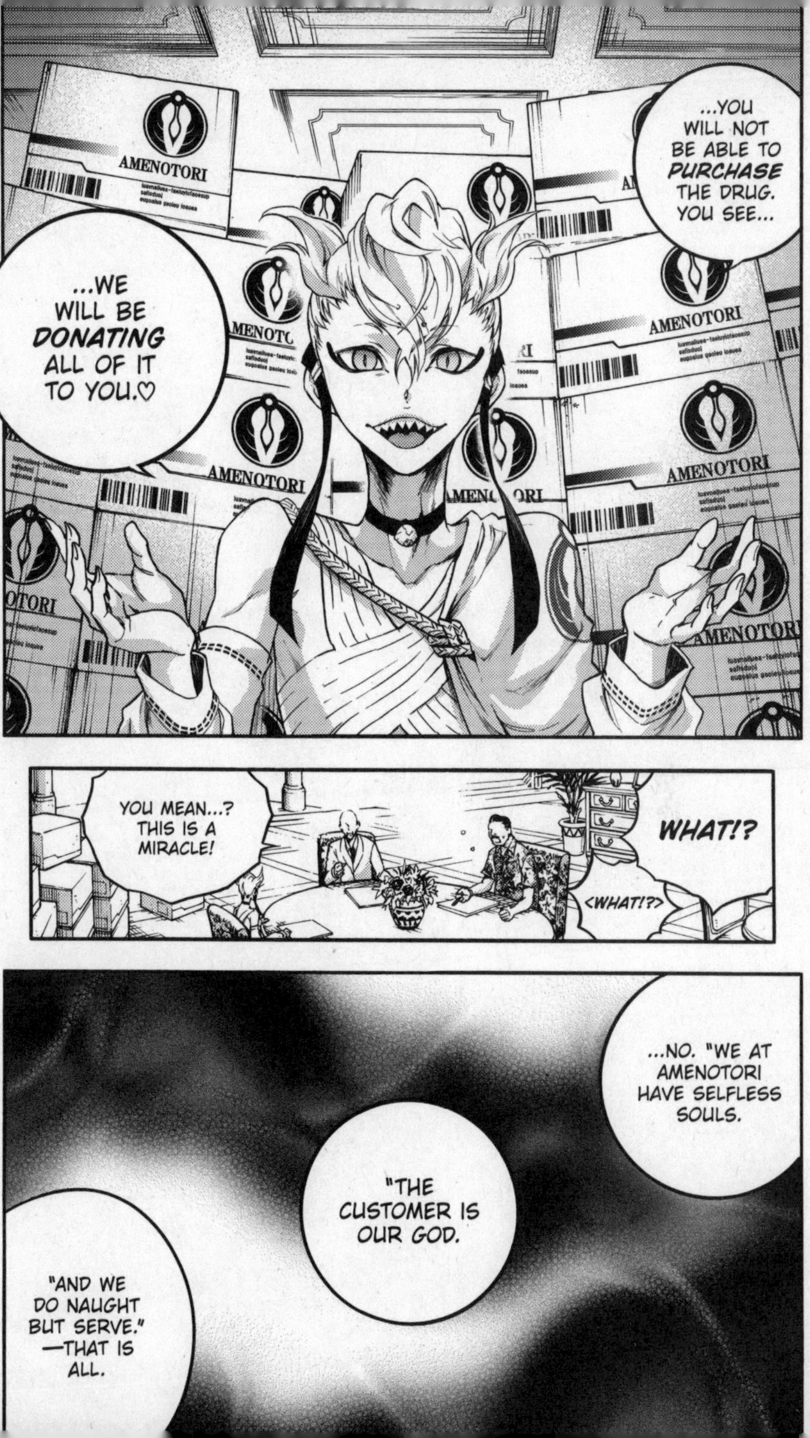
...YOU WILL NOT BE ABLE TO *PURCHASE* THE DRUG. YOU SEE...
...WE WILL BE *DONATING* ALL OF IT TO YOU.♡
WHAT!?
<WHAT!?>
YOU MEAN...? THIS IS A MIRACLE!
...NO. "WE AT AMENOTORI HAVE SELFLESS SOULS.
"THE CUSTOMER IS OUR GOD.
"AND WE DO NAUGHT BUT SERVE." —THAT IS ALL.

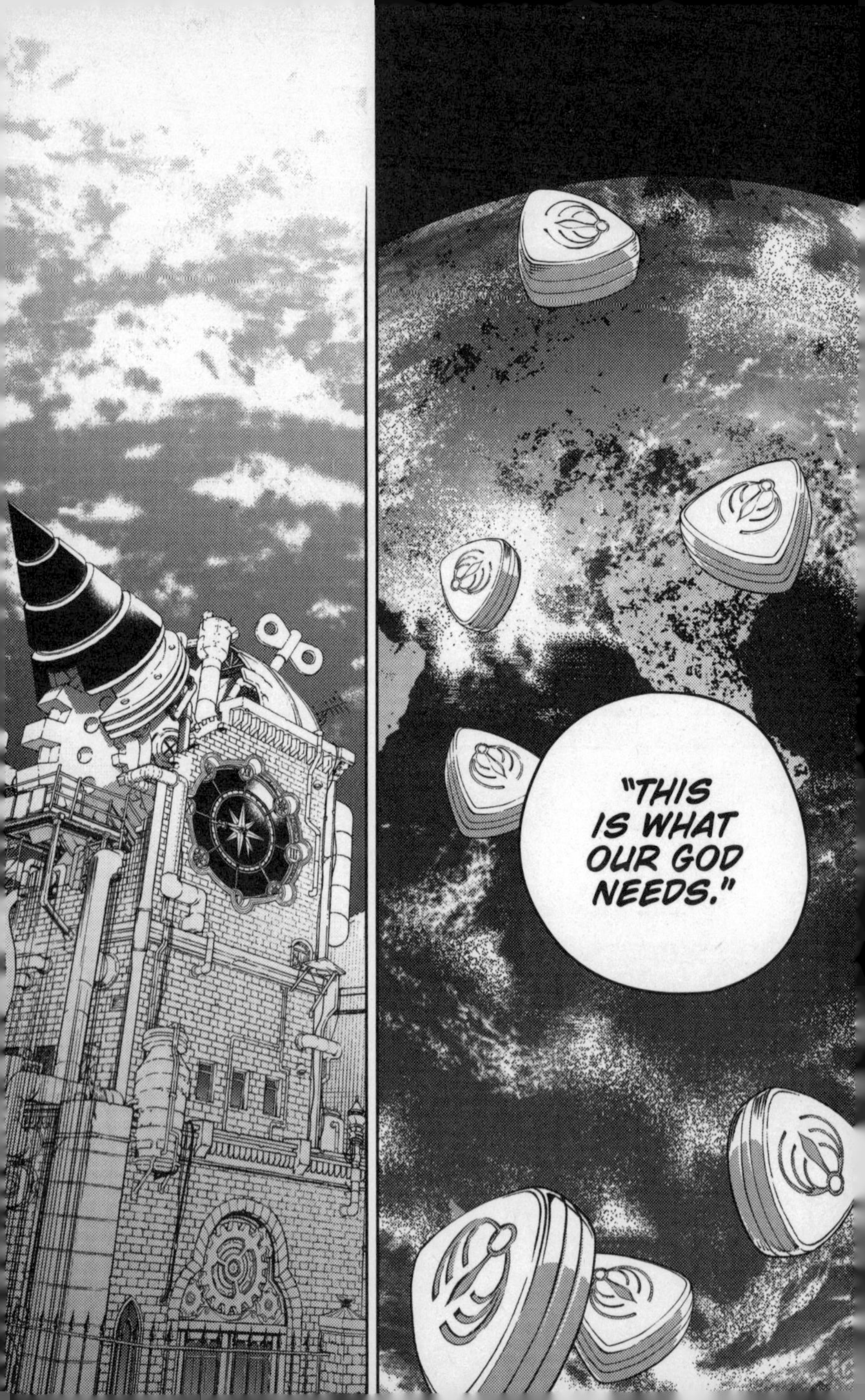
"THIS IS WHAT OUR GOD NEEDS."

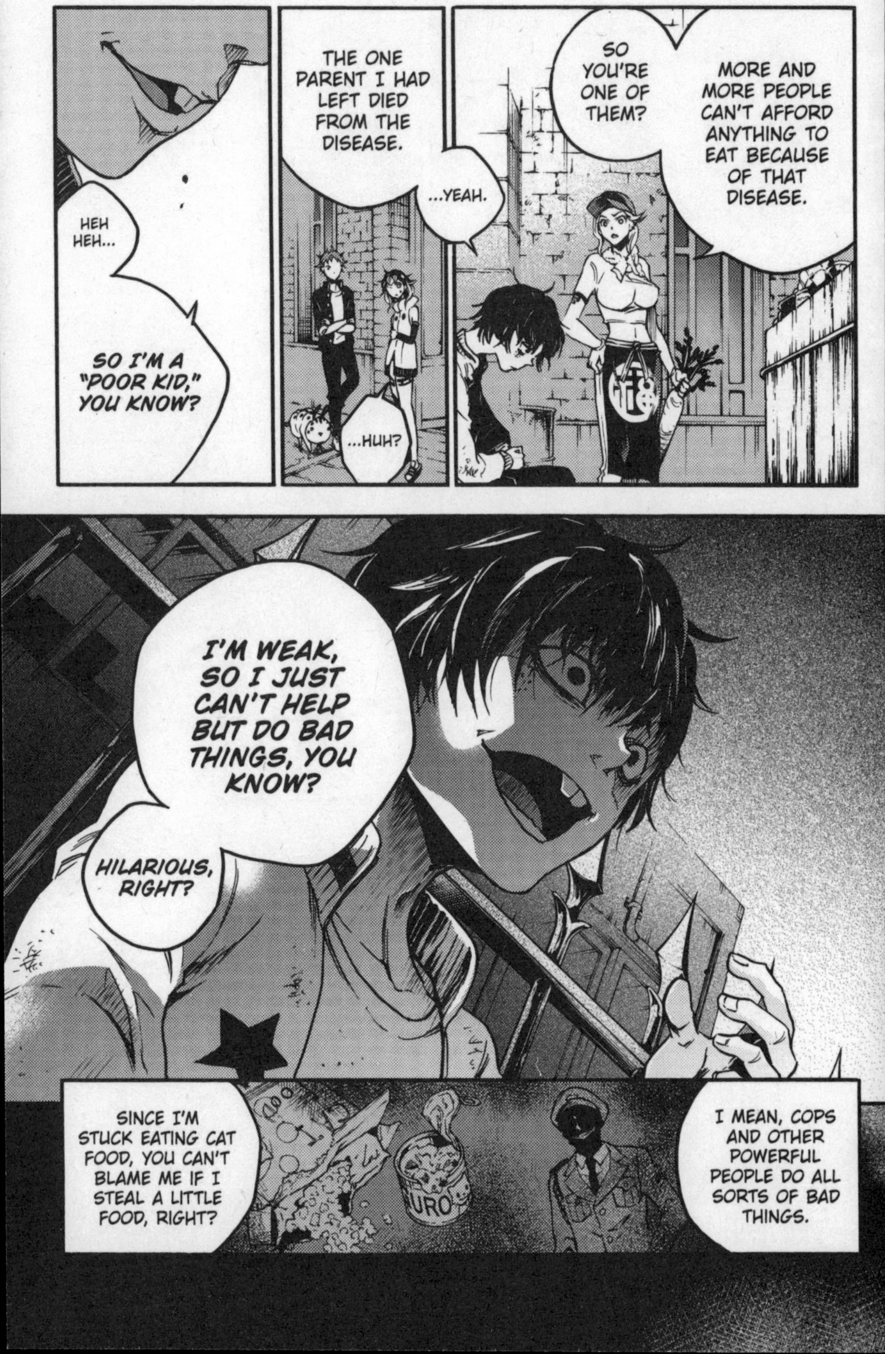
MORE AND MORE PEOPLE CAN'T AFFORD ANYTHING TO EAT BECAUSE OF THAT DISEASE.
SO YOU'RE ONE OF THEM?
...YEAH.
THE ONE PARENT I HAD LEFT DIED FROM THE DISEASE.
...HUH?
HEH HEH...
SO I'M A "POOR KID," YOU KNOW?
I'M WEAK, SO I JUST CAN'T HELP BUT DO BAD THINGS, YOU KNOW?
HILARIOUS, RIGHT?
I MEAN, COPS AND OTHER POWERFUL PEOPLE DO ALL SORTS OF BAD THINGS.
SINCE I'M STUCK EATING CAT FOOD, YOU CAN'T BLAME ME IF I STEAL A LITTLE FOOD, RIGHT?

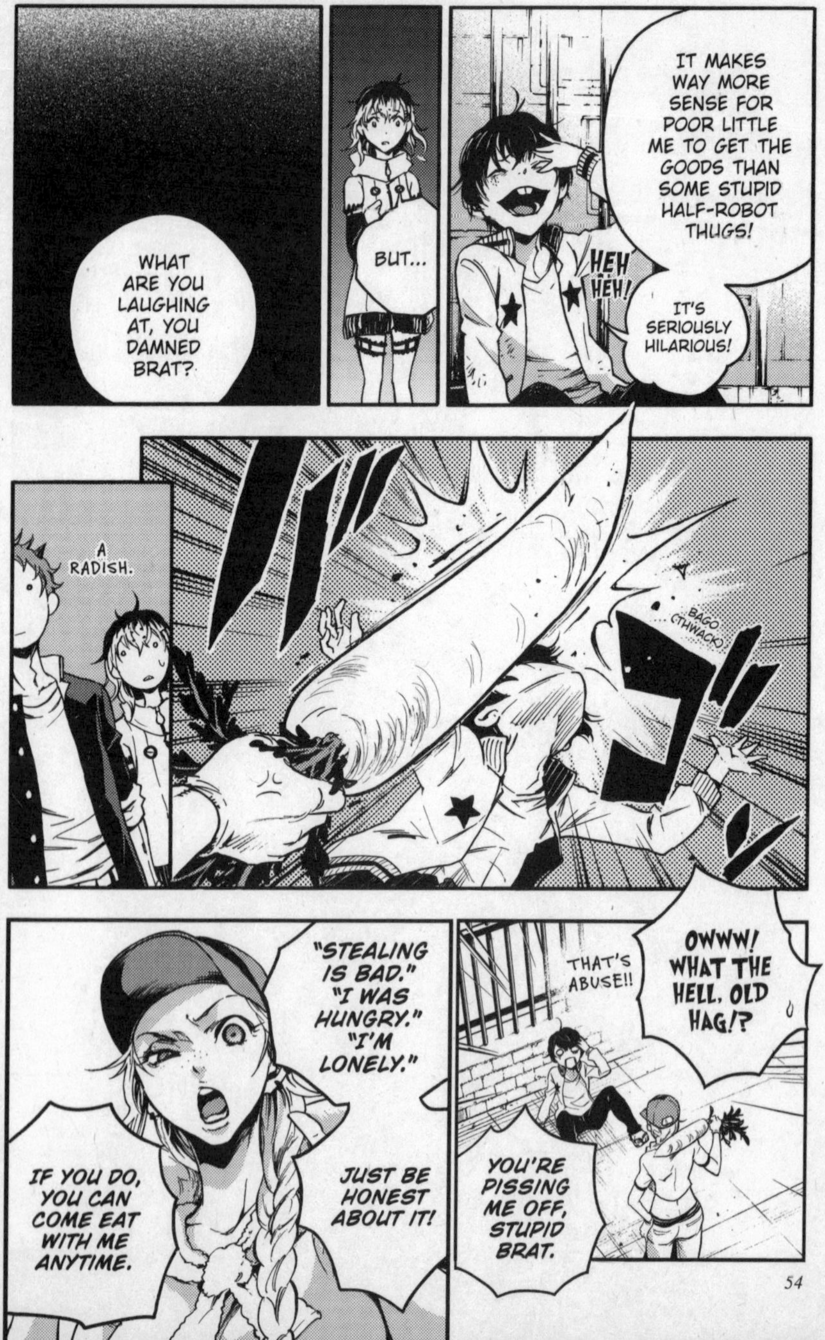
IT MAKES WAY MORE SENSE FOR POOR LITTLE ME TO GET THE GOODS THAN SOME STUPID HALF-ROBOT THUGS!
HEH HEH!
IT'S SERIOUSLY HILARIOUS!
BUT...
WHAT ARE YOU LAUGHING AT, YOU DAMNED BRAT?
BAGO (THWACK)
A RADISH.
OWWW! WHAT THE HELL, OLD HAG!?
THAT'S ABUSE!!
YOU'RE PISSING ME OFF, STUPID BRAT.
"STEALING IS BAD." "I WAS HUNGRY." "I'M LONELY."
JUST BE HONEST ABOUT IT!
IF YOU DO, YOU CAN COME EAT WITH ME ANYTIME.

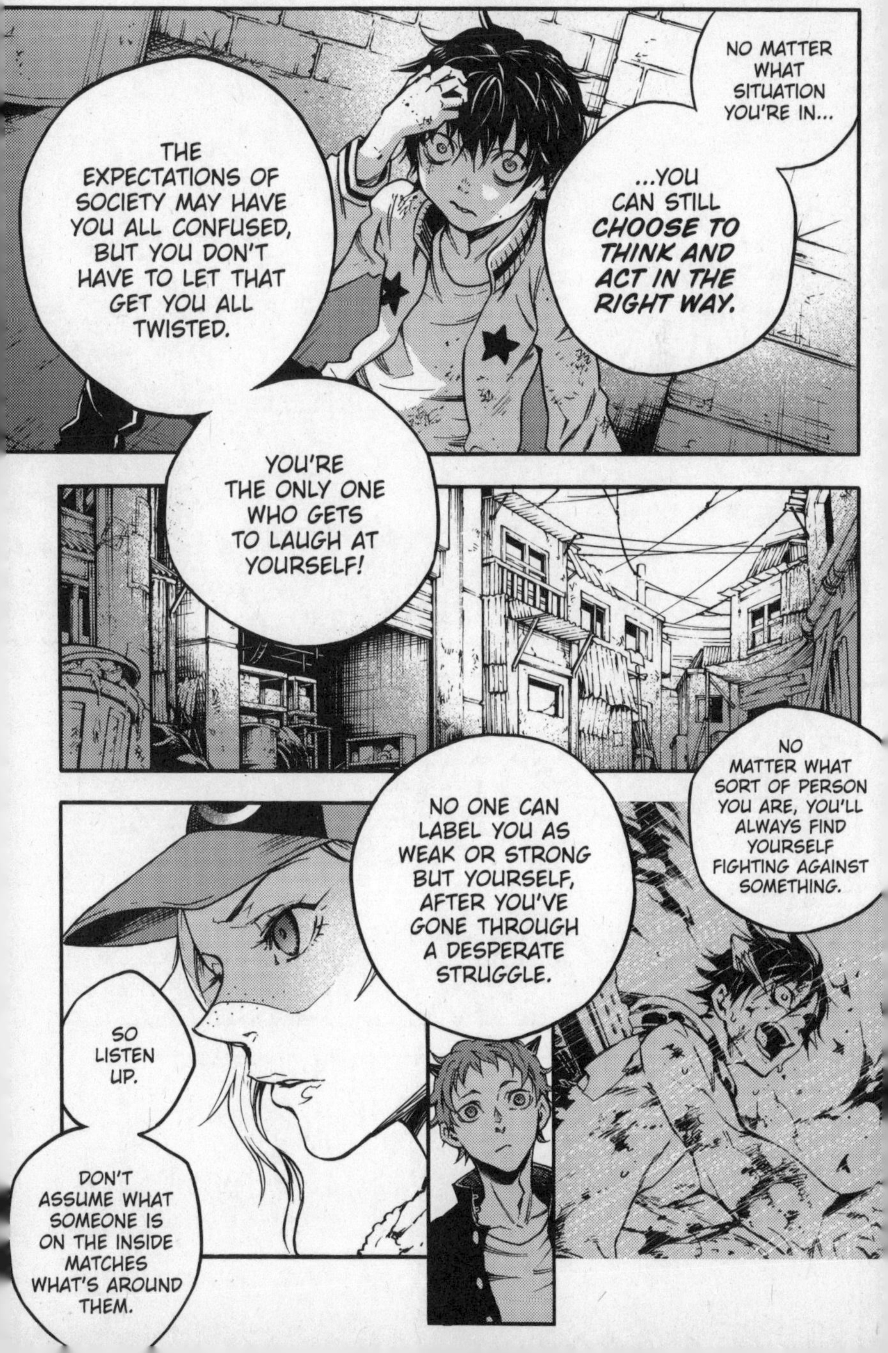
NO MATTER WHAT SITUATION YOU'RE IN...
...YOU CAN STILL *CHOOSE TO THINK AND ACT IN THE RIGHT WAY.*
THE EXPECTATIONS OF SOCIETY MAY HAVE YOU ALL CONFUSED, BUT YOU DON'T HAVE TO LET THAT GET YOU ALL TWISTED.
YOU'RE THE ONLY ONE WHO GETS TO LAUGH AT YOURSELF!
NO MATTER WHAT SORT OF PERSON YOU ARE, YOU'LL ALWAYS FIND YOURSELF FIGHTING AGAINST SOMETHING.
NO ONE CAN LABEL YOU AS WEAK OR STRONG BUT YOURSELF, AFTER YOU'VE GONE THROUGH A DESPERATE STRUGGLE.
SO LISTEN UP.
DON'T ASSUME WHAT SOMEONE IS ON THE INSIDE MATCHES WHAT'S AROUND THEM.

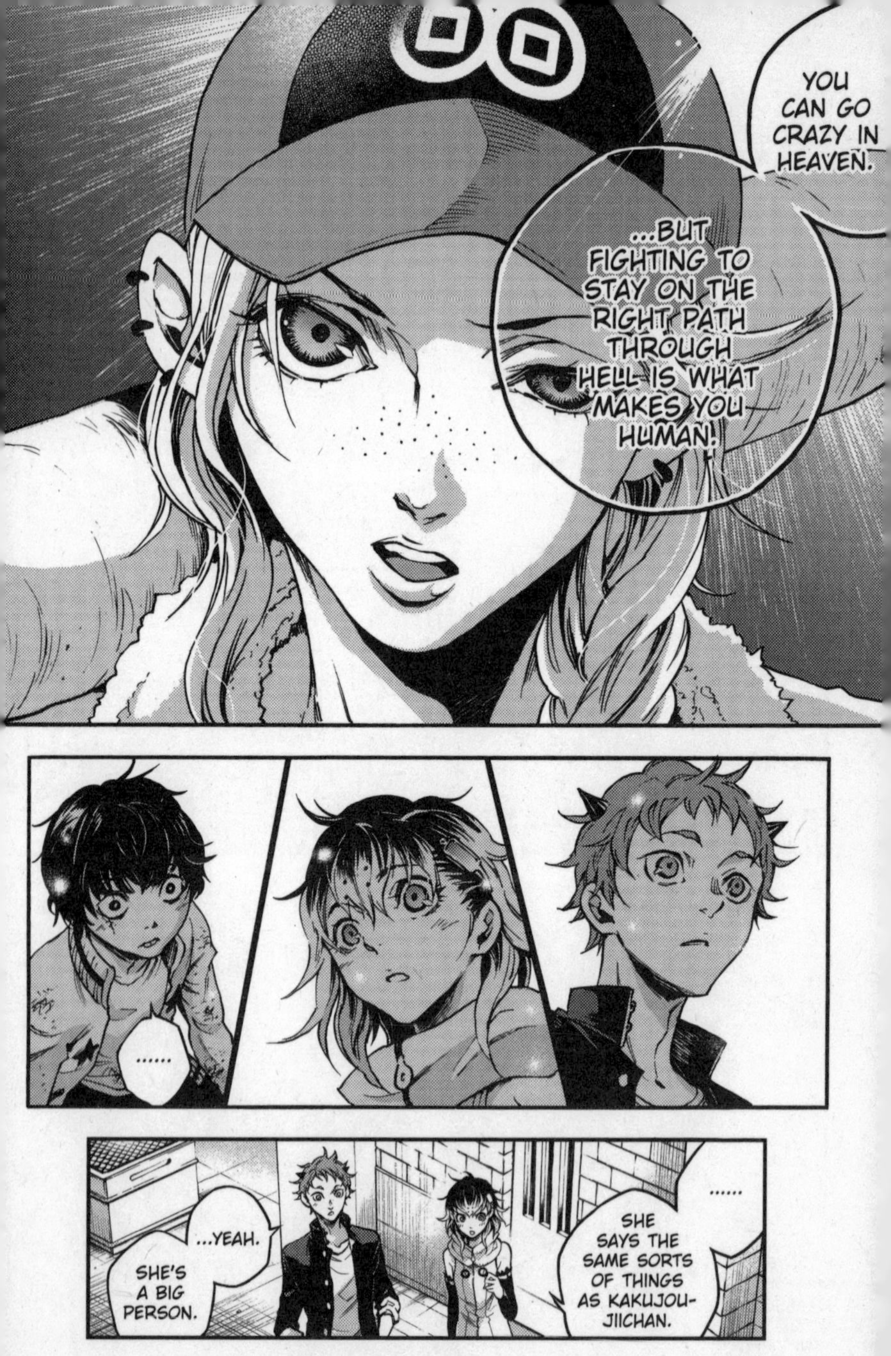
YOU CAN GO CRAZY IN HEAVEN.
...BUT FIGHTING TO STAY ON THE RIGHT PATH THROUGH HELL IS WHAT MAKES YOU HUMAN.
......
......
SHE SAYS THE SAME SORTS OF THINGS AS KAKUJOU-JIICHAN.
...YEAH.
SHE'S A BIG PERSON.

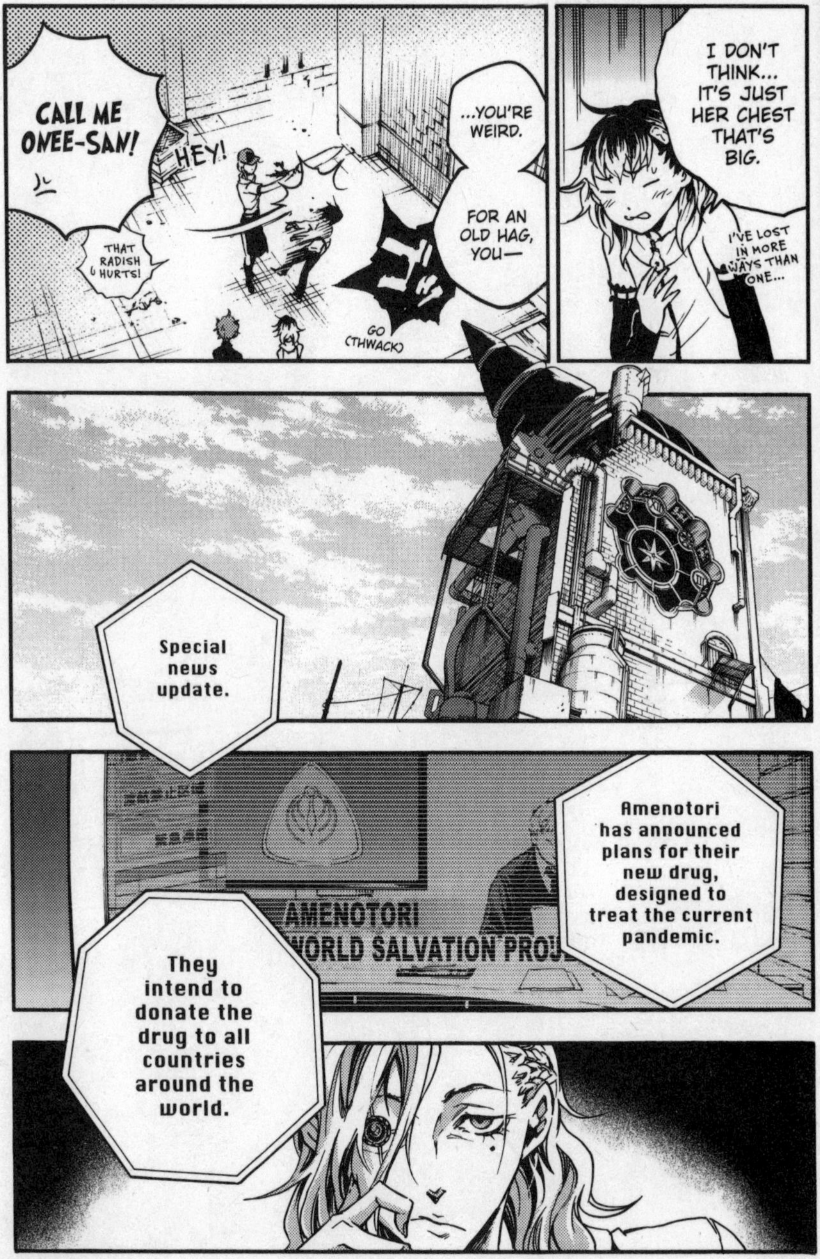
I DON'T THINK... IT'S JUST HER CHEST THAT'S BIG.
I'VE LOST IN MORE WAYS THAN ONE...
...YOU'RE WEIRD.
FOR AN OLD HAG, YOU—
GO (THWACK)
HEY!
CALL ME ONEE-SAN!
THAT RADISH HURTS!
Special news update.
Amenotori has announced plans for their new drug, designed to treat the current pandemic.
AMENOTORI
WORLD SALVATION PROJ
They intend to donate the drug to all countries around the world.

SIGN: LUCKY LUCKY SHOP

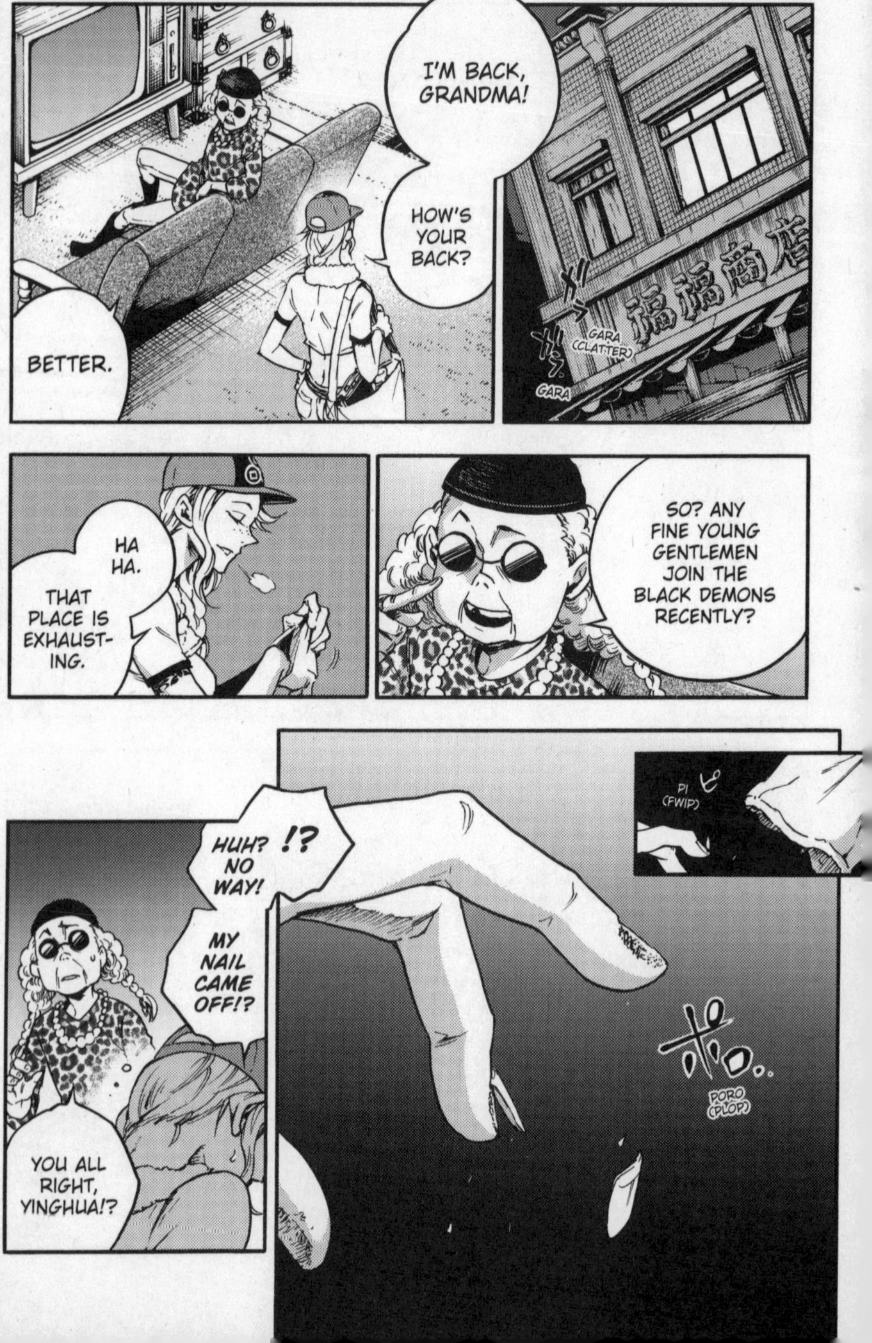
福福商店
GARA (CLATTER)
GARA
I'M BACK, GRANDMA!
HOW'S YOUR BACK?
BETTER.
SO? ANY FINE YOUNG GENTLEMEN JOIN THE BLACK DEMONS RECENTLY?
HA HA.
THAT PLACE IS EXHAUST-ING.
PI (FWIP)
HUH? !? NO WAY!
MY NAIL CAME OFF!?
PORO (PLOP)
YOU ALL RIGHT, YINGHUA!?

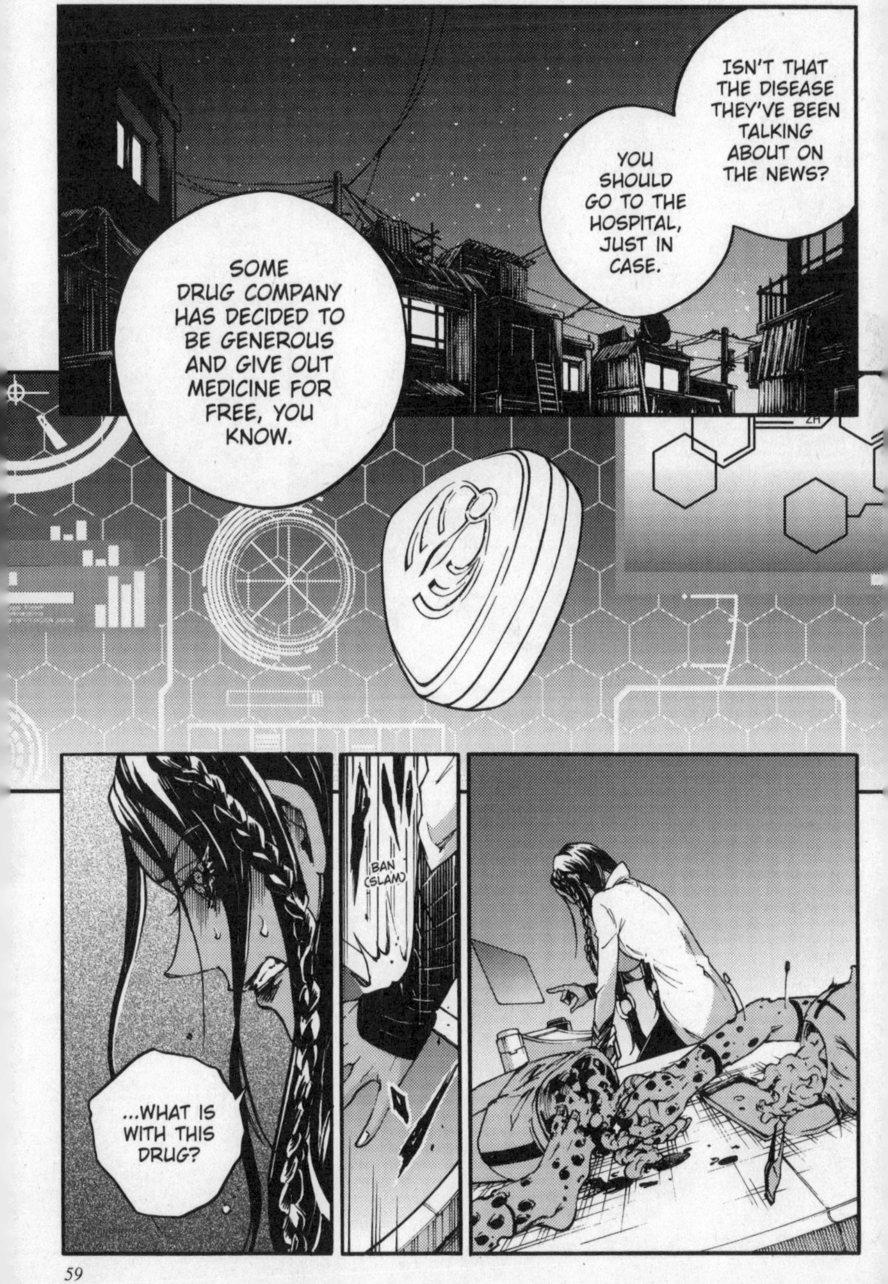
ISN'T THAT THE DISEASE THEY'VE BEEN TALKING ABOUT ON THE NEWS?
YOU SHOULD GO TO THE HOSPITAL, JUST IN CASE.
SOME DRUG COMPANY HAS DECIDED TO BE GENEROUS AND GIVE OUT MEDICINE FOR FREE, YOU KNOW.
BAN (SLAM)
...WHAT IS WITH THIS DRUG?

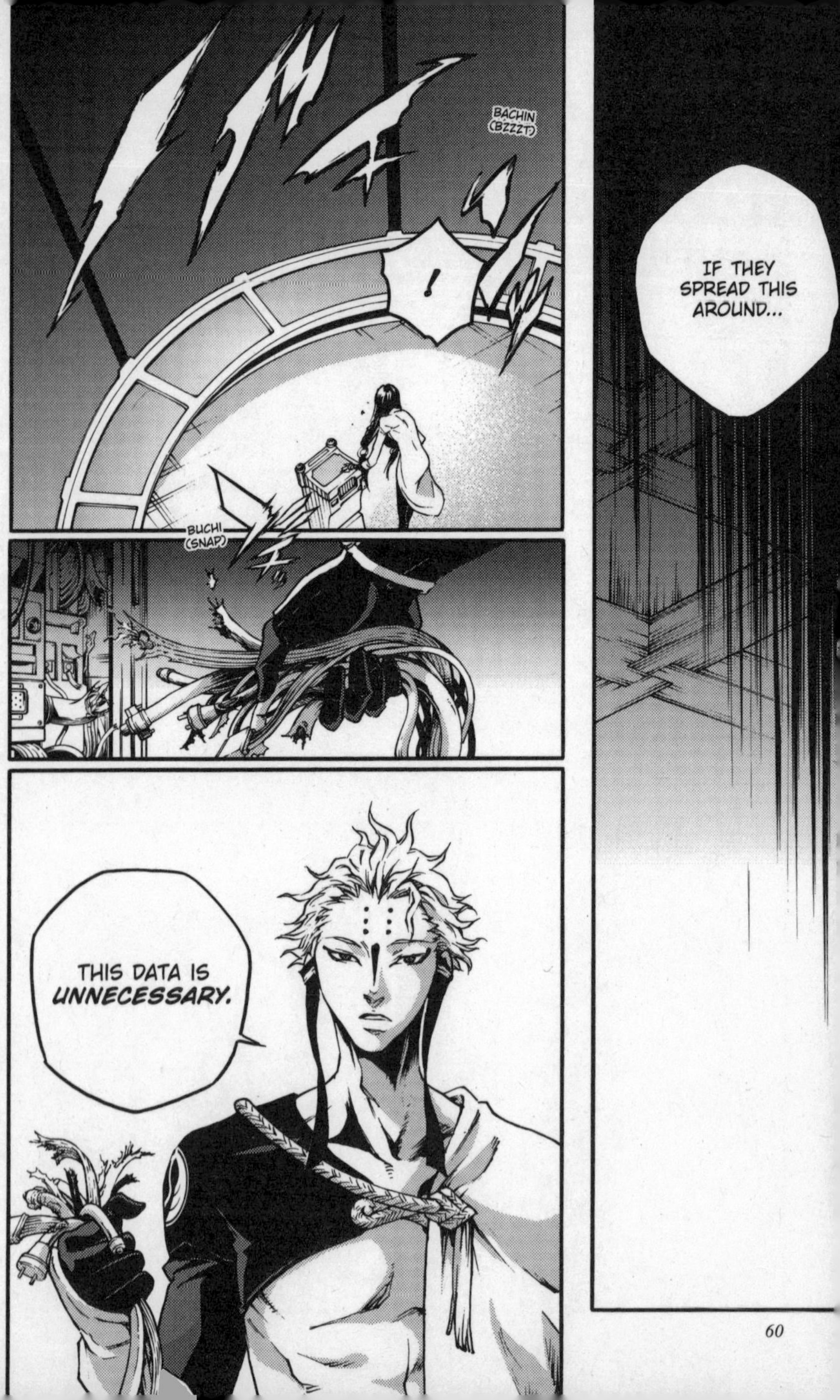
IF THEY SPREAD THIS AROUND...
BACHIN (BZZZT)
!
BUCHI (SNAP)
THIS DATA IS *UNNECESSARY.*

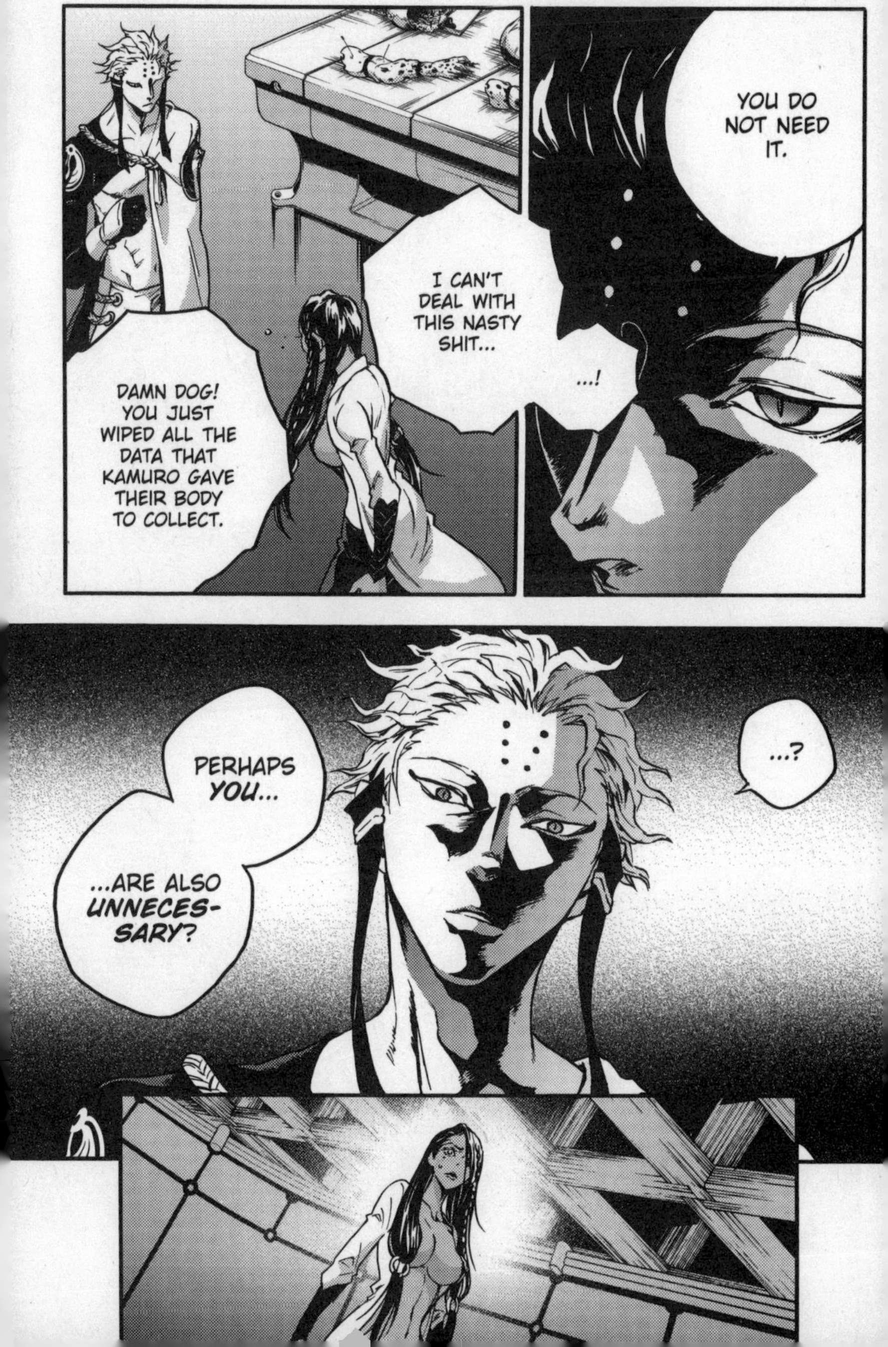
YOU DO NOT NEED IT.
...!
I CAN'T DEAL WITH THIS NASTY SHIT...
DAMN DOG! YOU JUST WIPED ALL THE DATA THAT KAMURO GAVE THEIR BODY TO COLLECT.
...?
PERHAPS *YOU*...
...ARE ALSO *UNNECES-SARY*?

THIS IS BAD.

AMENOTORI IS SUPPOSED TO BE THE GODS' DIVINE BOAT BOUND FOR HEAVEN.

BUT THIS BOAT...

...IS MORE LIKE...

HMM...

...WHILE I TOOK MY LITTLE TRIP UP NORTH...

...AMENOTORI WAS UP TO SOME PRETTY AWFUL STUFF.

...THIS IS ALMOST LIKE...

AMENOTORI WORLD SALVATION PRO

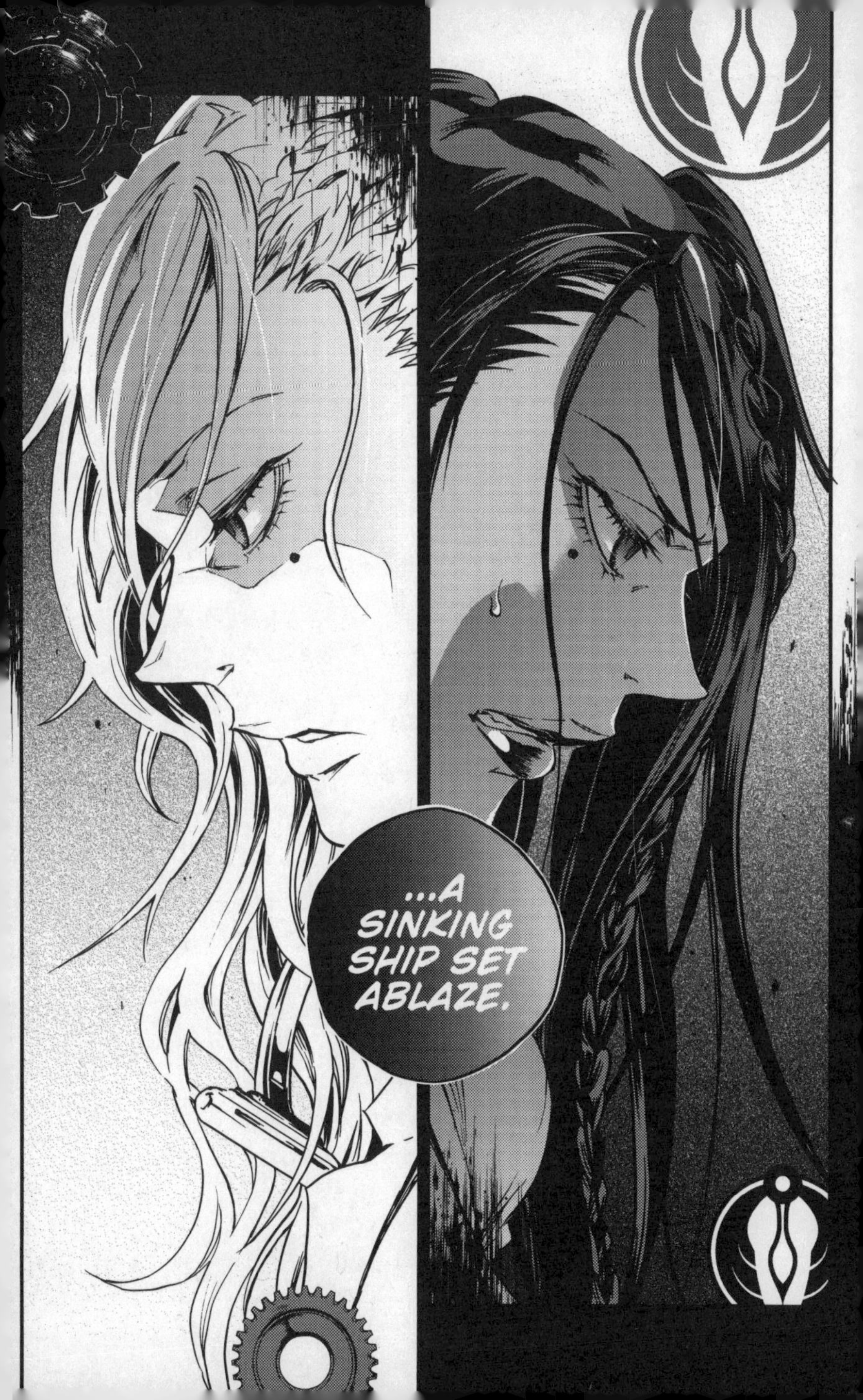
...A SINKING SHIP SET ABLAZE.

SMO 'KIN' PARADE

THE WORLD IS DEAD,

THE

PARADE

WILL START.

JINSEI KATAOKA

KAZUMA KONDOU

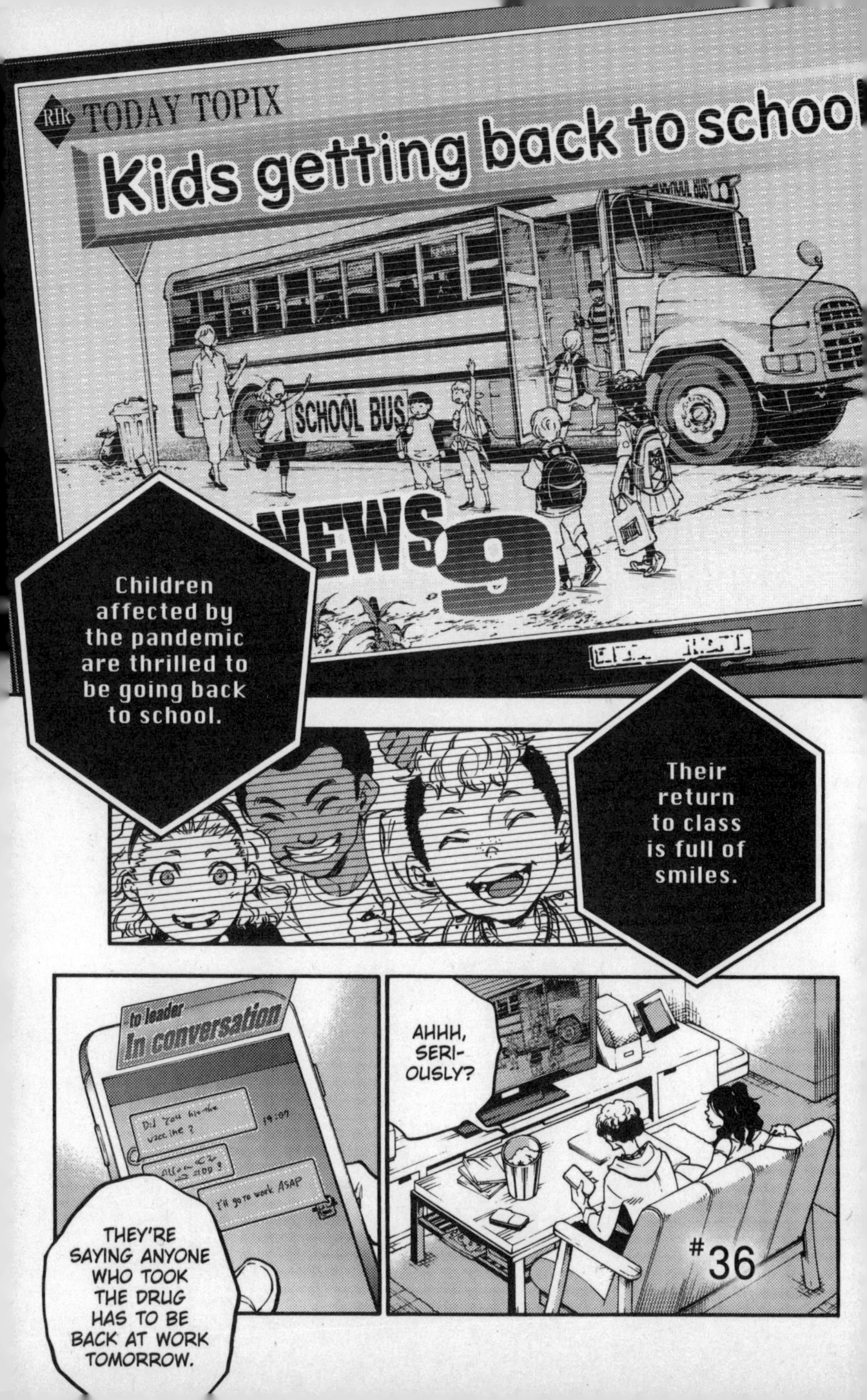
RIK TODAY TOPIX
Kids getting back to school
SCHOOL BUS
SCHOOL BUS
NEWS 9
Children affected by the pandemic are thrilled to be going back to school.
Their return to class is full of smiles.
AHHH, SERI-OUSLY?
#36
to leader
In conversation
I'll go to work ASAP
THEY'RE SAYING ANYONE WHO TOOK THE DRUG HAS TO BE BACK AT WORK TOMORROW.

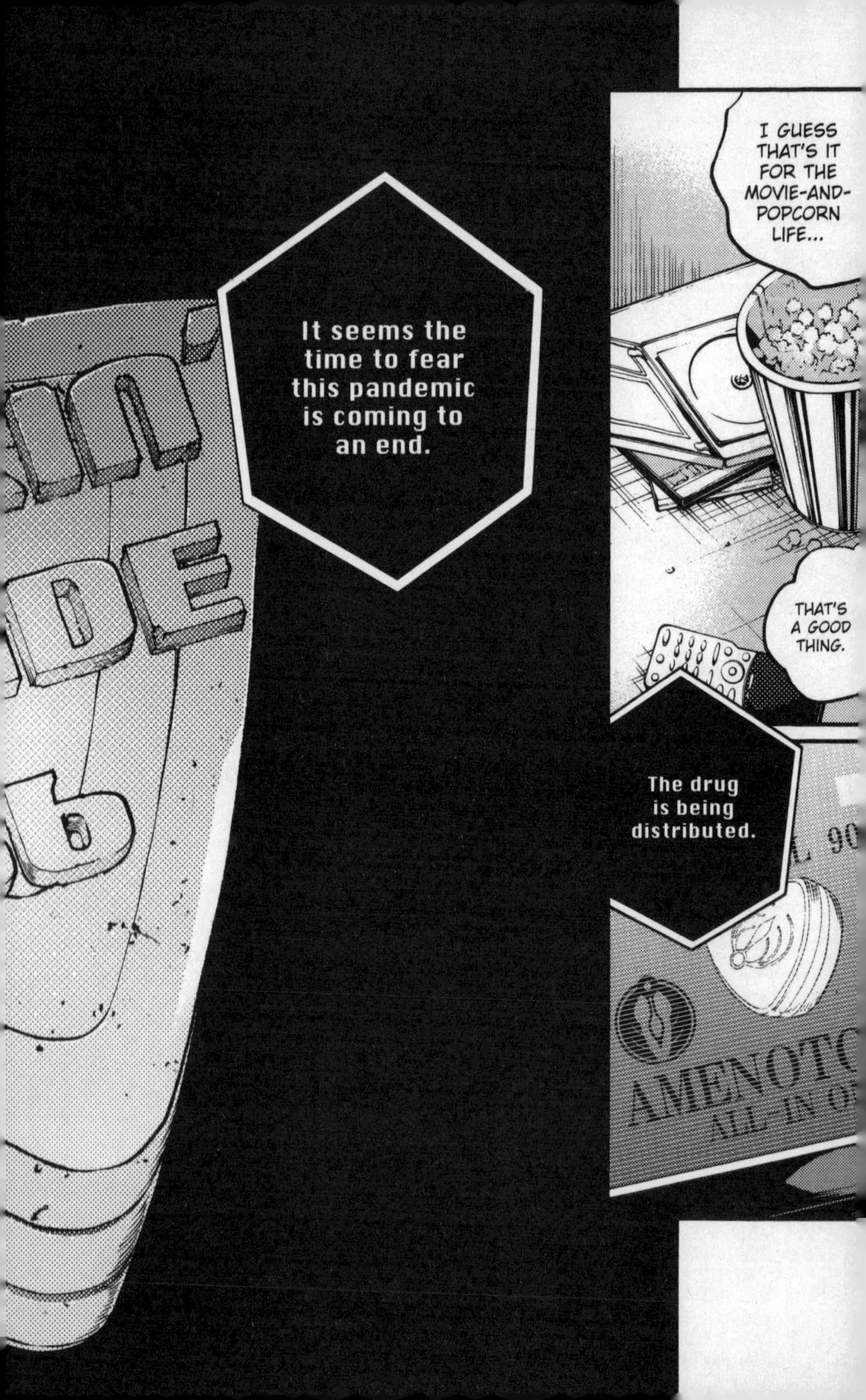
I GUESS THAT'S IT FOR THE MOVIE-AND-POPCORN LIFE...
THAT'S A GOOD THING.
The drug is being distributed.
It seems the time to fear this pandemic is coming to an end.

#36 ILL-PREPARED PANIC

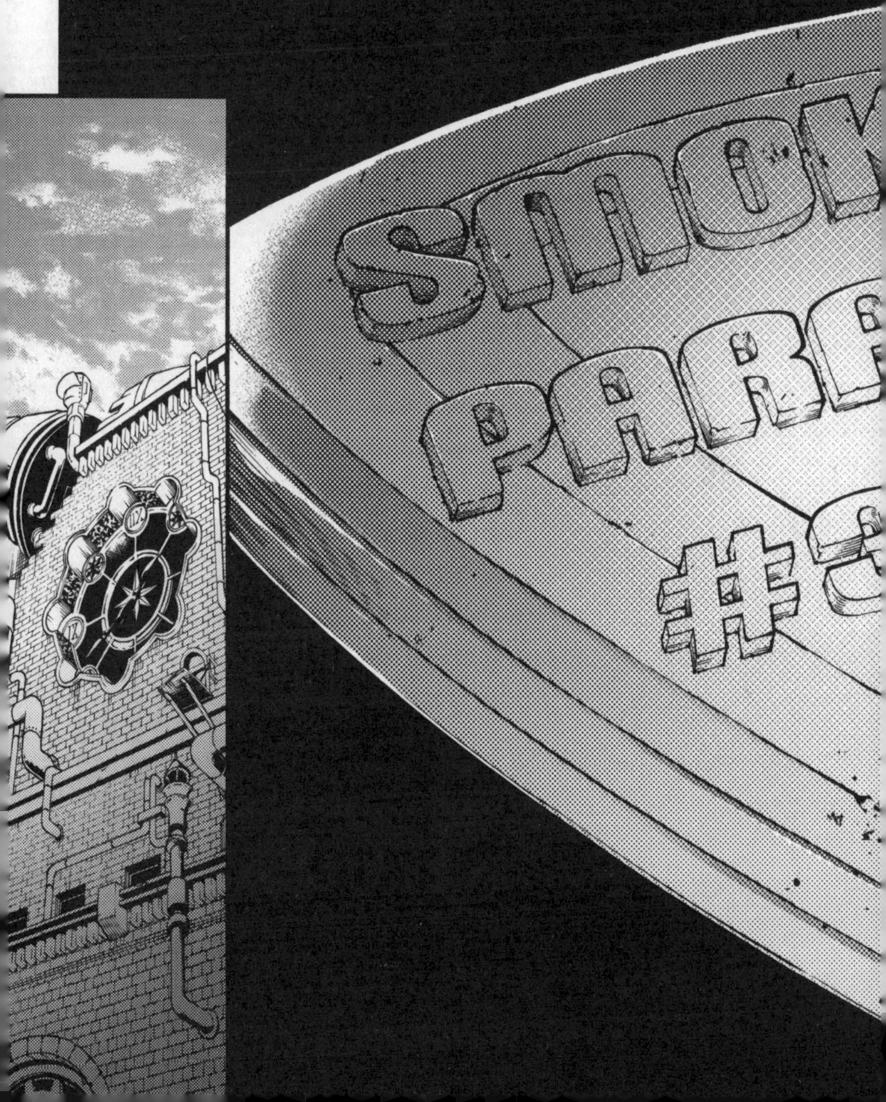

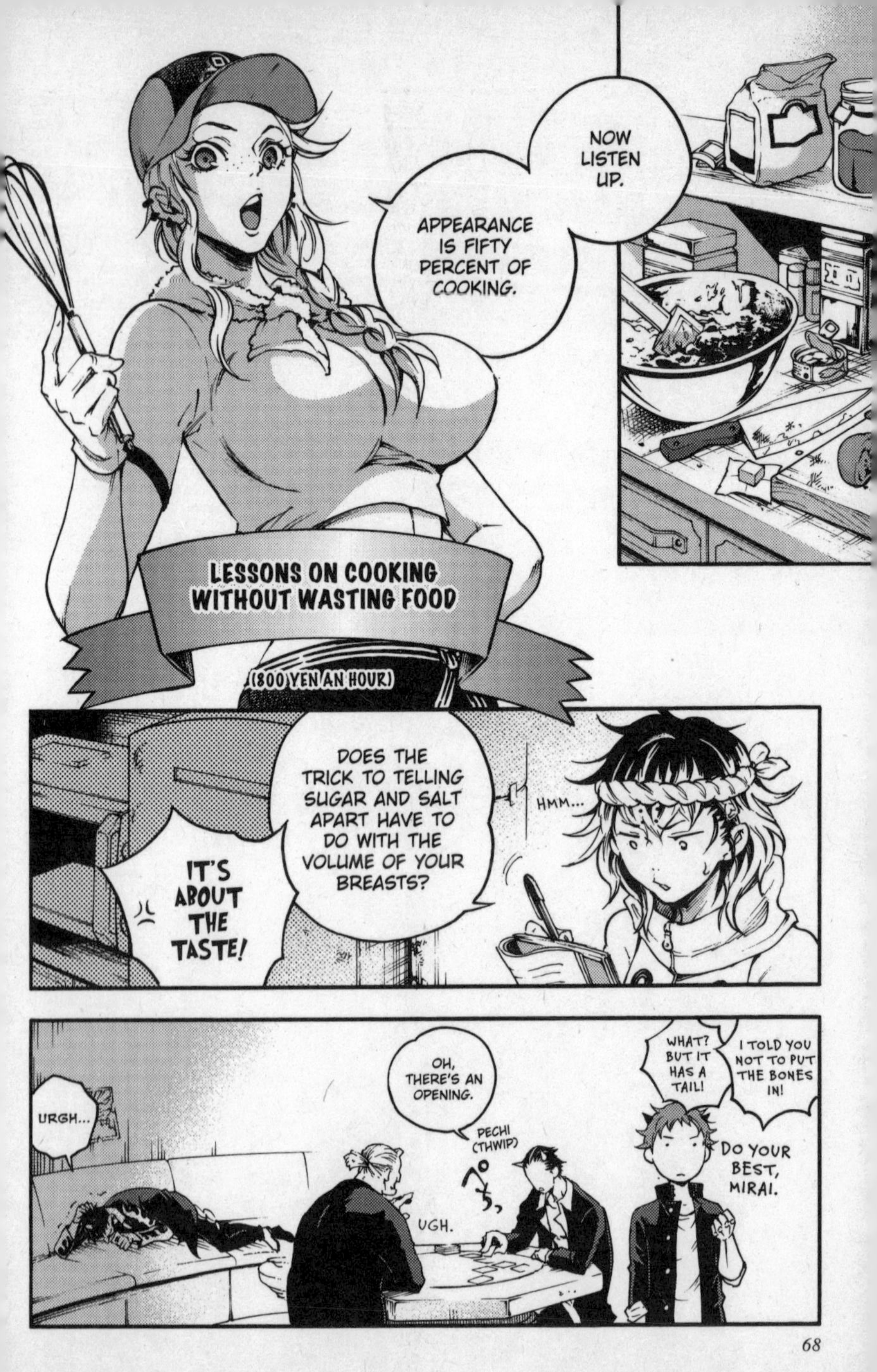
NOW LISTEN UP.
APPEARANCE IS FIFTY PERCENT OF COOKING.
LESSONS ON COOKING WITHOUT WASTING FOOD
(800 YEN AN HOUR)
HMM...
DOES THE TRICK TO TELLING SUGAR AND SALT APART HAVE TO DO WITH THE VOLUME OF YOUR BREASTS?
IT'S ABOUT THE TASTE!
I TOLD YOU NOT TO PUT THE BONES IN!
WHAT? BUT IT HAS A TAIL!
DO YOUR BEST, MIRAI.
PECHI (THWIP)
OH, THERE'S AN OPENING.
UGH.
URGH...

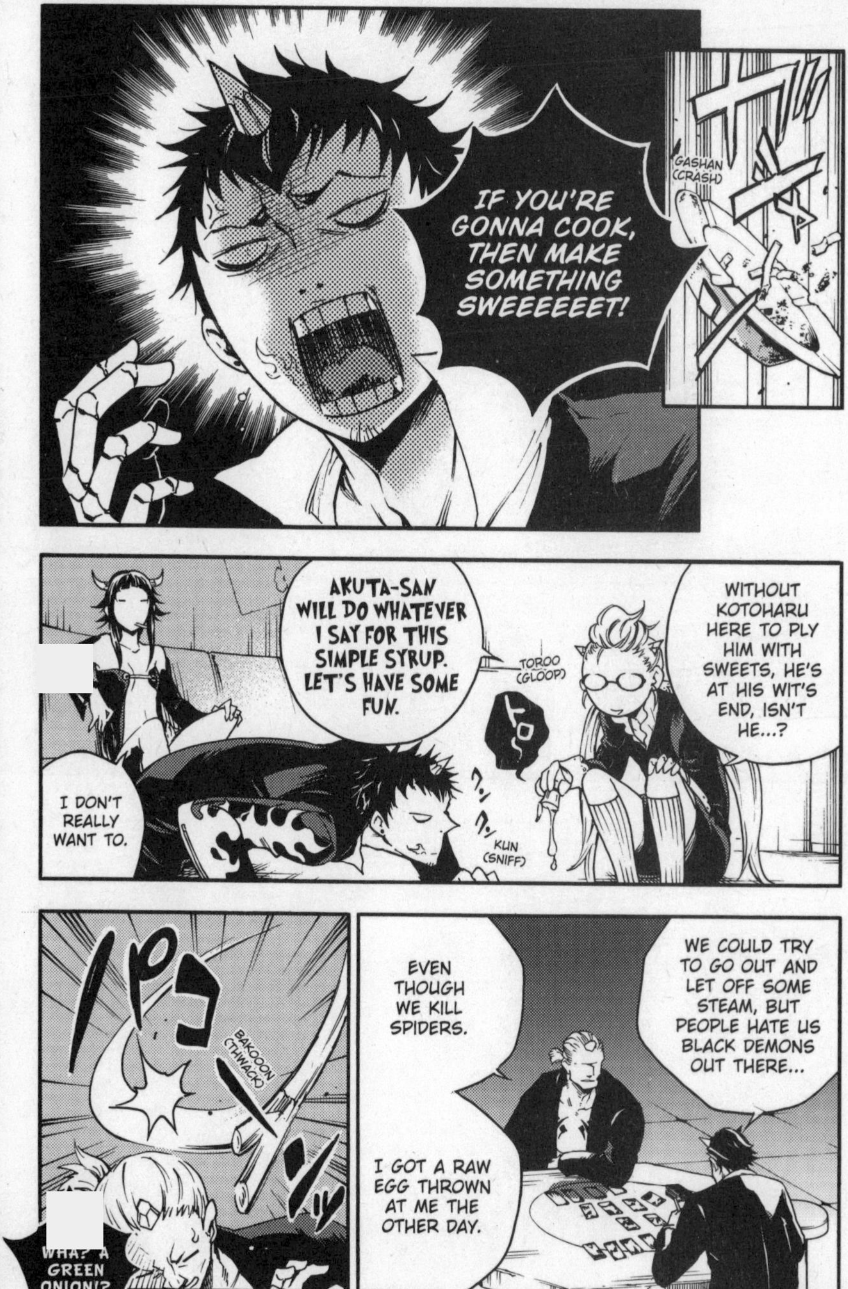

GASHAN (CRASH)
IF YOU'RE GONNA COOK, THEN MAKE SOMETHING SWEEEEEET!
WITHOUT KOTOHARU HERE TO PLY HIM WITH SWEETS, HE'S AT HIS WIT'S END, ISN'T HE...?
TOROO (GLOOP)
AKUTA-SAN WILL DO WHATEVER I SAY FOR THIS SIMPLE SYRUP. LET'S HAVE SOME FUN.
KUN (SNIFF)
I DON'T REALLY WANT TO.
WE COULD TRY TO GO OUT AND LET OFF SOME STEAM, BUT PEOPLE HATE US BLACK DEMONS OUT THERE...
EVEN THOUGH WE KILL SPIDERS.
I GOT A RAW EGG THROWN AT ME THE OTHER DAY.
BAKOOON (THWACK)
WHA? A GREEN ONION!?

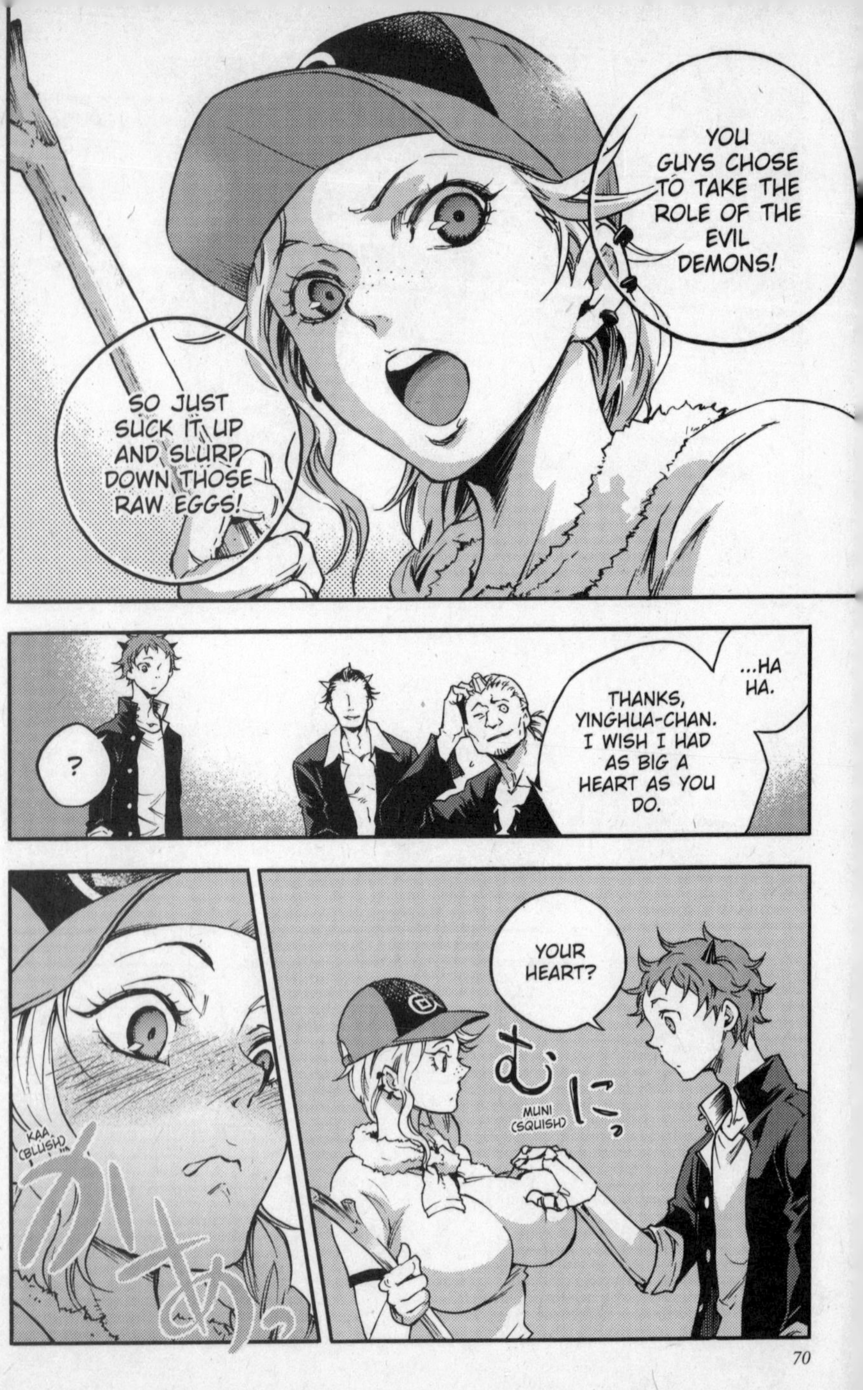
YOU GUYS CHOSE TO TAKE THE ROLE OF THE EVIL DEMONS!
SO JUST SUCK IT UP AND SLURP DOWN THOSE RAW EGGS!
...HA HA.
THANKS, YINGHUA-CHAN. I WISH I HAD AS BIG A HEART AS YOU DO.
?
YOUR HEART?
MUNI (SQUISH)
KAA (BLUSH)

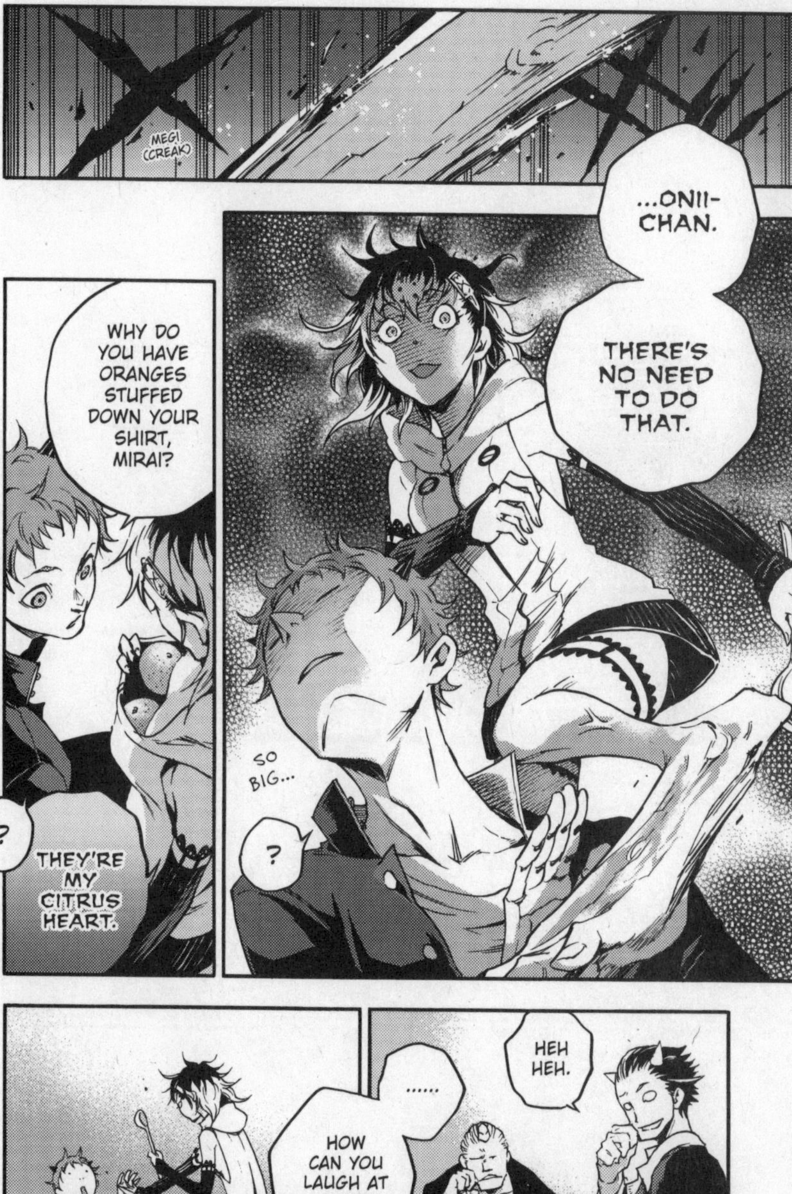
MEGI (CREAK)
...ONII-CHAN.
THERE'S NO NEED TO DO THAT.
SO BIG...
?
WHY DO YOU HAVE ORANGES STUFFED DOWN YOUR SHIRT, MIRAI?
?
THEY'RE MY CITRUS HEART.
HEH HEH.
......
HOW CAN YOU LAUGH AT THAT?

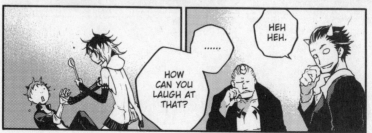

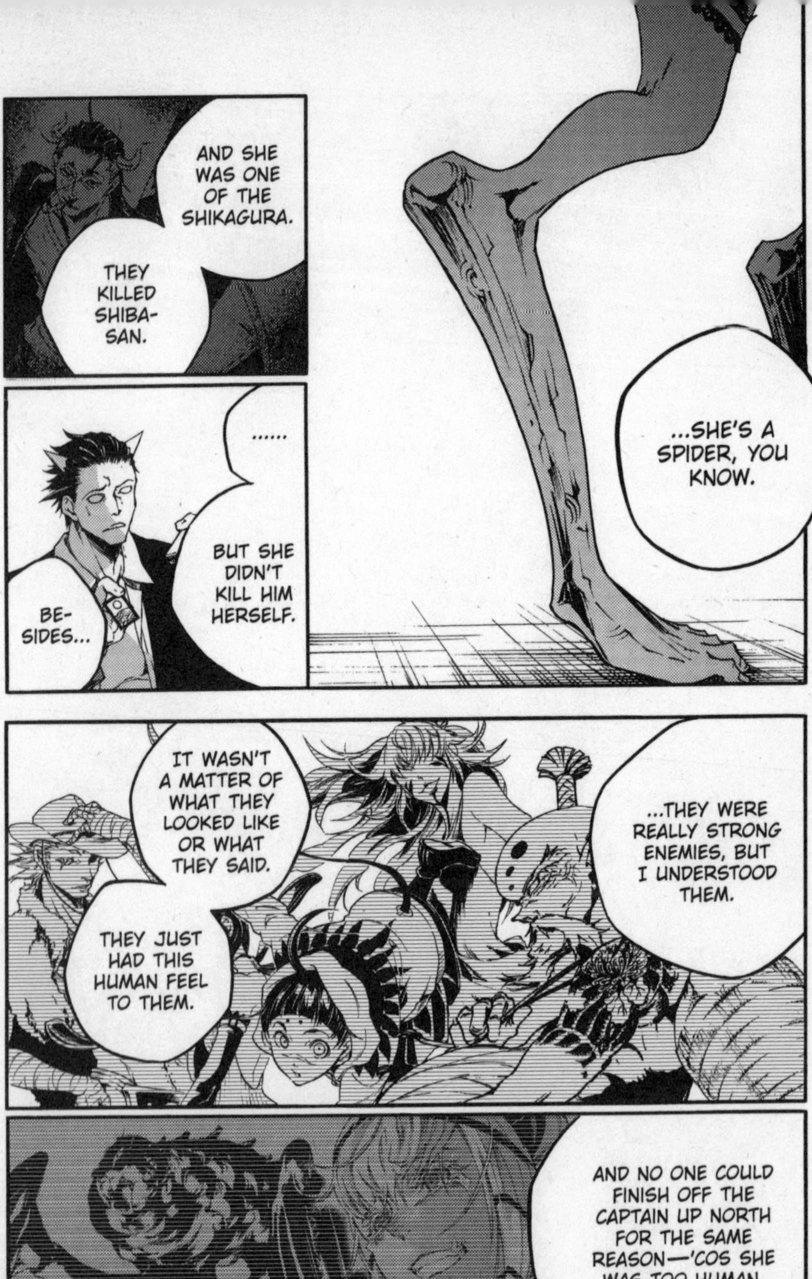
...SHE'S A SPIDER, YOU KNOW.
AND SHE WAS ONE OF THE SHIKAGURA.
THEY KILLED SHIBA-SAN.
......
BUT SHE DIDN'T KILL HIM HERSELF.
BE-SIDES...
...THEY WERE REALLY STRONG ENEMIES, BUT I UNDERSTOOD THEM.
IT WASN'T A MATTER OF WHAT THEY LOOKED LIKE OR WHAT THEY SAID.
THEY JUST HAD THIS HUMAN FEEL TO THEM.
AND NO ONE COULD FINISH OFF THE CAPTAIN UP NORTH FOR THE SAME REASON—'COS SHE WAS TOO HUMAN.

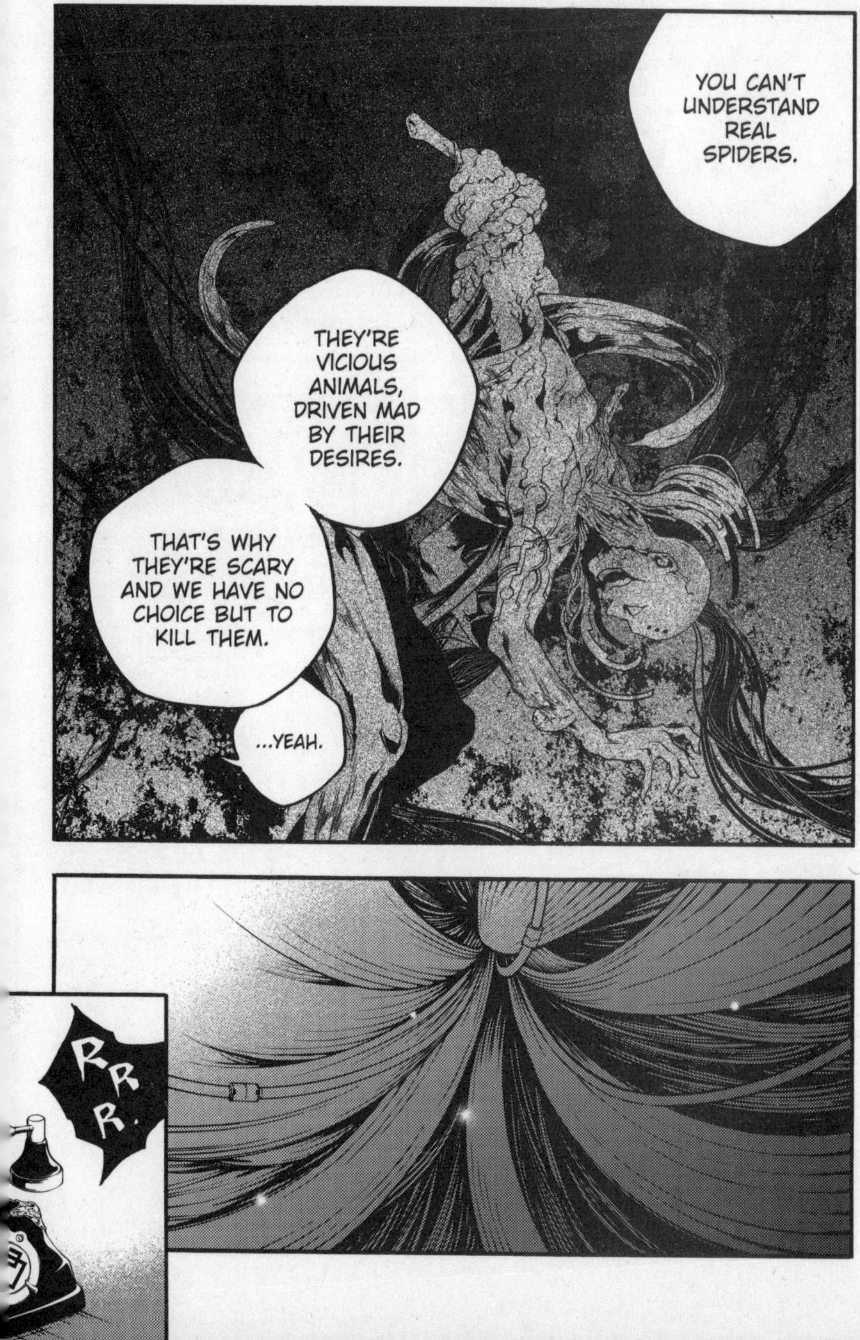
YOU CAN'T UNDERSTAND REAL SPIDERS.
THEY'RE VICIOUS ANIMALS, DRIVEN MAD BY THEIR DESIRES.
THAT'S WHY THEY'RE SCARY AND WE HAVE NO CHOICE BUT TO KILL THEM.
...YEAH.
RRR.

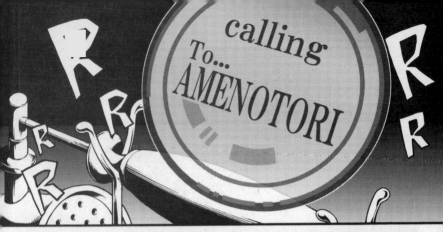

calling
To...
AMENOTORI

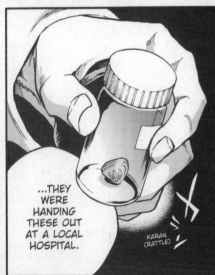

...THEY WERE HANDING THESE OUT AT A LOCAL HOSPITAL.

KARAN
(RATTLE)

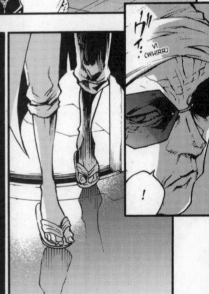

ヴィ
(WHIRR)

!

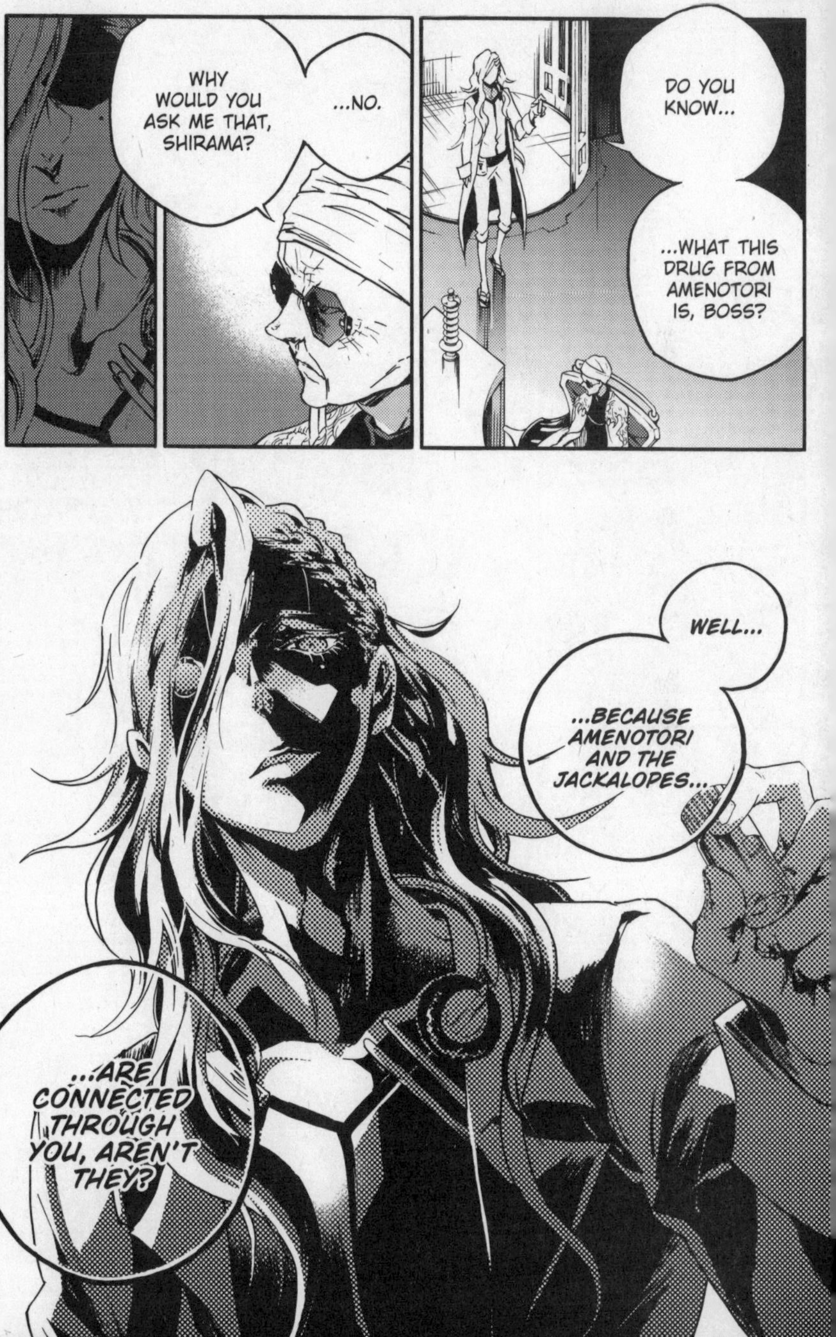
DO YOU KNOW...
...WHAT THIS DRUG FROM AMENOTORI IS, BOSS?
...NO.
WHY WOULD YOU ASK ME THAT, SHIRAMA?
WELL...
...BECAUSE AMENOTORI AND THE JACKALOPES...
...ARE CONNECTED THROUGH YOU, AREN'T THEY?

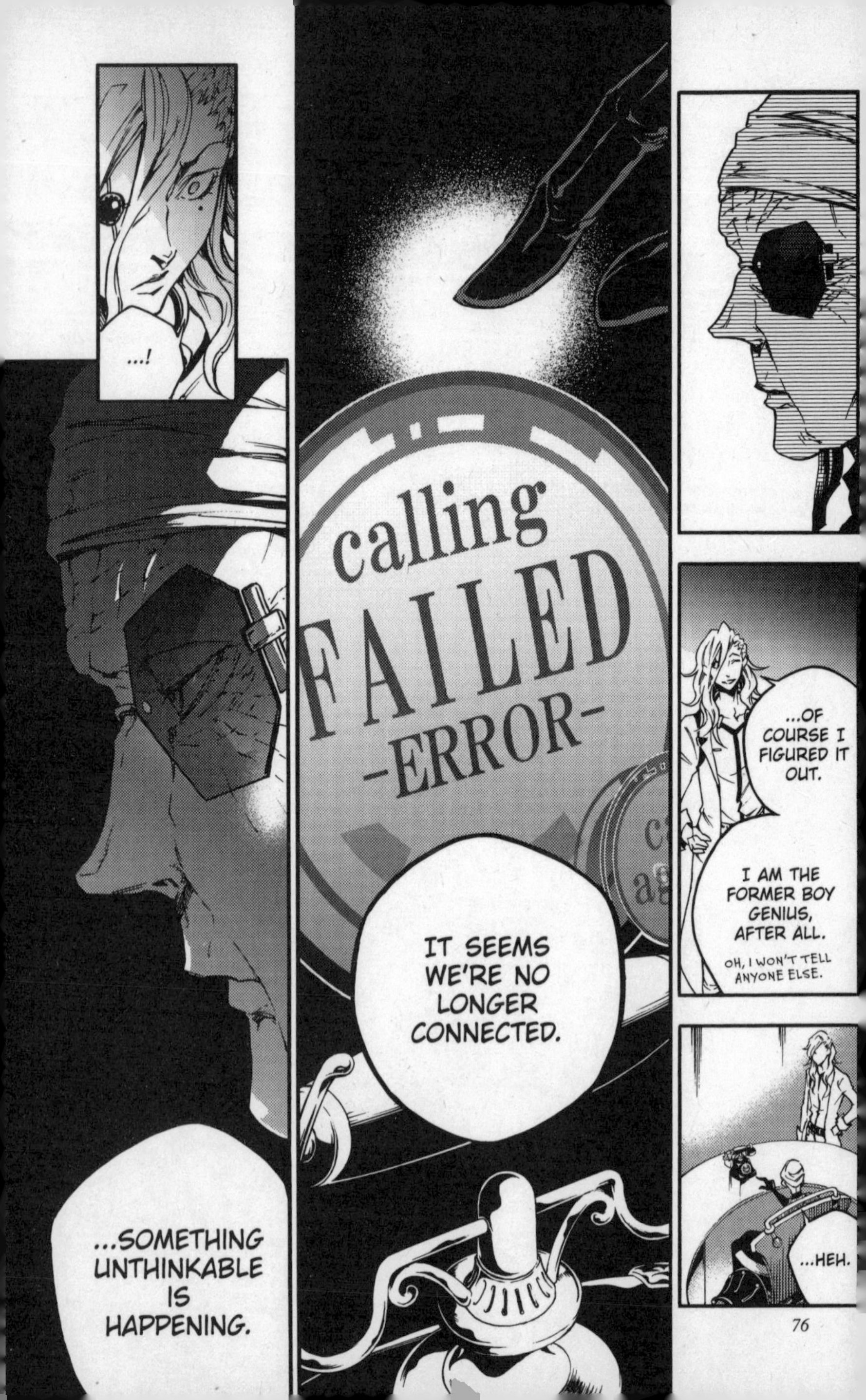
...OF COURSE I FIGURED IT OUT.
I AM THE FORMER BOY GENIUS, AFTER ALL.
OH, I WON'T TELL ANYONE ELSE.
...HEH.
calling
FAILED
-ERROR-
IT SEEMS WE'RE NO LONGER CONNECTED.
...!
...SOMETHING UNTHINKABLE IS HAPPENING.

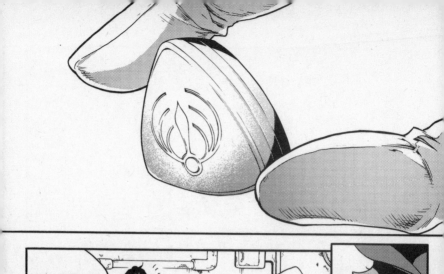

ARE YOU NOT FEELING WELL, WATERMELON-SAN?

IT'S YING-HUA!

HOO...

GOKUN (GULP)

FACKY LAND

......

I'LL BE RIGHT AS RAIN IF I GET SOME FOOD IN ME.

I'M JUST FINE.

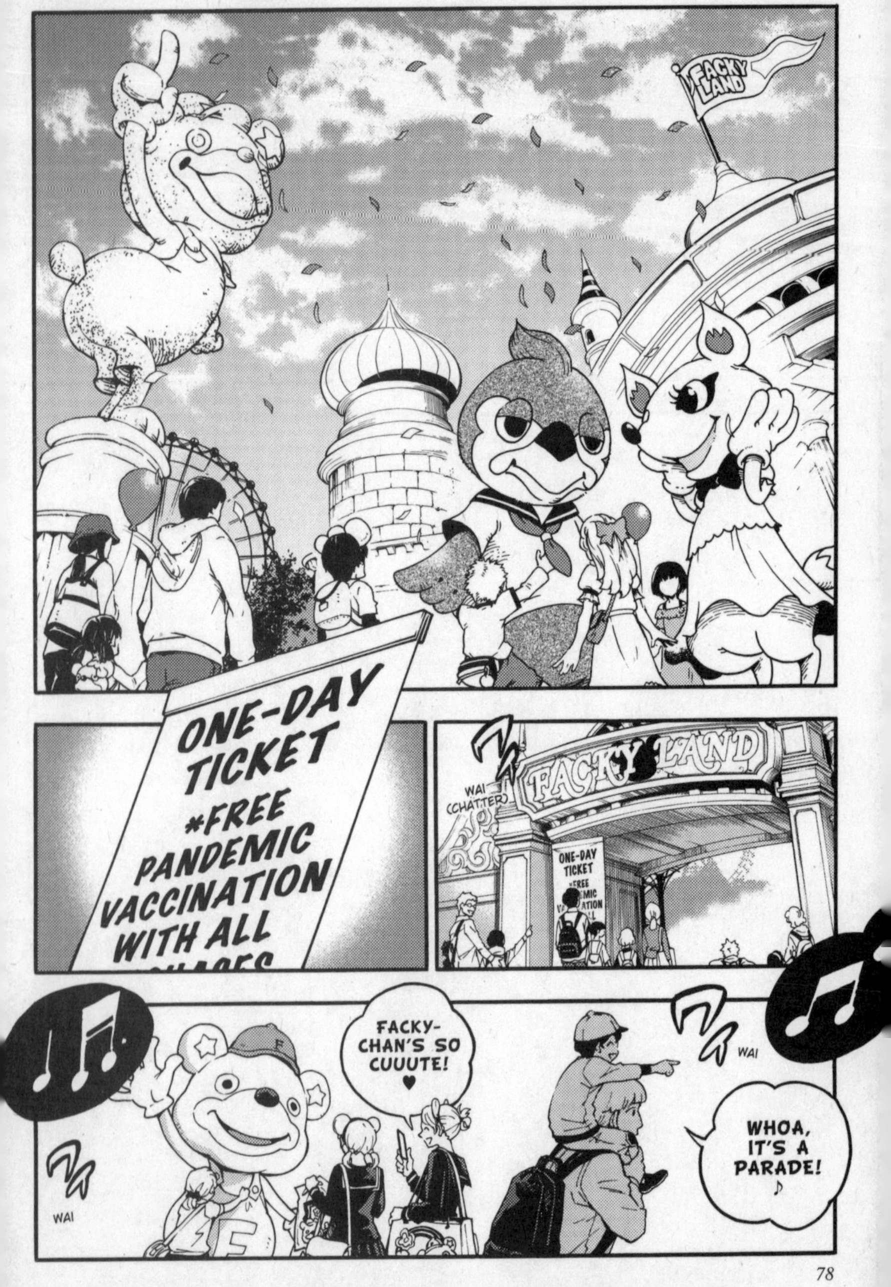
FACKY LAND
FACKY LAND
WAI (CHATTER)
ONE-DAY TICKET
ONE-DAY TICKET *FREE PANDEMIC VACCINATION WITH ALL
WAI
WHOA, IT'S A PARADE! ♪
FACKY-CHAN'S SO CUUUTE! ♥
WAI

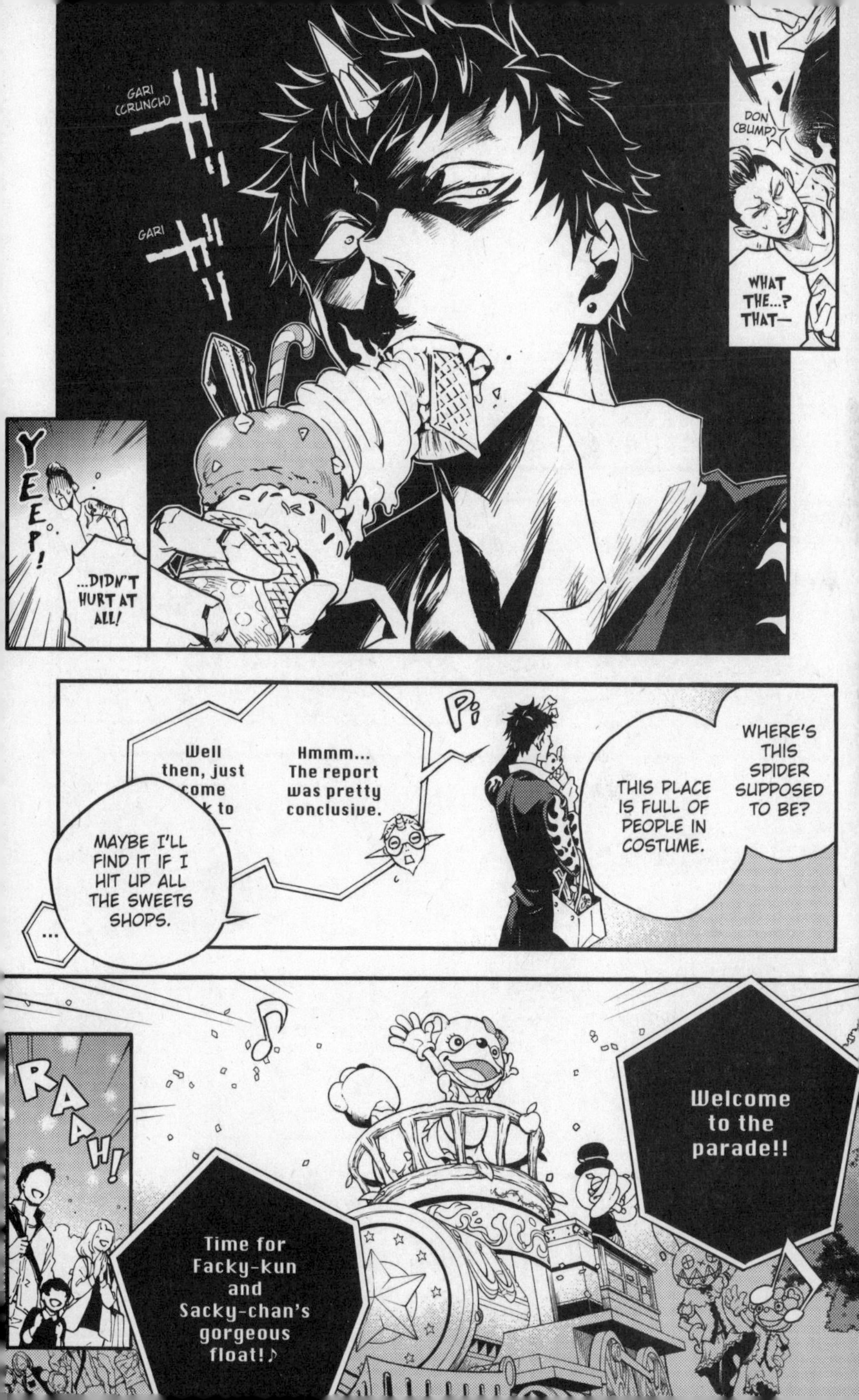
DON (BUMP)
WHAT THE...? THAT—
GARI (CRUNCH)
GARI
YEEP!
...DIDN'T HURT AT ALL!
Pi
WHERE'S THIS SPIDER SUPPOSED TO BE?
THIS PLACE IS FULL OF PEOPLE IN COSTUME.
Hmmm... The report was pretty conclusive.
Well then, just come
MAYBE I'LL FIND IT IF I HIT UP ALL THE SWEETS SHOPS.
...
Welcome to the parade!!
Time for Facky-kun and Sacky-chan's gorgeous float!♪
RAAH!

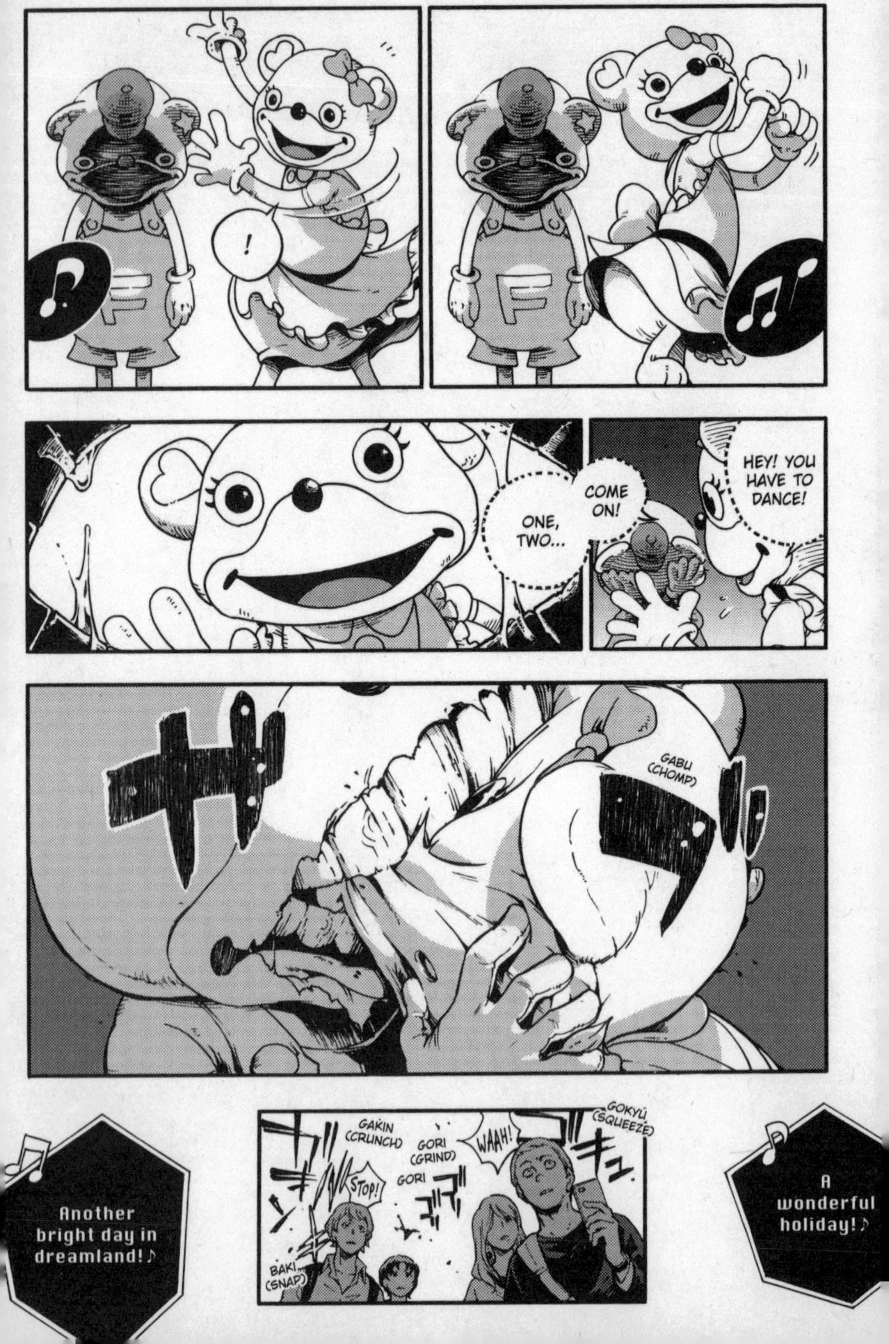
!
HEY! YOU HAVE TO DANCE!
COME ON!
ONE, TWO...
GABU (CHOMP)
A wonderful holiday!♪
GOKYŪ (SQUEEZE)
WAAH!
GORI (GRIND)
GORI
GAKIN (CRUNCH)
STOP!
BAKI (SNAP)
Another bright day in dreamland!♪

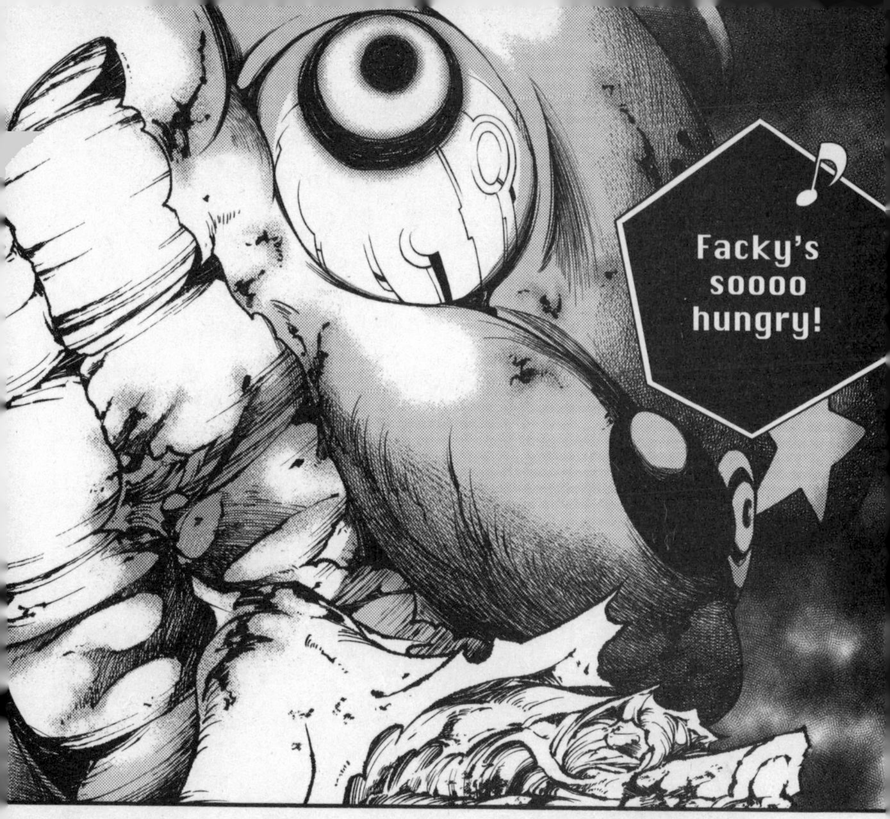
Facky's soooo hungry!

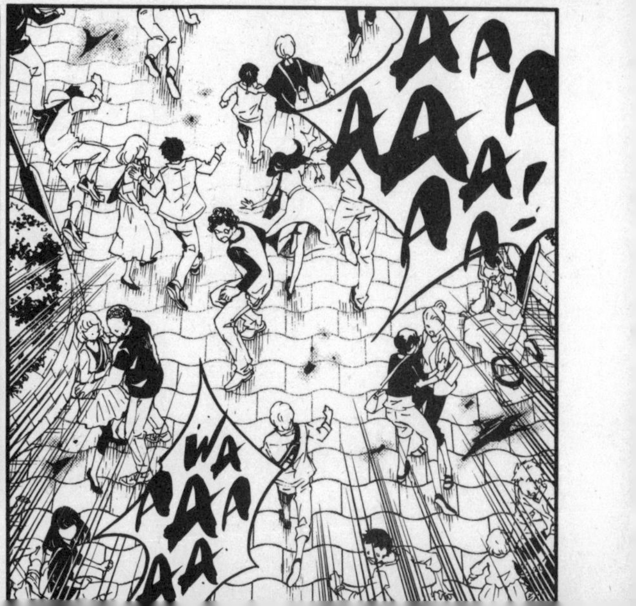
AAAAAAAA!
WAAAAAAA

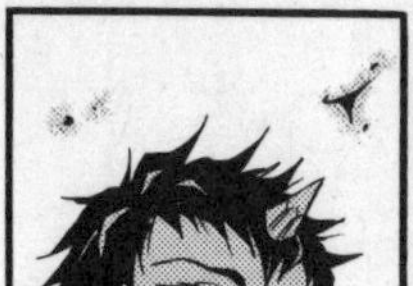
FOUND THE TARGET.

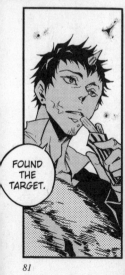

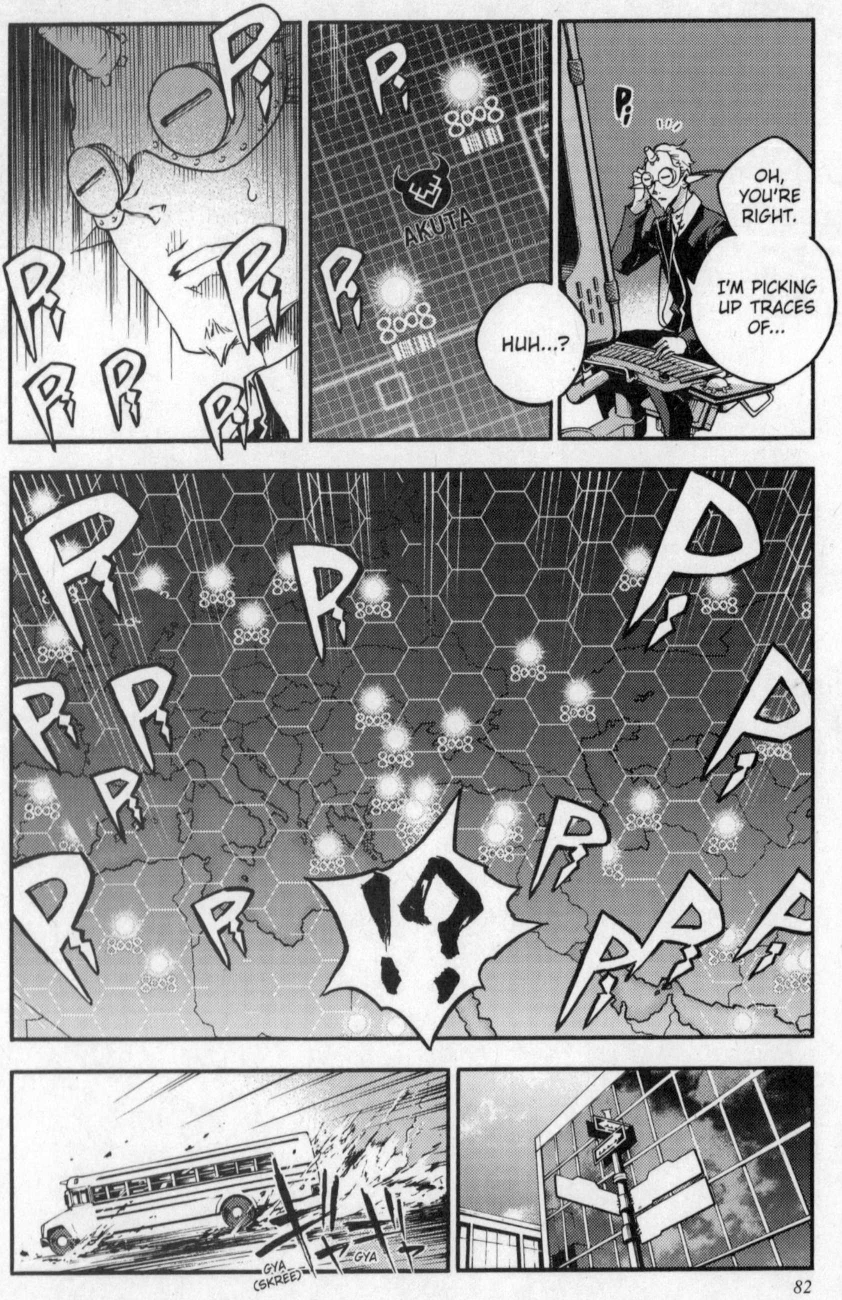
Pi
OH, YOU'RE RIGHT.
I'M PICKING UP TRACES OF...
HUH...?
Pi
AKUTA
Pi
Pi
Pi
!?
GYA
(SKREE)
GYA

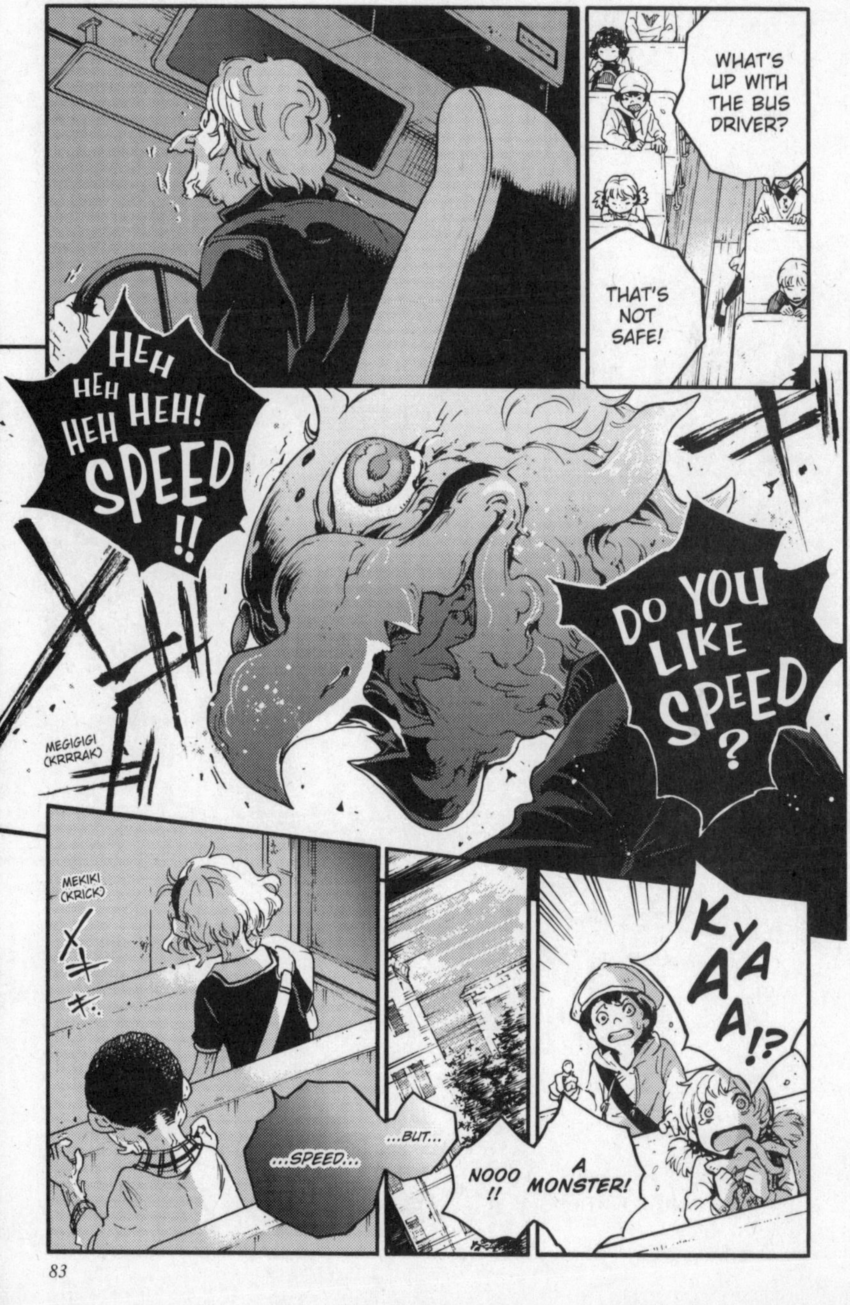
WHAT'S UP WITH THE BUS DRIVER?
THAT'S NOT SAFE!
HEH HEH HEH HEH! SPEED!!
DO YOU LIKE SPEED?
MEGIGIGI (KRRRAK)
KYAAAA!?
A MONSTER!
NOOO!!
...BUT...
MEKIKI (KRICK)
...SPEED...

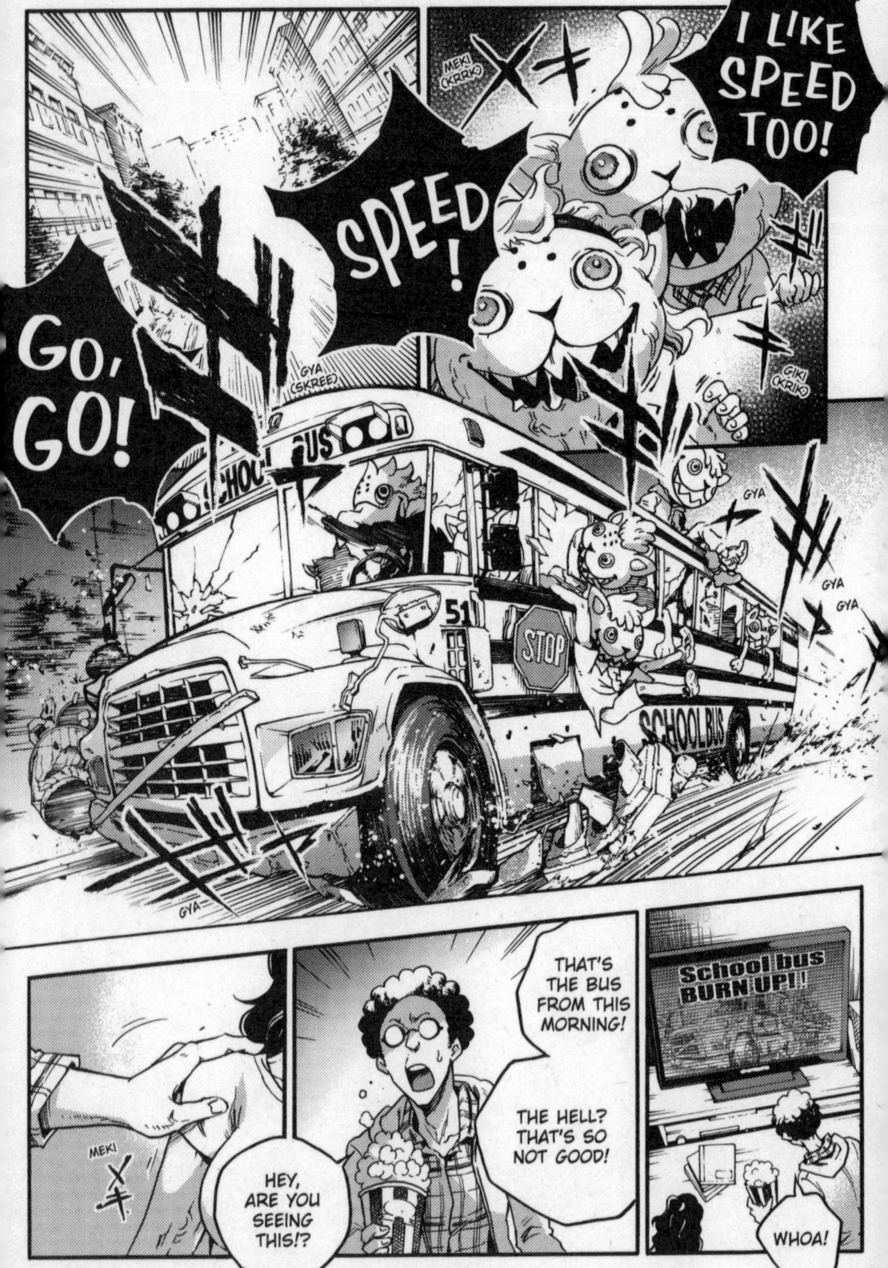
MEKI (KRRK)
I LIKE SPEED TOO!
GIKI (KRIK)
SPEED!
GO, GO!
GYA (SKREE)
SCHOOL BUS
GYA
GYA
GYA
51
STOP
SCHOOLBUS
GYA
School bus BURN UP!!
WHOA!
THAT'S THE BUS FROM THIS MORNING!
THE HELL? THAT'S SO NOT GOOD!
HEY, ARE YOU SEEING THIS!?
MEKI

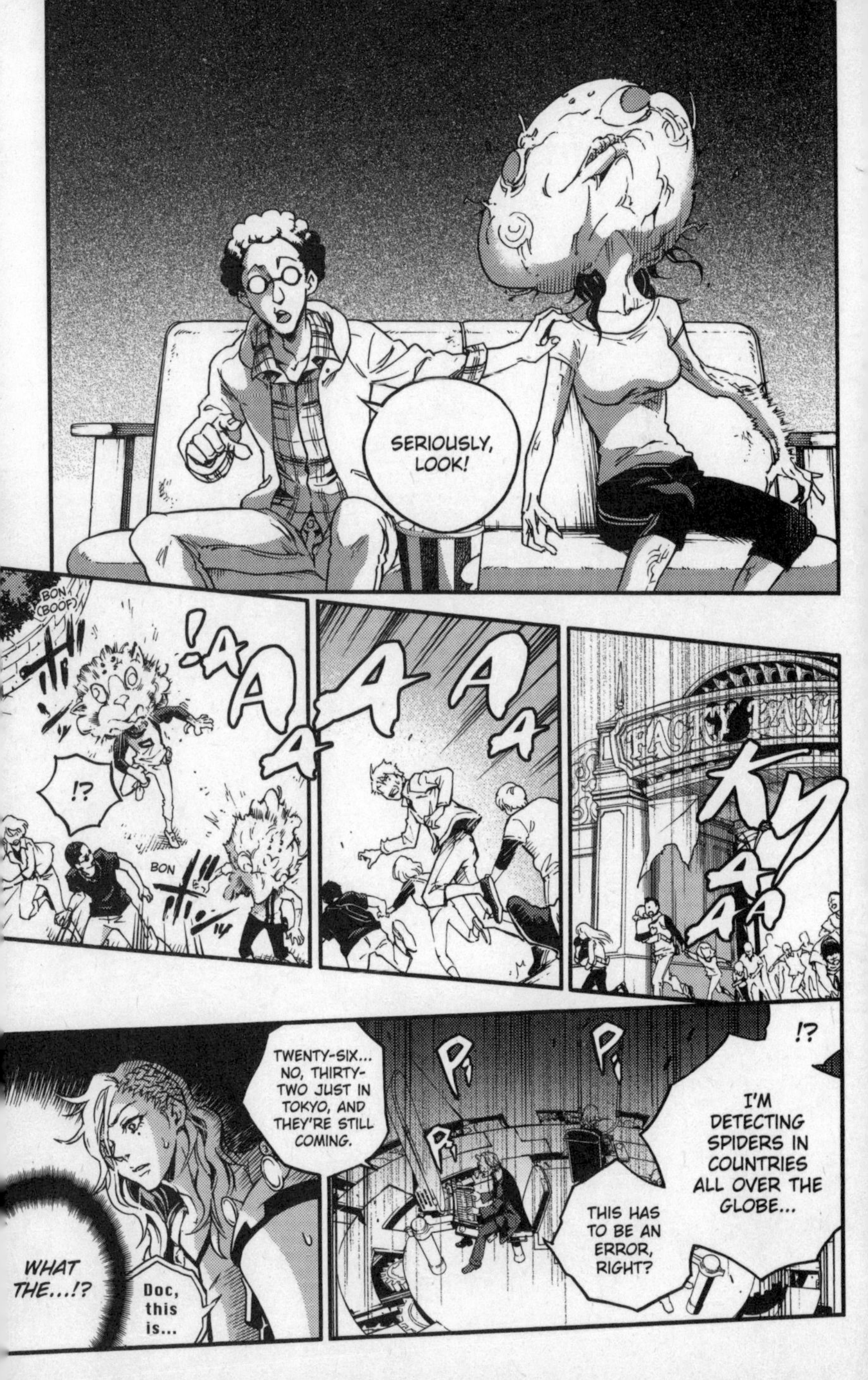
SERIOUSLY, LOOK!
KYAAA!
AAAA
AA!
BON (BOOF)
!?
BON
!?
I'M DETECTING SPIDERS IN COUNTRIES ALL OVER THE GLOBE...
THIS HAS TO BE AN ERROR, RIGHT?
TWENTY-SIX... NO, THIRTY-TWO JUST IN TOKYO, AND THEY'RE STILL COMING.
Doc, this is...
WHAT THE...!?

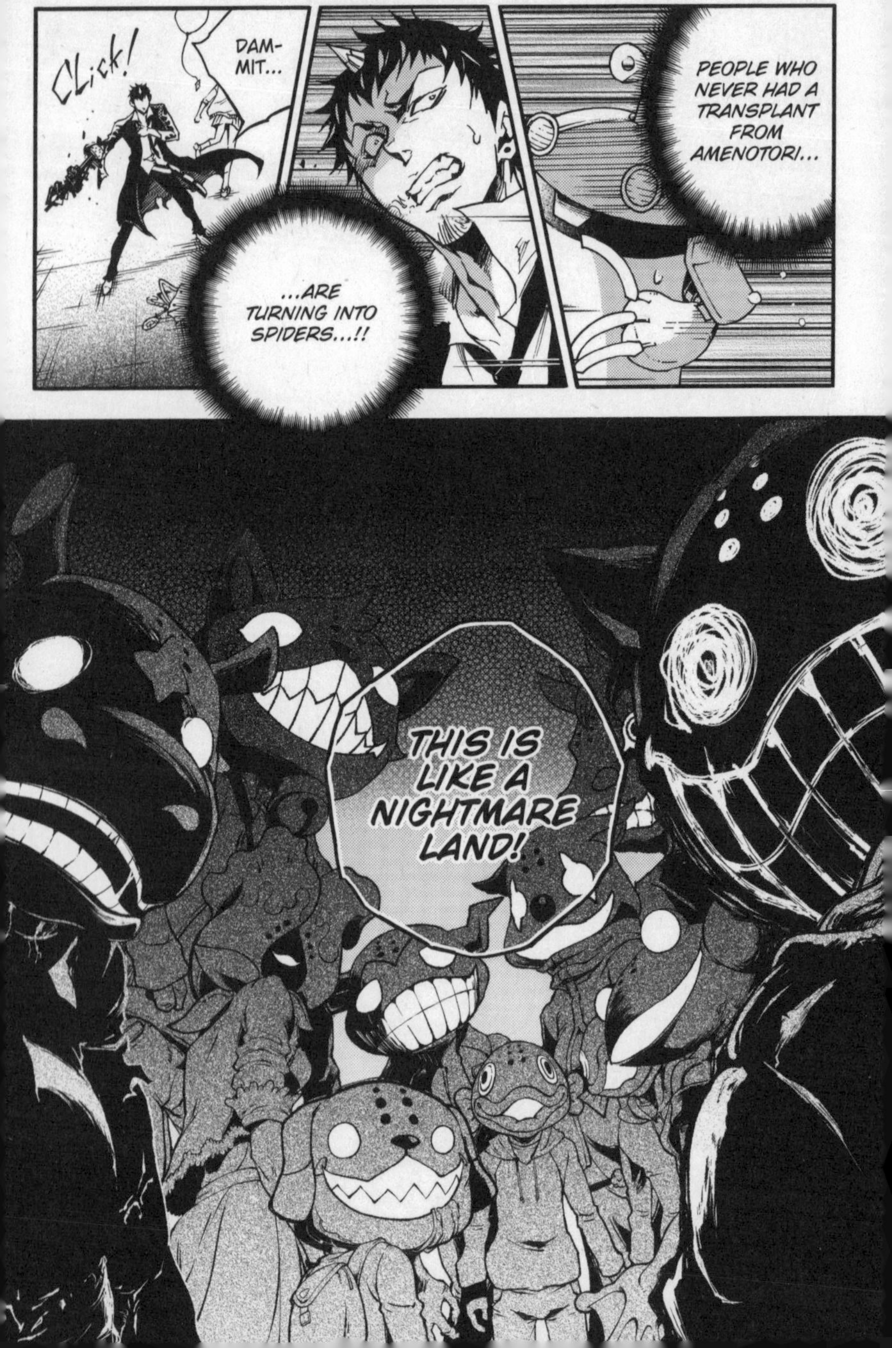
PEOPLE WHO NEVER HAD A TRANSPLANT FROM AMENOTORI...
...ARE TURNING INTO SPIDERS...!!
DAM-MIT...
CLick!
THIS IS LIKE A NIGHTMARE LAND!

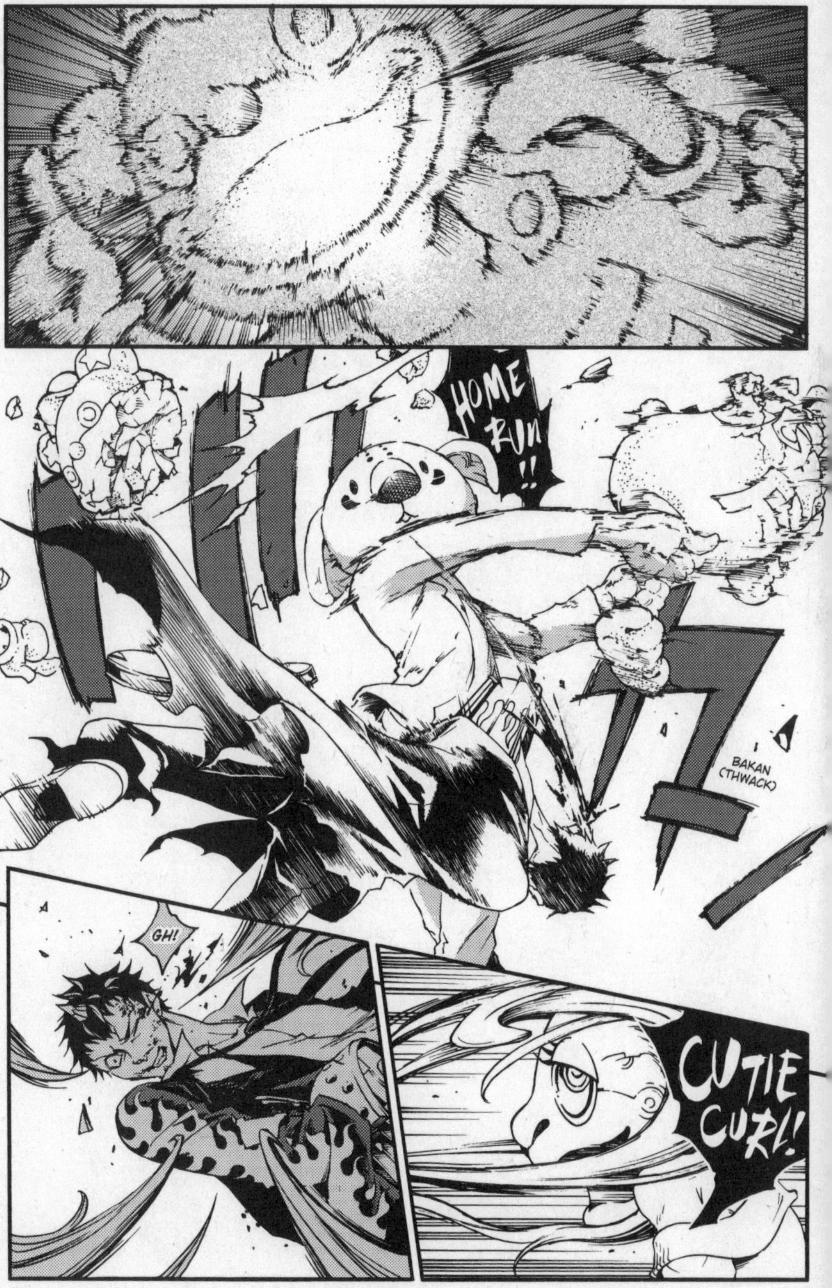
HOME RUN!!
BAKAN (THWACK)
CUTIE CURL!
GH!

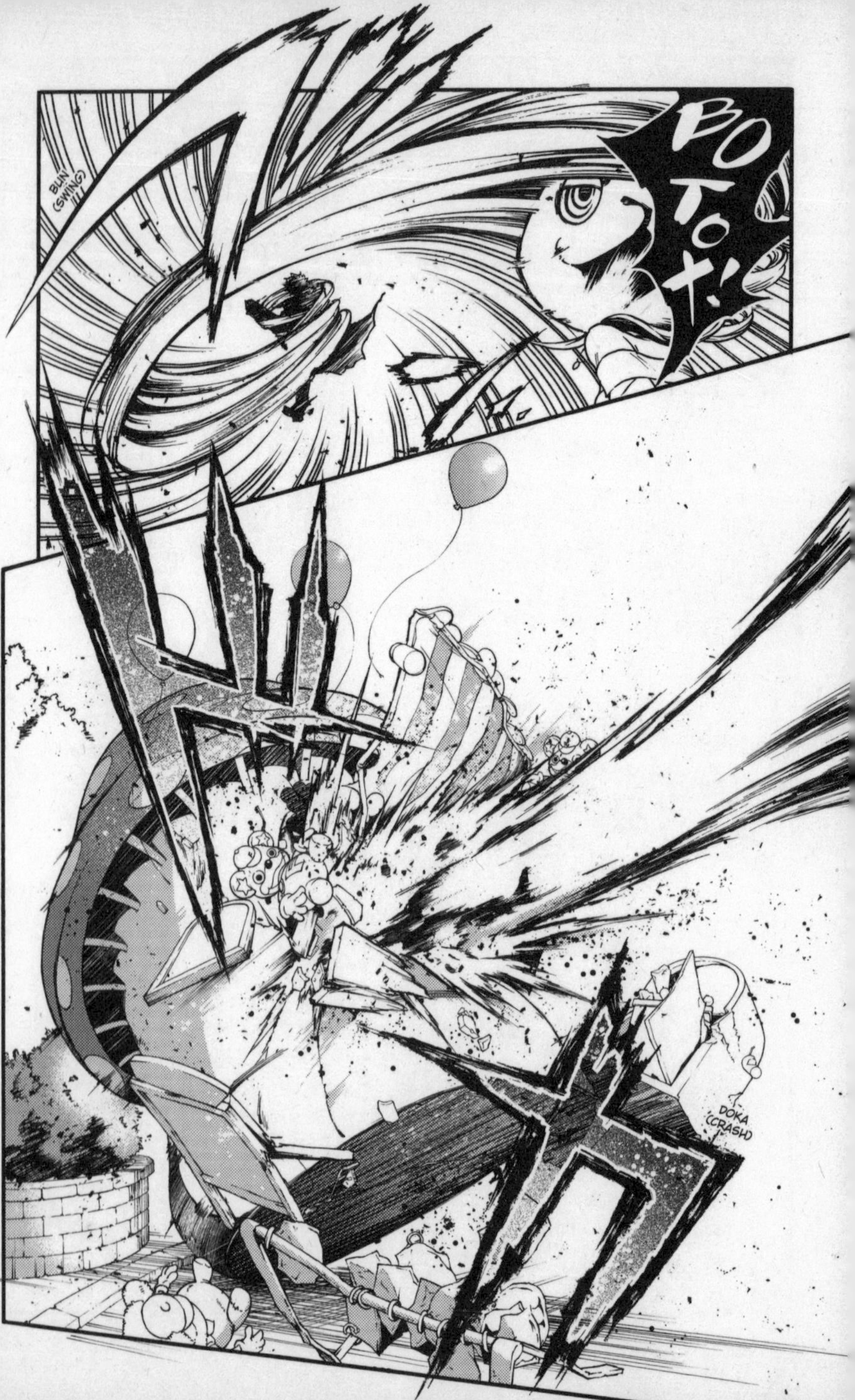
BOTOX!
BUN (SWING)
DOKA (CRASH)

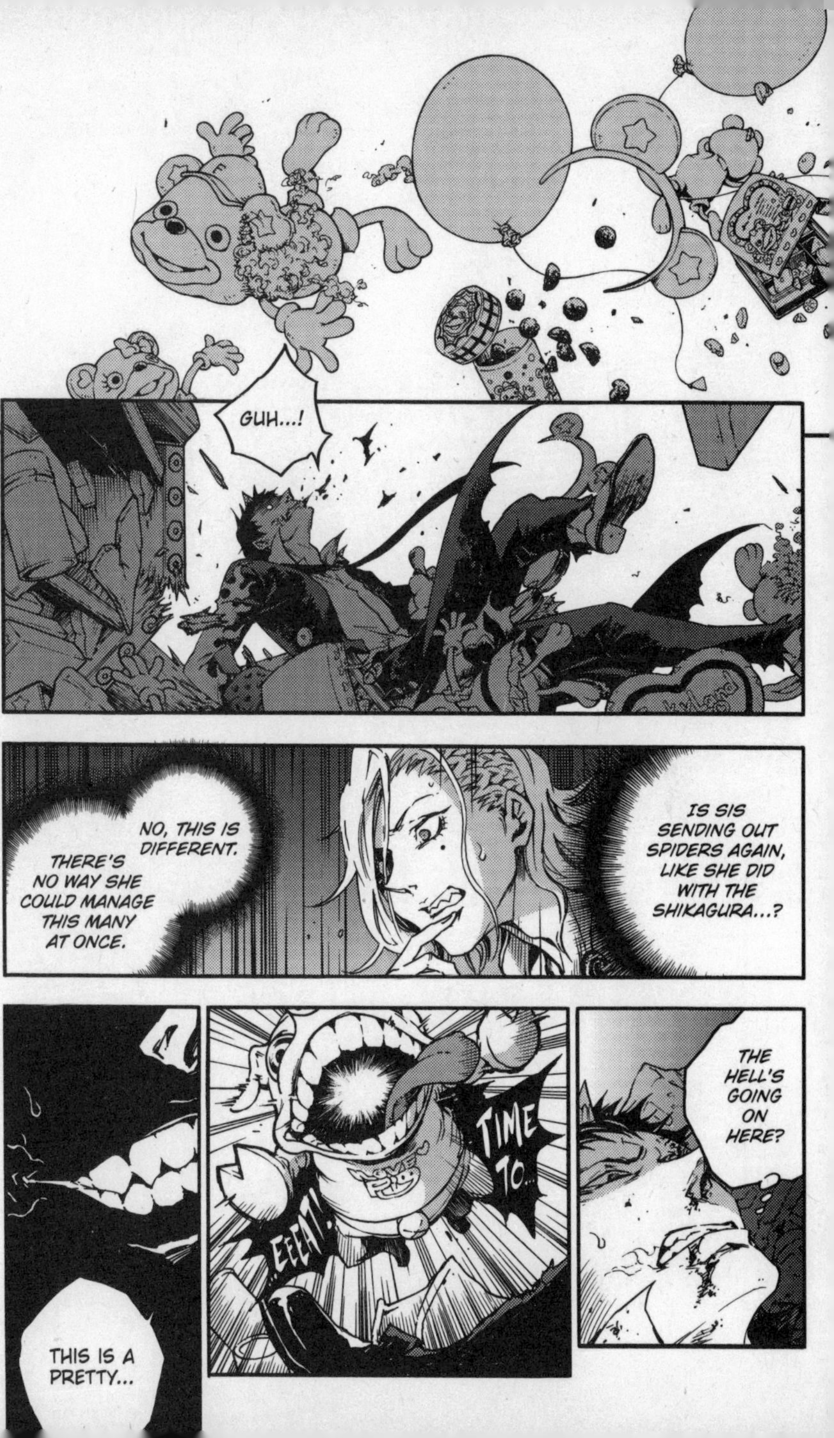
GUH...!
IS SIS SENDING OUT SPIDERS AGAIN, LIKE SHE DID WITH THE SHIKAGURA...?
NO, THIS IS DIFFERENT.
THERE'S NO WAY SHE COULD MANAGE THIS MANY AT ONCE.
THE HELL'S GOING ON HERE?
TIME TO...
EEEAT!
THIS IS A PRETTY...

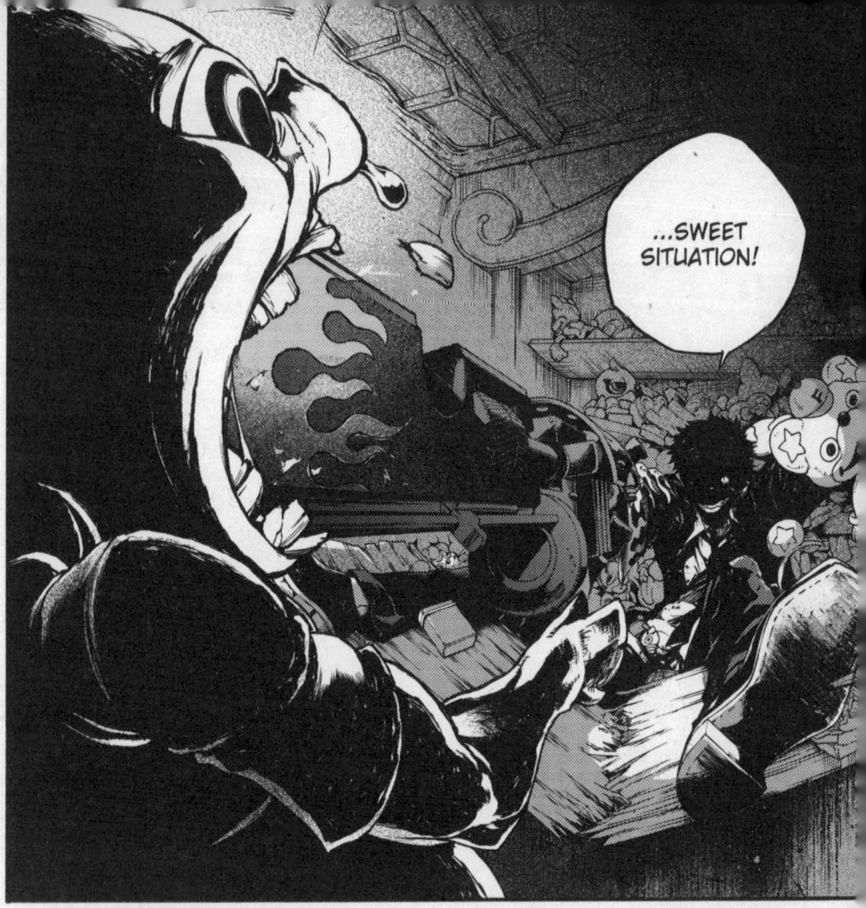
...SWEET SITUATION!

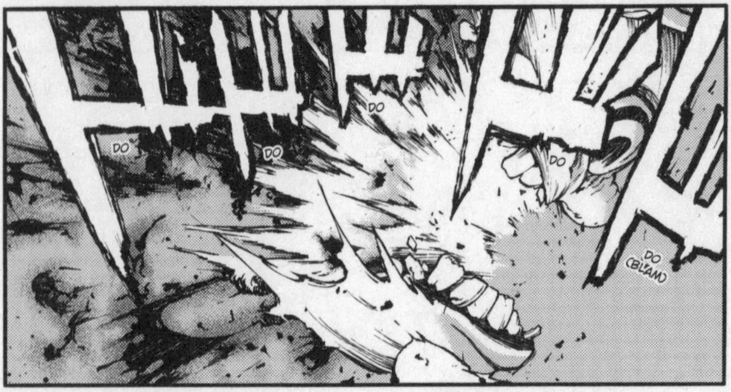
DO
DO
DO
DO
DO
(BLAM)

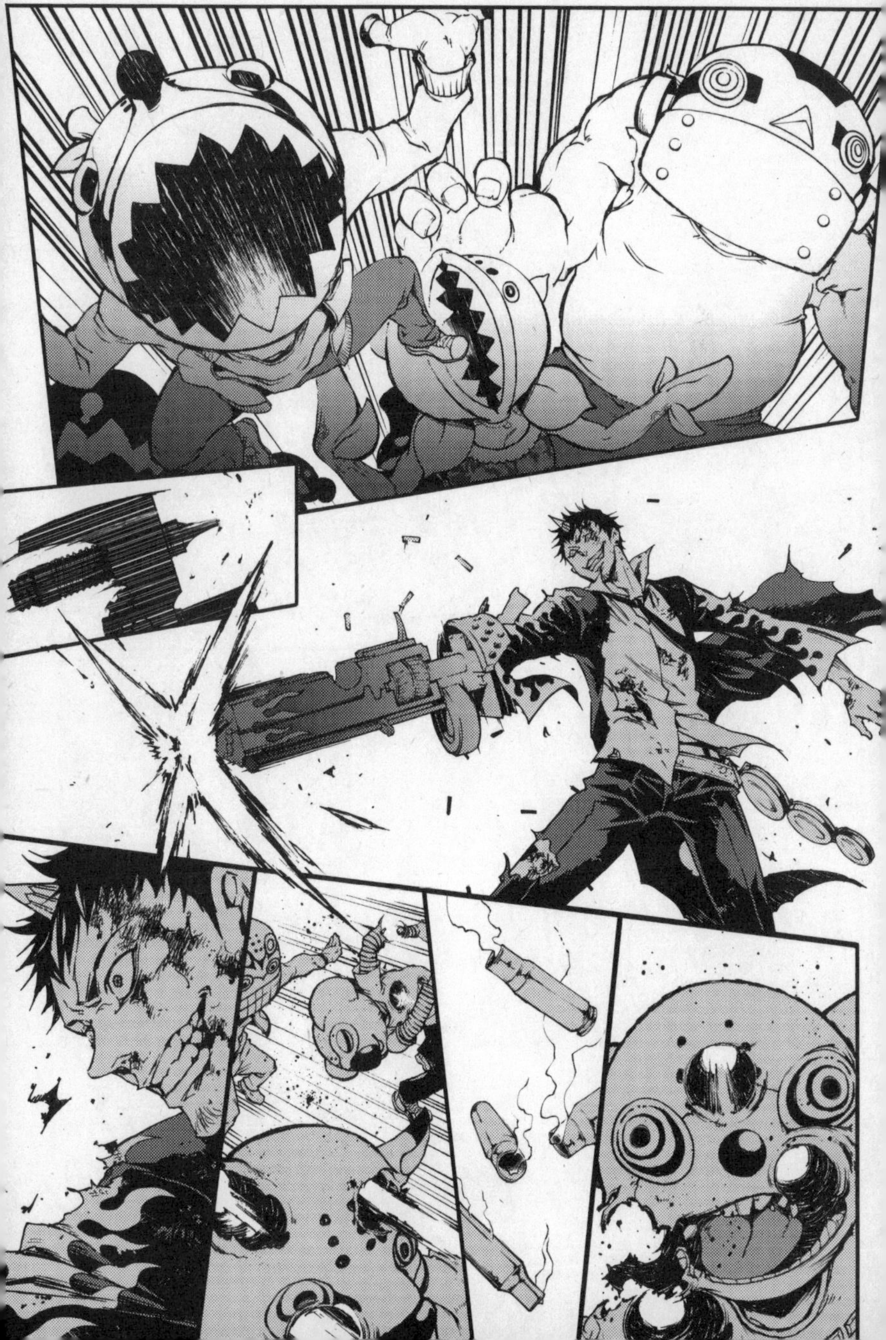

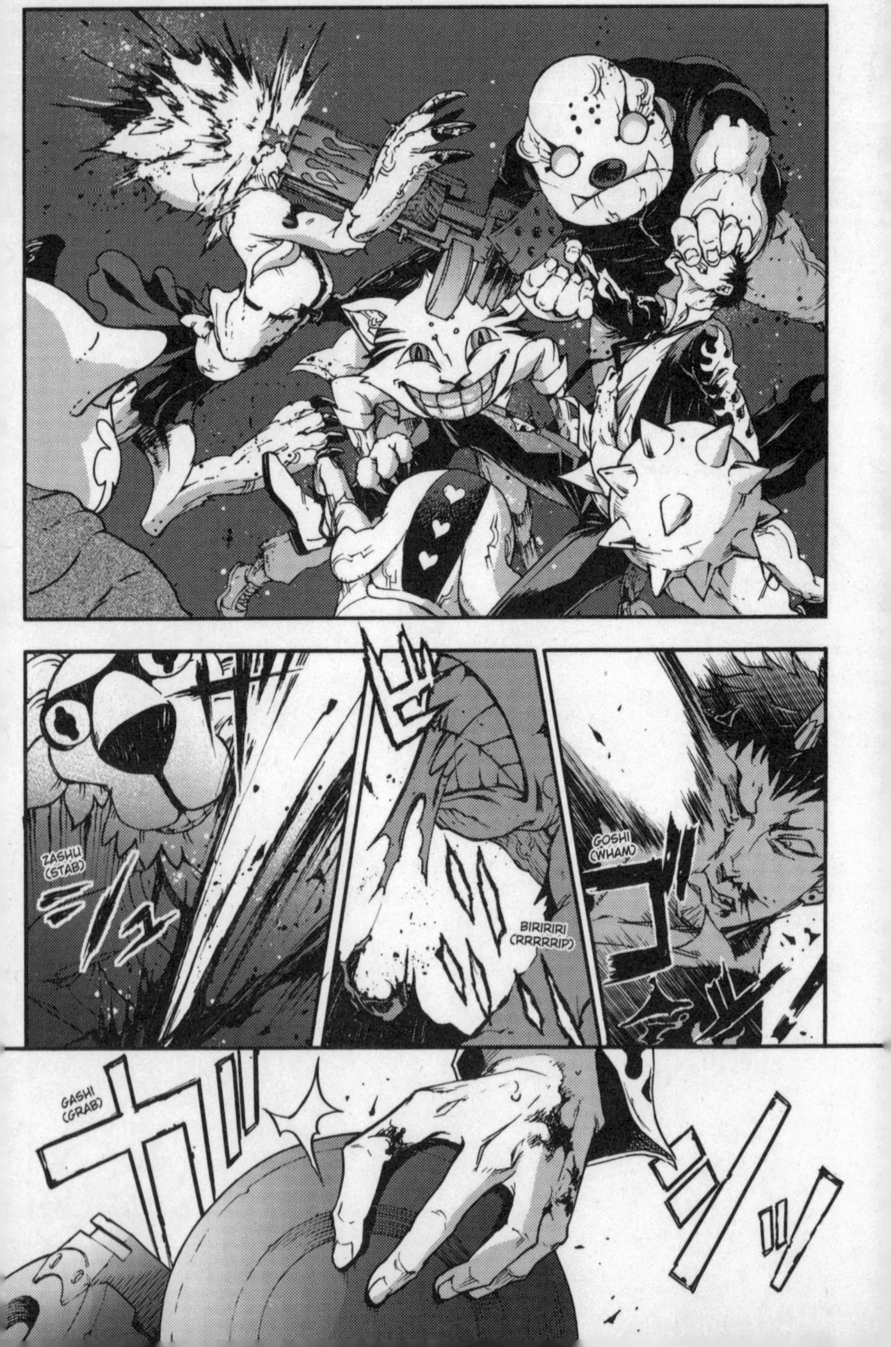
GOSHI (WHAM)
BIRIRIRI (RRRRRIP)
ZASHU (STAB)
GASHI (GRAB)

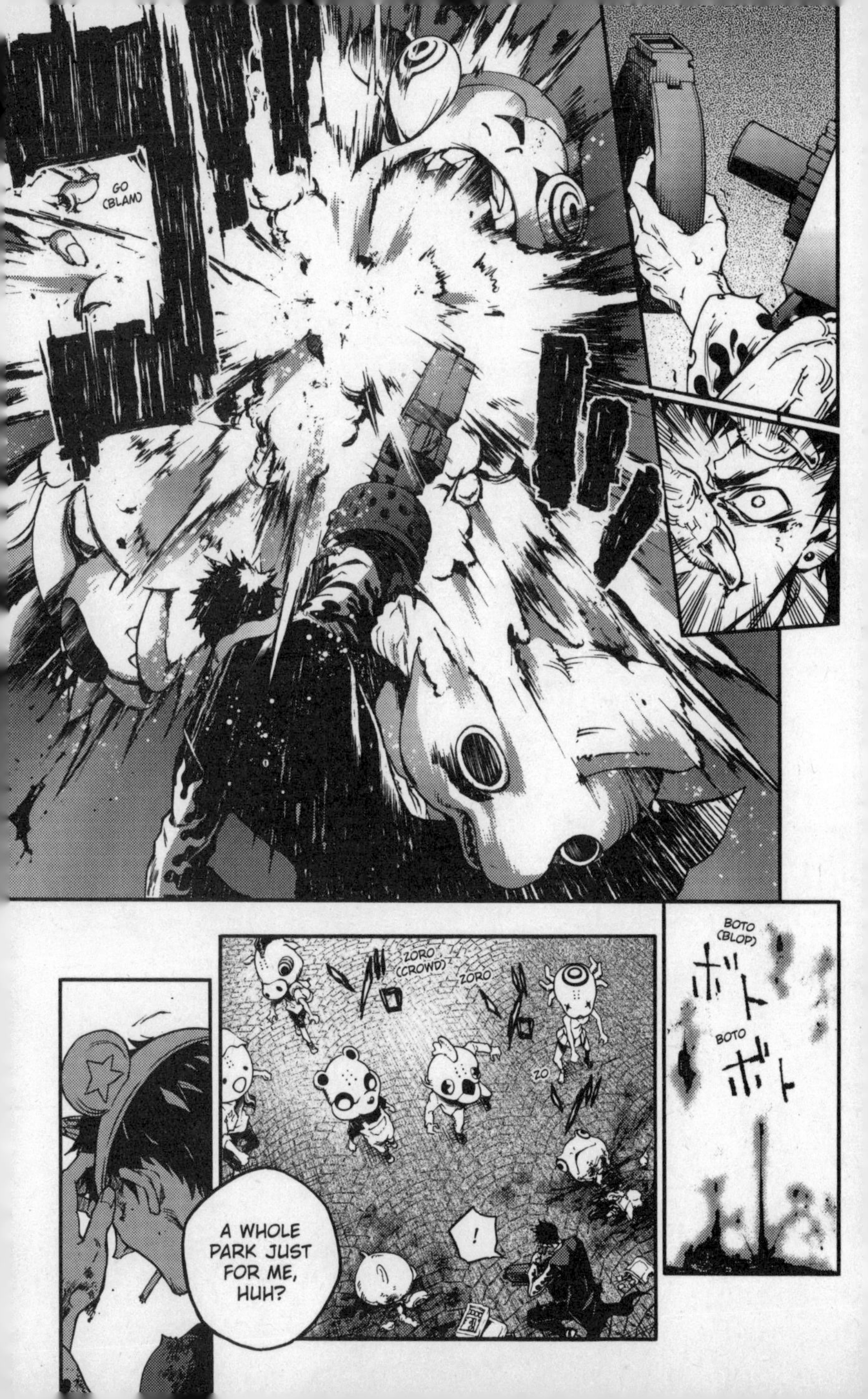
GO
(BLAM)
BOTO
(BLOP)
ボト
BOTO
ボト
ZORO
(CROWD)
ZORO
ZO
!
A WHOLE PARK JUST FOR ME, HUH?

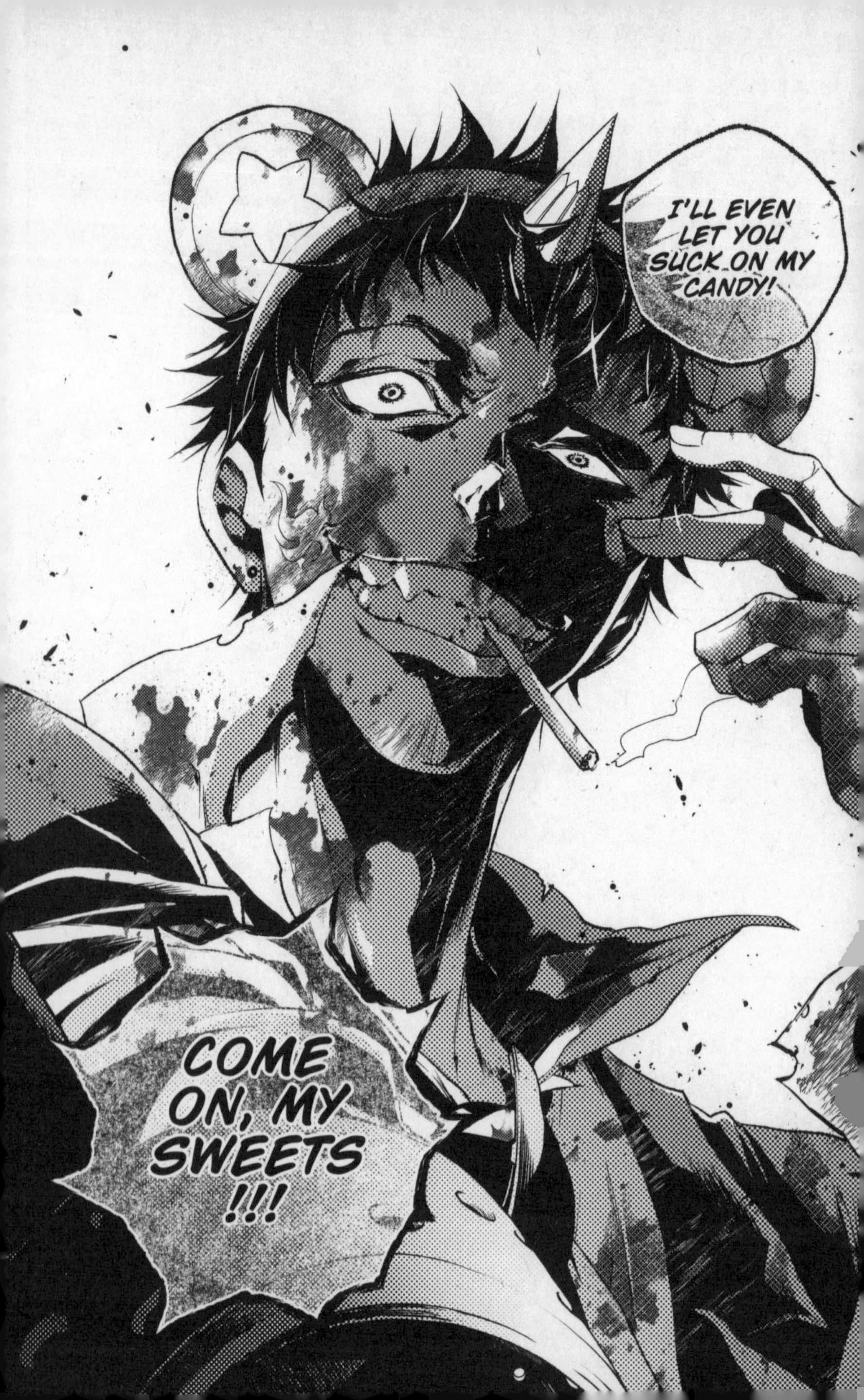
I'LL EVEN LET YOU SUCK ON MY CANDY!
COME ON, MY SWEETS !!!

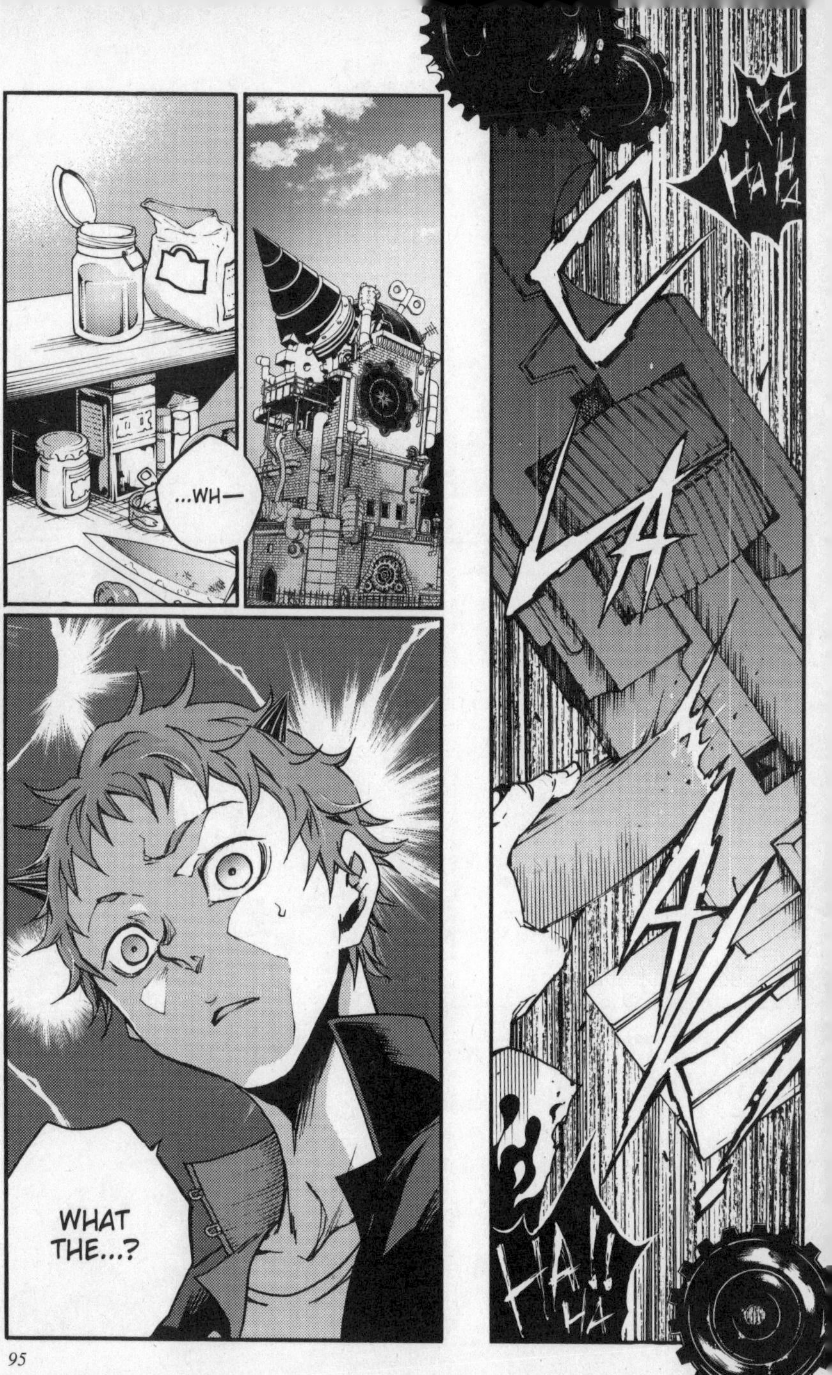
HA HAHA
HA!! HA
...WH—
WHAT THE...?

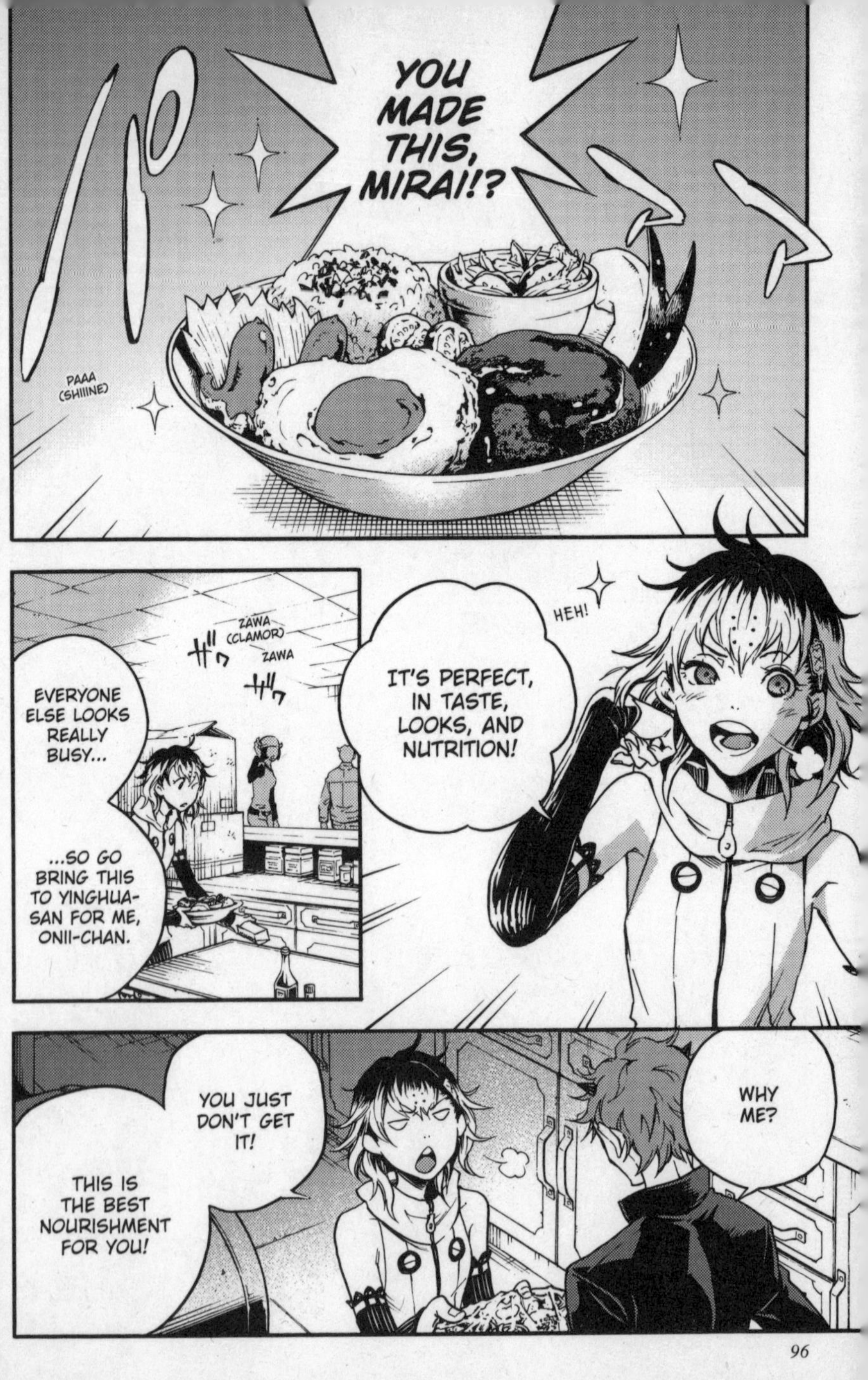
YOU MADE THIS, MIRAI!?
PAAA (SHIIINE)
HEH!
IT'S PERFECT, IN TASTE, LOOKS, AND NUTRITION!
ZAWA (CLAMOR) ZAWA
EVERYONE ELSE LOOKS REALLY BUSY...
...SO GO BRING THIS TO YINGHUA-SAN FOR ME, ONII-CHAN.
WHY ME?
YOU JUST DON'T GET IT!
THIS IS THE BEST NOURISHMENT FOR YOU!

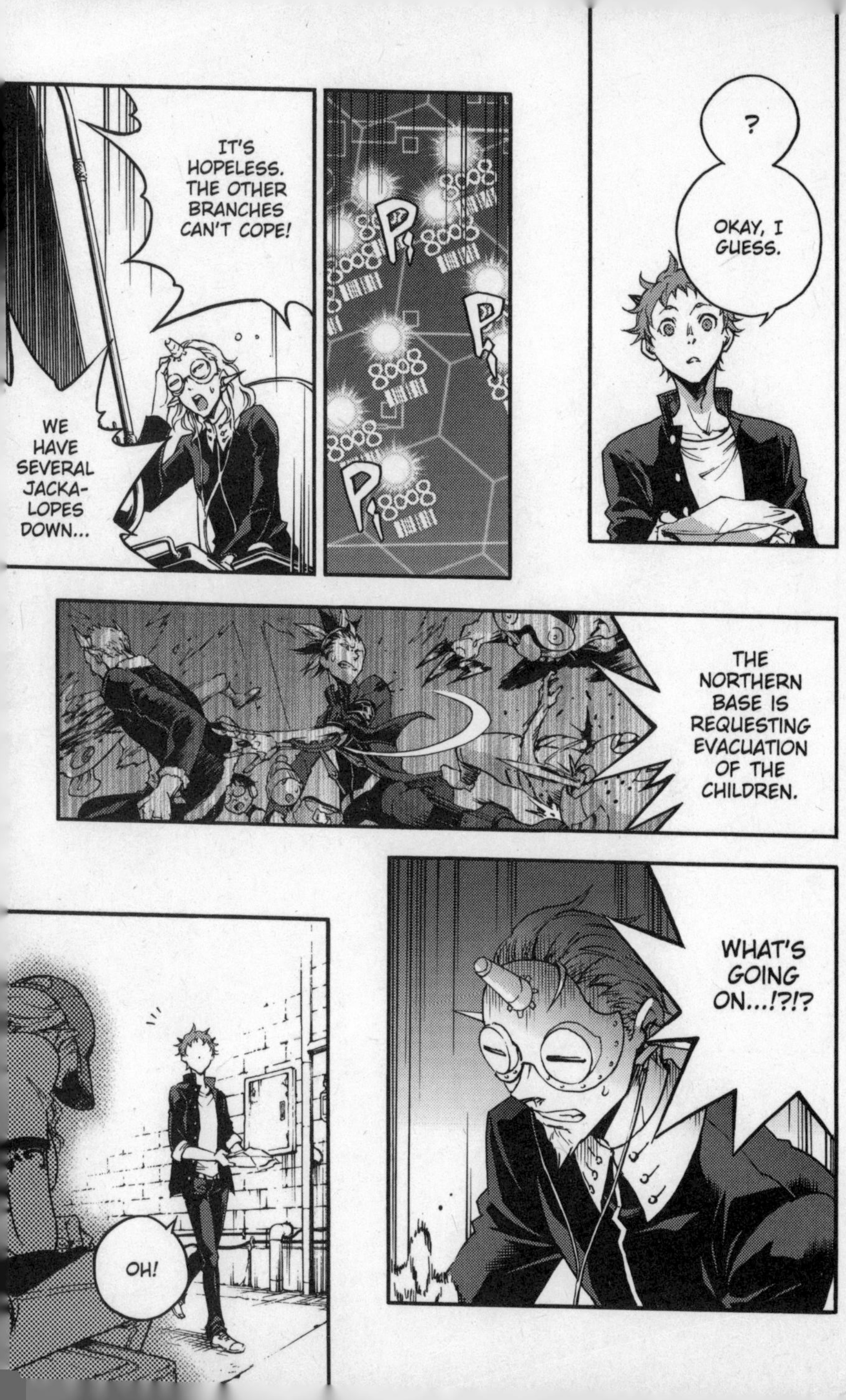
?
OKAY, I GUESS.
IT'S HOPELESS. THE OTHER BRANCHES CAN'T COPE!
WE HAVE SEVERAL JACKA-LOPES DOWN...
THE NORTHERN BASE IS REQUESTING EVACUATION OF THE CHILDREN.
WHAT'S GOING ON...!?!?
OH!

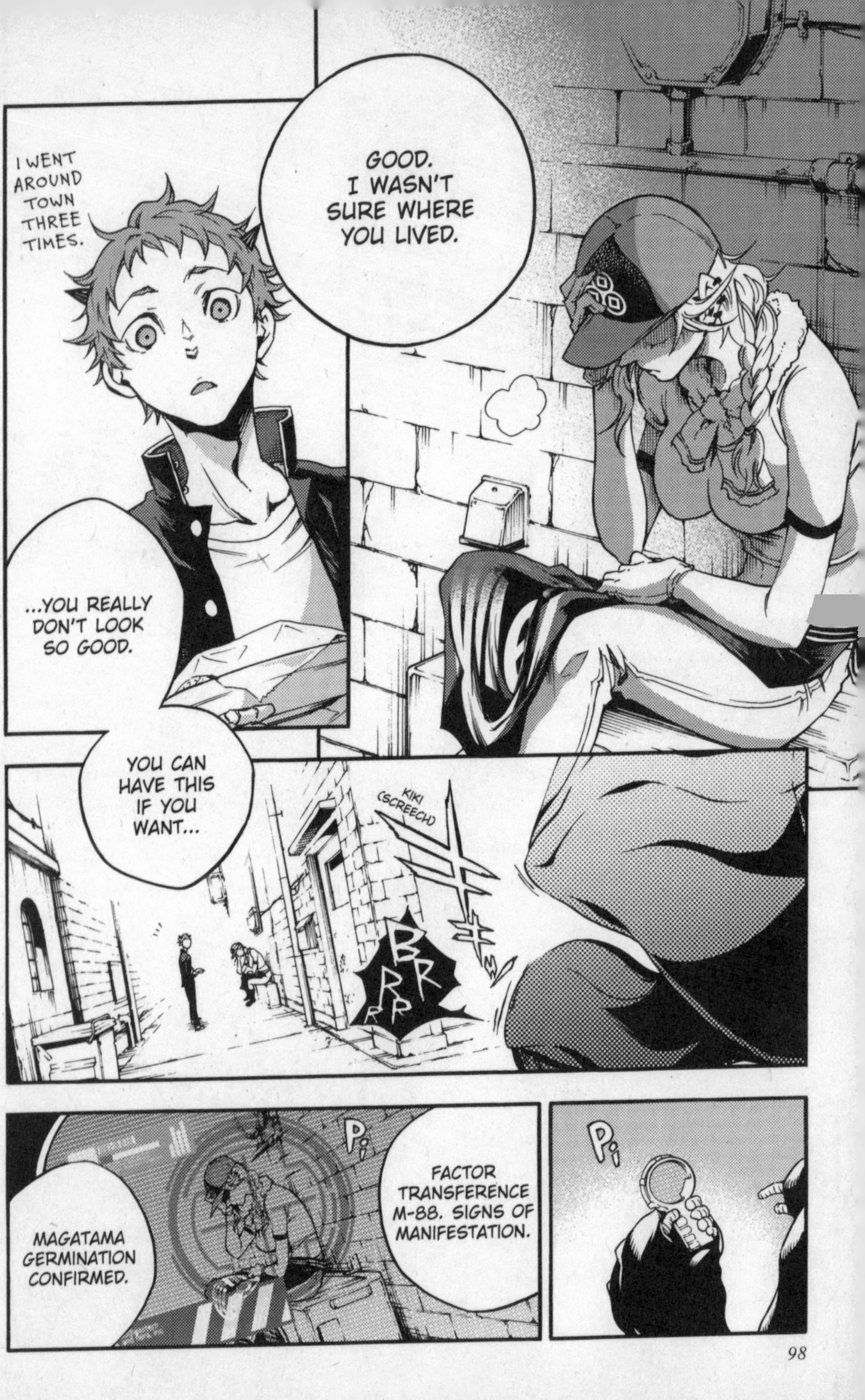
GOOD. I WASN'T SURE WHERE YOU LIVED.
I WENT AROUND TOWN THREE TIMES.
...YOU REALLY DON'T LOOK SO GOOD.
YOU CAN HAVE THIS IF YOU WANT...
KIKI (SCREECH)
BRRR
Pi
Pi
FACTOR TRANSFERENCE M-88. SIGNS OF MANIFESTATION.
MAGATAMA GERMINATION CONFIRMED.

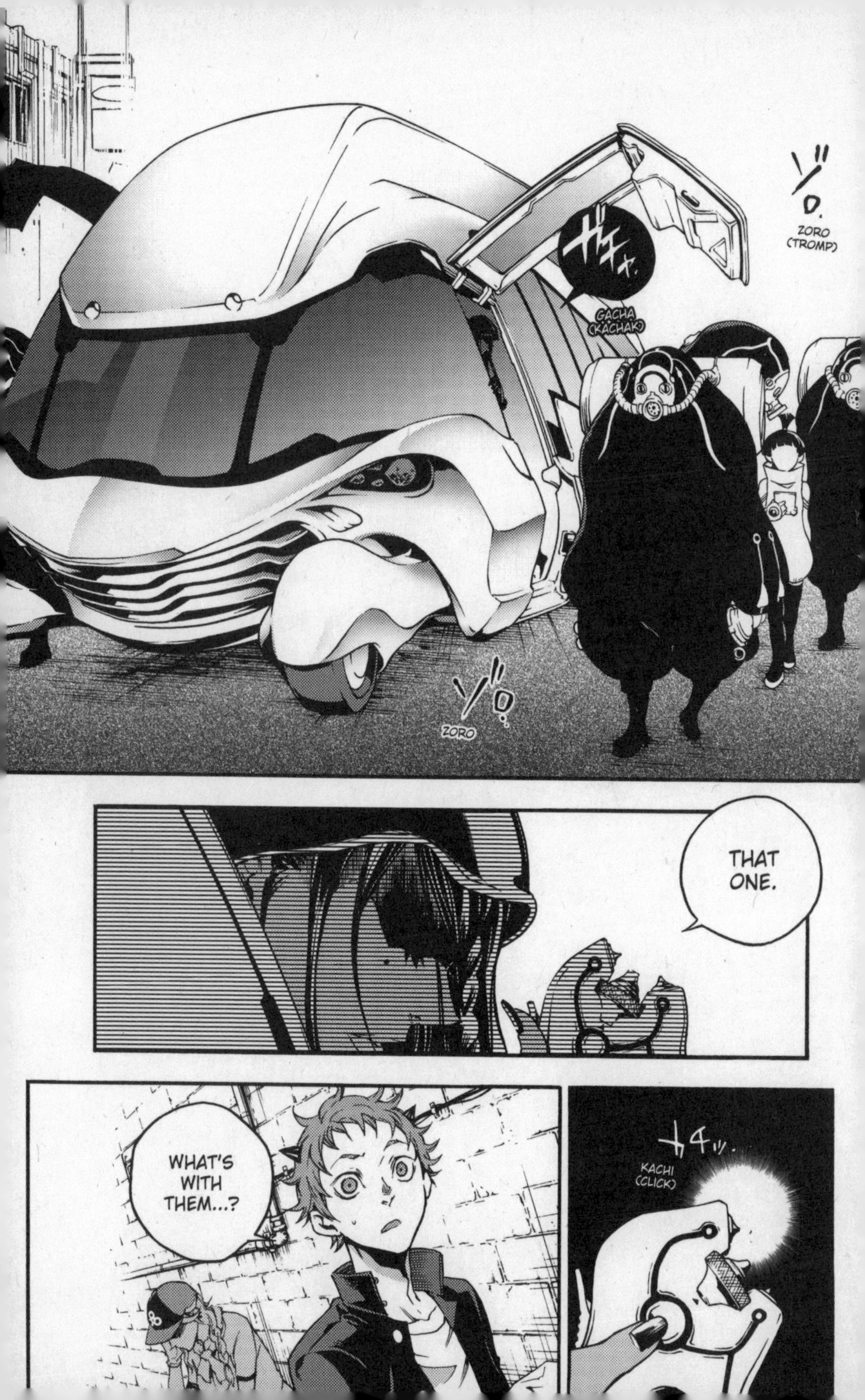
ZORO (TROMP)
GACHA (KACHAK)
ZORO
THAT ONE.
KACHI (CLICK)
WHAT'S WITH THEM...?

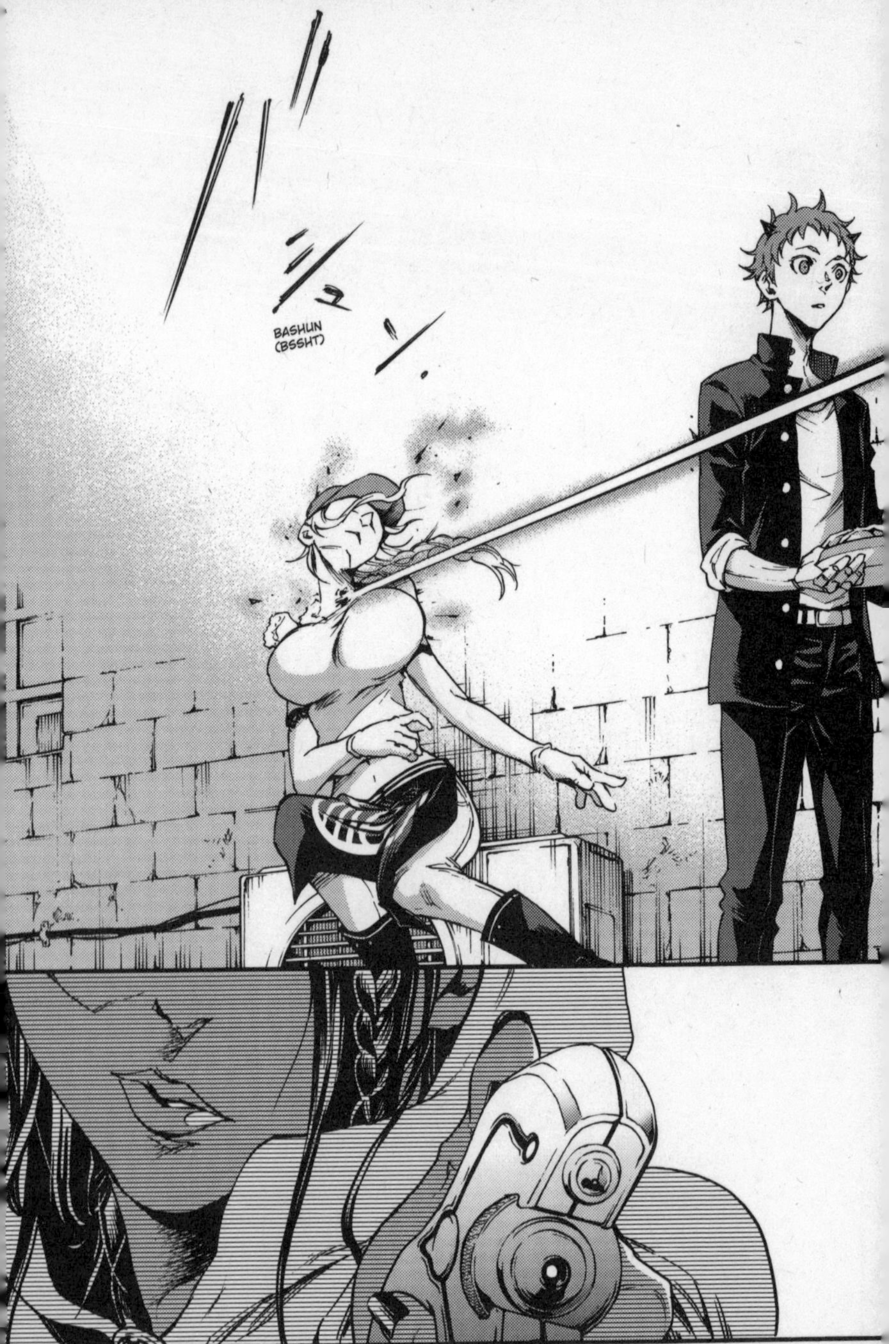
シュン.
BASHUN
(BSSHT)

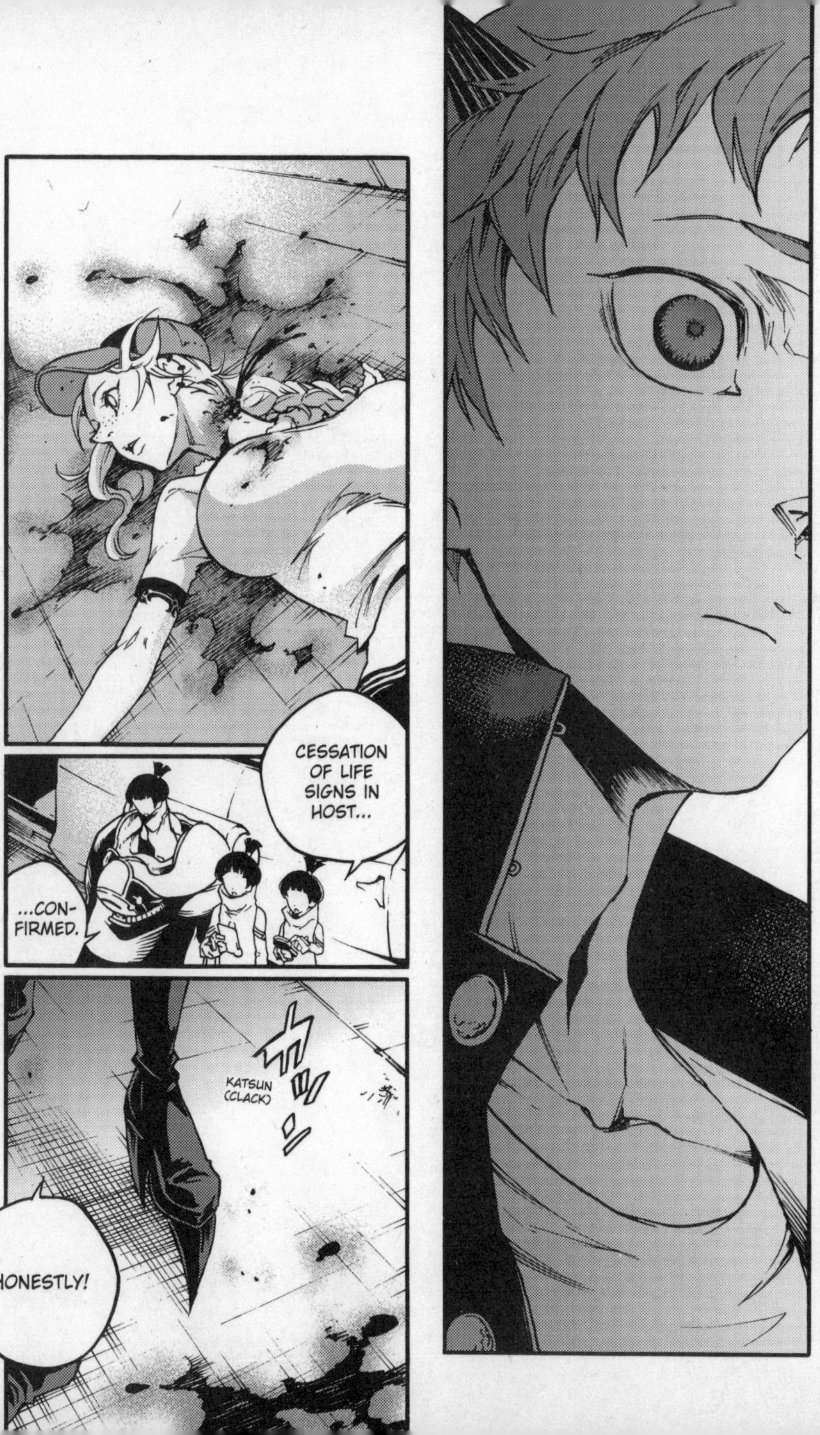
CESSATION OF LIFE SIGNS IN HOST...
...CON-FIRMED.
KATSUN (CLACK)
HONESTLY!

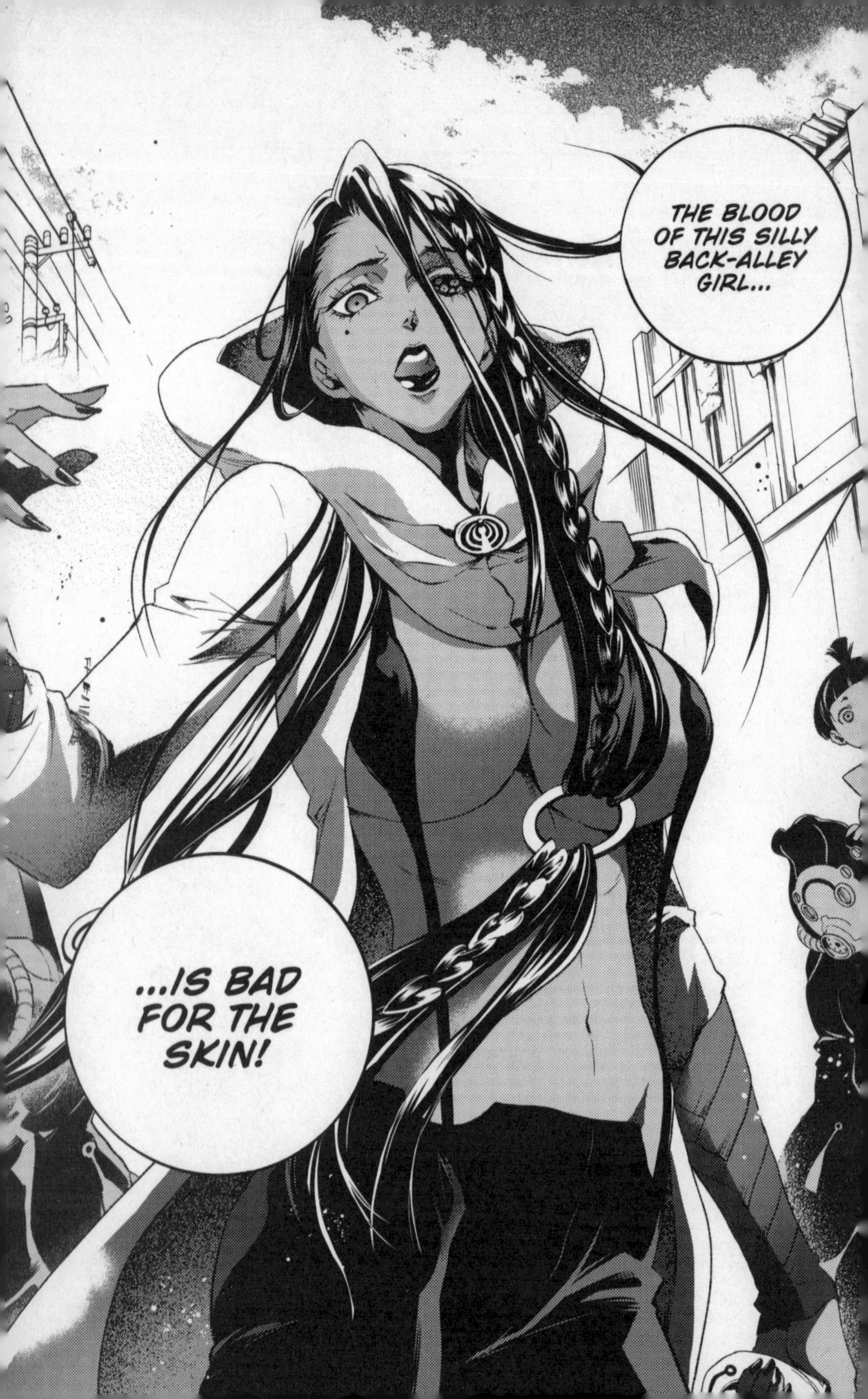
THE BLOOD OF THIS SILLY BACK-ALLEY GIRL...
...IS BAD FOR THE SKIN!

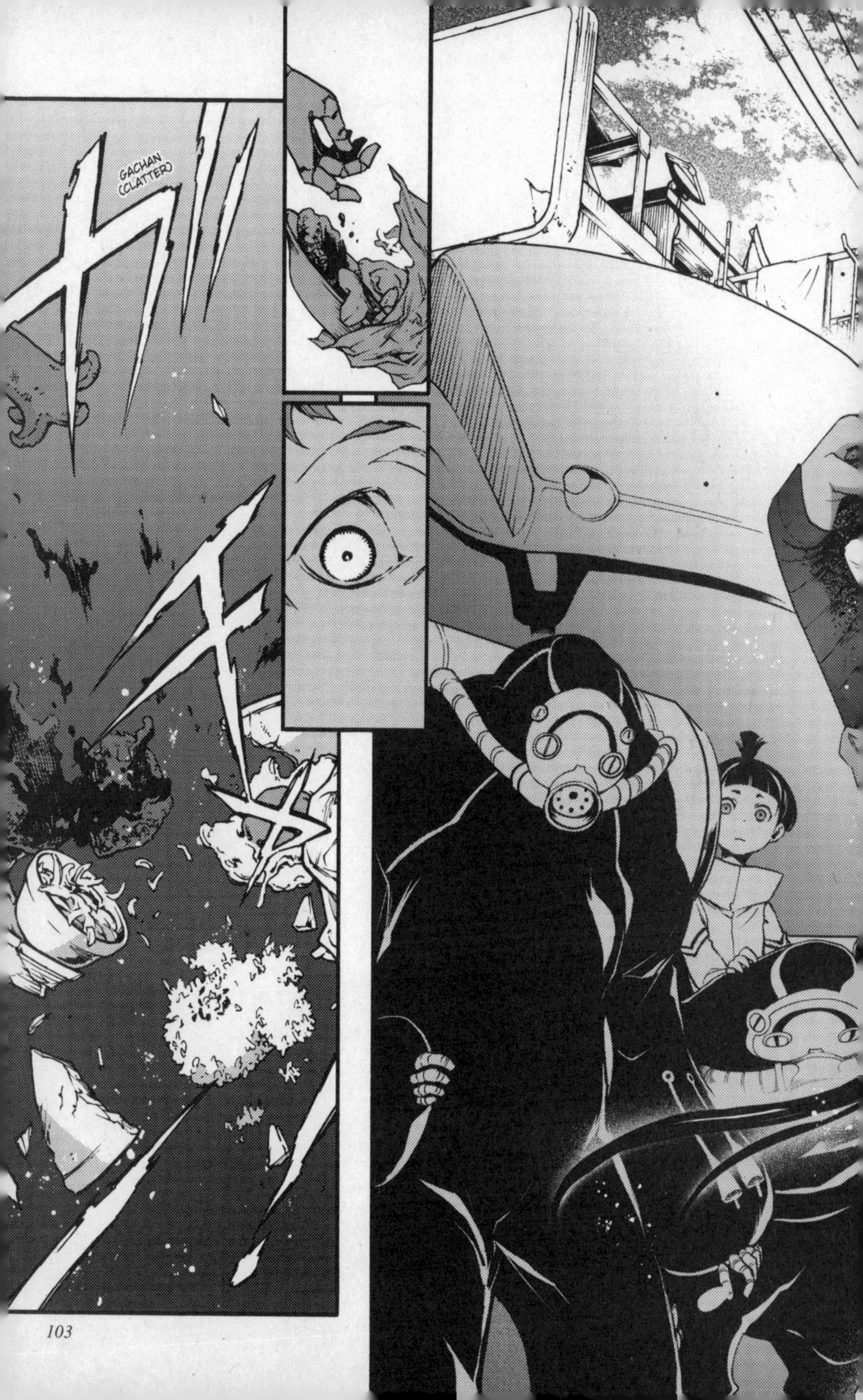
GACHAN
(CLATTER)

THE WORLD IS DI

SMOKIN' PARADE

JINSEI KATAOKA

KAZUMA KONDOU

THE PARADE
WILL
START.

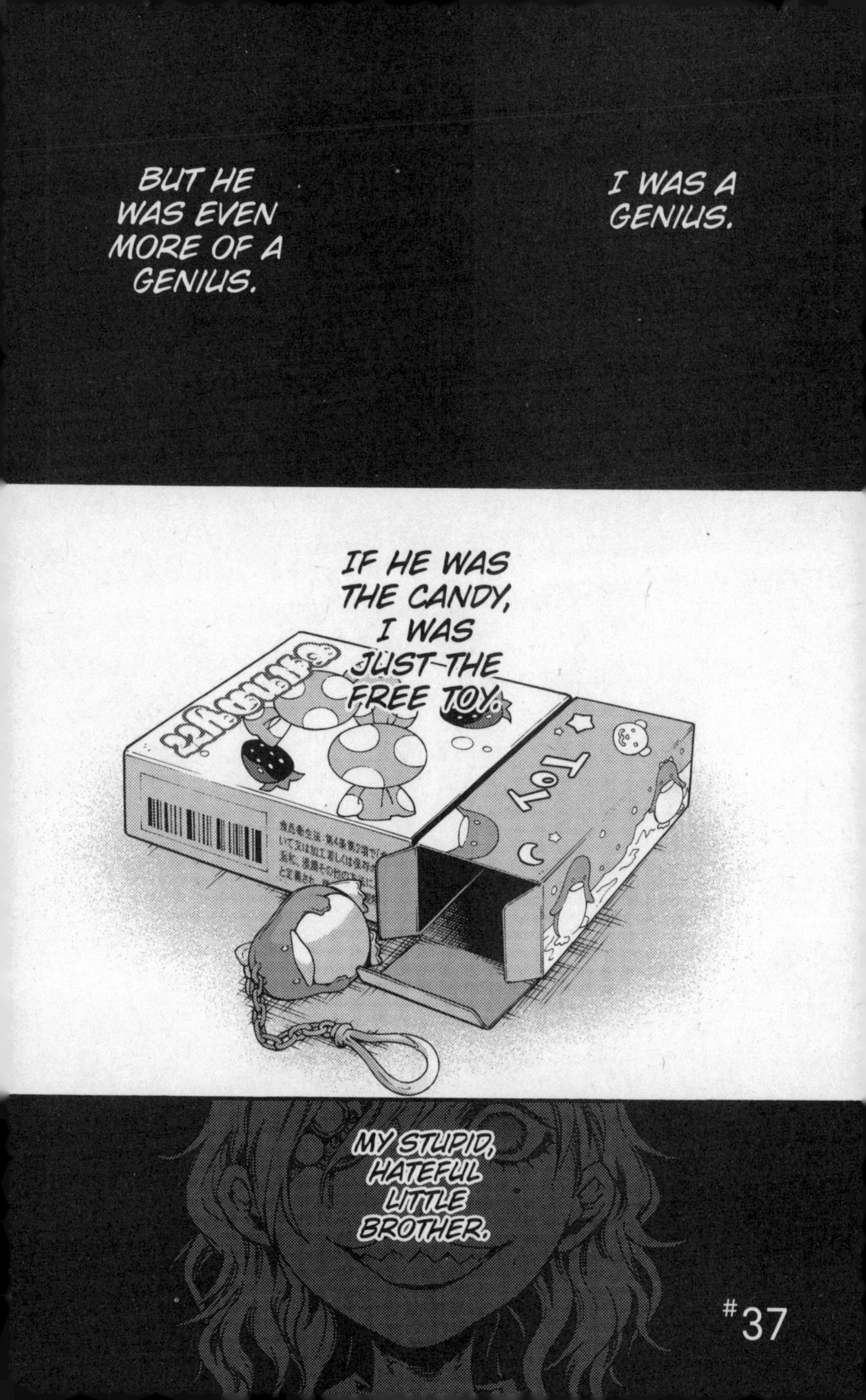
I WAS A GENIUS.
BUT HE WAS EVEN MORE OF A GENIUS.
IF HE WAS THE CANDY, I WAS JUST THE FREE TOY.
MY STUPID, HATEFUL LITTLE BROTHER.
#37

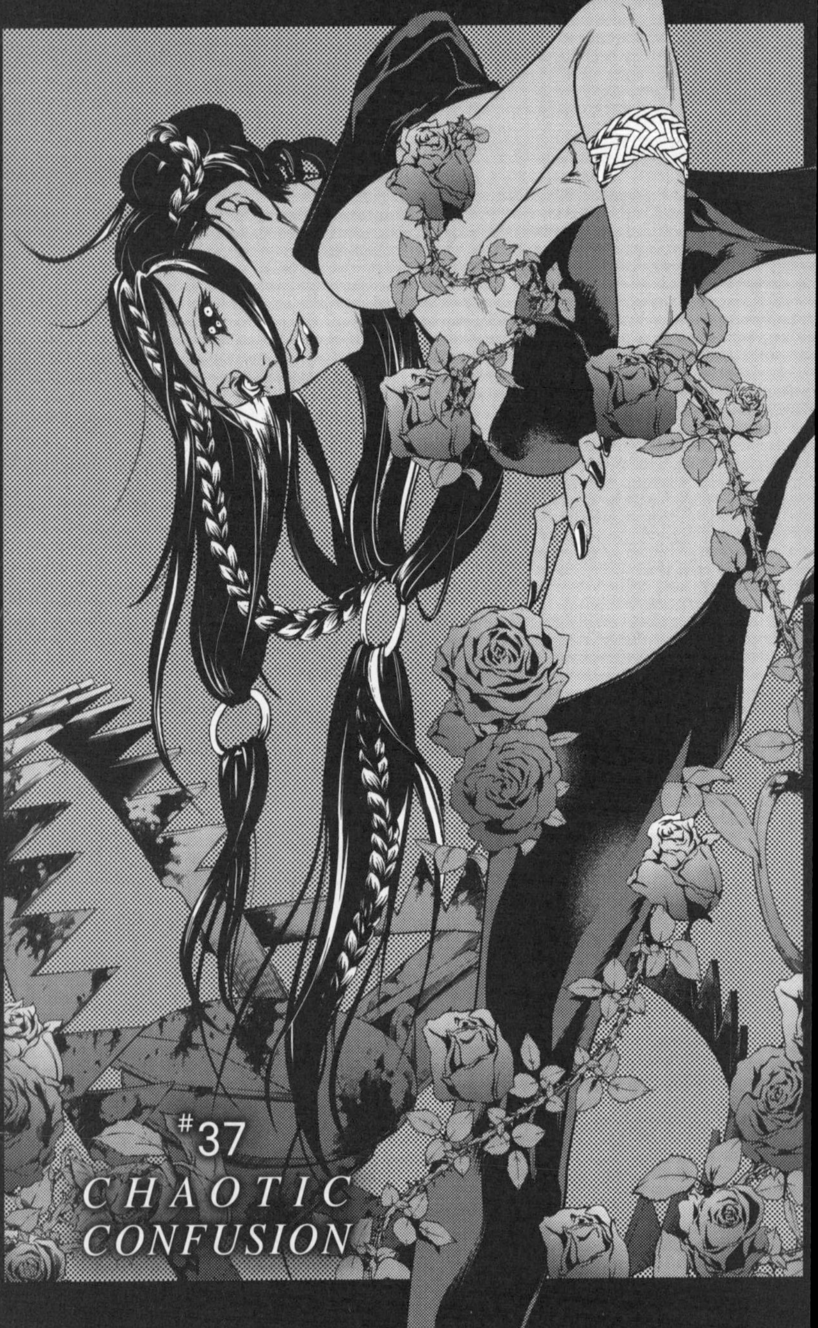

#37 CHAOTIC CONFUSION

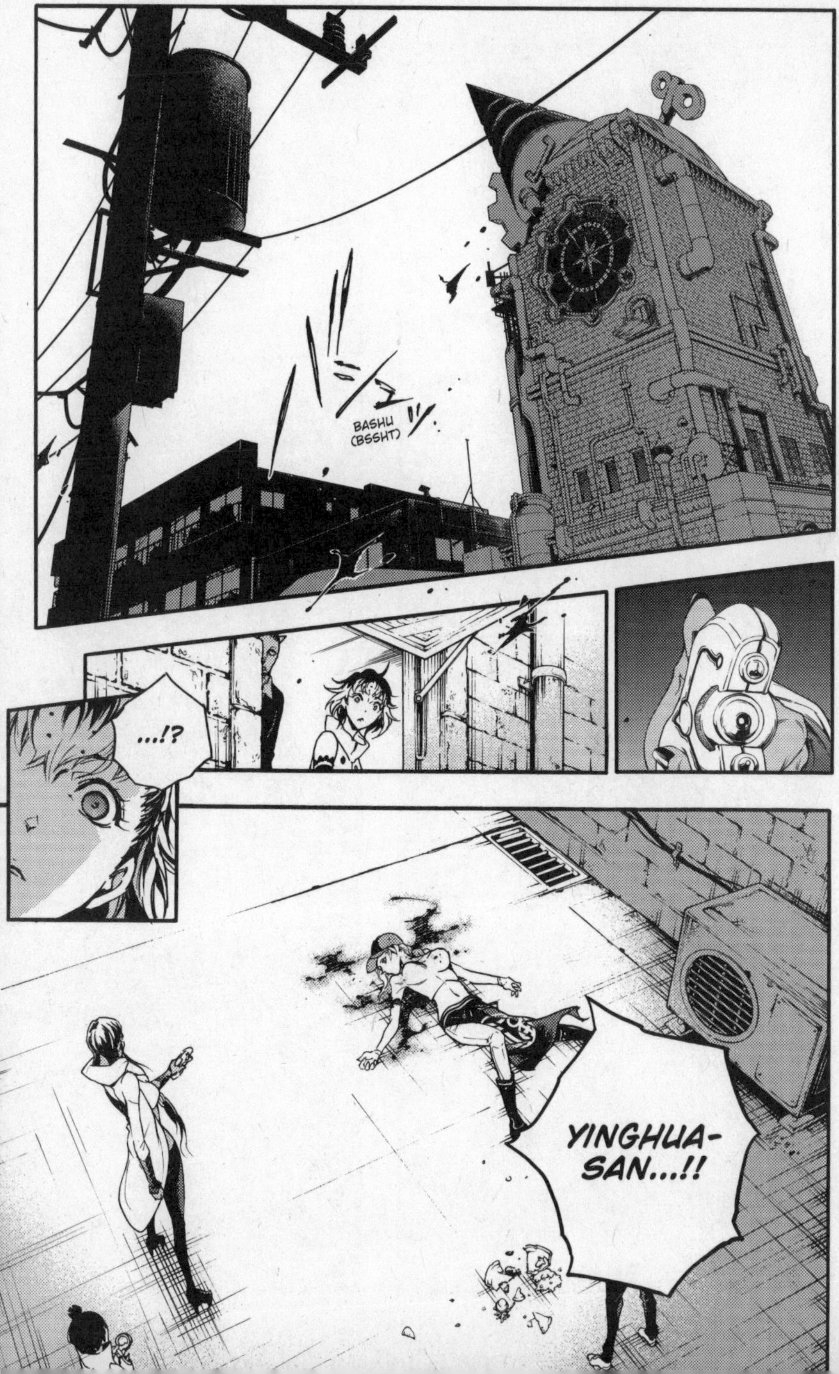
BASHU
(BSSHT)
...!?
YINGHUA-SAN...!!

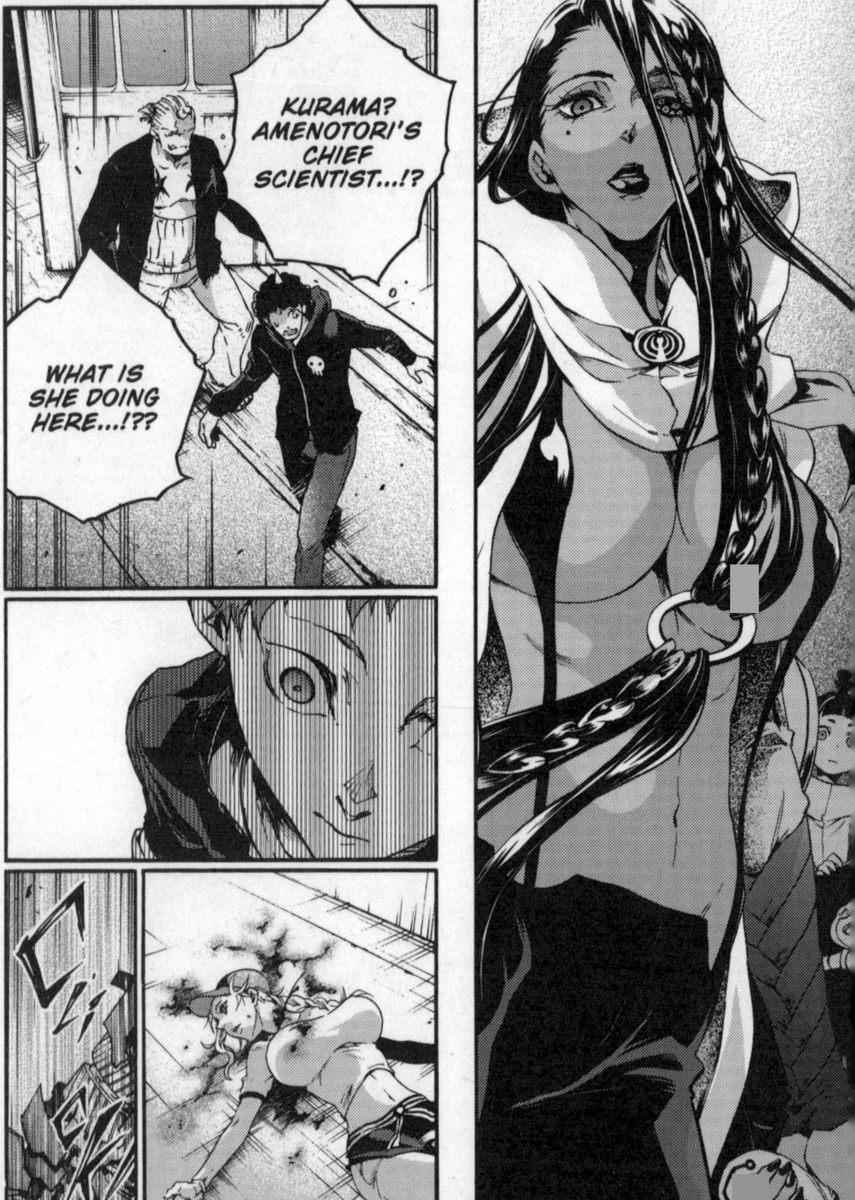
KURAMA? AMENOTORI'S CHIEF SCIENTIST...!?
WHAT IS SHE DOING HERE...!??

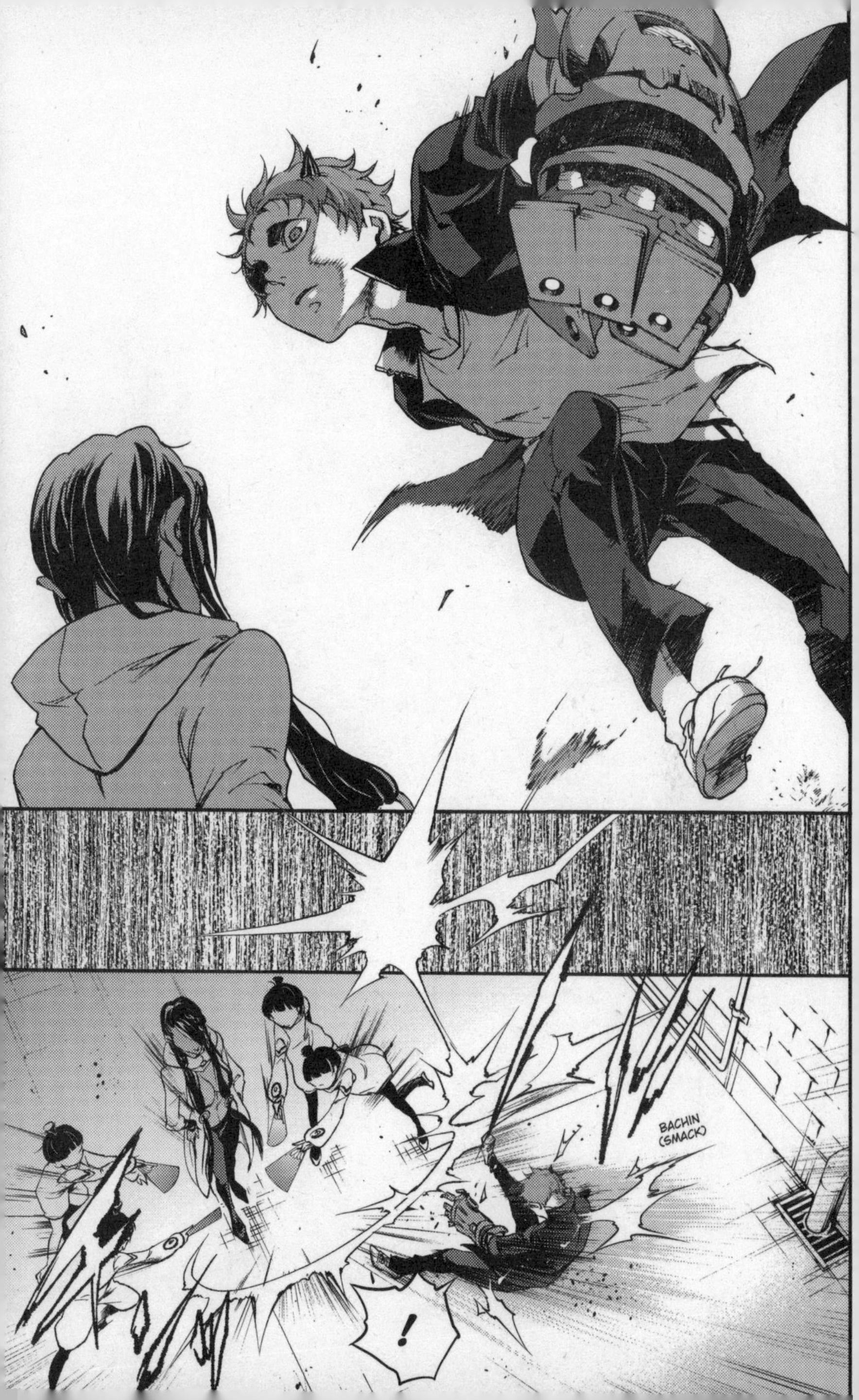
BACHIN
(SMACK)
!

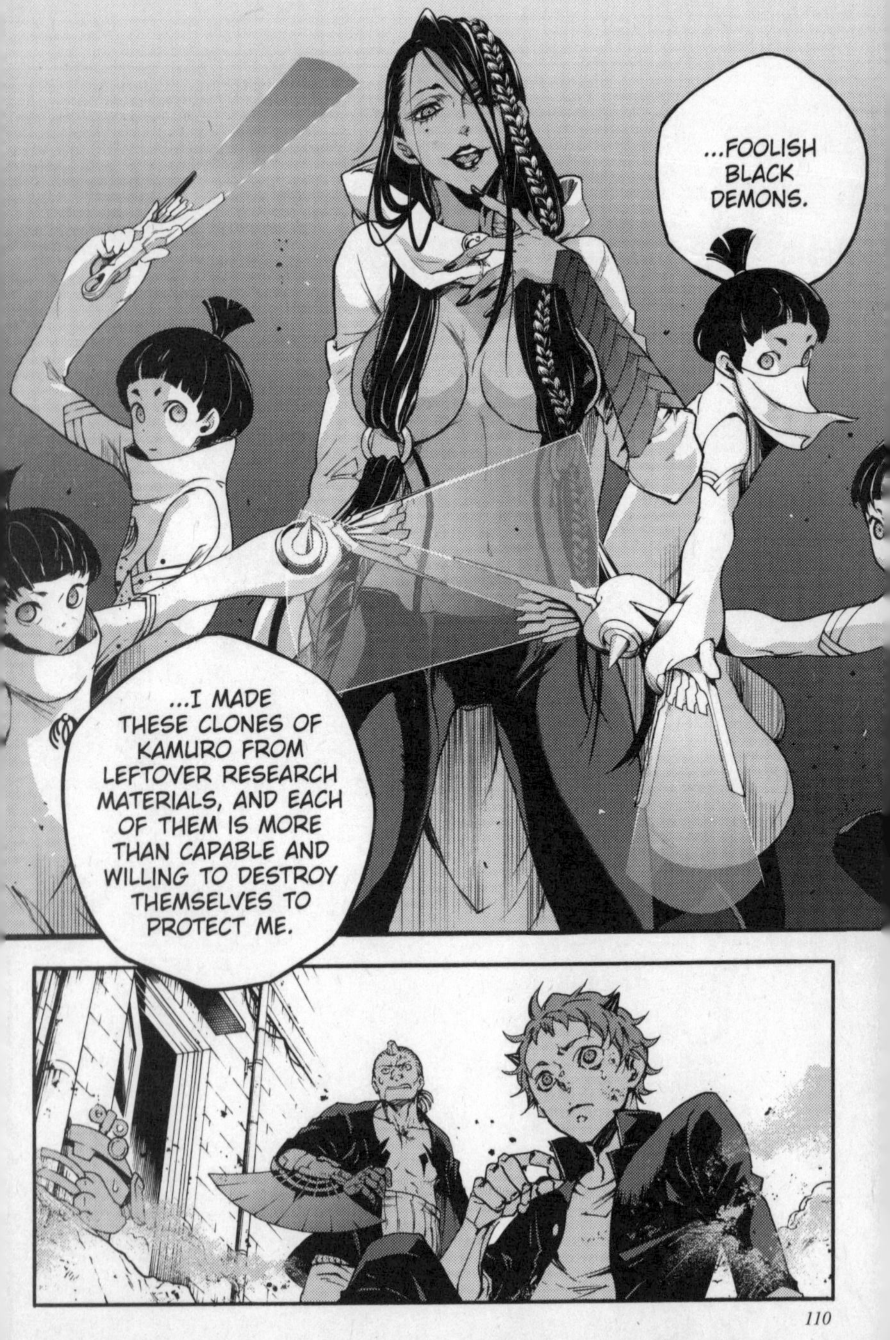
...FOOLISH BLACK DEMONS.
...I MADE THESE CLONES OF KAMURO FROM LEFTOVER RESEARCH MATERIALS, AND EACH OF THEM IS MORE THAN CAPABLE AND WILLING TO DESTROY THEMSELVES TO PROTECT ME.

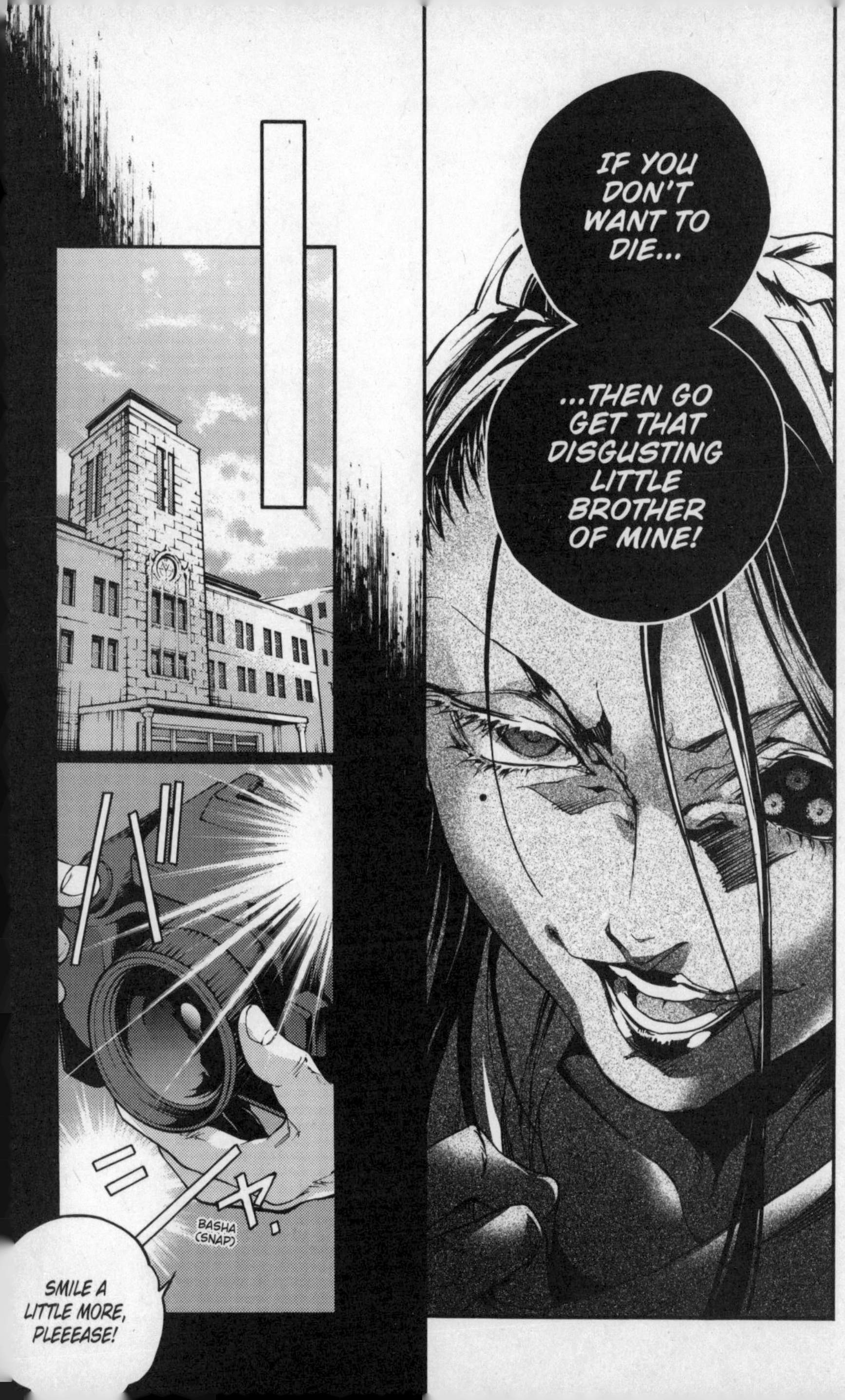
IF YOU DON'T WANT TO DIE...
...THEN GO GET THAT DISGUSTING LITTLE BROTHER OF MINE!
BASHA (SNAP)
SMILE A LITTLE MORE, PLEEEASE!

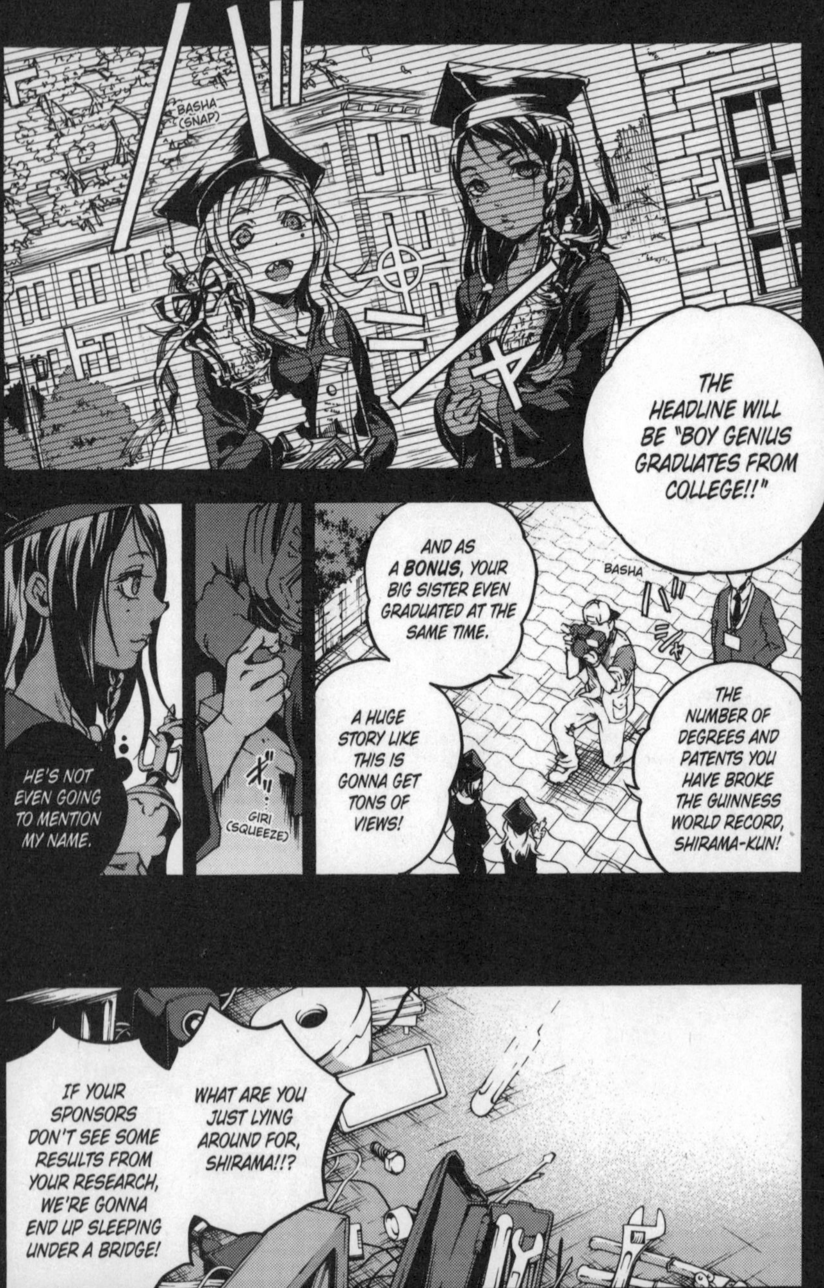
THE HEADLINE WILL BE "BOY GENIUS GRADUATES FROM COLLEGE!!"
BASHA (SNAP)
BASHA
THE NUMBER OF DEGREES AND PATENTS YOU HAVE BROKE THE GUINNESS WORLD RECORD, SHIRAMA-KUN!
AND AS A **BONUS**, YOUR BIG SISTER EVEN GRADUATED AT THE SAME TIME.
A HUGE STORY LIKE THIS IS GONNA GET TONS OF VIEWS!
GIRI (SQUEEZE)
HE'S NOT EVEN GOING TO MENTION MY NAME.
WHAT ARE YOU JUST LYING AROUND FOR, SHIRAMA!!?
IF YOUR SPONSORS DON'T SEE SOME RESULTS FROM YOUR RESEARCH, WE'RE GONNA END UP SLEEPING UNDER A BRIDGE!

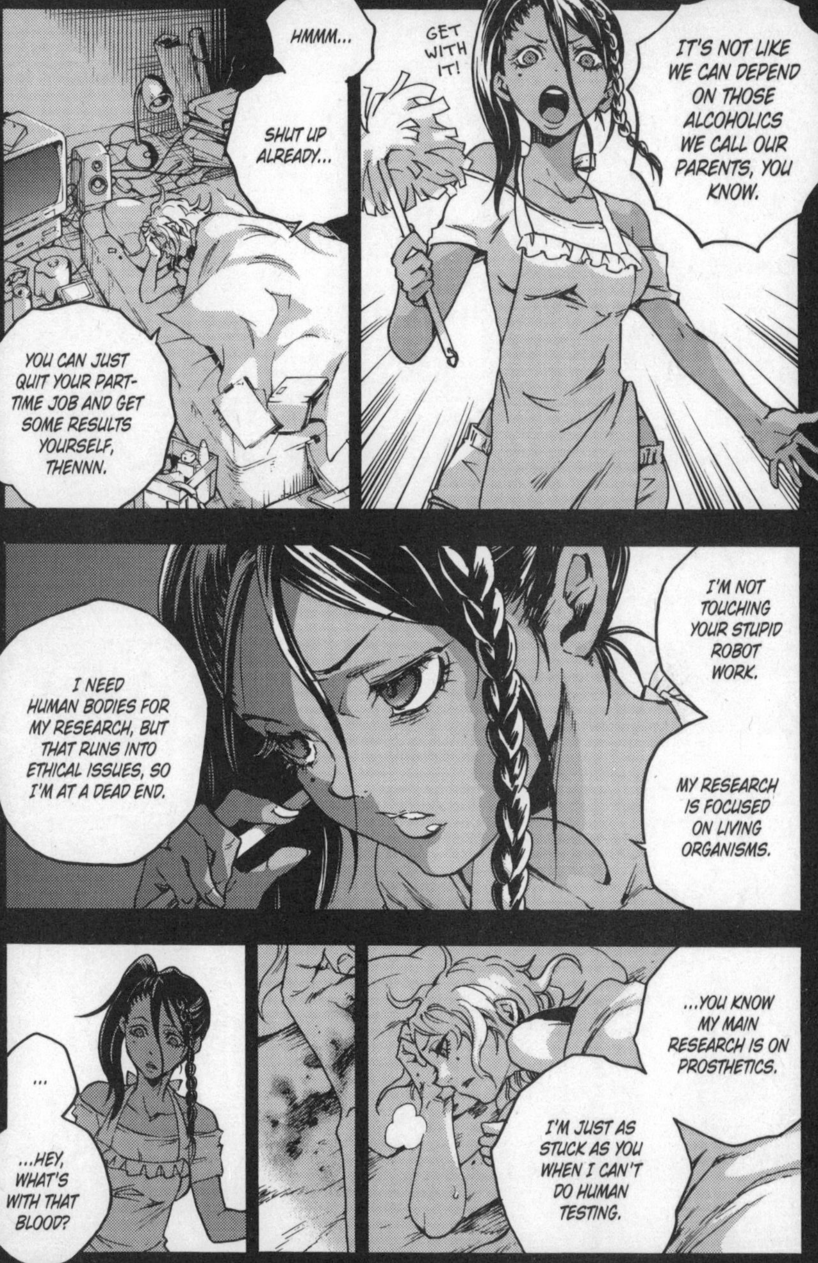
IT'S NOT LIKE WE CAN DEPEND ON THOSE ALCOHOLICS WE CALL OUR PARENTS, YOU KNOW.
GET WITH IT!
HMMM...
SHUT UP ALREADY...
YOU CAN JUST QUIT YOUR PART-TIME JOB AND GET SOME RESULTS YOURSELF, THENNN.
I'M NOT TOUCHING YOUR STUPID ROBOT WORK.
MY RESEARCH IS FOCUSED ON LIVING ORGANISMS.
I NEED HUMAN BODIES FOR MY RESEARCH, BUT THAT RUNS INTO ETHICAL ISSUES, SO I'M AT A DEAD END.
...YOU KNOW MY MAIN RESEARCH IS ON PROSTHETICS.
I'M JUST AS STUCK AS YOU WHEN I CAN'T DO HUMAN TESTING.
...
...HEY, WHAT'S WITH THAT BLOOD?

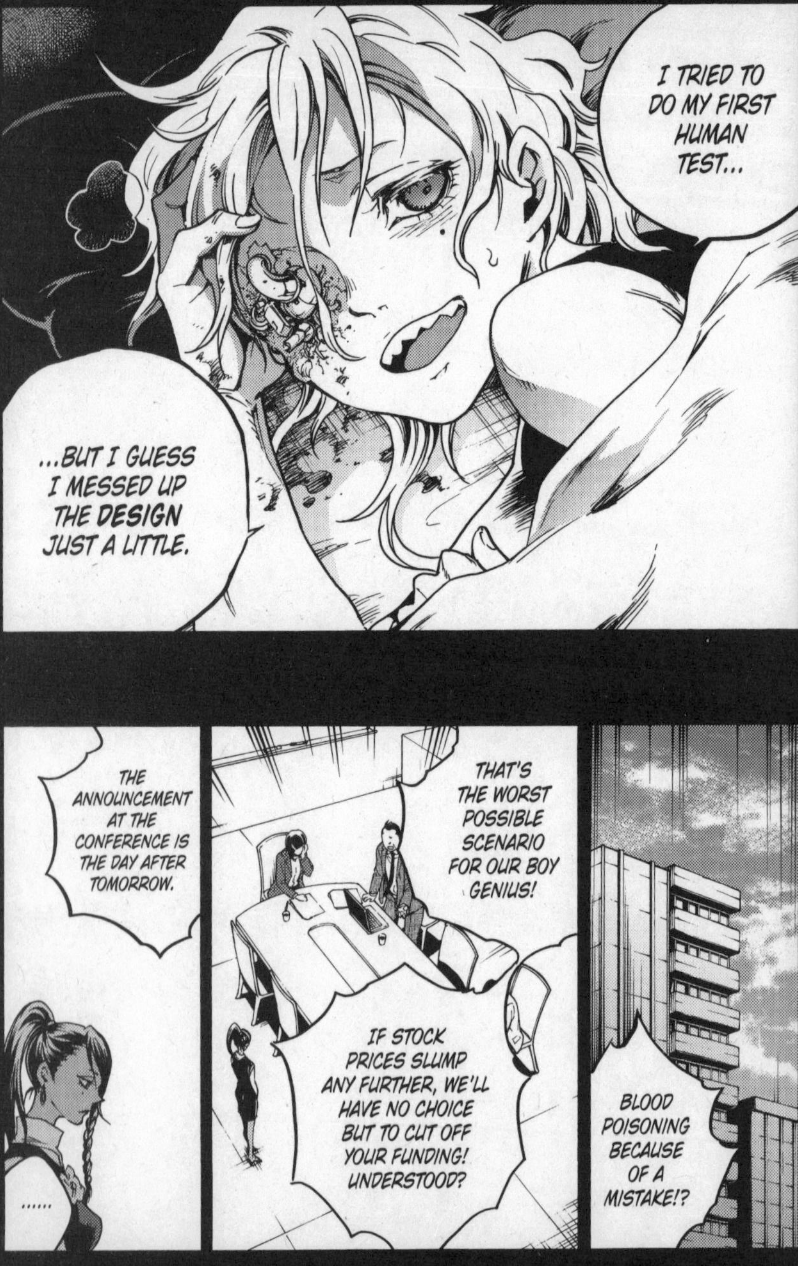
I TRIED TO DO MY FIRST HUMAN TEST...
...BUT I GUESS I MESSED UP THE DESIGN JUST A LITTLE.
BLOOD POISONING BECAUSE OF A MISTAKE!?
THAT'S THE WORST POSSIBLE SCENARIO FOR OUR BOY GENIUS!
IF STOCK PRICES SLUMP ANY FURTHER, WE'LL HAVE NO CHOICE BUT TO CUT OFF YOUR FUNDING! UNDERSTOOD?
THE ANNOUNCEMENT AT THE CONFERENCE IS THE DAY AFTER TOMORROW.
......

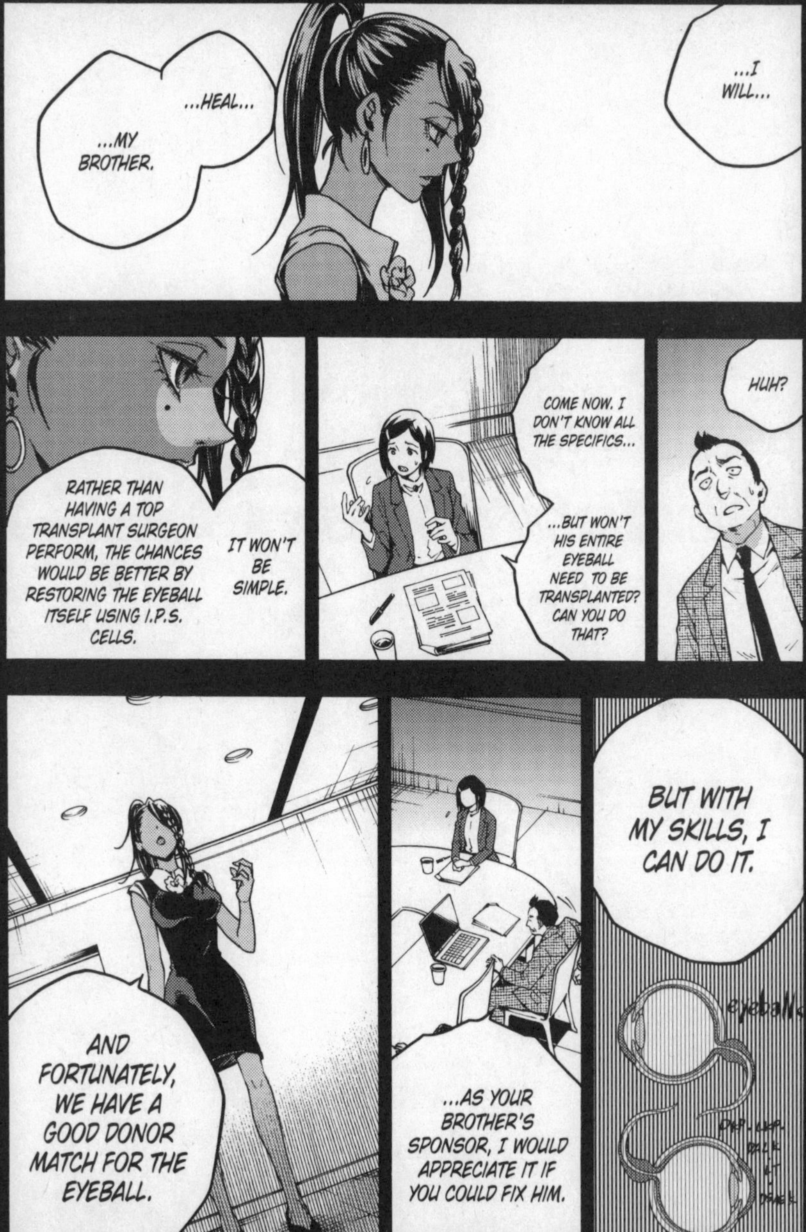
...I WILL...
...HEAL...
...MY BROTHER.
HUH?
COME NOW. I DON'T KNOW ALL THE SPECIFICS...
...BUT WON'T HIS ENTIRE EYEBALL NEED TO BE TRANSPLANTED? CAN YOU DO THAT?
IT WON'T BE SIMPLE.
RATHER THAN HAVING A TOP TRANSPLANT SURGEON PERFORM, THE CHANCES WOULD BE BETTER BY RESTORING THE EYEBALL ITSELF USING I.P.S. CELLS.
BUT WITH MY SKILLS, I CAN DO IT.
eyeball
...AS YOUR BROTHER'S SPONSOR, I WOULD APPRECIATE IT IF YOU COULD FIX HIM.
AND FORTUNATELY, WE HAVE A GOOD DONOR MATCH FOR THE EYEBALL.

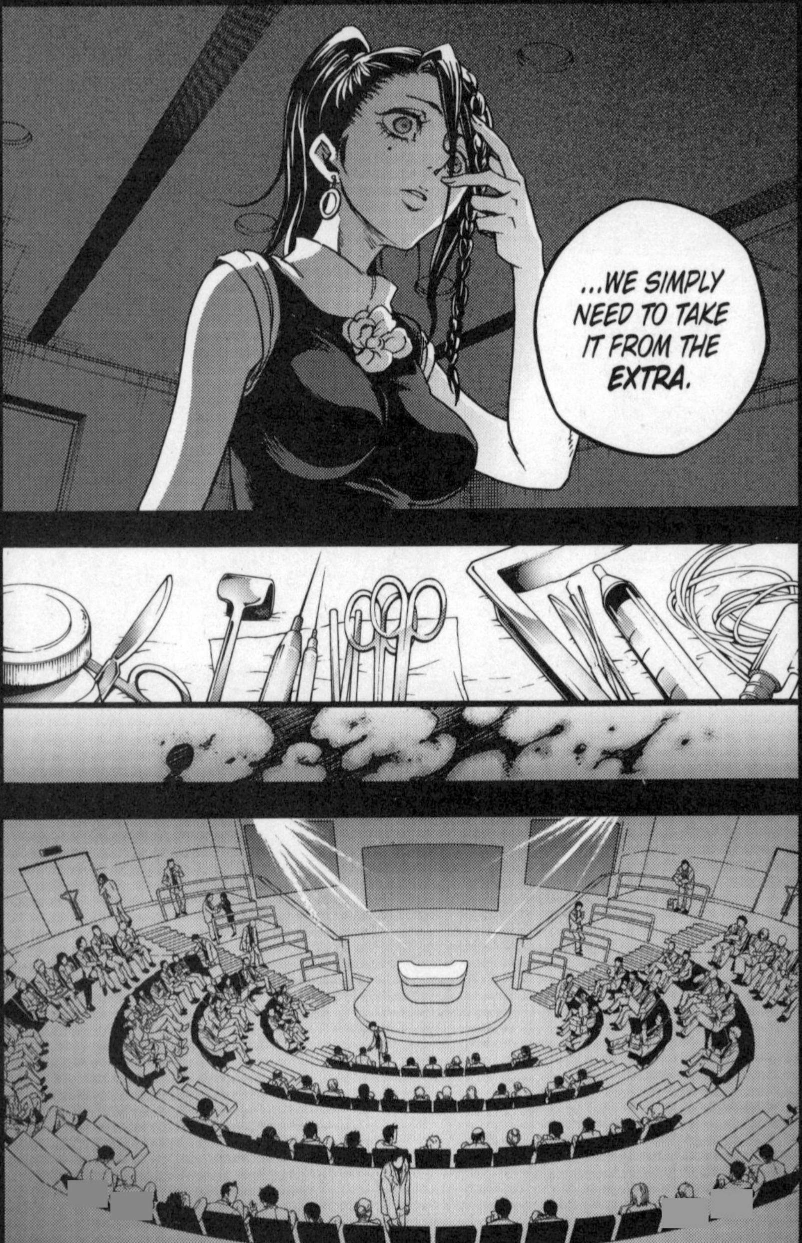
...WE SIMPLY NEED TO TAKE IT FROM THE EXTRA.

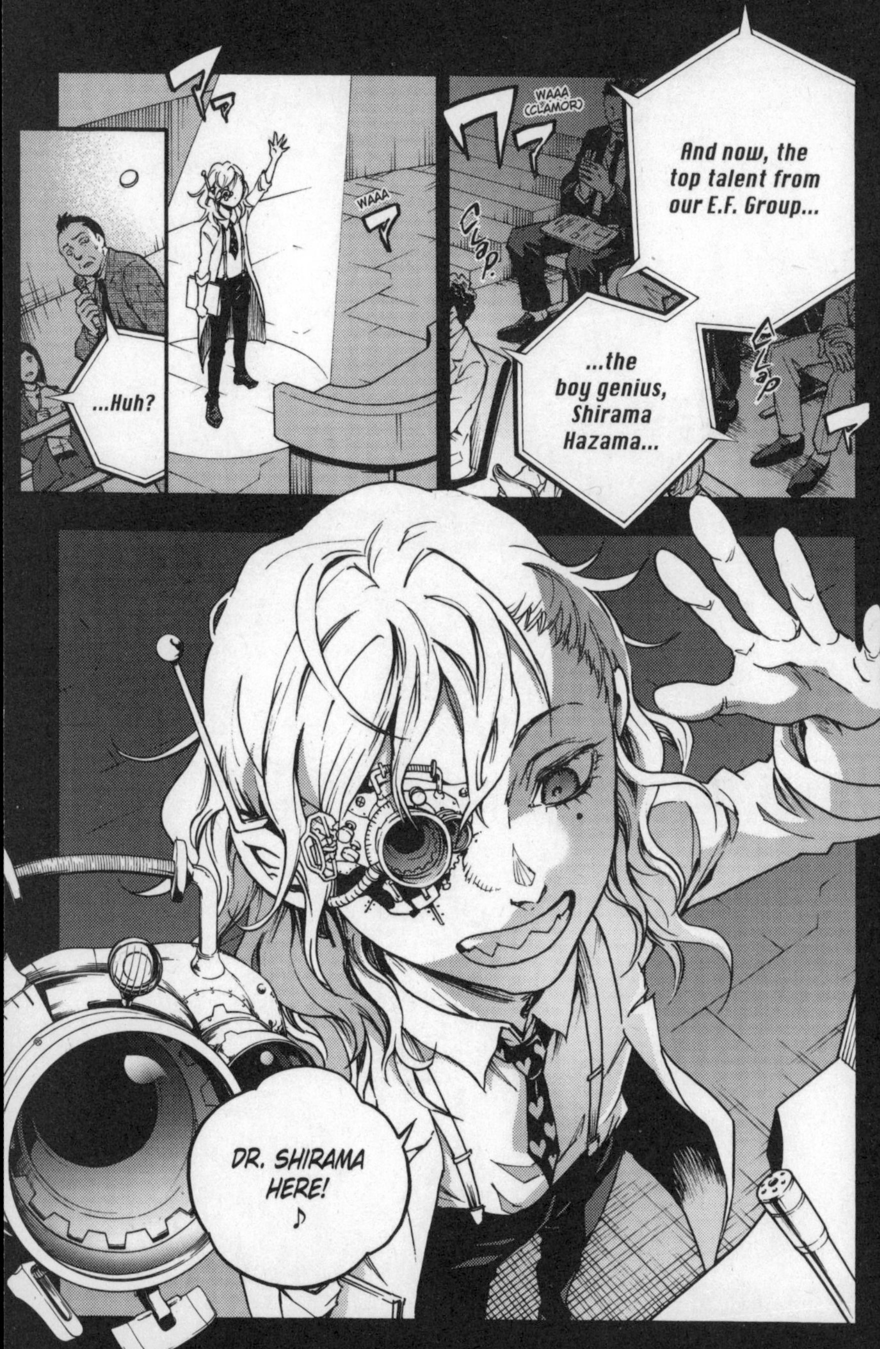
WAAA (CLAMOR)
And now, the top talent from our E.F. Group...
Clap
...the boy genius, Shirama Hazama...
Clap
WAAA
...Huh?
DR. SHIRAMA HERE! ♪

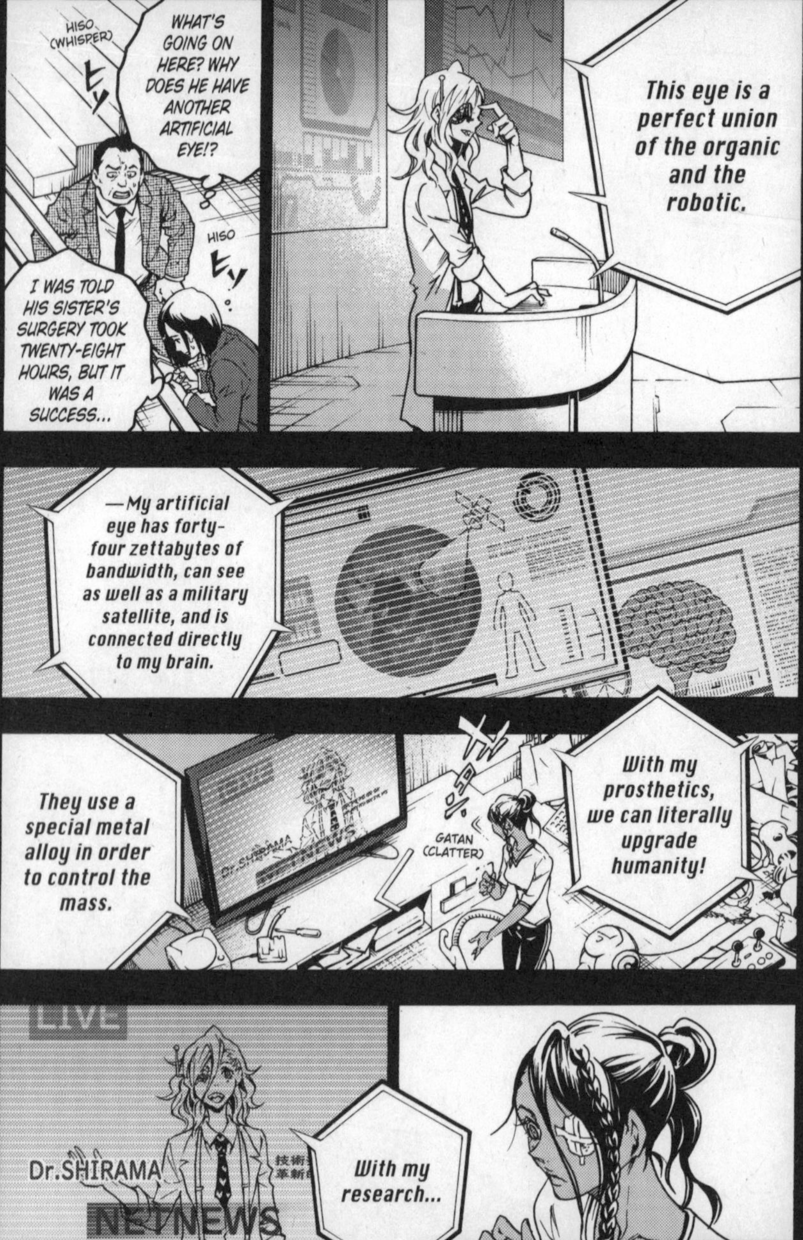
This eye is a perfect union of the organic and the robotic.
HISO (WHISPER)
WHAT'S GOING ON HERE? WHY DOES HE HAVE ANOTHER ARTIFICIAL EYE!?
HISO
I WAS TOLD HIS SISTER'S SURGERY TOOK TWENTY-EIGHT HOURS, BUT IT WAS A SUCCESS...
—My artificial eye has forty-four zettabytes of bandwidth, can see as well as a military satellite, and is connected directly to my brain.
With my prosthetics, we can literally upgrade humanity!
GATAN (CLATTER)
They use a special metal alloy in order to control the mass.
LIVE
Dr.SHIRAMA
NETNEWS
With my research...

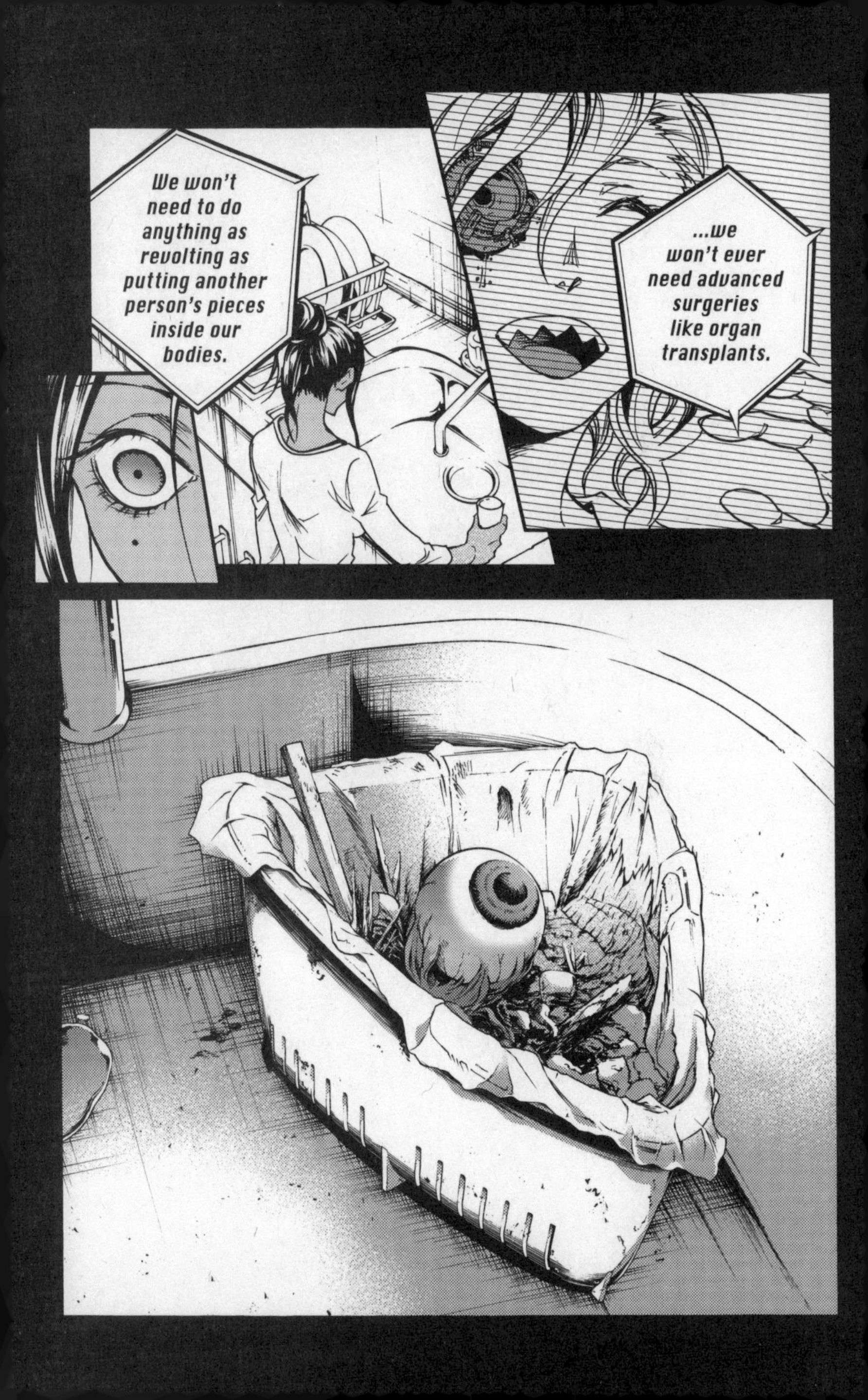
...we won't ever need advanced surgeries like organ transplants.
We won't need to do anything as revolting as putting another person's pieces inside our bodies.

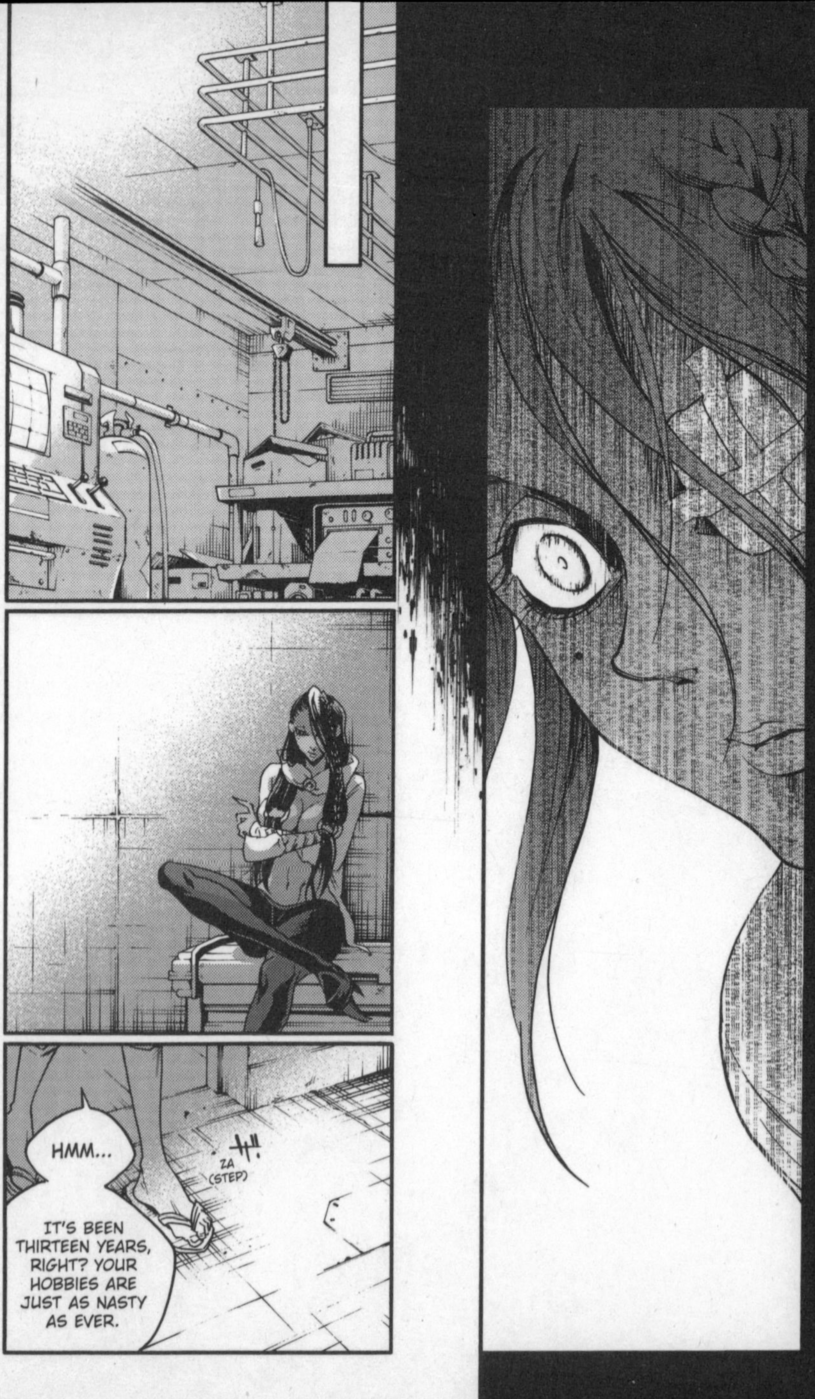
ZA (STEP)
HMM...
IT'S BEEN THIRTEEN YEARS, RIGHT? YOUR HOBBIES ARE JUST AS NASTY AS EVER.

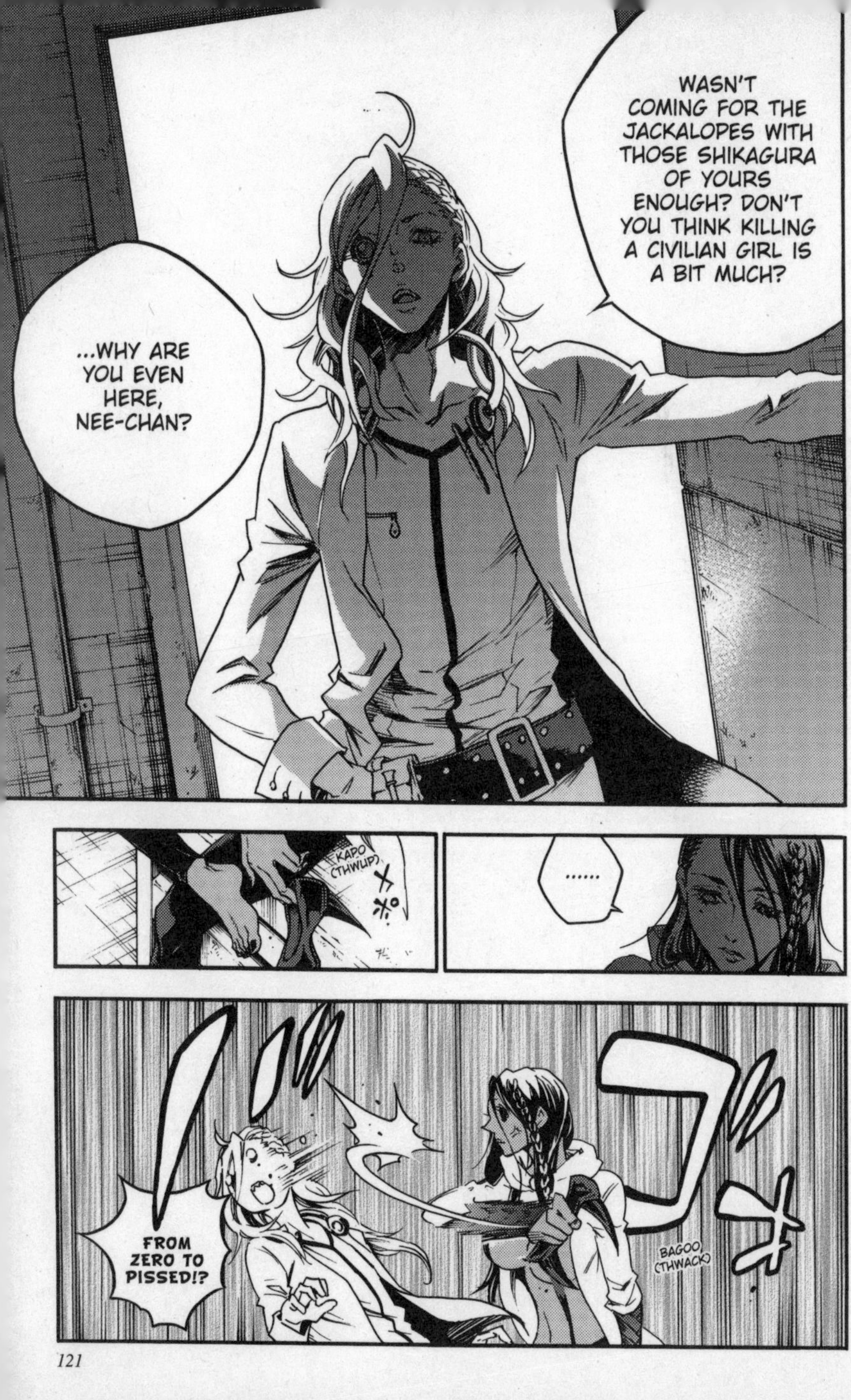
WASN'T COMING FOR THE JACKALOPES WITH THOSE SHIKAGURA OF YOURS ENOUGH? DON'T YOU THINK KILLING A CIVILIAN GIRL IS A BIT MUCH?
...WHY ARE YOU EVEN HERE, NEE-CHAN?
......
KAPO (THWUP)
BAGOO (THWACK)
FROM ZERO TO PISSED!?

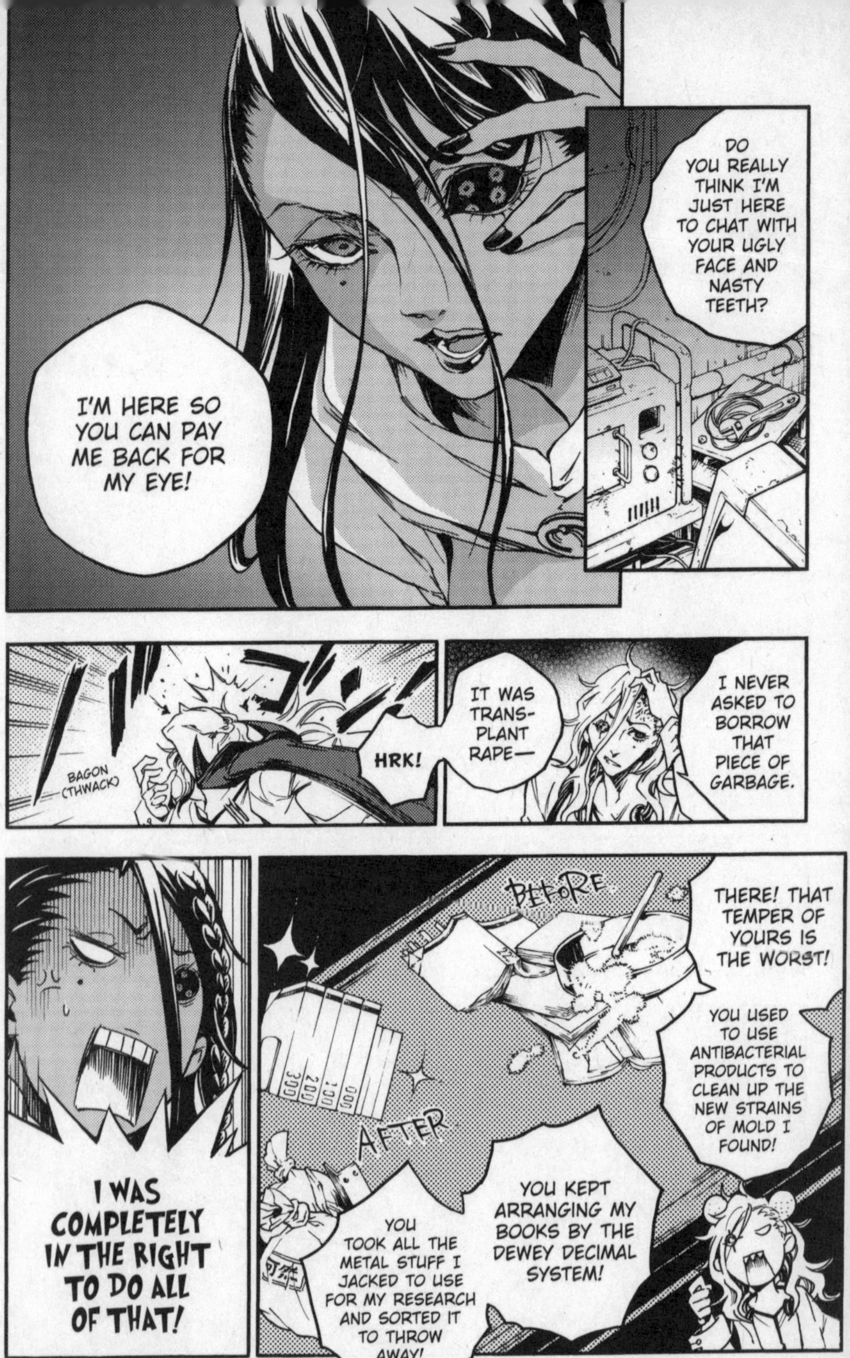
DO YOU REALLY THINK I'M JUST HERE TO CHAT WITH YOUR UGLY FACE AND NASTY TEETH?
I'M HERE SO YOU CAN PAY ME BACK FOR MY EYE!
I NEVER ASKED TO BORROW THAT PIECE OF GARBAGE.
IT WAS TRANS-PLANT RAPE—
HRK!
BAGON (THWACK)
BEFORE
THERE! THAT TEMPER OF YOURS IS THE WORST!
YOU USED TO USE ANTIBACTERIAL PRODUCTS TO CLEAN UP THE NEW STRAINS OF MOLD I FOUND!
AFTER
YOU KEPT ARRANGING MY BOOKS BY THE DEWEY DECIMAL SYSTEM!
YOU TOOK ALL THE METAL STUFF I JACKED TO USE FOR MY RESEARCH AND SORTED IT TO THROW AWAY!
I WAS COMPLETELY IN THE RIGHT TO DO ALL OF THAT!

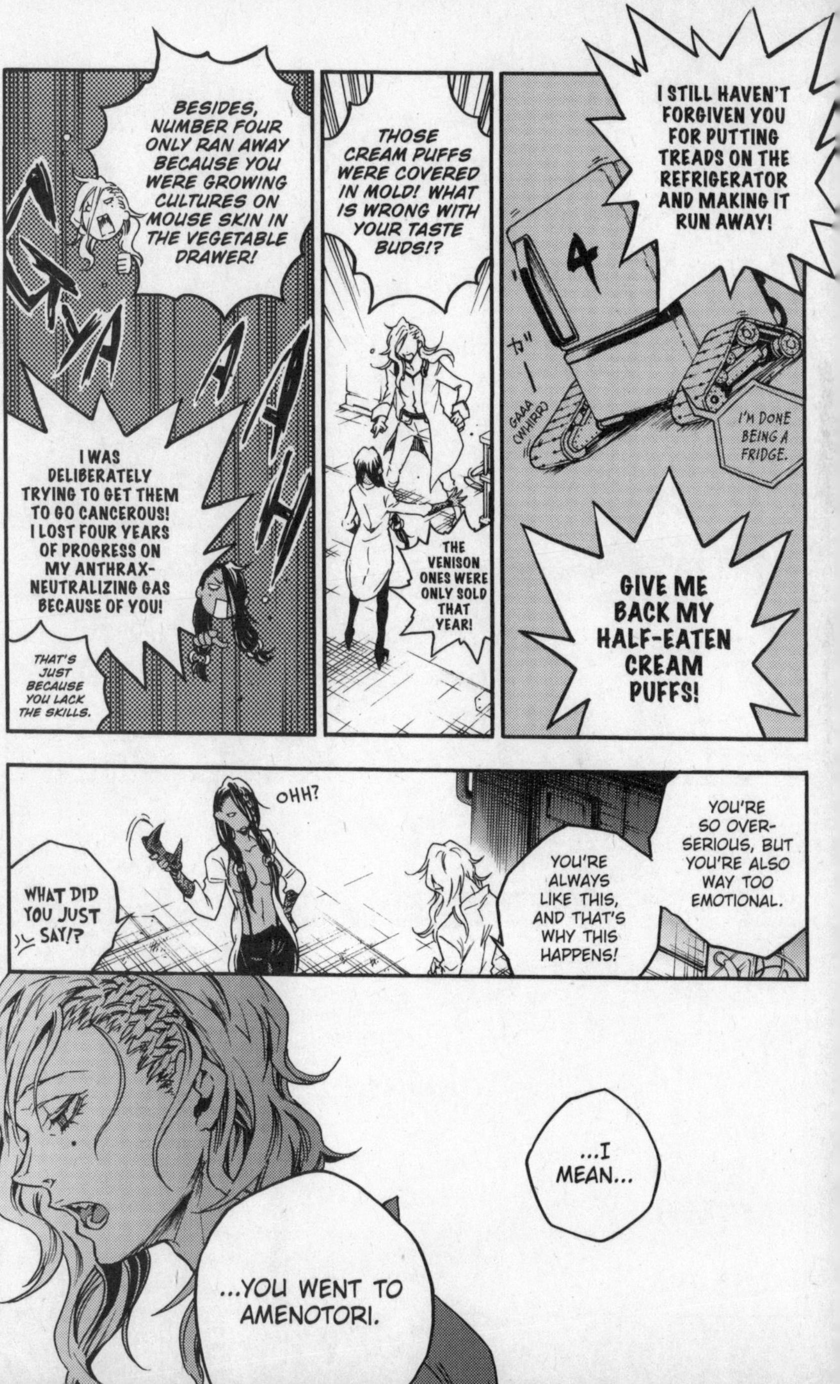
I STILL HAVEN'T FORGIVEN YOU FOR PUTTING TREADS ON THE REFRIGERATOR AND MAKING IT RUN AWAY!
GAAA (WHIRR)
I'M DONE BEING A FRIDGE.
GIVE ME BACK MY HALF-EATEN CREAM PUFFS!
THOSE CREAM PUFFS WERE COVERED IN MOLD! WHAT IS WRONG WITH YOUR TASTE BUDS!?
THE VENISON ONES WERE ONLY SOLD THAT YEAR!
BESIDES, NUMBER FOUR ONLY RAN AWAY BECAUSE YOU WERE GROWING CULTURES ON MOUSE SKIN IN THE VEGETABLE DRAWER!
KYAAAH
I WAS DELIBERATELY TRYING TO GET THEM TO GO CANCEROUS! I LOST FOUR YEARS OF PROGRESS ON MY ANTHRAX-NEUTRALIZING GAS BECAUSE OF YOU!
THAT'S JUST BECAUSE YOU LACK THE SKILLS.
YOU'RE SO OVER-SERIOUS, BUT YOU'RE ALSO WAY TOO EMOTIONAL.
YOU'RE ALWAYS LIKE THIS, AND THAT'S WHY THIS HAPPENS!
OHH?
WHAT DID YOU JUST SAY!?
...I MEAN...
...YOU WENT TO AMENOTORI.

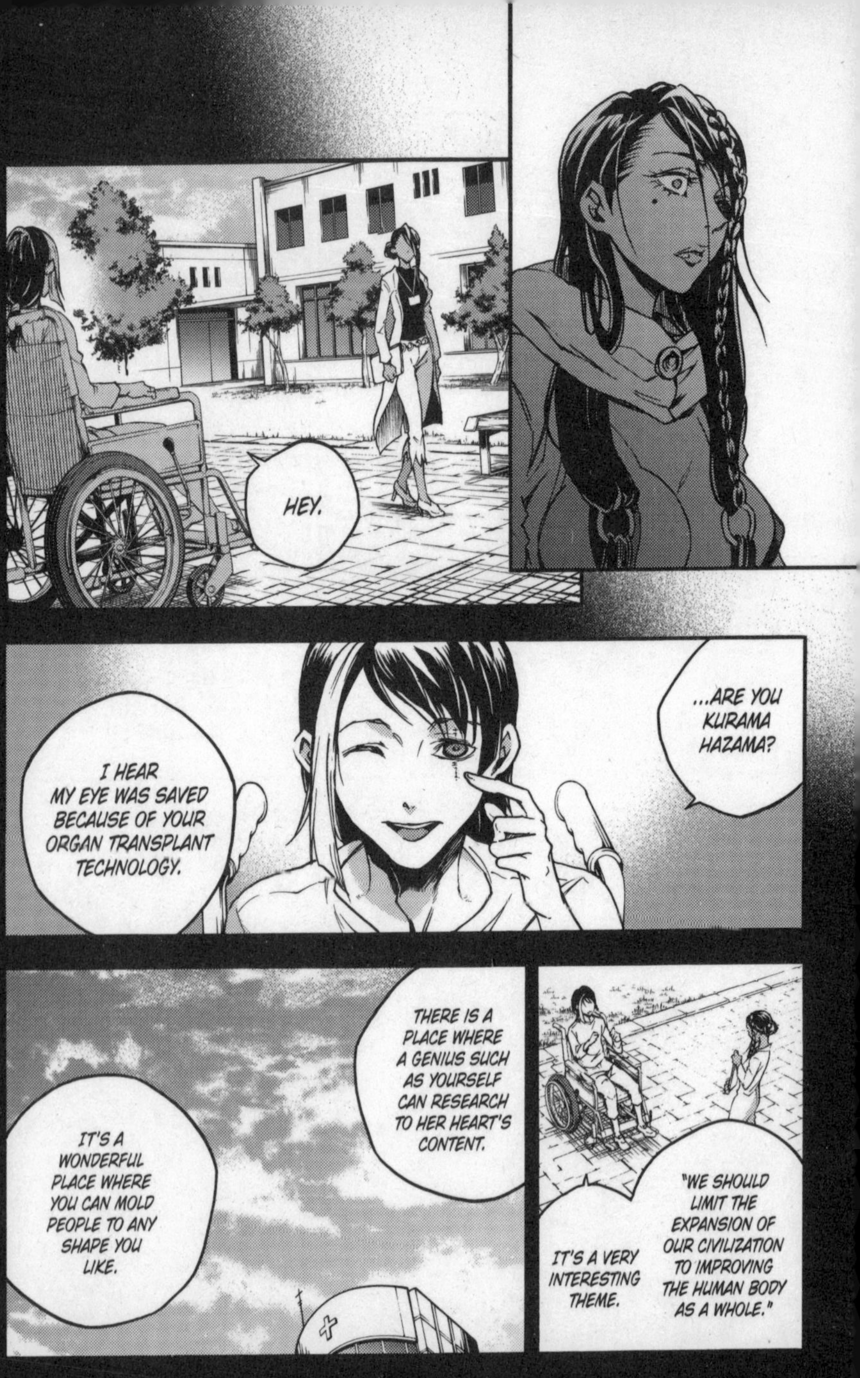
HEY.
...ARE YOU KURAMA HAZAMA?
I HEAR MY EYE WAS SAVED BECAUSE OF YOUR ORGAN TRANSPLANT TECHNOLOGY.
"WE SHOULD LIMIT THE EXPANSION OF OUR CIVILIZATION TO IMPROVING THE HUMAN BODY AS A WHOLE."
IT'S A VERY INTERESTING THEME.
THERE IS A PLACE WHERE A GENIUS SUCH AS YOURSELF CAN RESEARCH TO HER HEART'S CONTENT.
IT'S A WONDERFUL PLACE WHERE YOU CAN MOLD PEOPLE TO ANY SHAPE YOU LIKE.

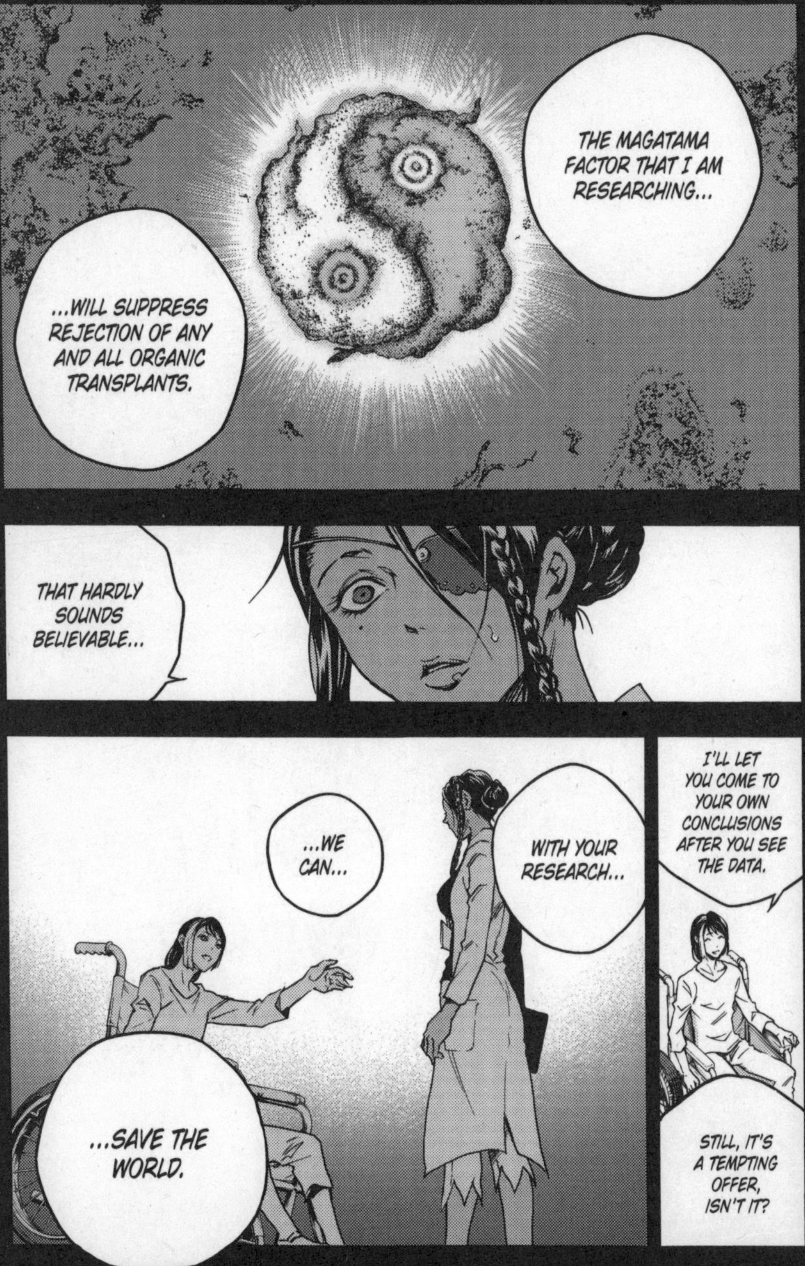
THE MAGATAMA FACTOR THAT I AM RESEARCHING...
...WILL SUPPRESS REJECTION OF ANY AND ALL ORGANIC TRANSPLANTS.
THAT HARDLY SOUNDS BELIEVABLE...
I'LL LET YOU COME TO YOUR OWN CONCLUSIONS AFTER YOU SEE THE DATA.
STILL, IT'S A TEMPTING OFFER, ISN'T IT?
WITH YOUR RESEARCH...
...WE CAN...
...SAVE THE WORLD.

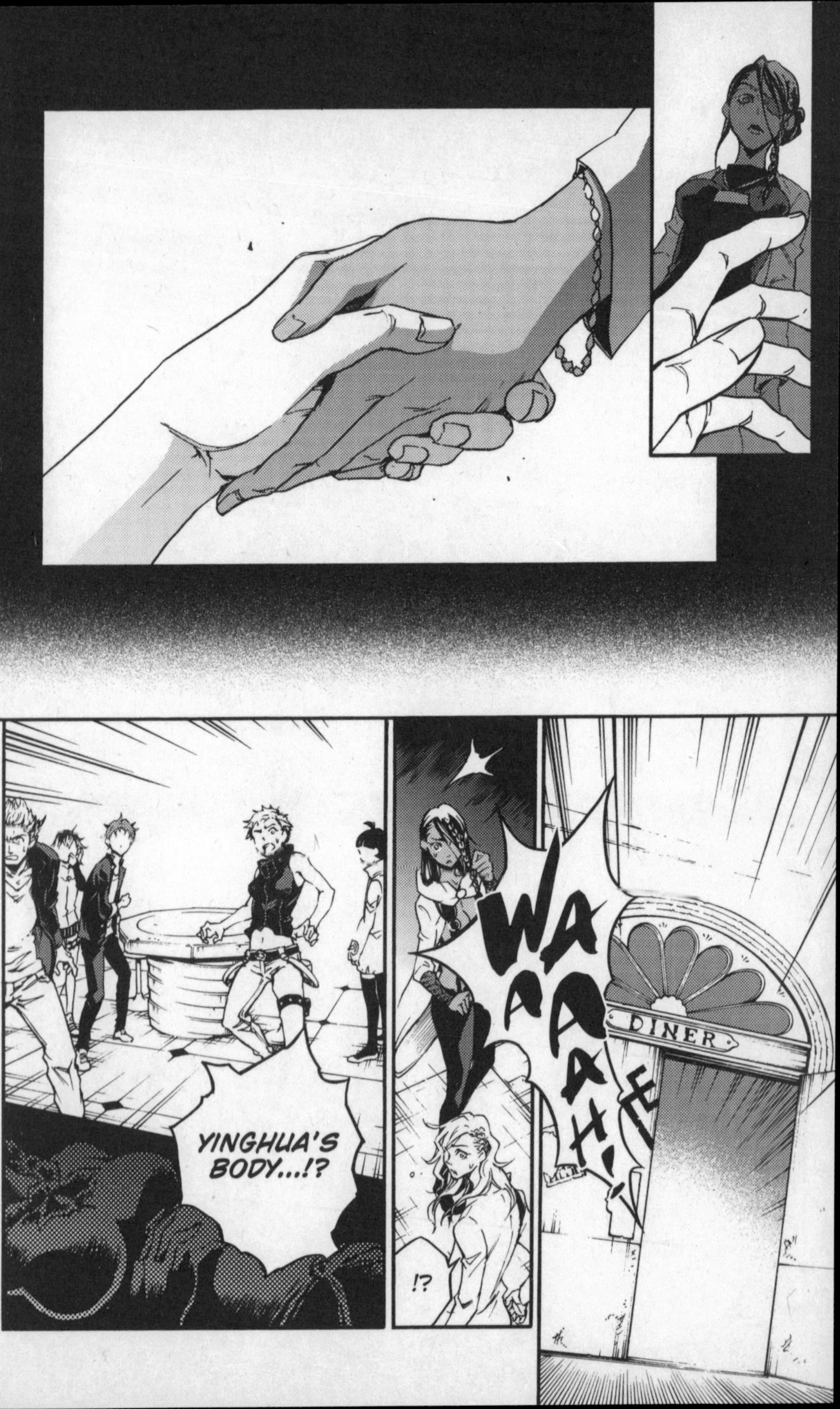
DINER
WAAAAH!
!?
YINGHUA'S BODY...!?

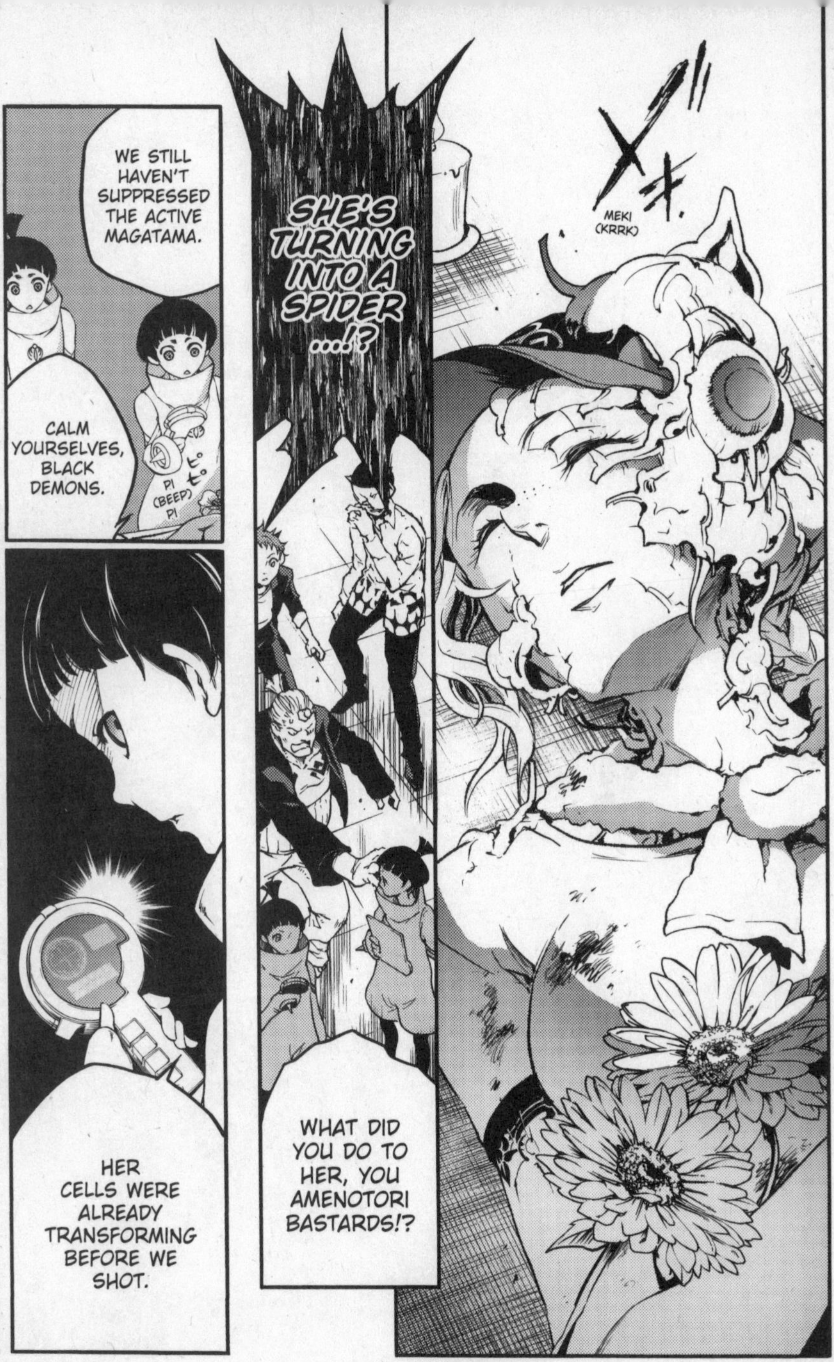
MEKI (KRRK)
SHE'S TURNING INTO A SPIDER ...!?
WHAT DID YOU DO TO HER, YOU AMENOTORI BASTARDS!?
WE STILL HAVEN'T SUPPRESSED THE ACTIVE MAGATAMA.
CALM YOURSELVES, BLACK DEMONS.
PI (BEEP) PI
HER CELLS WERE ALREADY TRANSFORMING BEFORE WE SHOT.

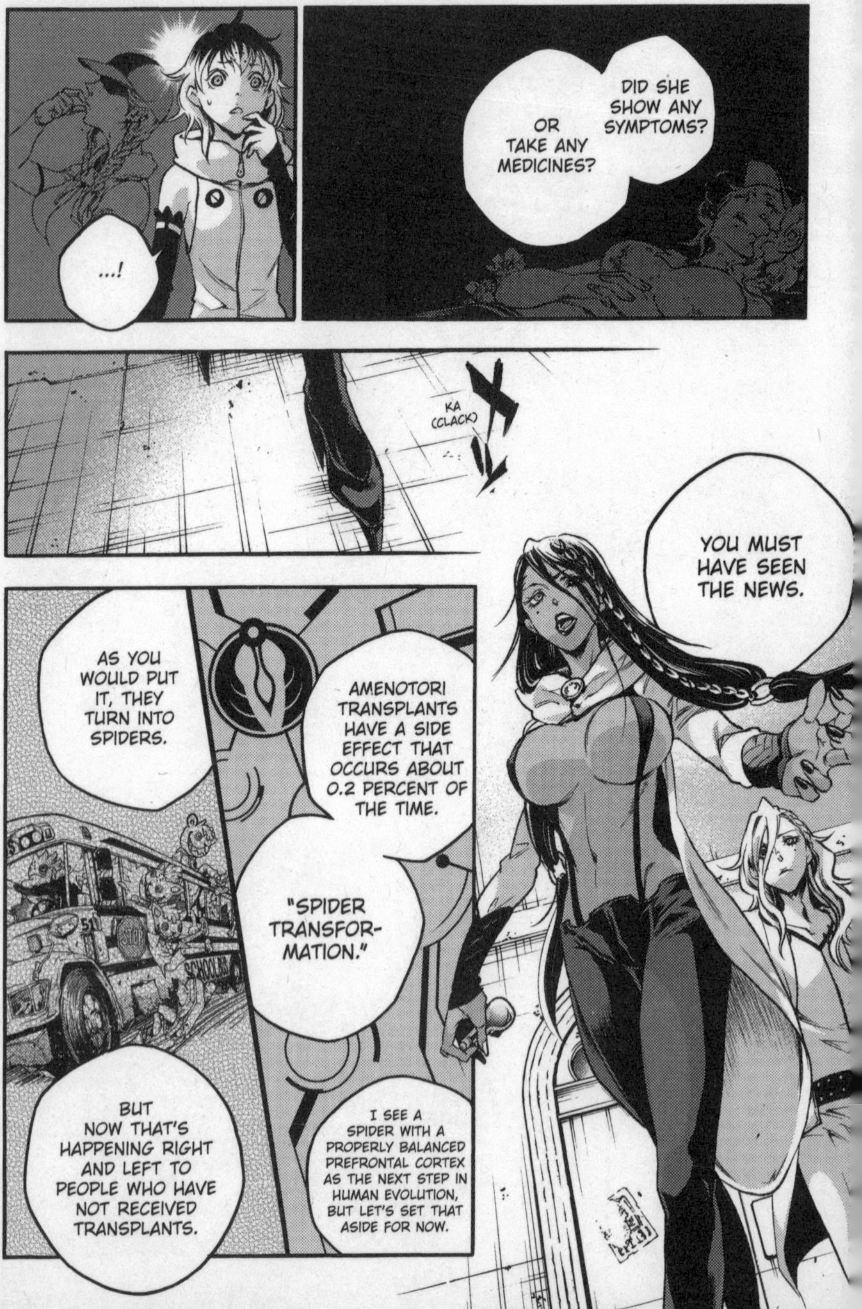
DID SHE SHOW ANY SYMPTOMS?
OR TAKE ANY MEDICINES?
...!
KA (CLACK)
YOU MUST HAVE SEEN THE NEWS.
AMENOTORI TRANSPLANTS HAVE A SIDE EFFECT THAT OCCURS ABOUT 0.2 PERCENT OF THE TIME.
"SPIDER TRANSFORMATION."
AS YOU WOULD PUT IT, THEY TURN INTO SPIDERS.
I SEE A SPIDER WITH A PROPERLY BALANCED PREFRONTAL CORTEX AS THE NEXT STEP IN HUMAN EVOLUTION, BUT LET'S SET THAT ASIDE FOR NOW.
BUT NOW THAT'S HAPPENING RIGHT AND LEFT TO PEOPLE WHO HAVE NOT RECEIVED TRANSPLANTS.

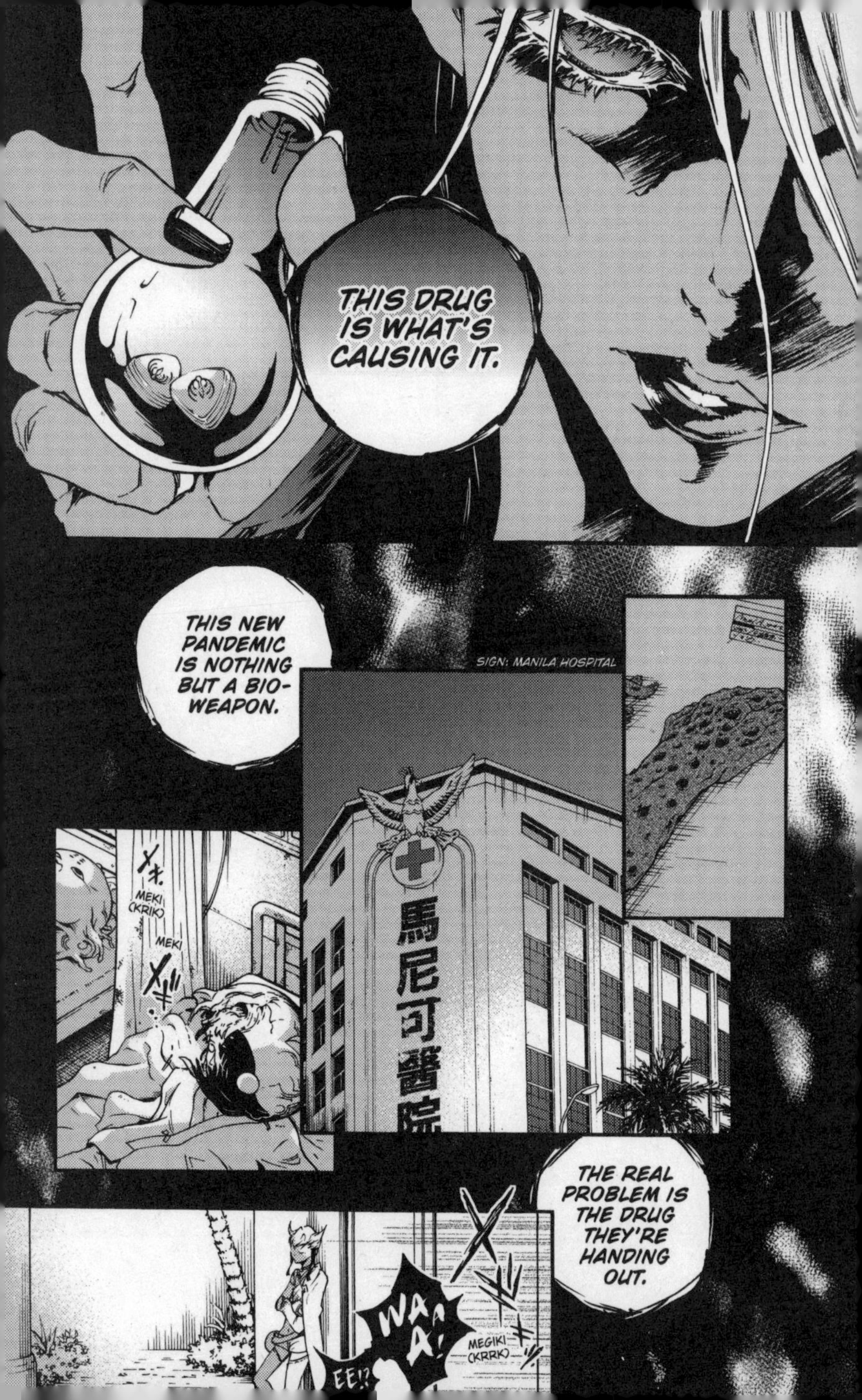
THIS DRUG IS WHAT'S CAUSING IT.
THIS NEW PANDEMIC IS NOTHING BUT A BIO-WEAPON.
SIGN: MANILA HOSPITAL
馬尼可醫院
MEKI (KRIK)
MEKI
THE REAL PROBLEM IS THE DRUG THEY'RE HANDING OUT.
MEGIKI (KRRK)
WAAA!
EE!?

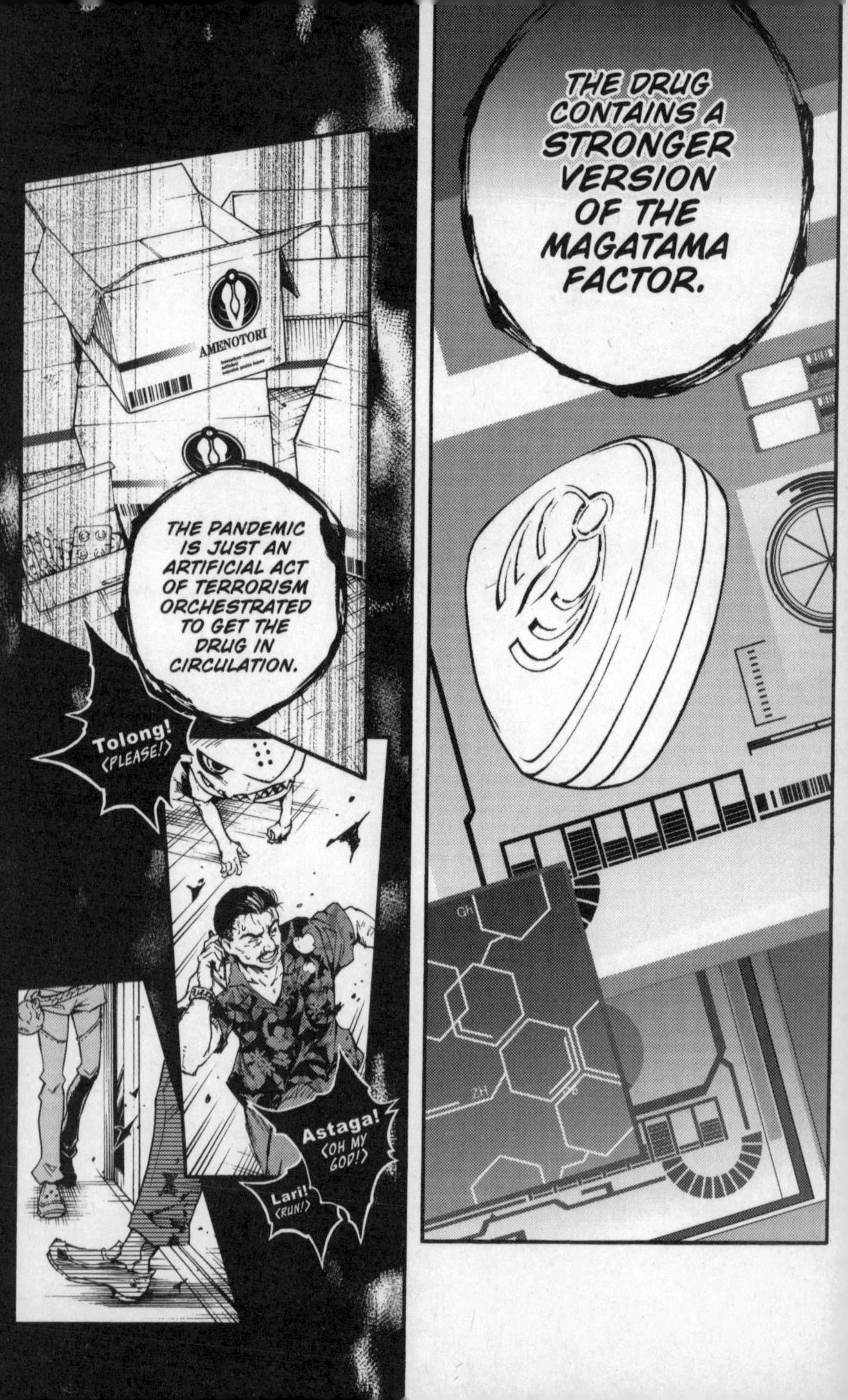
THE DRUG CONTAINS A STRONGER VERSION OF THE MAGATAMA FACTOR.
AMENOTORI
THE PANDEMIC IS JUST AN ARTIFICIAL ACT OF TERRORISM ORCHESTRATED TO GET THE DRUG IN CIRCULATION.
Tolong! ⟨PLEASE!⟩
Astaga! ⟨OH MY GOD!⟩
Lari! ⟨RUN!⟩

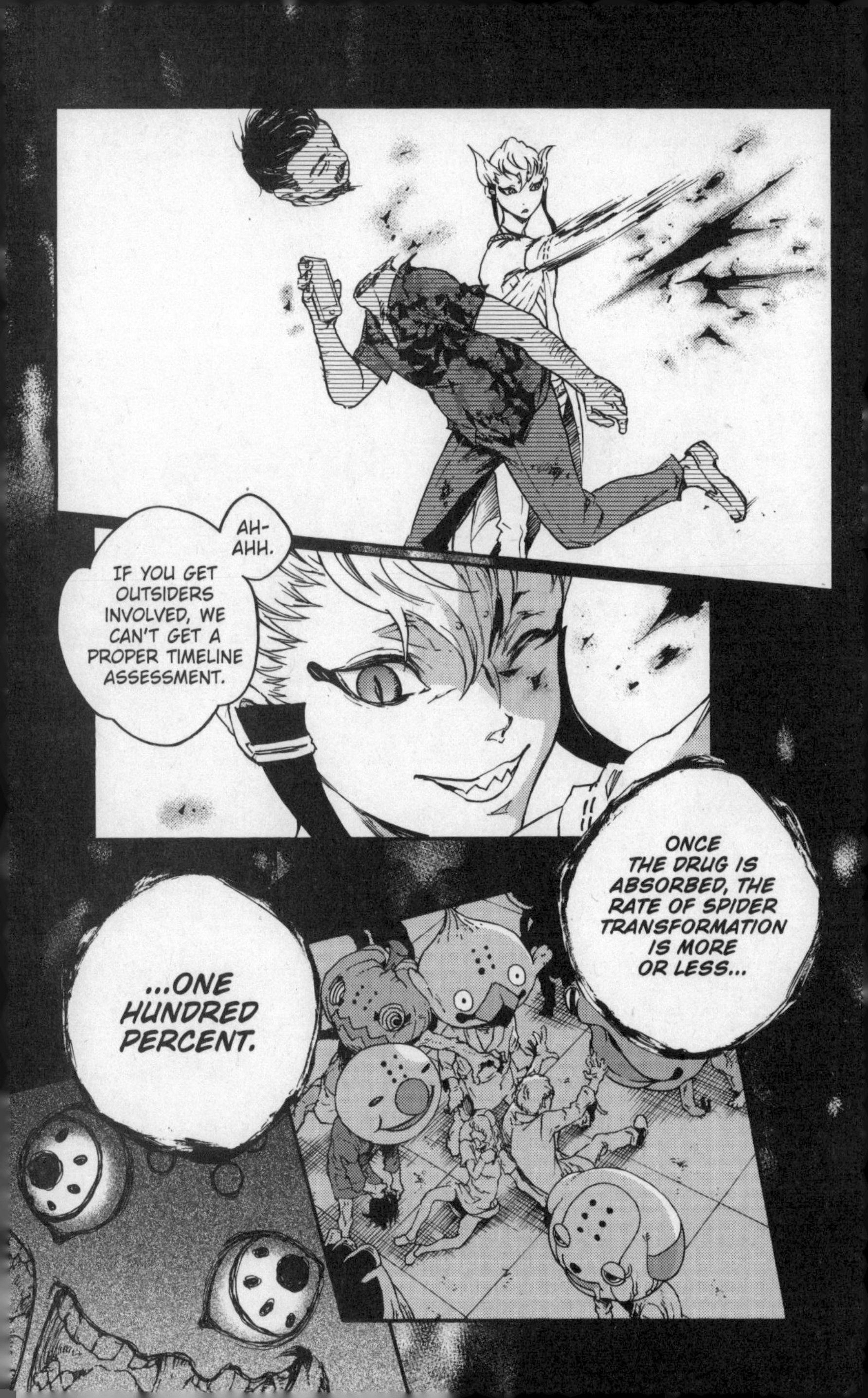
AH-AHH.
IF YOU GET OUTSIDERS INVOLVED, WE CAN'T GET A PROPER TIMELINE ASSESSMENT.
ONCE THE DRUG IS ABSORBED, THE RATE OF SPIDER TRANSFORMATION IS MORE OR LESS...
...ONE HUNDRED PERCENT.

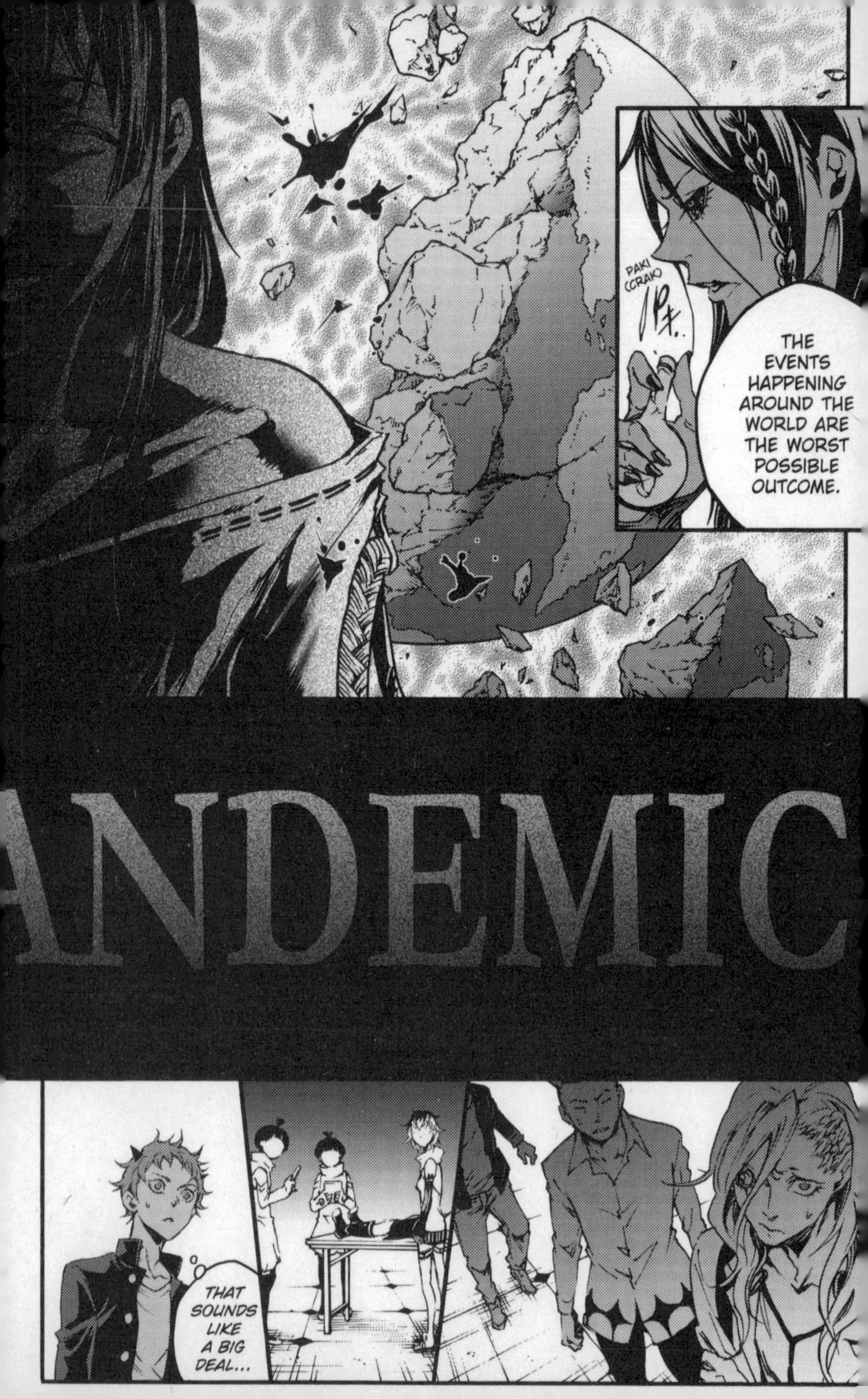
PAKI (CRAK)
THE EVENTS HAPPENING AROUND THE WORLD ARE THE WORST POSSIBLE OUTCOME.
ANDEMIC
THAT SOUNDS LIKE A BIG DEAL...

THE PRESIDENT OF AMENOTORI, UTSUWA MUNOMIYA...

...HAS ENGINEERED A GLOBAL CATASTROPHE.

SPIDER P.

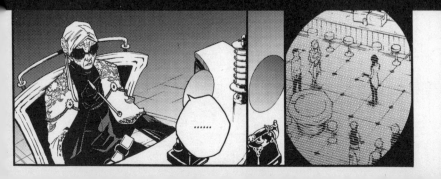

......

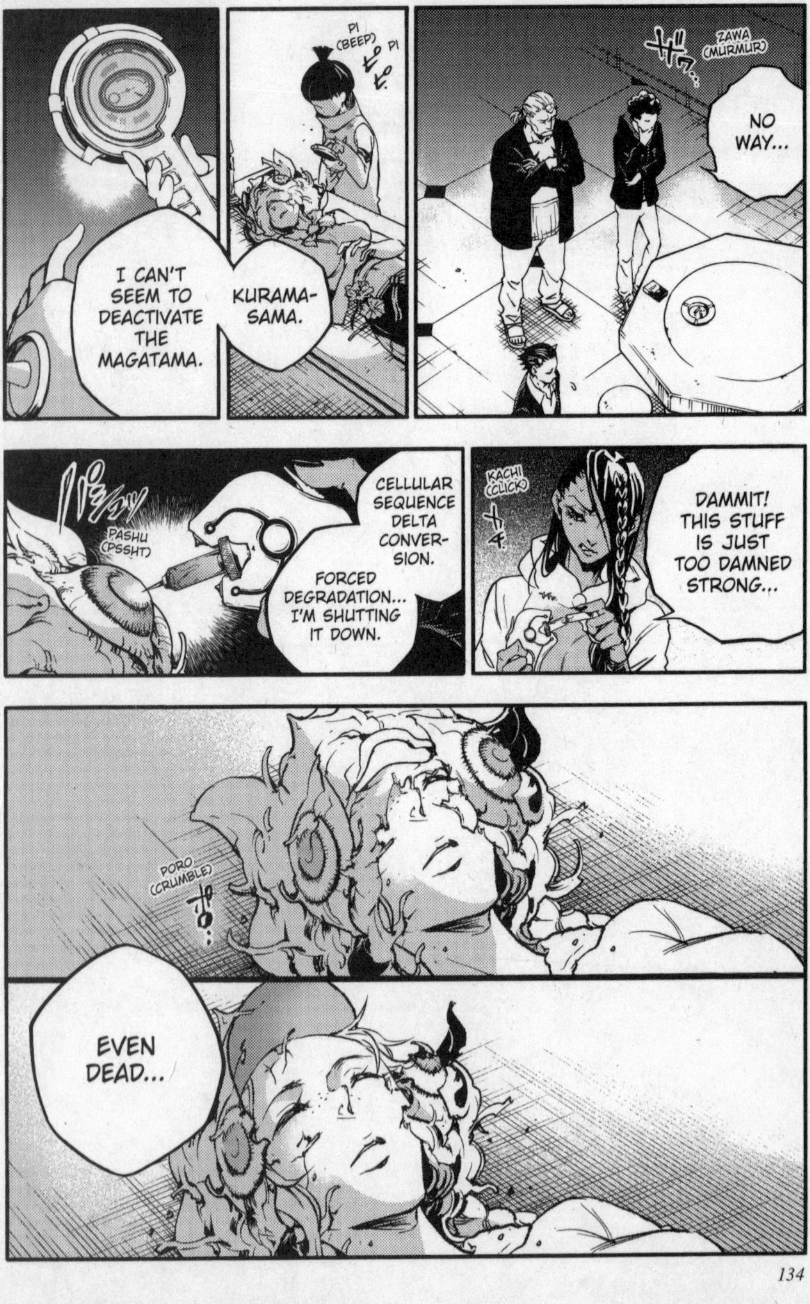
ZAWA (MURMUR)
NO WAY...
PI (BEEP) PI
KURAMA-SAMA.
I CAN'T SEEM TO DEACTIVATE THE MAGATAMA.
KACHI (CLICK)
DAMMIT! THIS STUFF IS JUST TOO DAMNED STRONG...
CELLULAR SEQUENCE DELTA CONVERSION.
FORCED DEGRADATION... I'M SHUTTING IT DOWN.
PASHU (PSSHT)
PORO (CRUMBLE)
EVEN DEAD...

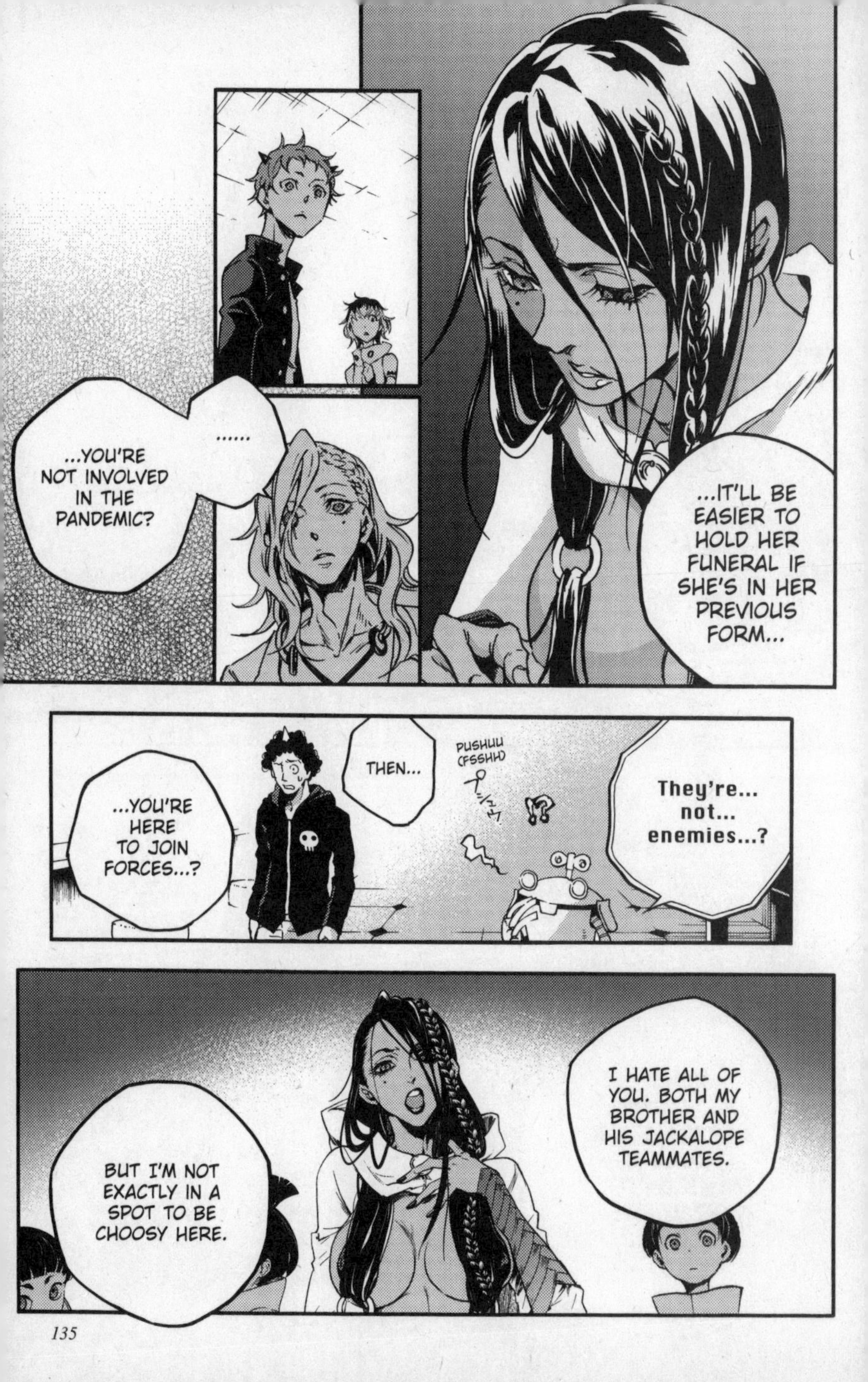
...IT'LL BE EASIER TO HOLD HER FUNERAL IF SHE'S IN HER PREVIOUS FORM...
......
...YOU'RE NOT INVOLVED IN THE PANDEMIC?
They're... not... enemies...?
PUSHUU (FSSHH)
THEN...
...YOU'RE HERE TO JOIN FORCES...?
I HATE ALL OF YOU. BOTH MY BROTHER AND HIS JACKALOPE TEAMMATES.
BUT I'M NOT EXACTLY IN A SPOT TO BE CHOOSY HERE.

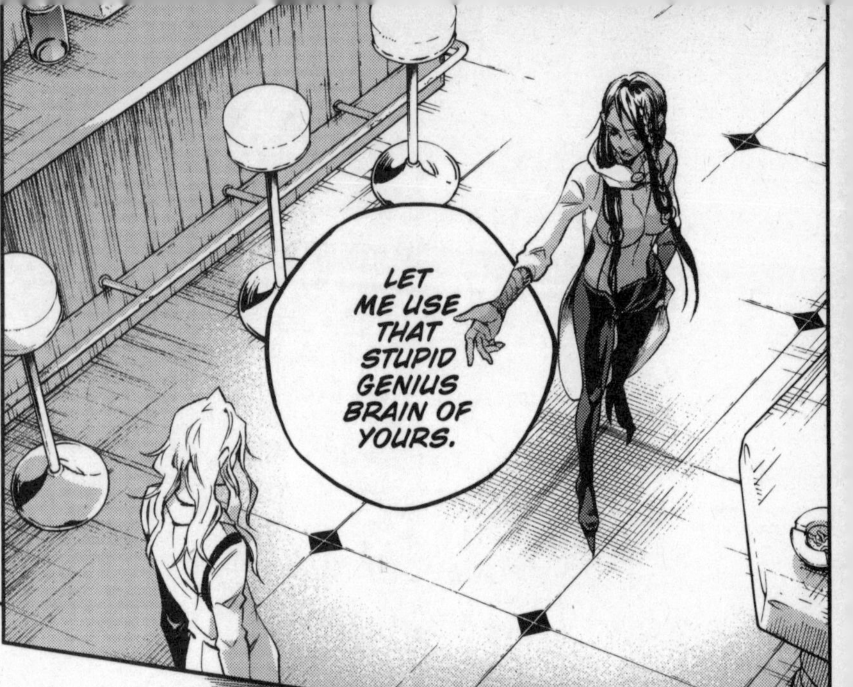
LET ME USE THAT STUPID GENIUS BRAIN OF YOURS.
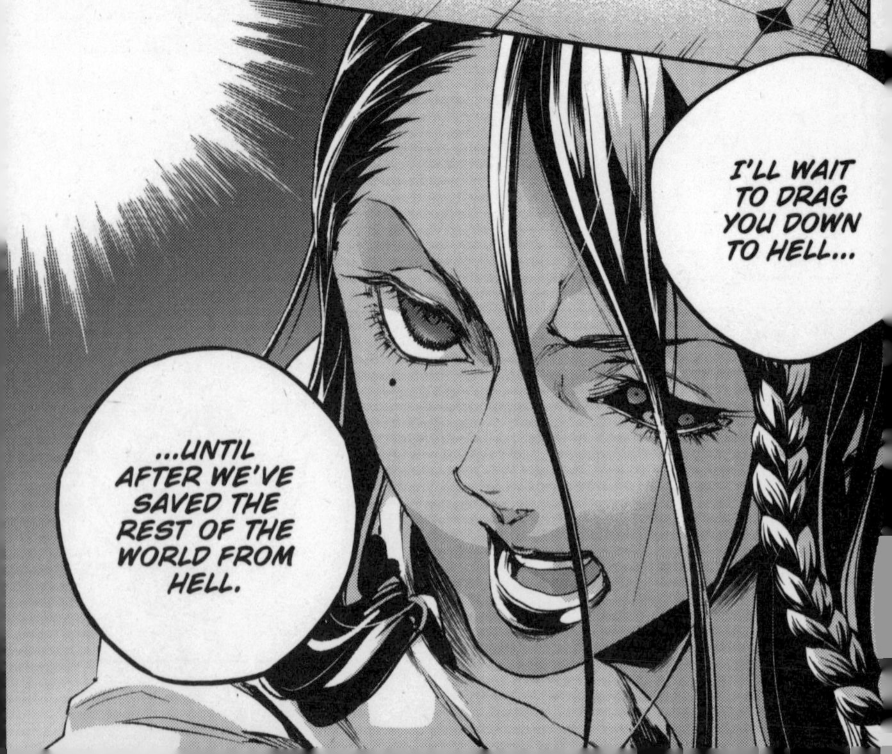
I'LL WAIT TO DRAG YOU DOWN TO HELL...
...UNTIL AFTER WE'VE SAVED THE REST OF THE WORLD FROM HELL.

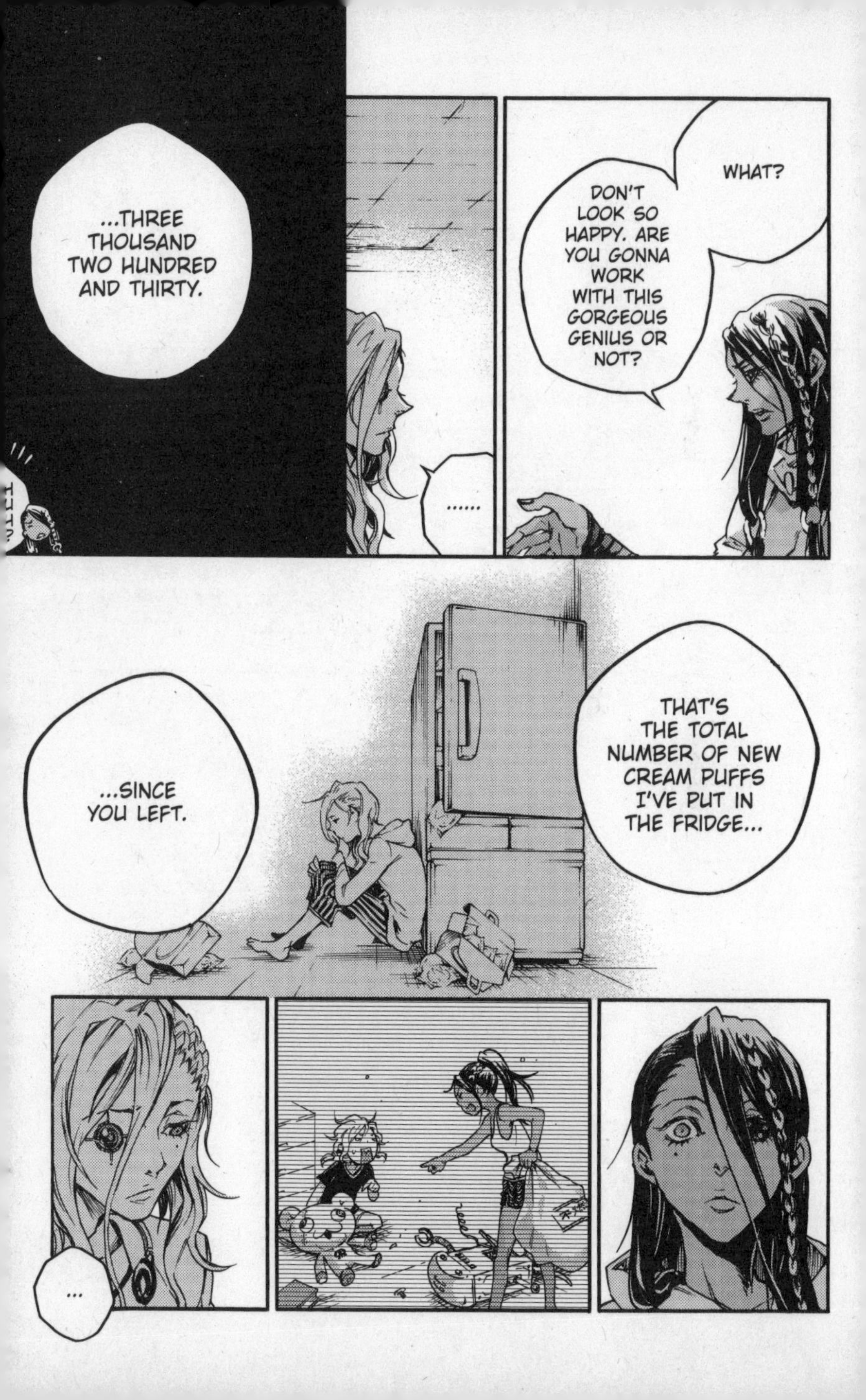
WHAT?
DON'T LOOK SO HAPPY. ARE YOU GONNA WORK WITH THIS GORGEOUS GENIUS OR NOT?
......
...THREE THOUSAND TWO HUNDRED AND THIRTY.
THAT'S THE TOTAL NUMBER OF NEW CREAM PUFFS I'VE PUT IN THE FRIDGE...
...SINCE YOU LEFT.
...

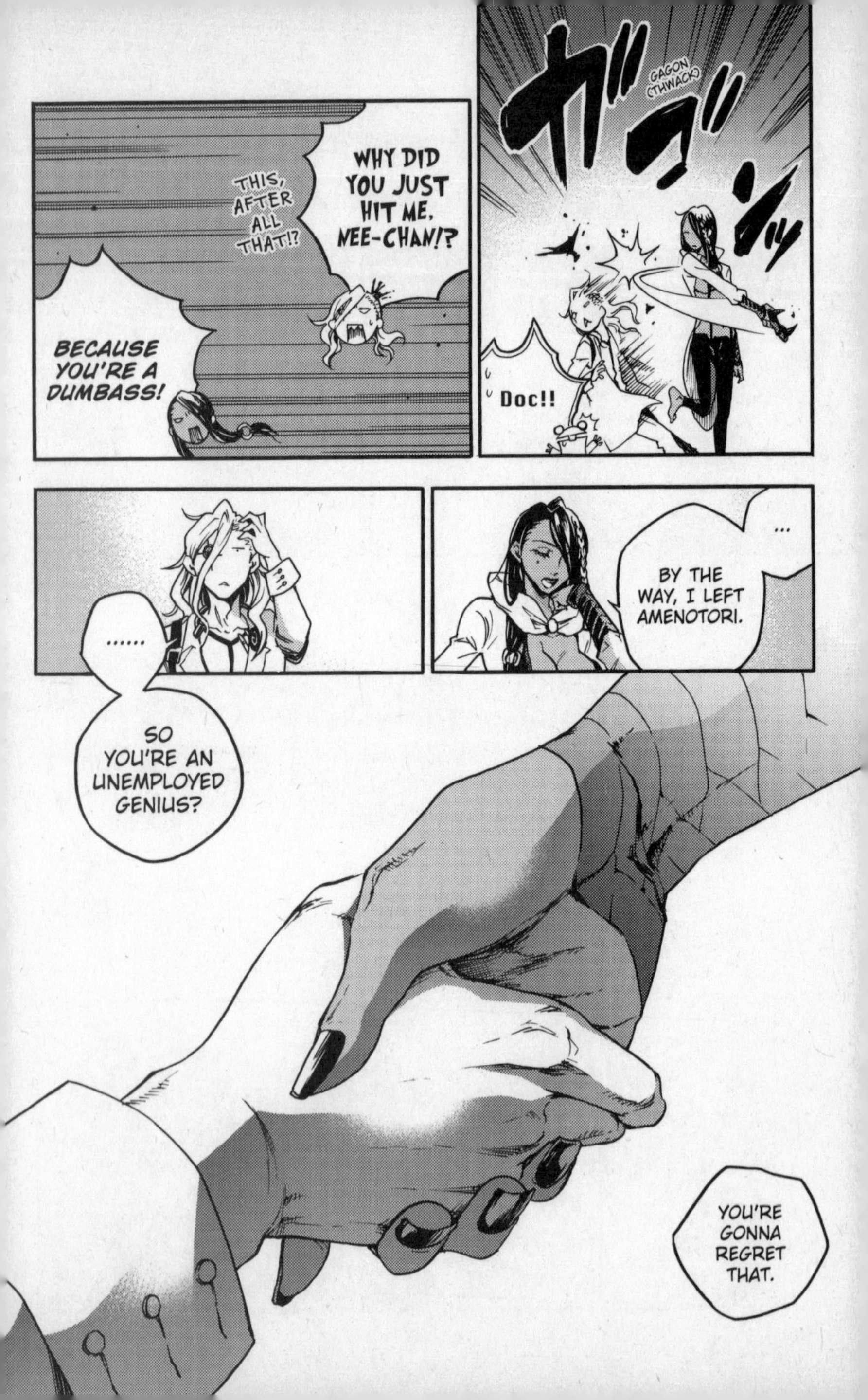
GAGON (THWACK)
Doc!!
WHY DID YOU JUST HIT ME, NEE-CHAN!?
THIS, AFTER ALL THAT!?
BECAUSE YOU'RE A DUMBASS!
...
BY THE WAY, I LEFT AMENOTORI.
......
SO YOU'RE AN UNEMPLOYED GENIUS?
YOU'RE GONNA REGRET THAT.

SMOKIN' PARADE

SMOKIN' PARADE

THE WORLD IS DEAD, THE PARADE WILL START.

JINSEI KATAOKA, KAZUMA KONDOU

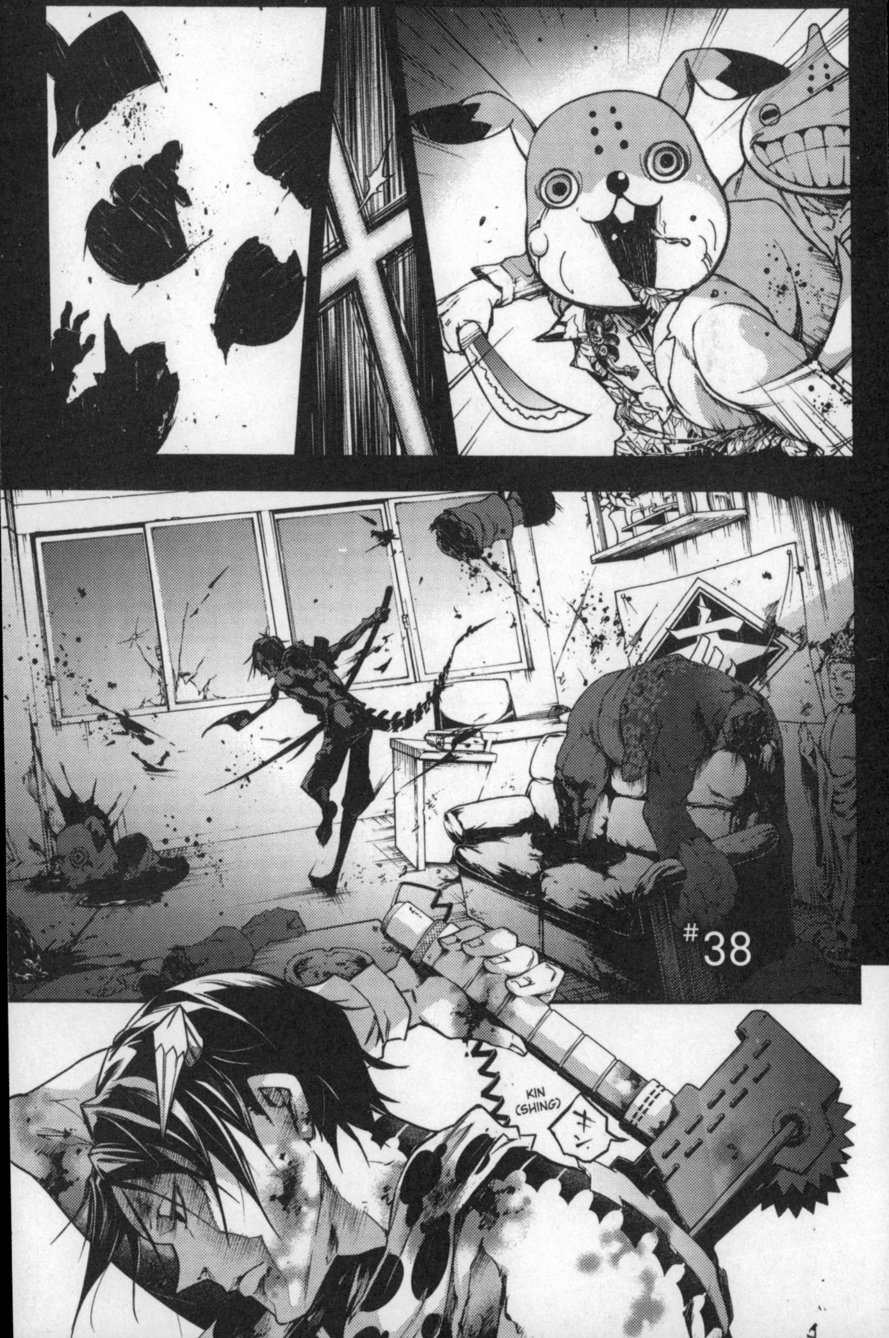
#38
KIN (SHING)

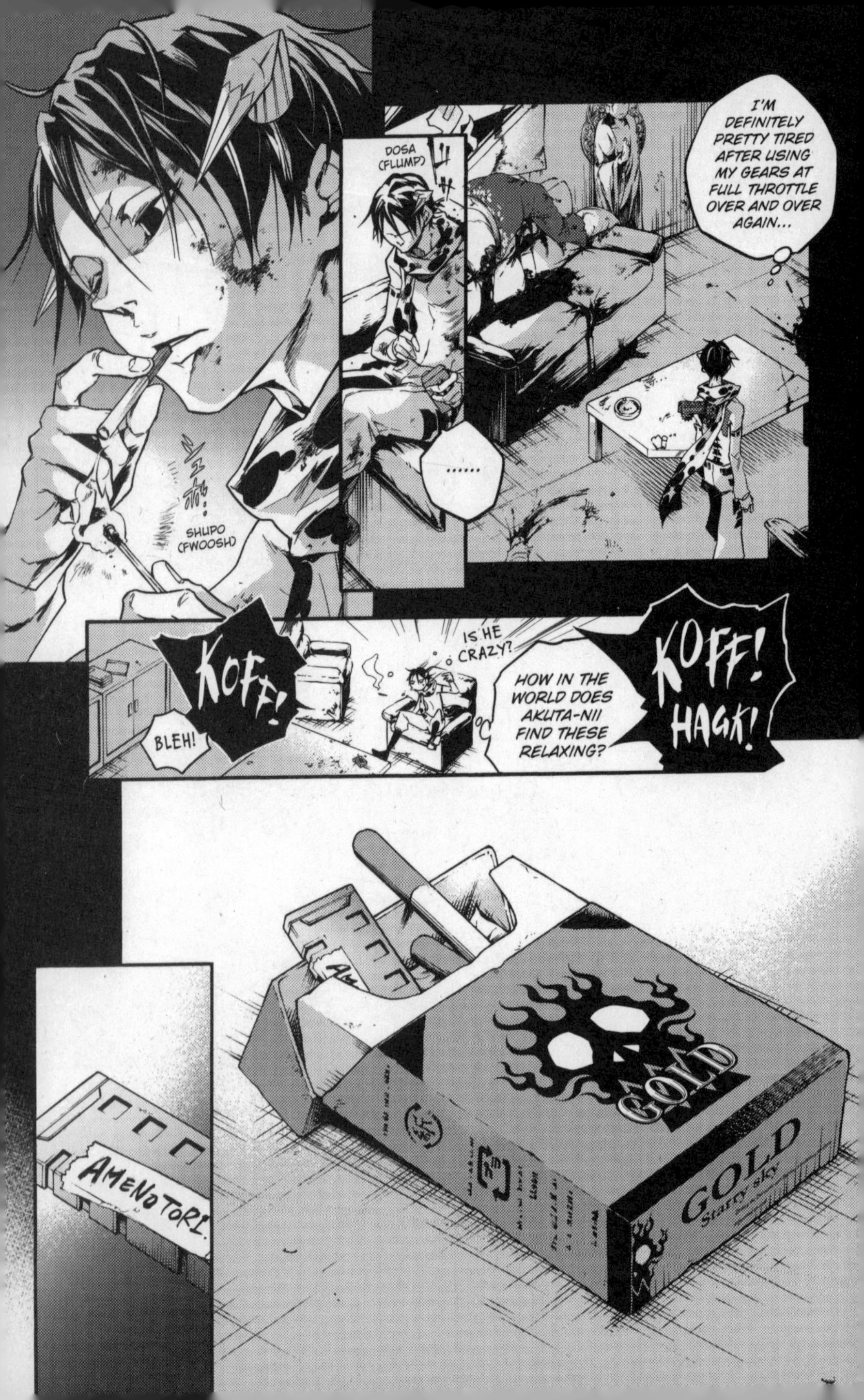
I'M DEFINITELY PRETTY TIRED AFTER USING MY GEARS AT FULL THROTTLE OVER AND OVER AGAIN...
......
DOSA (FLUMP)
SHUPO (FWOOSH)
KOFF! HAGK!
HOW IN THE WORLD DOES AKUTA-NII FIND THESE RELAXING?
IS HE CRAZY?
KOFF!
BLEH!
GOLD
GOLD
Starry sky
AMENOTORI

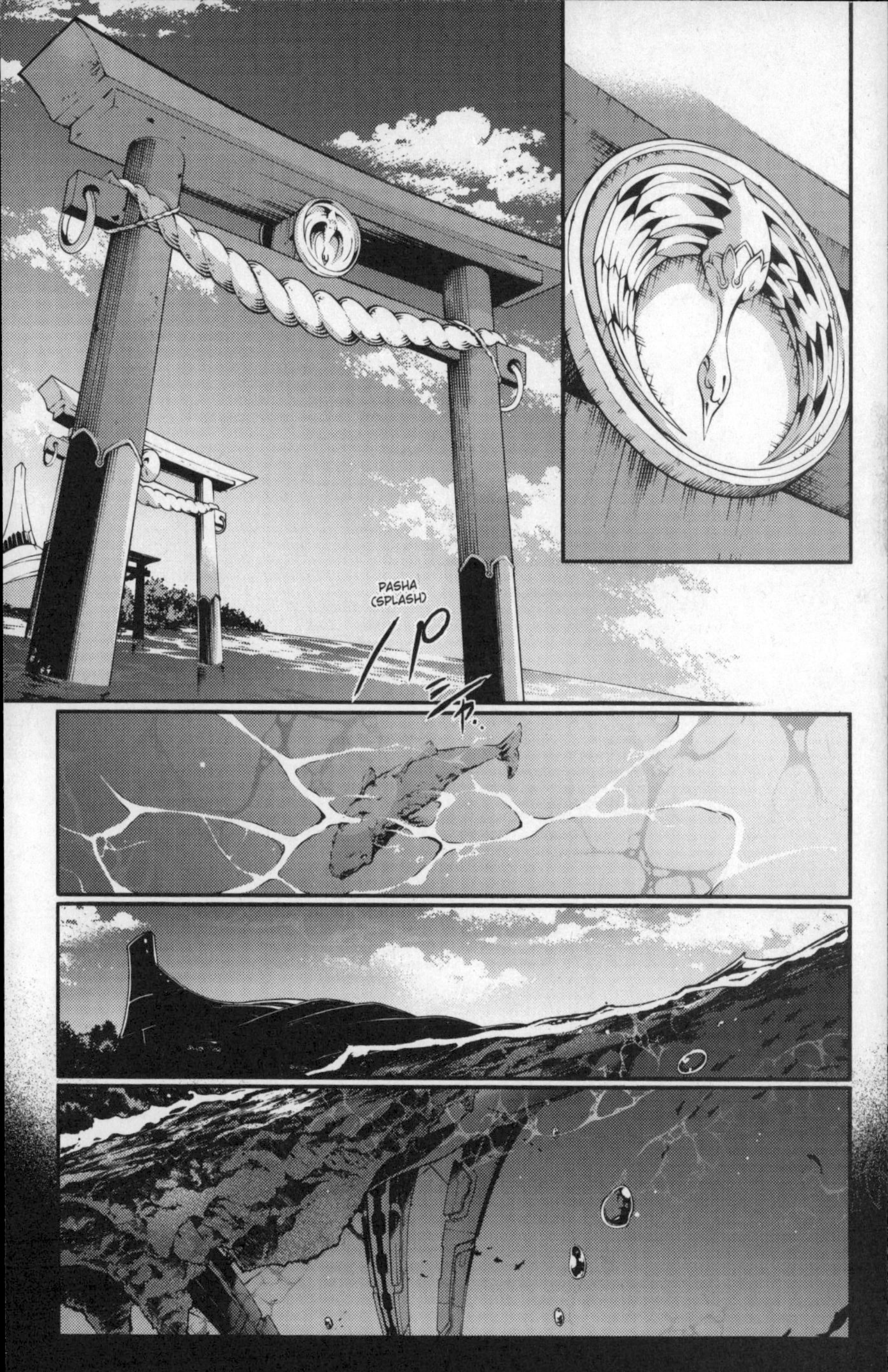
PASHA (SPLASH)
パシャ…

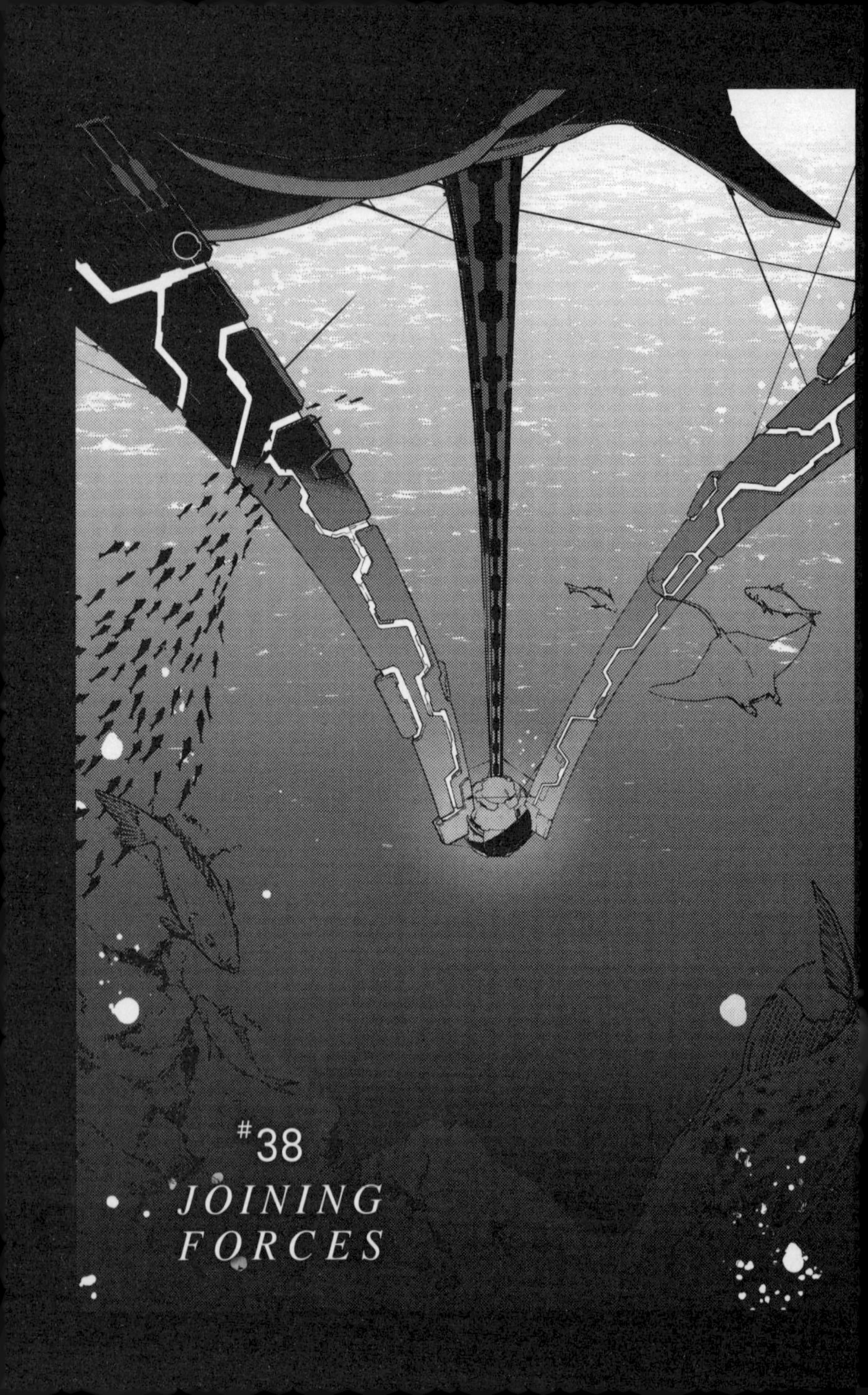
#38
JOINING
FORCES

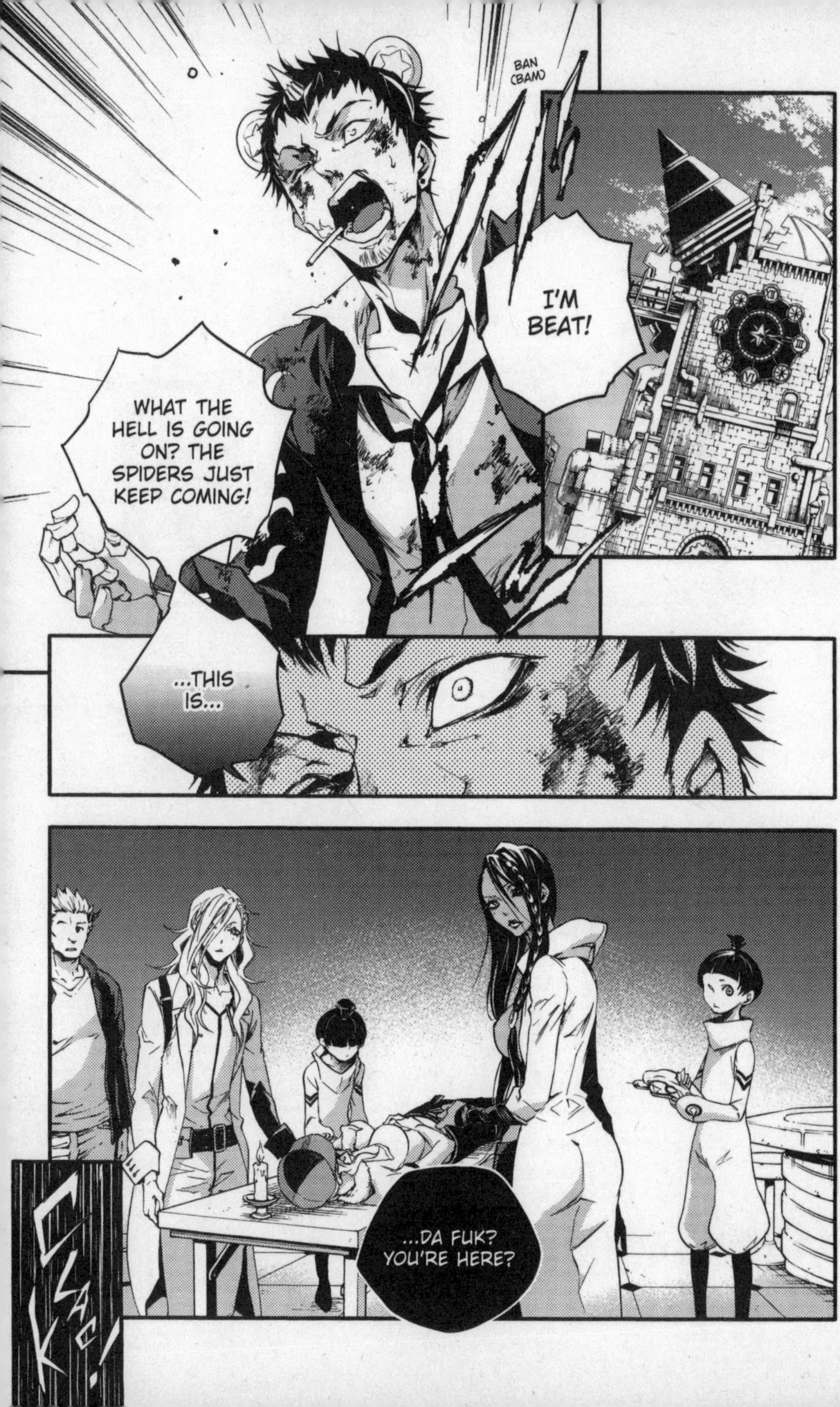
BAN (BAM)
I'M BEAT!
WHAT THE HELL IS GOING ON? THE SPIDERS JUST KEEP COMING!
...THIS IS...
...DA FUK? YOU'RE HERE?
CLACK!

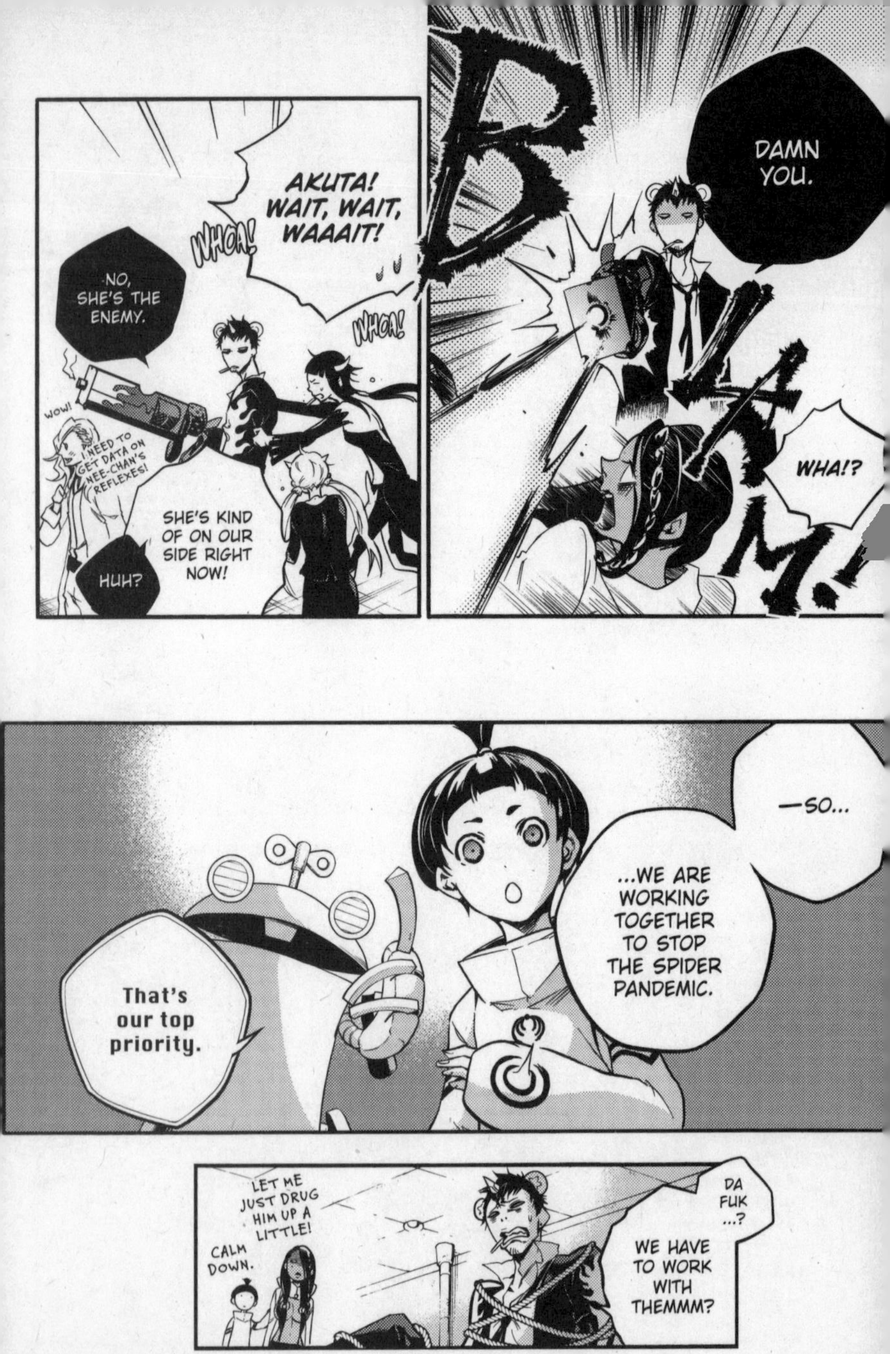
DAMN YOU.
BLAM!
WHA!?
AKUTA! WAIT, WAIT, WAAAIT!
WHOA!
WHOA!
NO, SHE'S THE ENEMY.
SHE'S KIND OF ON OUR SIDE RIGHT NOW!
WOW!
I NEED TO GET DATA ON NEE-CHAN'S REFLEXES!
HUH?
—SO...
...WE ARE WORKING TOGETHER TO STOP THE SPIDER PANDEMIC.
That's our top priority.
DA FUK ...?
WE HAVE TO WORK WITH THEMMM?
LET ME JUST DRUG HIM UP A LITTLE!
CALM DOWN.

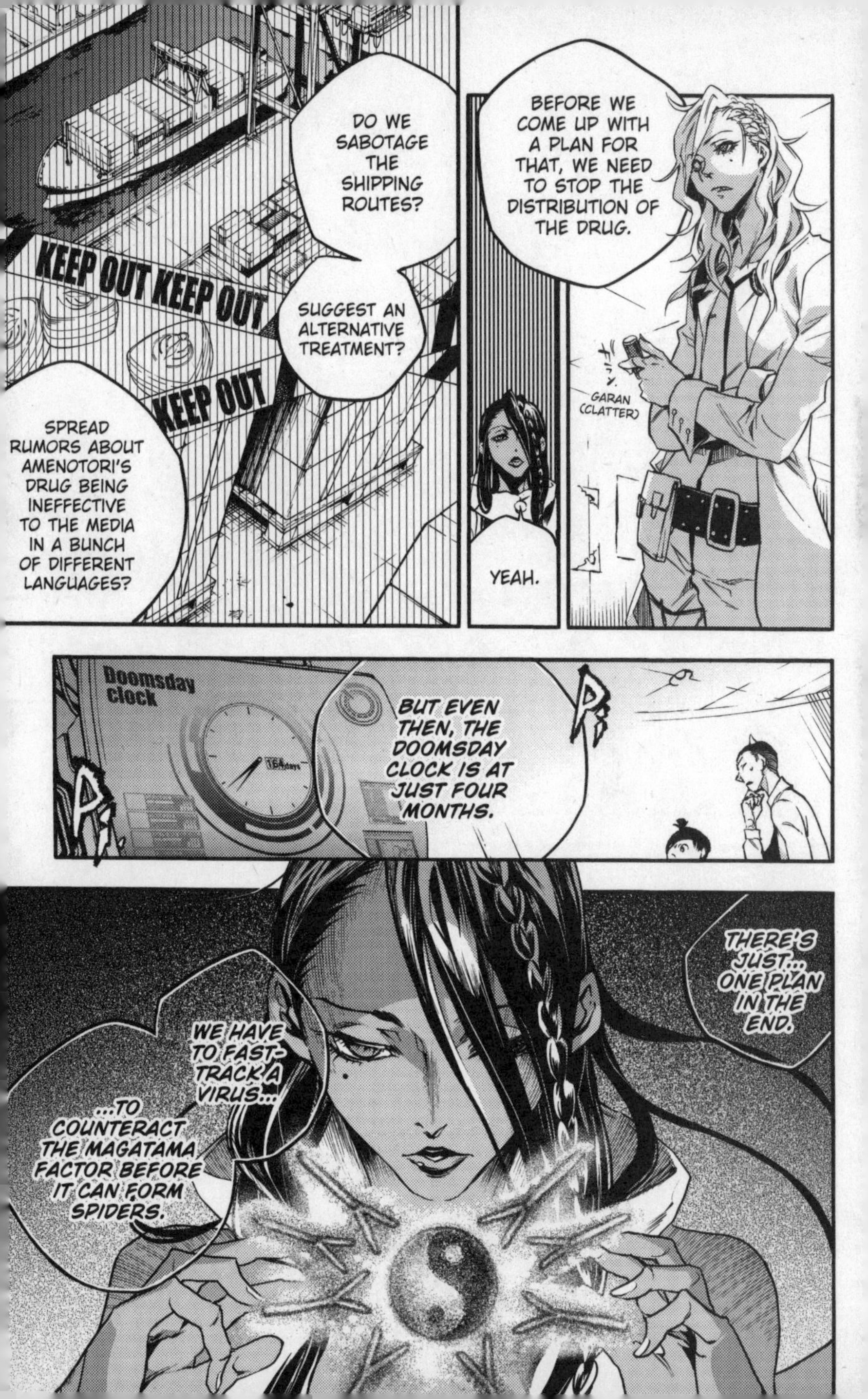

BEFORE WE COME UP WITH A PLAN FOR THAT, WE NEED TO STOP THE DISTRIBUTION OF THE DRUG.
GARAN (CLATTER)
YEAH.
DO WE SABOTAGE THE SHIPPING ROUTES?
SUGGEST AN ALTERNATIVE TREATMENT?
KEEP OUT KEEP OUT
KEEP OUT
SPREAD RUMORS ABOUT AMENOTORI'S DRUG BEING INEFFECTIVE TO THE MEDIA IN A BUNCH OF DIFFERENT LANGUAGES?
BUT EVEN THEN, THE DOOMSDAY CLOCK IS AT JUST FOUR MONTHS.
Doomsday clock
164 days
THERE'S JUST... ONE PLAN IN THE END.
WE HAVE TO FAST-TRACK A VIRUS...
...TO COUNTERACT THE MAGATAMA FACTOR BEFORE IT CAN FORM SPIDERS.

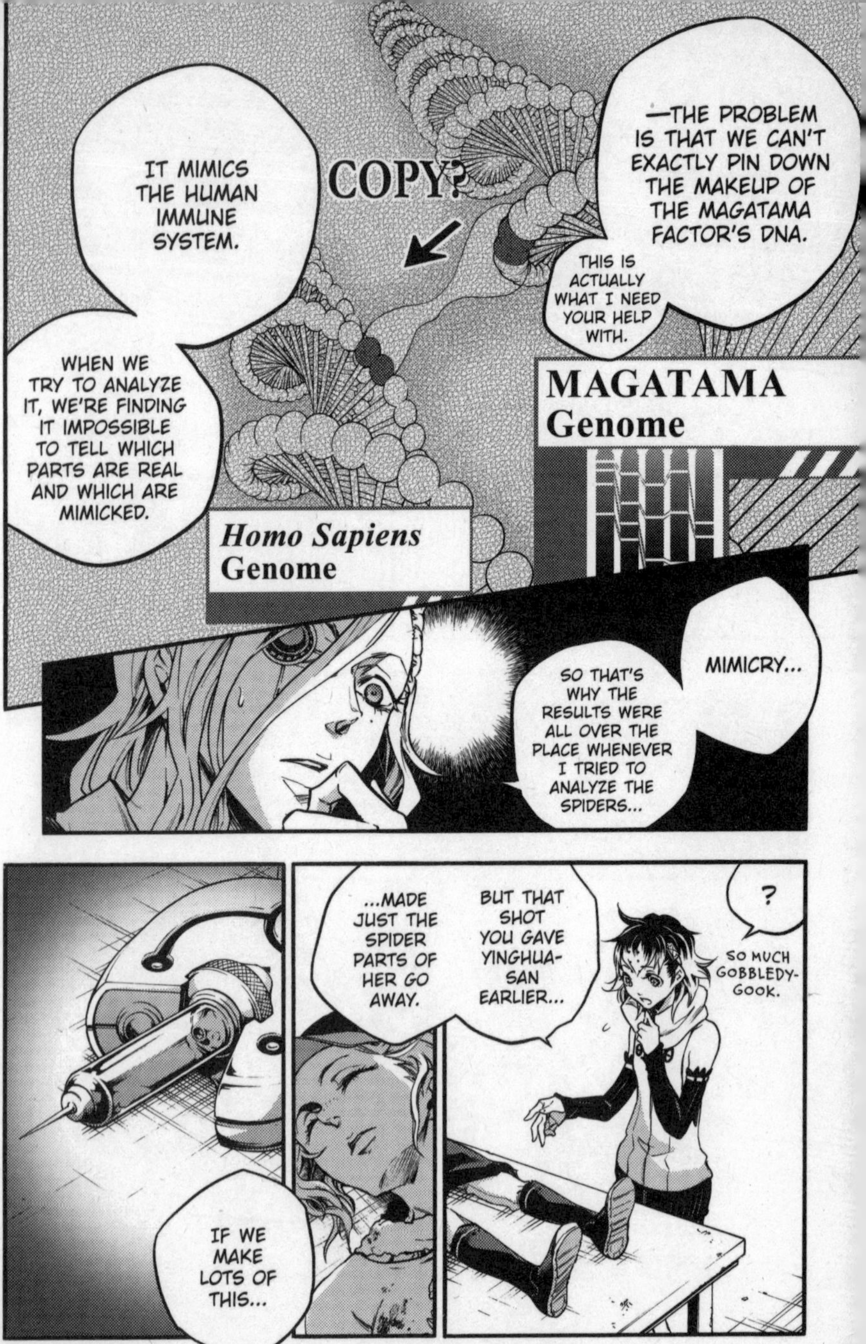
—THE PROBLEM IS THAT WE CAN'T EXACTLY PIN DOWN THE MAKEUP OF THE MAGATAMA FACTOR'S DNA.
THIS IS ACTUALLY WHAT I NEED YOUR HELP WITH.
COPY?
IT MIMICS THE HUMAN IMMUNE SYSTEM.
MAGATAMA Genome
WHEN WE TRY TO ANALYZE IT, WE'RE FINDING IT IMPOSSIBLE TO TELL WHICH PARTS ARE REAL AND WHICH ARE MIMICKED.
Homo Sapiens Genome
MIMICRY...
SO THAT'S WHY THE RESULTS WERE ALL OVER THE PLACE WHENEVER I TRIED TO ANALYZE THE SPIDERS...
?
SO MUCH GOBBLEDYGOOK.
BUT THAT SHOT YOU GAVE YINGHUA-SAN EARLIER...
...MADE JUST THE SPIDER PARTS OF HER GO AWAY.
IF WE MAKE LOTS OF THIS...

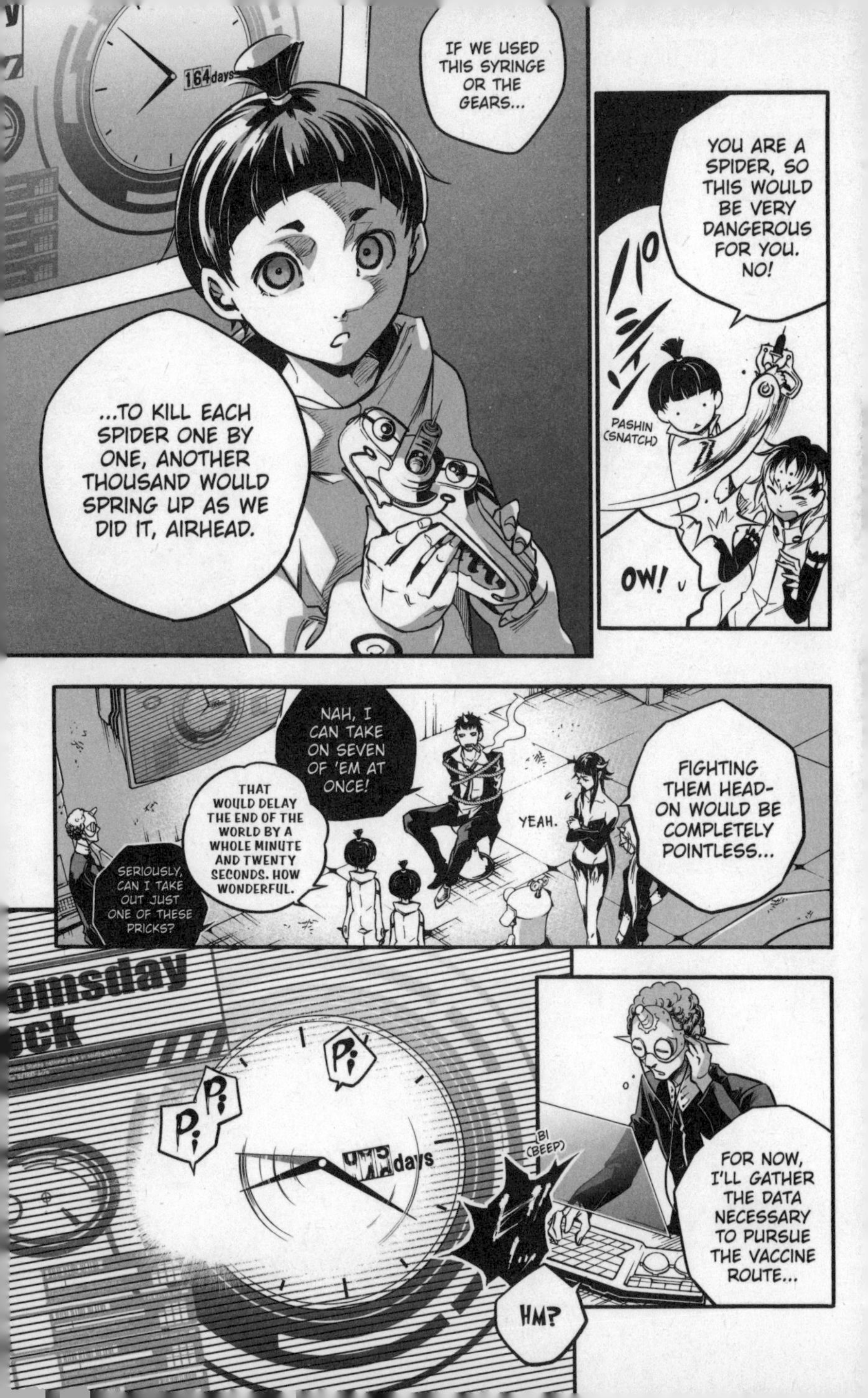
YOU ARE A SPIDER, SO THIS WOULD BE VERY DANGEROUS FOR YOU. NO!
PASHIN (SNATCH)
OW!
164days
IF WE USED THIS SYRINGE OR THE GEARS...
...TO KILL EACH SPIDER ONE BY ONE, ANOTHER THOUSAND WOULD SPRING UP AS WE DID IT, AIRHEAD.
FIGHTING THEM HEAD-ON WOULD BE COMPLETELY POINTLESS...
YEAH.
NAH, I CAN TAKE ON SEVEN OF 'EM AT ONCE!
THAT WOULD DELAY THE END OF THE WORLD BY A WHOLE MINUTE AND TWENTY SECONDS. HOW WONDERFUL.
SERIOUSLY, CAN I TAKE OUT JUST ONE OF THESE PRICKS?
FOR NOW, I'LL GATHER THE DATA NECESSARY TO PURSUE THE VACCINE ROUTE...
BI (BEEP)
HM?
Pi
Pi
Pi
days

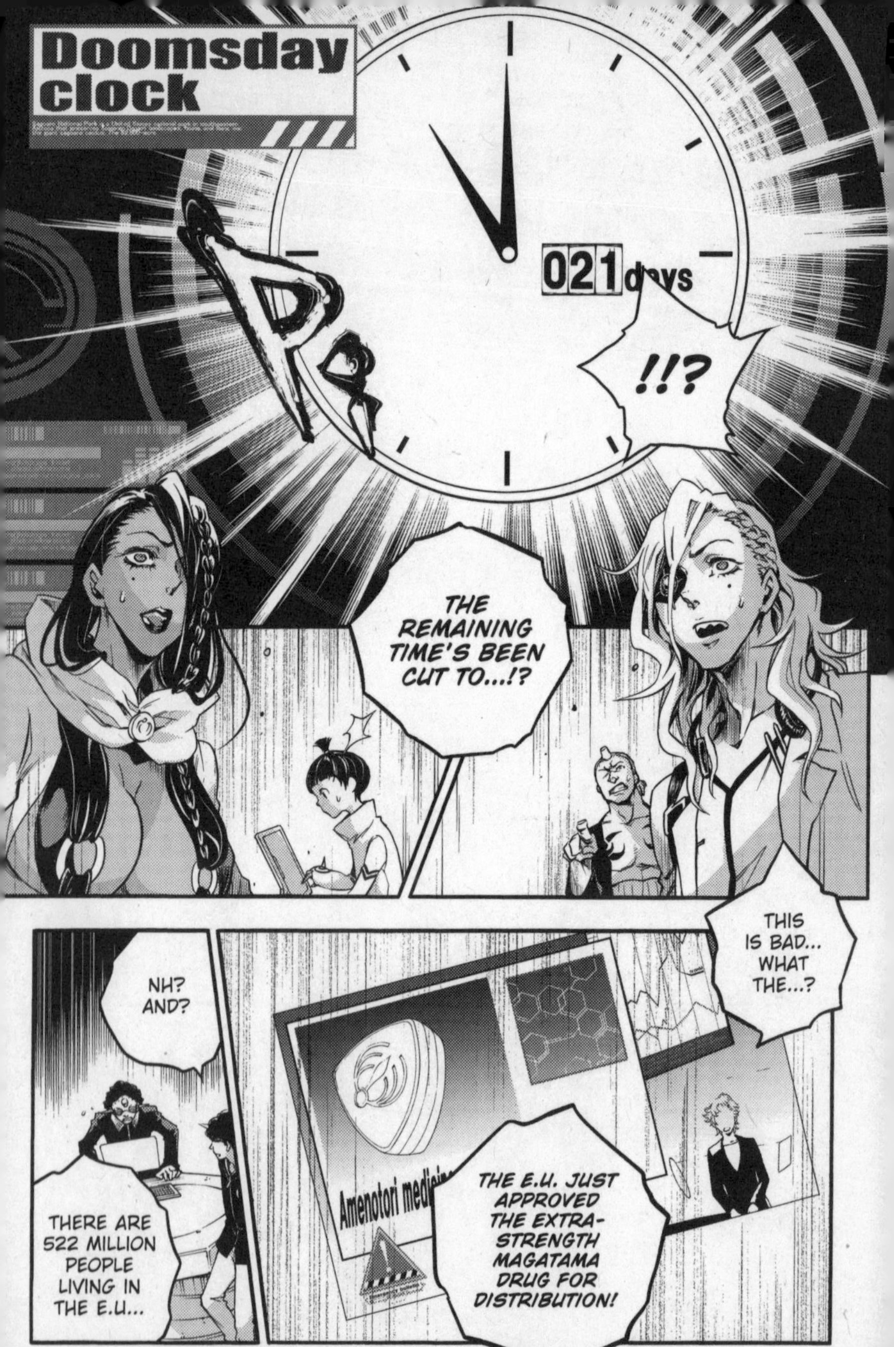
Doomsday clock
021 days
!!?
THE REMAINING TIME'S BEEN CUT TO...!?
THIS IS BAD... WHAT THE...?
Amenotori medi
THE E.U. JUST APPROVED THE EXTRA-STRENGTH MAGATAMA DRUG FOR DISTRIBUTION!
NH? AND?
THERE ARE 522 MILLION PEOPLE LIVING IN THE E.U...

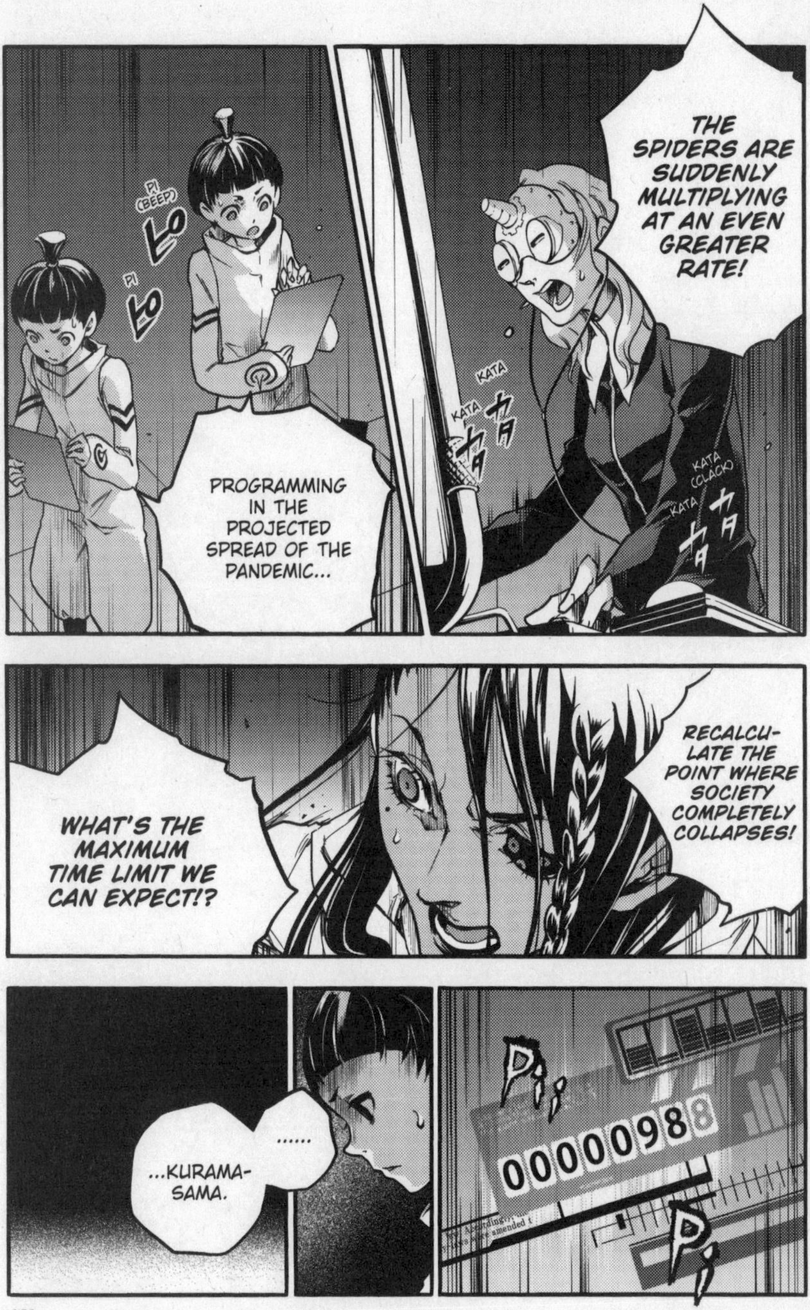
THE SPIDERS ARE SUDDENLY MULTIPLYING AT AN EVEN GREATER RATE!
KATA
KATA
KATA (CLACK)
KATA
PI (BEEP)
PI
PROGRAMMING IN THE PROJECTED SPREAD OF THE PANDEMIC...
RECALCULATE THE POINT WHERE SOCIETY COMPLETELY COLLAPSES!
WHAT'S THE MAXIMUM TIME LIMIT WE CAN EXPECT!?
Pi
00000988
Pi
......
...KURAMA-SAMA.

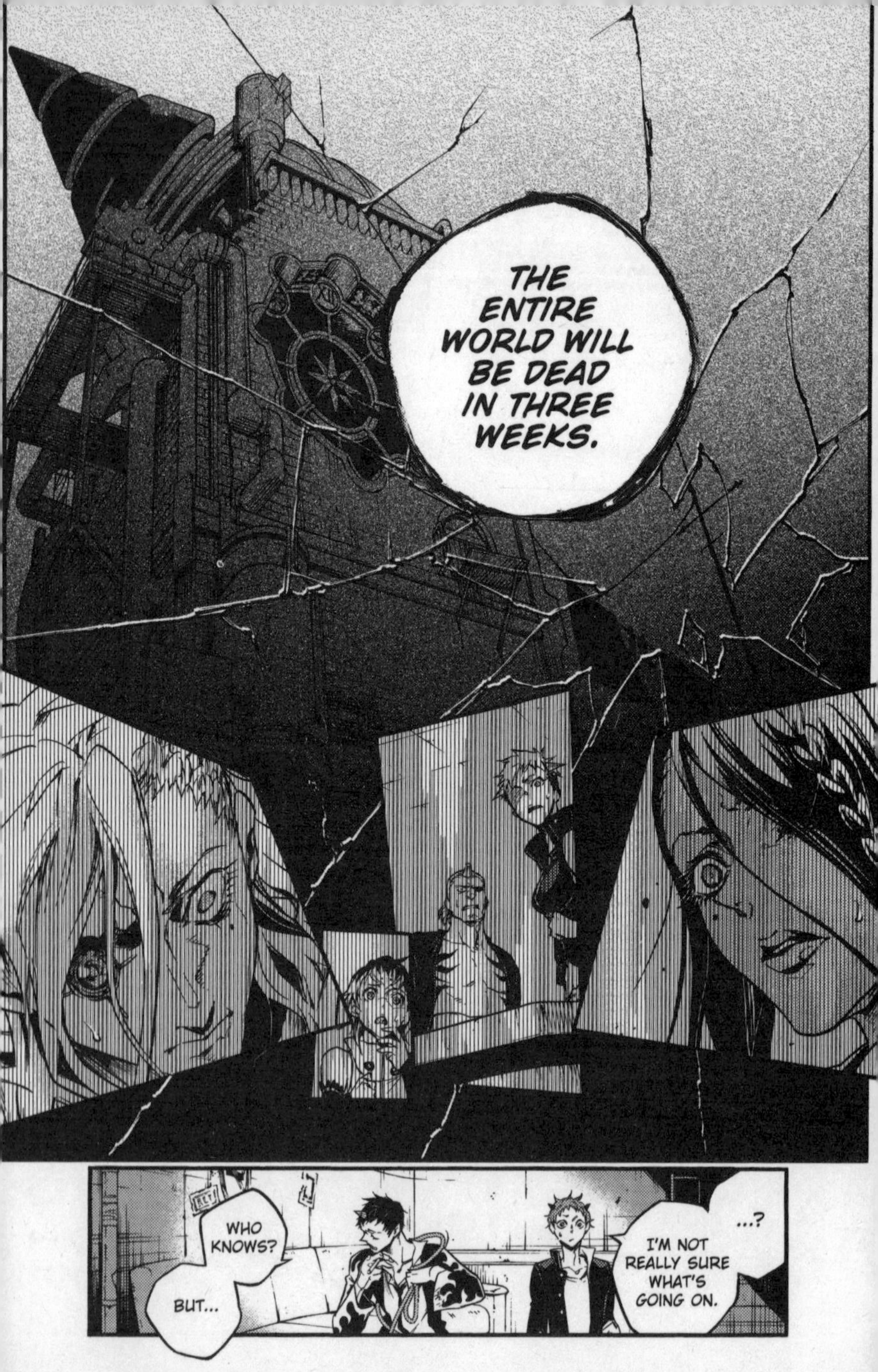
THE ENTIRE WORLD WILL BE DEAD IN THREE WEEKS.
...?
I'M NOT REALLY SURE WHAT'S GOING ON.
WHO KNOWS?
BUT...

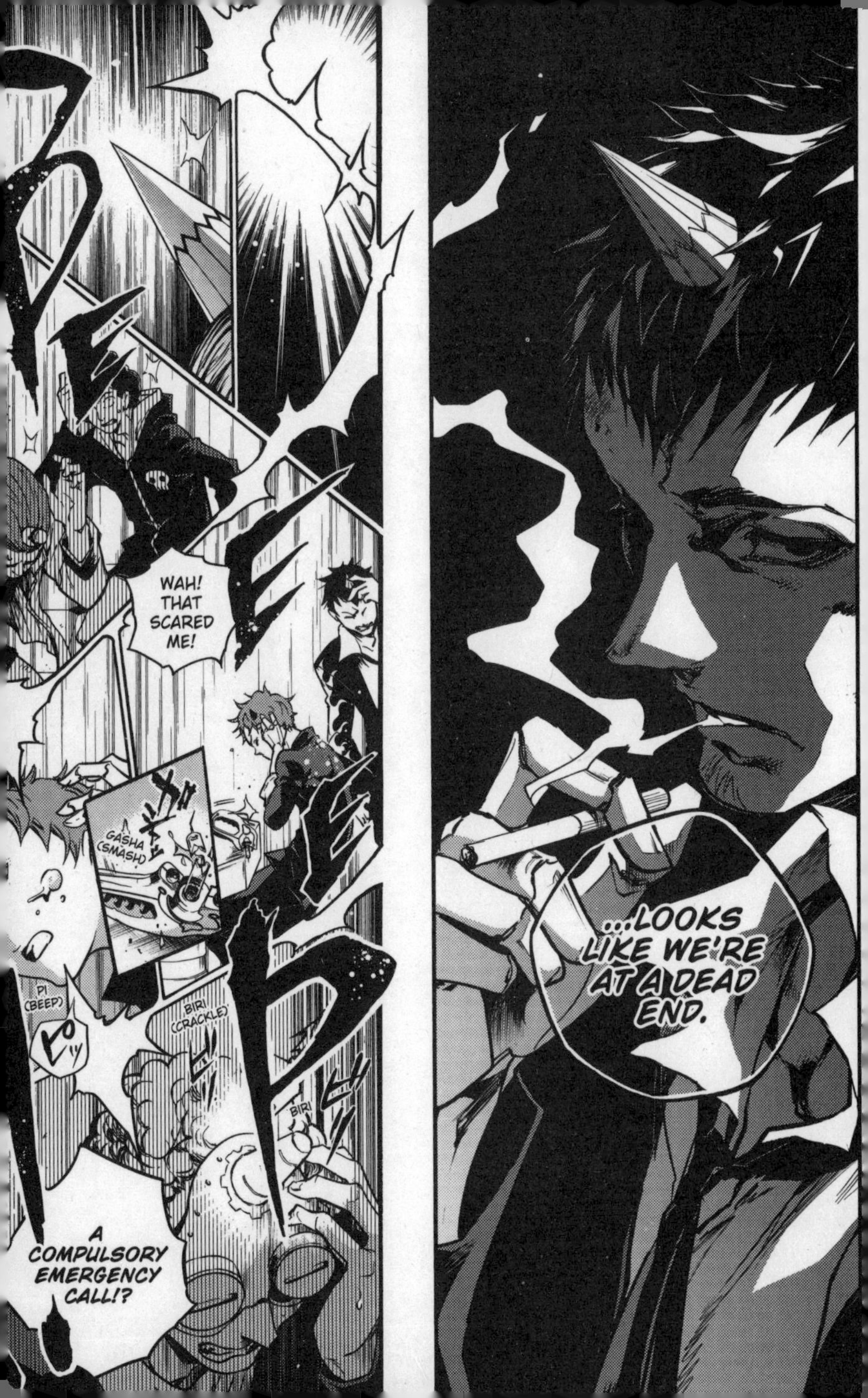
...LOOKS LIKE WE'RE AT A DEAD END.
WAH! THAT SCARED ME!
GASHA (SMASH)
PI (BEEP)
BIRI (CRACKLE)
BIRI
A COMPULSORY EMERGENCY CALL!?

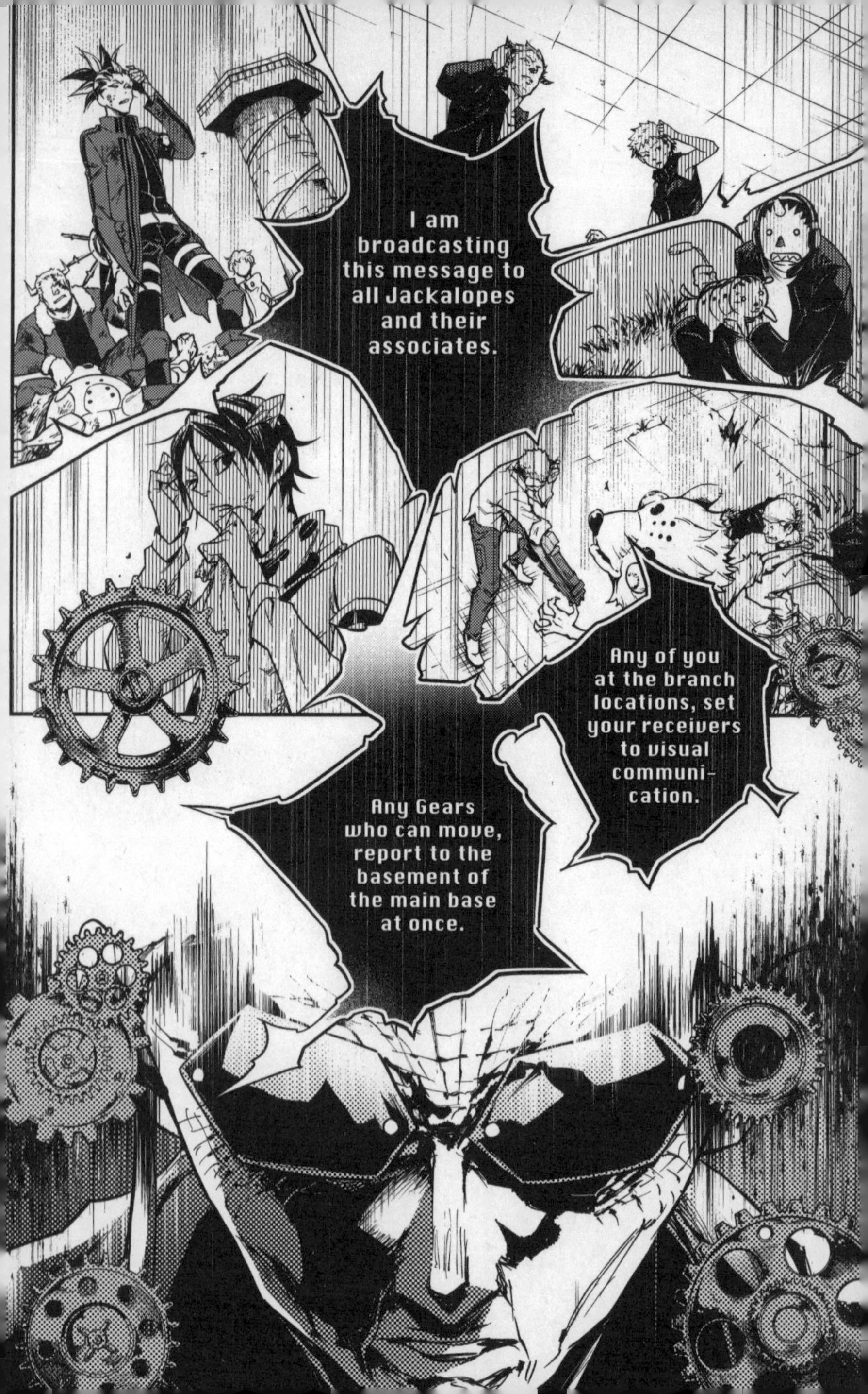
I am broadcasting this message to all Jackalopes and their associates.
Any of you at the branch locations, set your receivers to visual communi-cation.
Any Gears who can move, report to the basement of the main base at once.

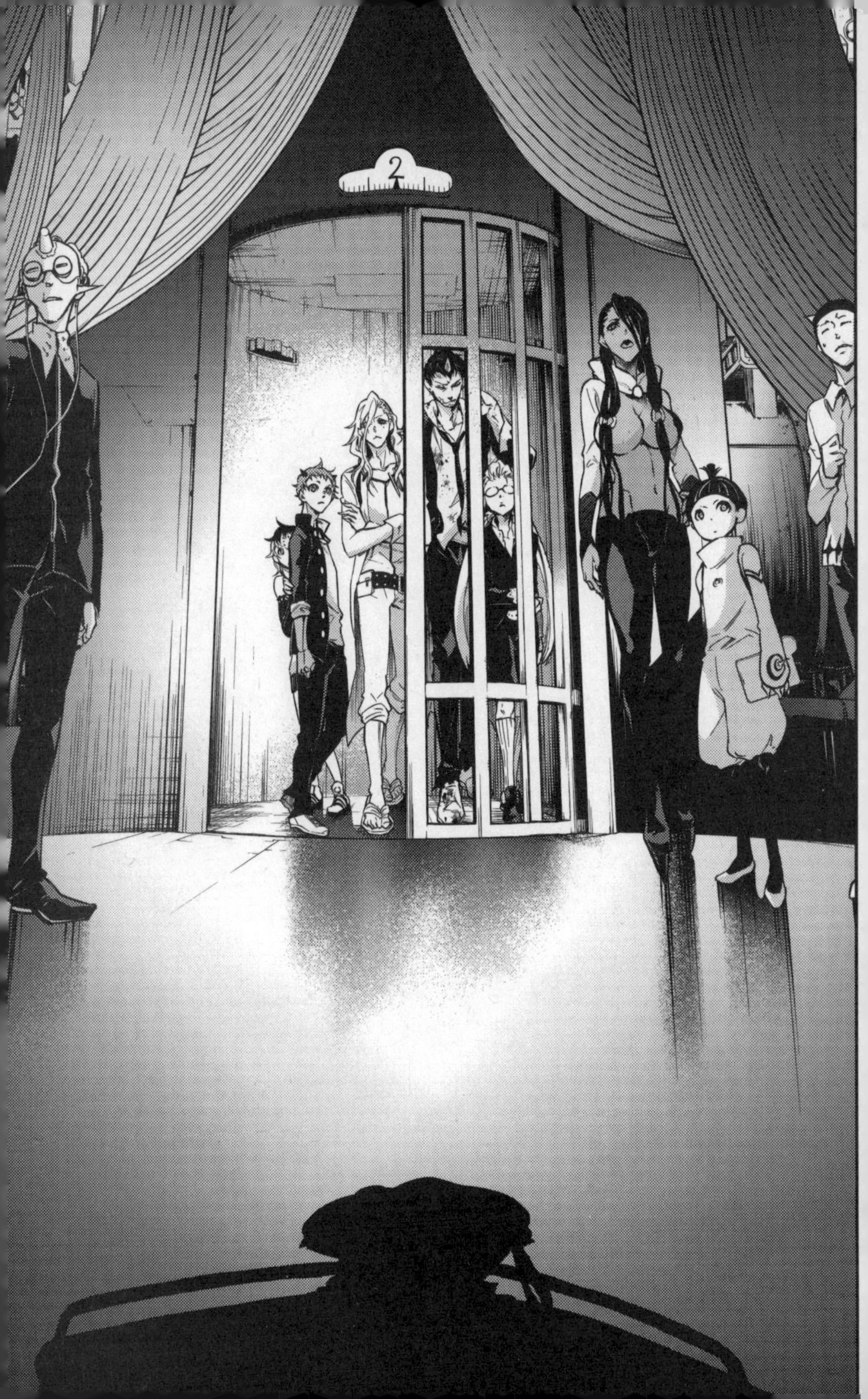
2

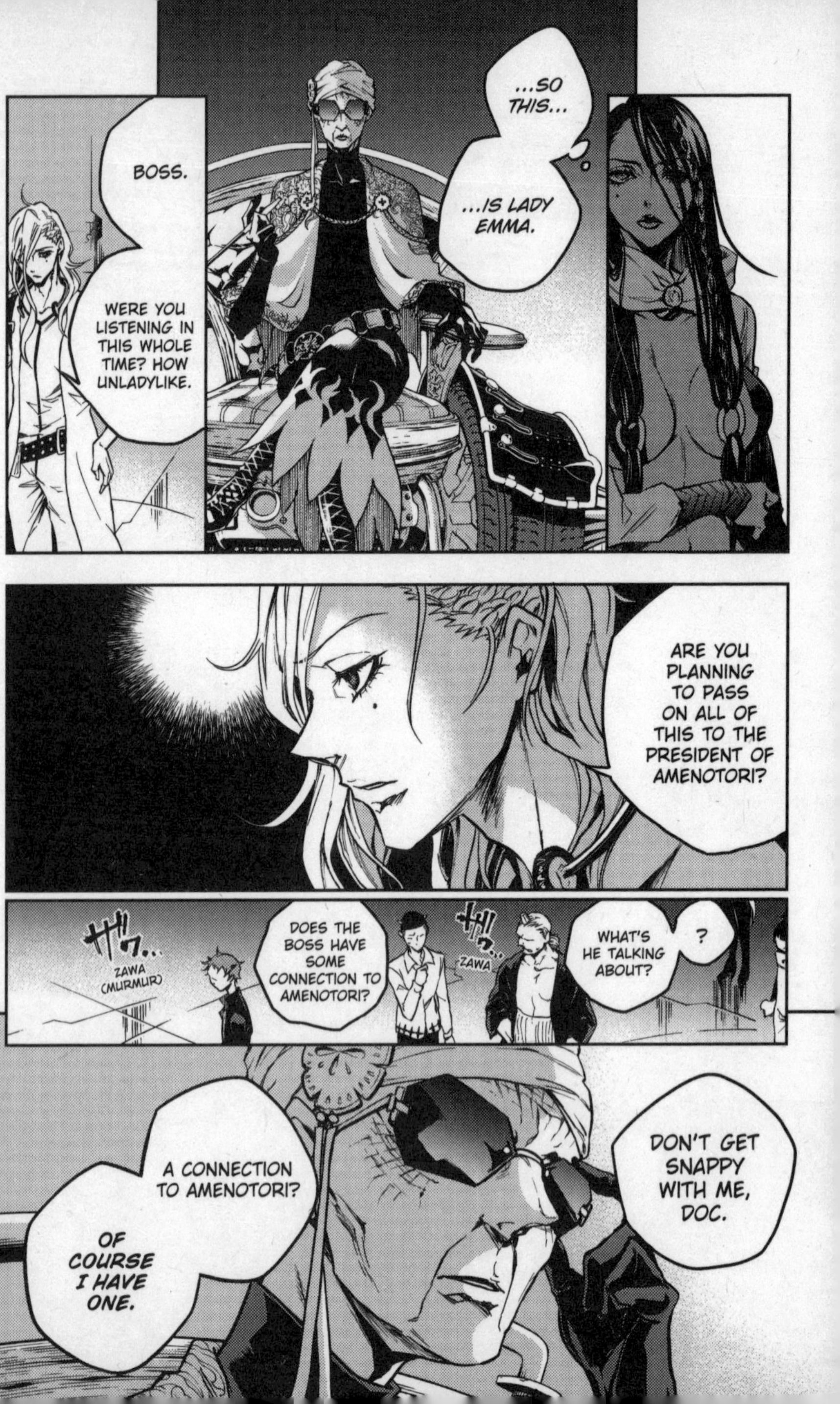
...SO THIS...
...IS LADY EMMA.
BOSS.
WERE YOU LISTENING IN THIS WHOLE TIME? HOW UNLADYLIKE.
ARE YOU PLANNING TO PASS ON ALL OF THIS TO THE PRESIDENT OF AMENOTORI?
?
WHAT'S HE TALKING ABOUT?
ZAWA
DOES THE BOSS HAVE SOME CONNECTION TO AMENOTORI?
ZAWA (MURMUR)
DON'T GET SNAPPY WITH ME, DOC.
A CONNECTION TO AMENOTORI?
OF COURSE I HAVE ONE.

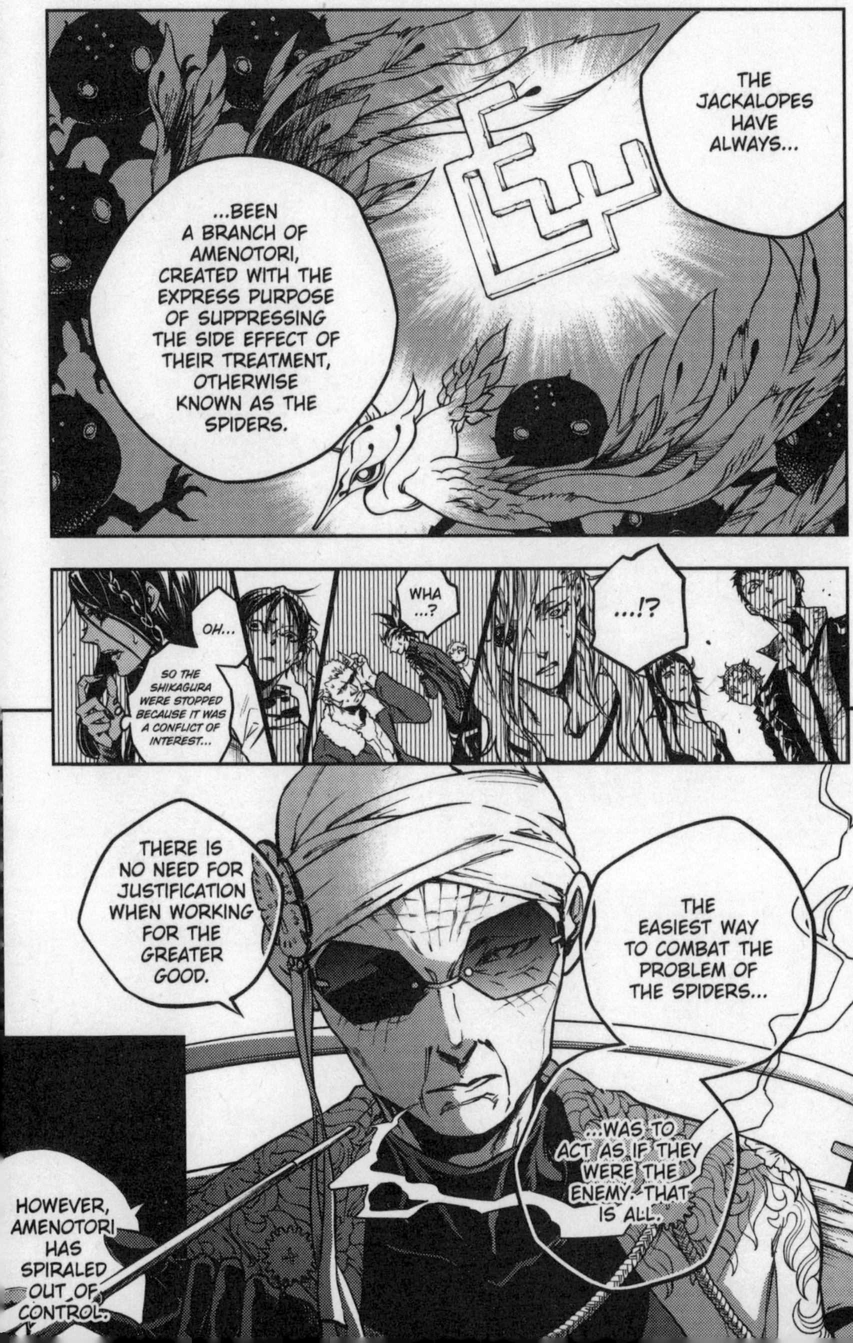
THE JACKALOPES HAVE ALWAYS...
...BEEN A BRANCH OF AMENOTORI, CREATED WITH THE EXPRESS PURPOSE OF SUPPRESSING THE SIDE EFFECT OF THEIR TREATMENT, OTHERWISE KNOWN AS THE SPIDERS.
...!?
WHA ...?
OH...
SO THE SHIKAGURA WERE STOPPED BECAUSE IT WAS A CONFLICT OF INTEREST...
THE EASIEST WAY TO COMBAT THE PROBLEM OF THE SPIDERS...
...WAS TO ACT AS IF THEY WERE THE ENEMY. THAT IS ALL.
THERE IS NO NEED FOR JUSTIFICATION WHEN WORKING FOR THE GREATER GOOD.
HOWEVER, AMENOTORI HAS SPIRALED OUT OF CONTROL.

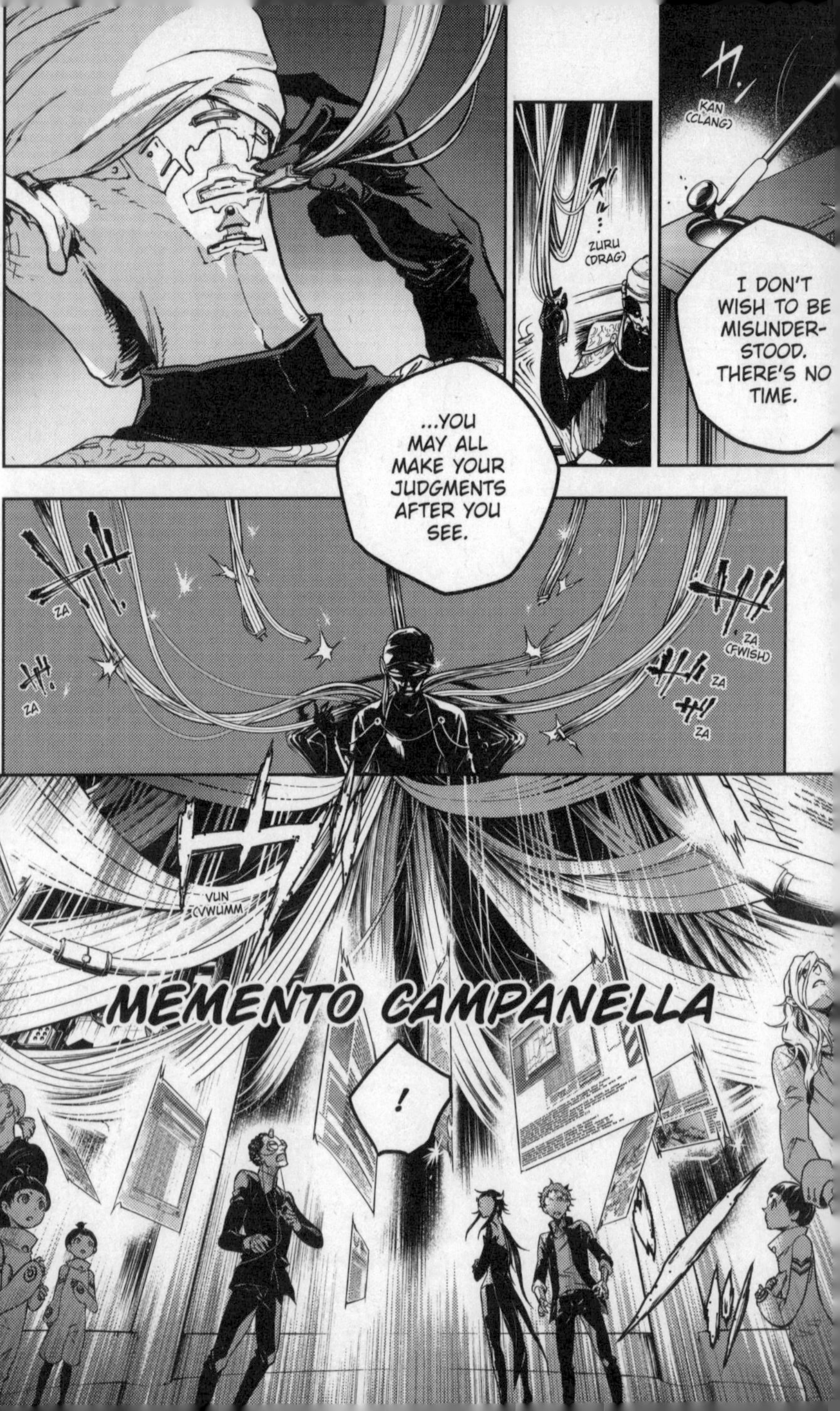

KAN (CLANG)
I DON'T WISH TO BE MISUNDER-STOOD. THERE'S NO TIME.
ZURU (DRAG)
...YOU MAY ALL MAKE YOUR JUDGMENTS AFTER YOU SEE.
ZA (FWISH)
ZA
ZA
ZA
ZA
VUN (VWUMM)
MEMENTO CAMPANELLA
!

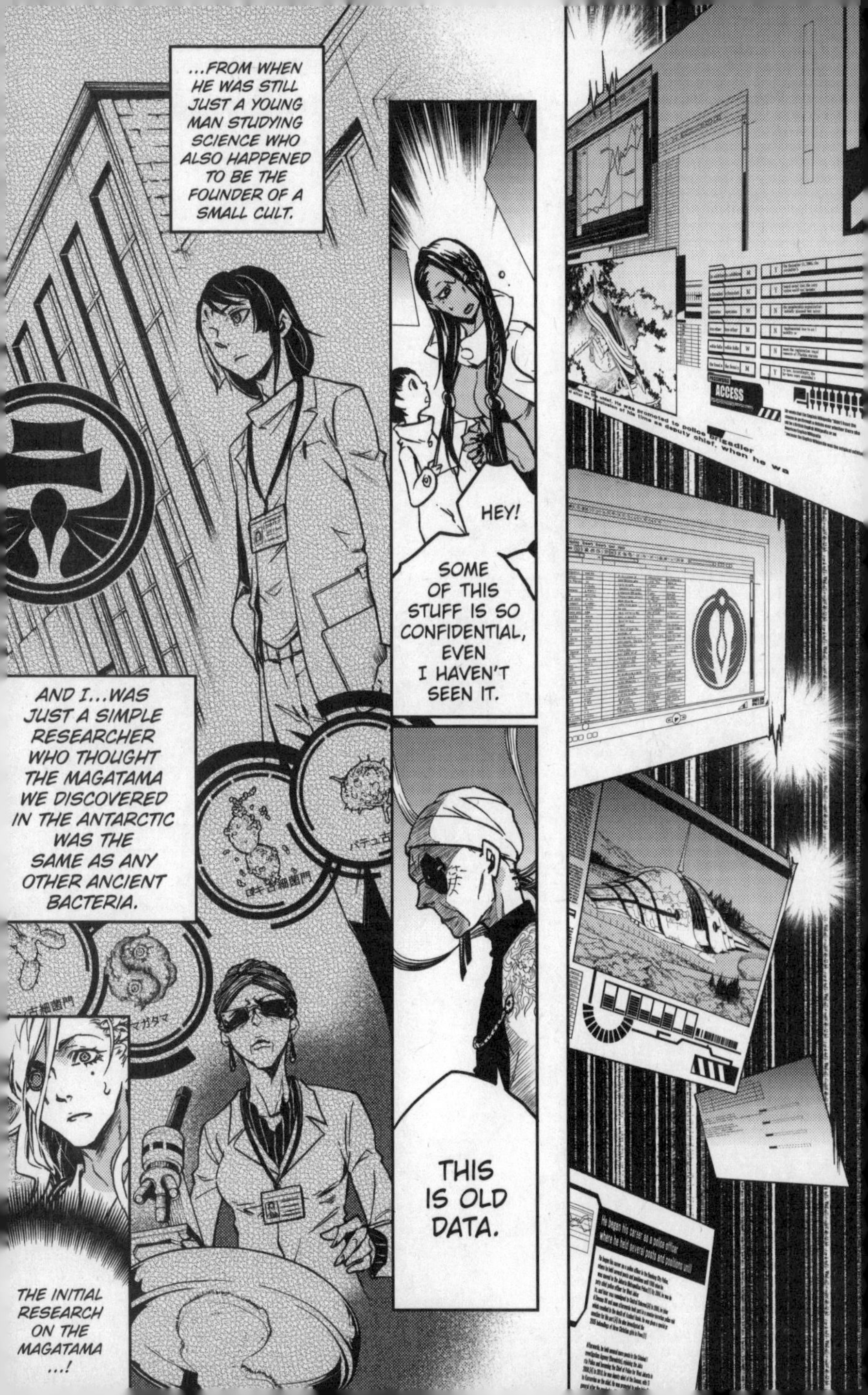
ACCESS
HEY!
SOME OF THIS STUFF IS SO CONFIDENTIAL, EVEN I HAVEN'T SEEN IT.
THIS IS OLD DATA.
...FROM WHEN HE WAS STILL JUST A YOUNG MAN STUDYING SCIENCE WHO ALSO HAPPENED TO BE THE FOUNDER OF A SMALL CULT.
AND I...WAS JUST A SIMPLE RESEARCHER WHO THOUGHT THE MAGATAMA WE DISCOVERED IN THE ANTARCTIC WAS THE SAME AS ANY OTHER ANCIENT BACTERIA.
THE INITIAL RESEARCH ON THE MAGATAMA...!

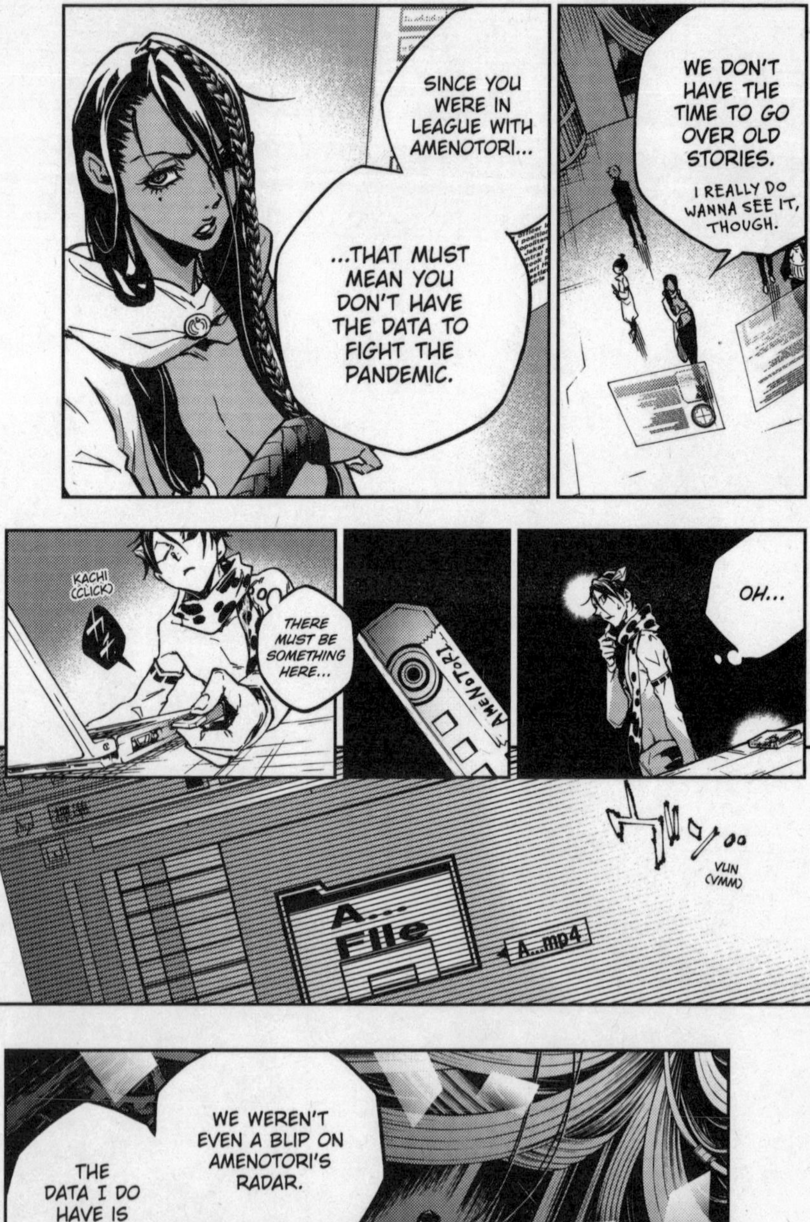
WE DON'T HAVE THE TIME TO GO OVER OLD STORIES.
I REALLY DO WANNA SEE IT, THOUGH.
SINCE YOU WERE IN LEAGUE WITH AMENOTORI...
...THAT MUST MEAN YOU DON'T HAVE THE DATA TO FIGHT THE PANDEMIC.
OH...
AMENOTORI
KACHI (CLICK)
THERE MUST BE SOMETHING HERE...
VUN (VMM)
A... File
A...mp4
WE WEREN'T EVEN A BLIP ON AMENOTORI'S RADAR.
THE DATA I DO HAVE IS MINIMAL.

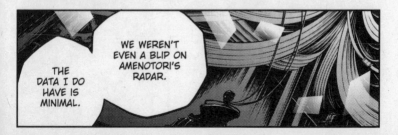

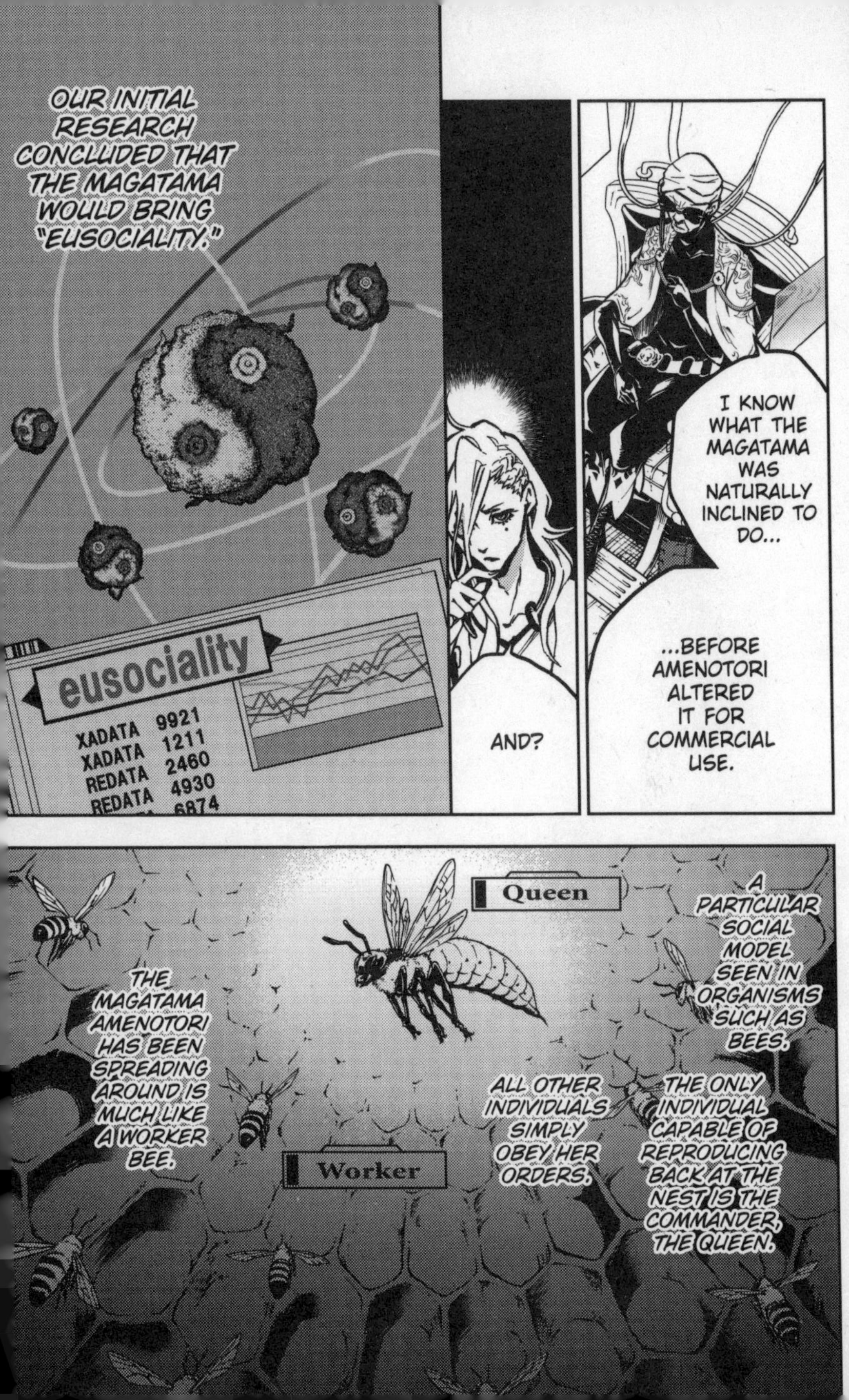
I KNOW WHAT THE MAGATAMA WAS NATURALLY INCLINED TO DO...
...BEFORE AMENOTORI ALTERED IT FOR COMMERCIAL USE.
AND?
OUR INITIAL RESEARCH CONCLUDED THAT THE MAGATAMA WOULD BRING "EUSOCIALITY."
eusociality
XADATA 9921
XADATA 1211
REDATA 2460
REDATA 4930
A PARTICULAR SOCIAL MODEL SEEN IN ORGANISMS SUCH AS BEES.
Queen
THE ONLY INDIVIDUAL CAPABLE OF REPRODUCING BACK AT THE NEST IS THE COMMANDER, THE QUEEN.
ALL OTHER INDIVIDUALS SIMPLY OBEY HER ORDERS.
THE MAGATAMA AMENOTORI HAS BEEN SPREADING AROUND IS MUCH LIKE A WORKER BEE.
Worker

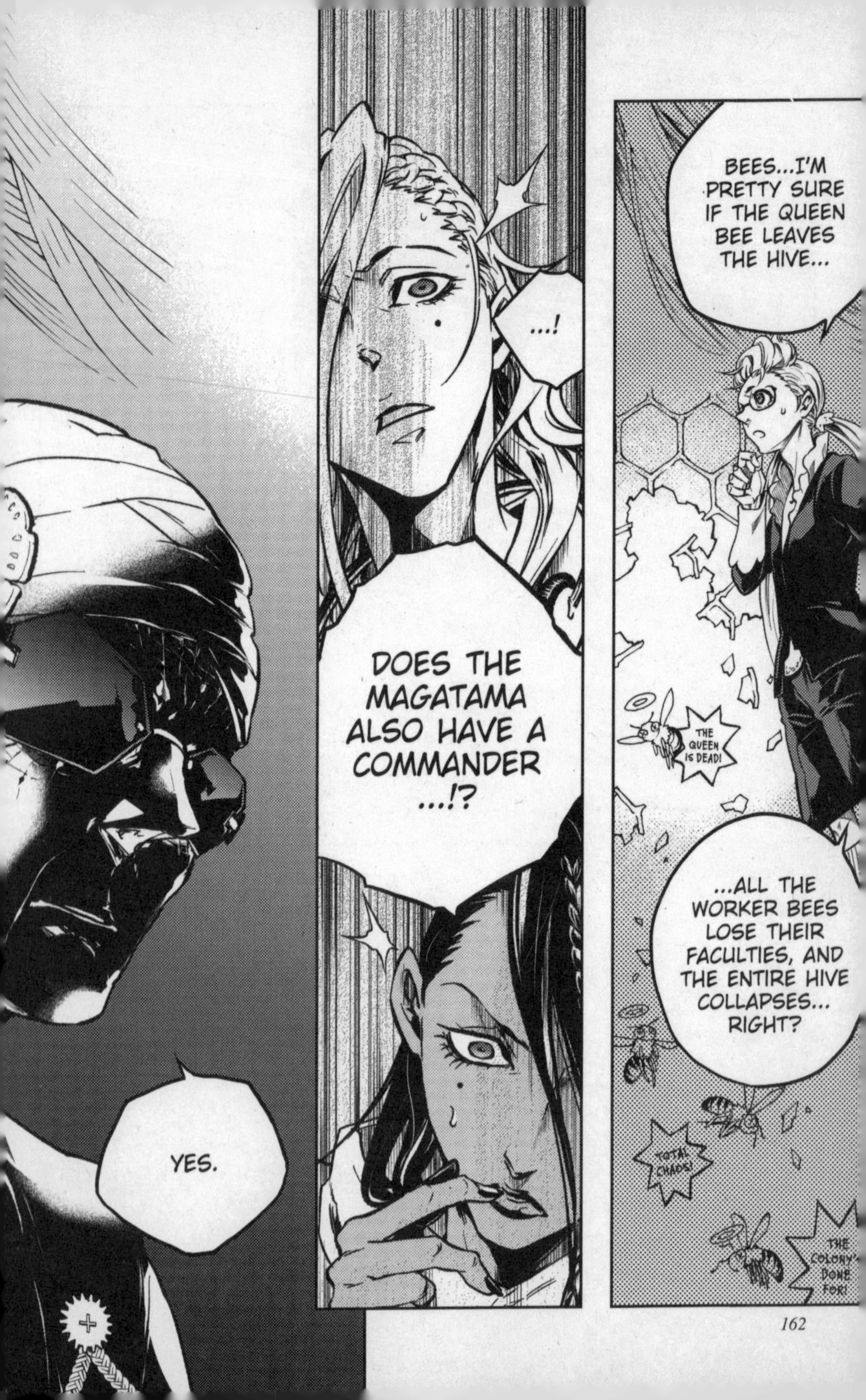
BEES...I'M PRETTY SURE IF THE QUEEN BEE LEAVES THE HIVE...
THE QUEEN IS DEAD!
...ALL THE WORKER BEES LOSE THEIR FACULTIES, AND THE ENTIRE HIVE COLLAPSES... RIGHT?
TOTAL CHAOS!
THE COLONY'S DONE FOR!
...!
DOES THE MAGATAMA ALSO HAVE A COMMANDER ...!?
YES.

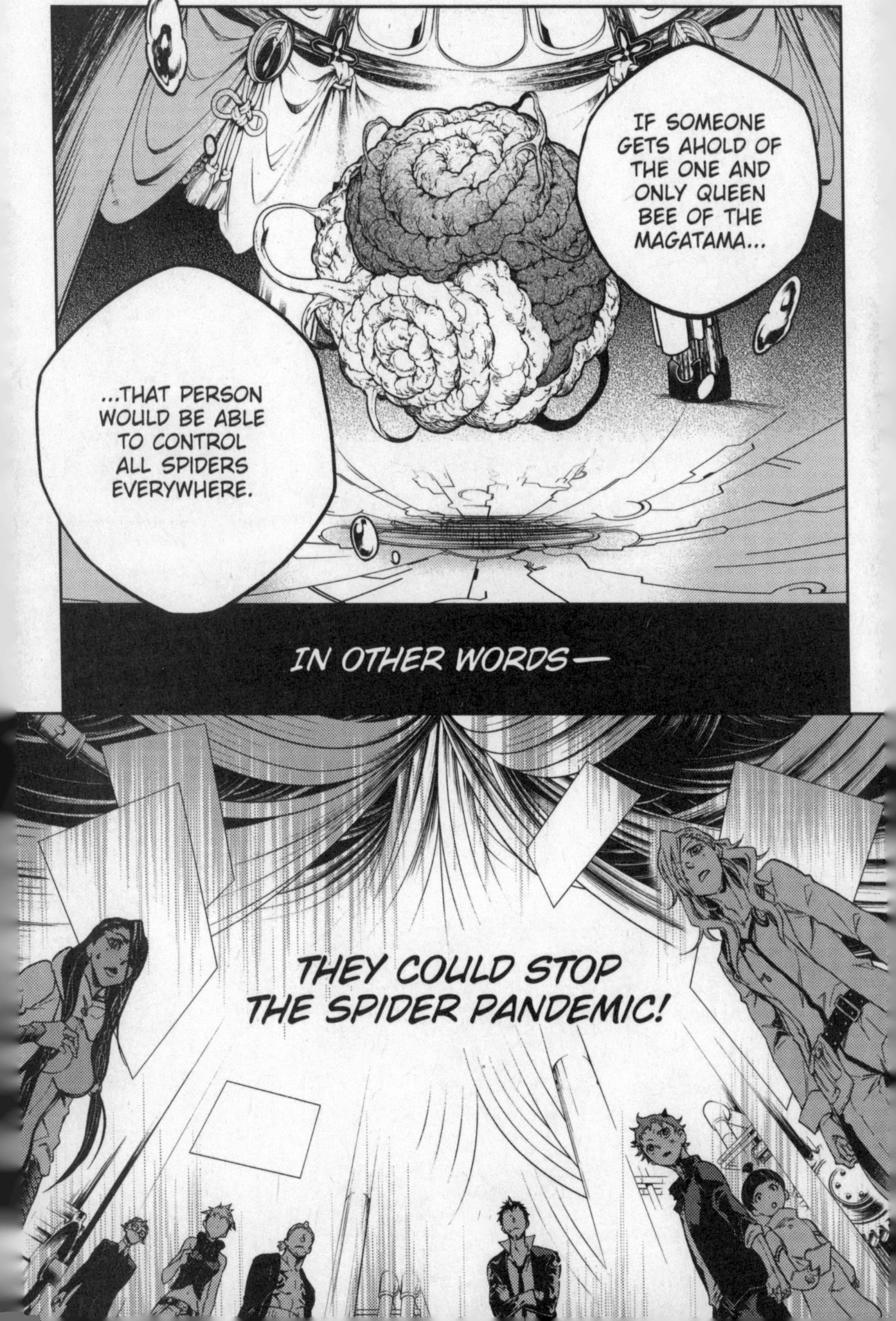
IF SOMEONE GETS AHOLD OF THE ONE AND ONLY QUEEN BEE OF THE MAGATAMA...
...THAT PERSON WOULD BE ABLE TO CONTROL ALL SPIDERS EVERYWHERE.
IN OTHER WORDS—
THEY COULD STOP THE SPIDER PANDEMIC!

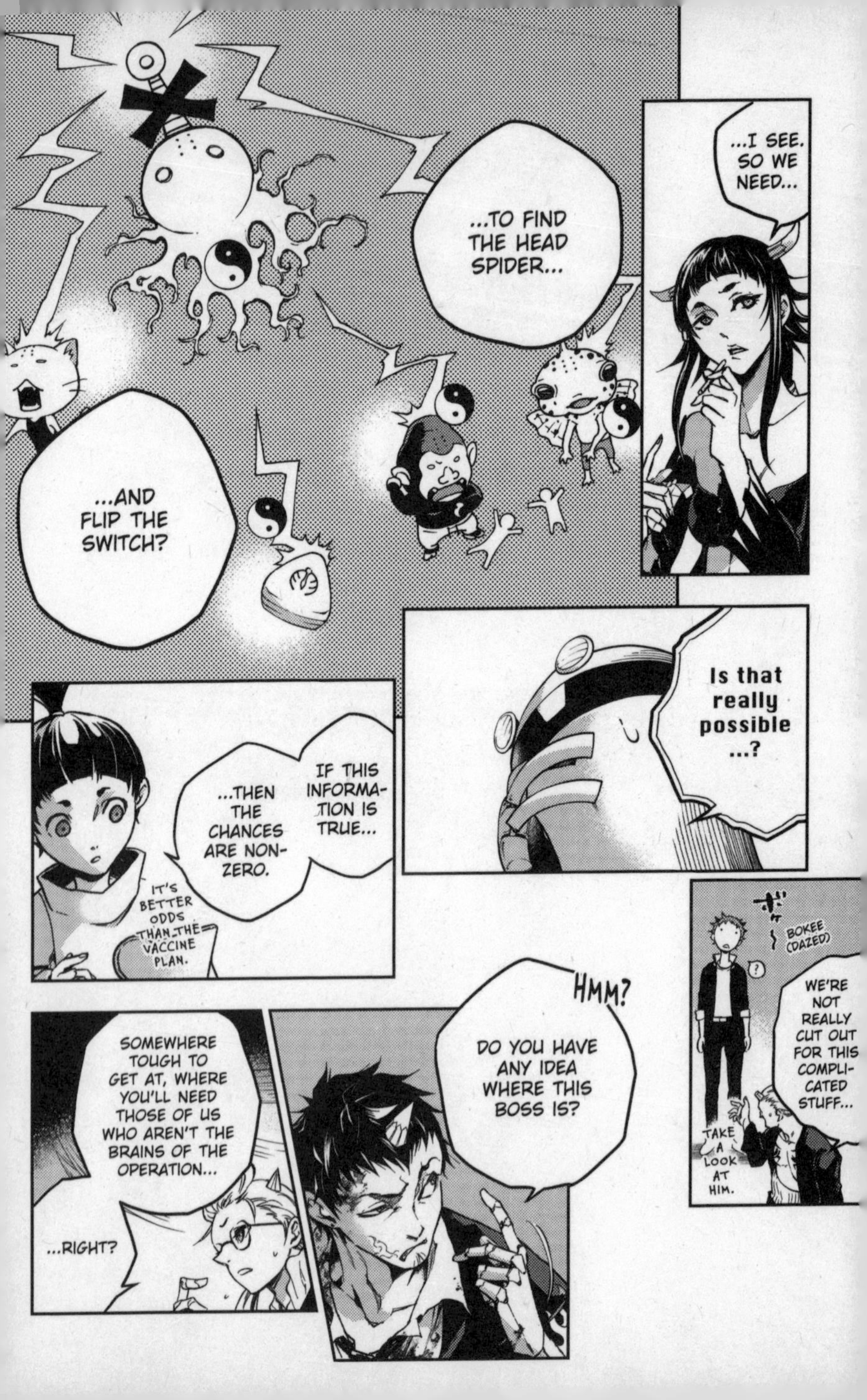
...I SEE. SO WE NEED...
...TO FIND THE HEAD SPIDER...
...AND FLIP THE SWITCH?
Is that really possible ...?
IF THIS INFORMATION IS TRUE...
...THEN THE CHANCES ARE NON-ZERO.
IT'S BETTER ODDS THAN THE VACCINE PLAN.
BOKEE (DAZED)
WE'RE NOT REALLY CUT OUT FOR THIS COMPLICATED STUFF...
TAKE A LOOK AT HIM.
HMM?
DO YOU HAVE ANY IDEA WHERE THIS BOSS IS?
SOMEWHERE TOUGH TO GET AT, WHERE YOU'LL NEED THOSE OF US WHO AREN'T THE BRAINS OF THE OPERATION...
...RIGHT?

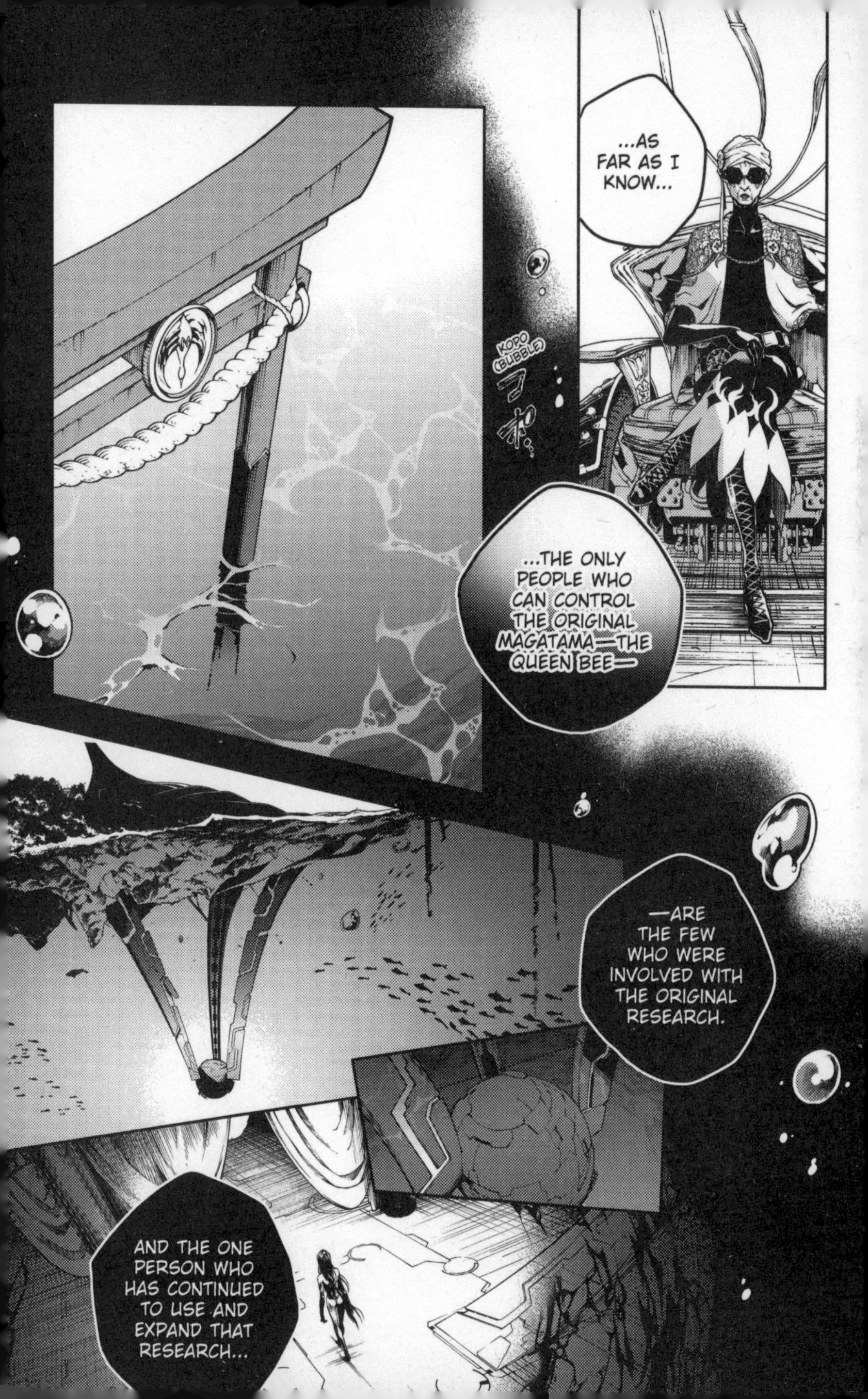
...AS FAR AS I KNOW...
KOPO (BUBBLE)
...THE ONLY PEOPLE WHO CAN CONTROL THE ORIGINAL MAGATAMA—THE QUEEN BEE—
—ARE THE FEW WHO WERE INVOLVED WITH THE ORIGINAL RESEARCH.
AND THE ONE PERSON WHO HAS CONTINUED TO USE AND EXPAND THAT RESEARCH...

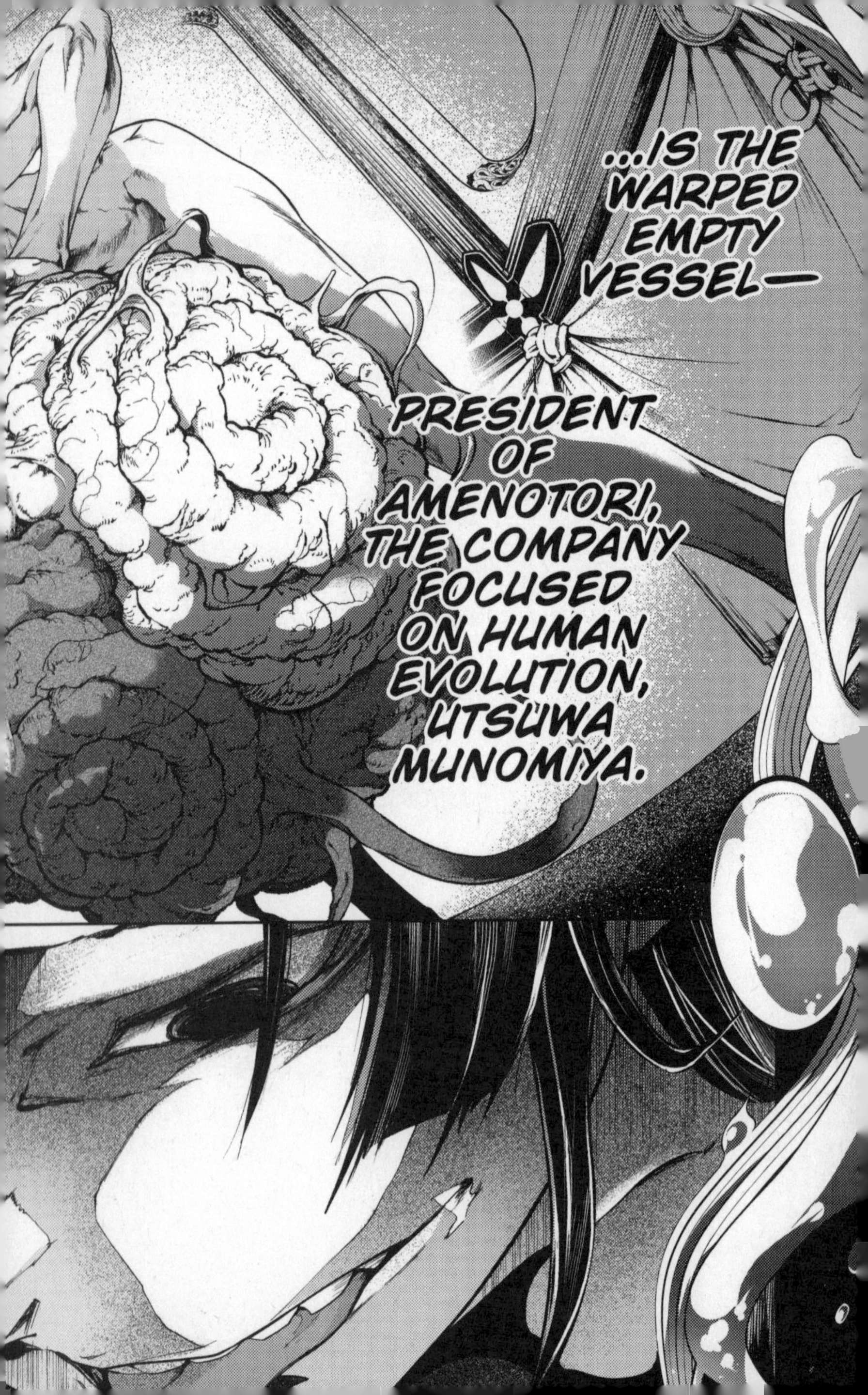
...IS THE WARPED EMPTY VESSEL—
PRESIDENT OF AMENOTORI, THE COMPANY FOCUSED ON HUMAN EVOLUTION, UTSUWA MUNOMIYA.

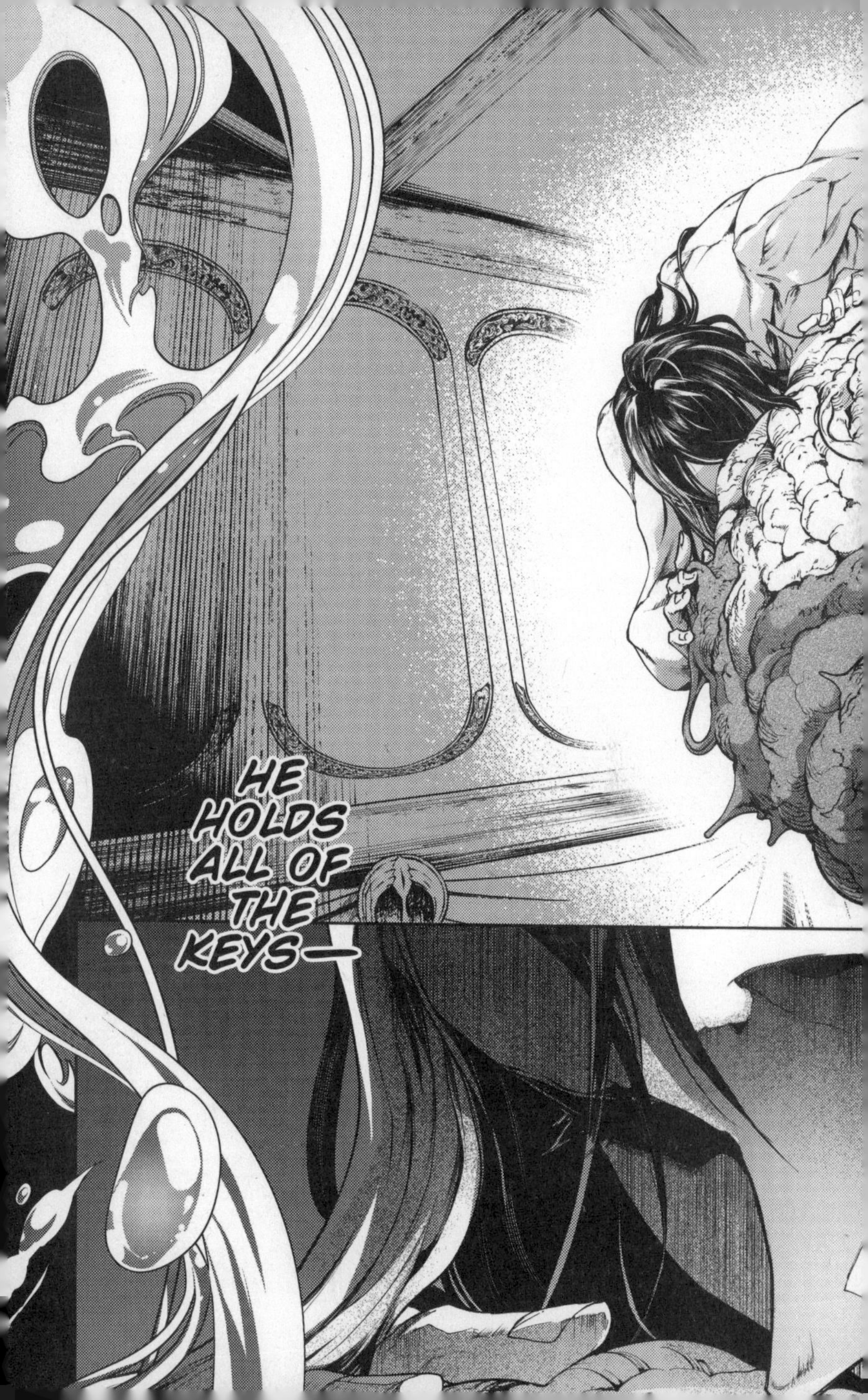
HE HOLDS ALL OF THE KEYS—

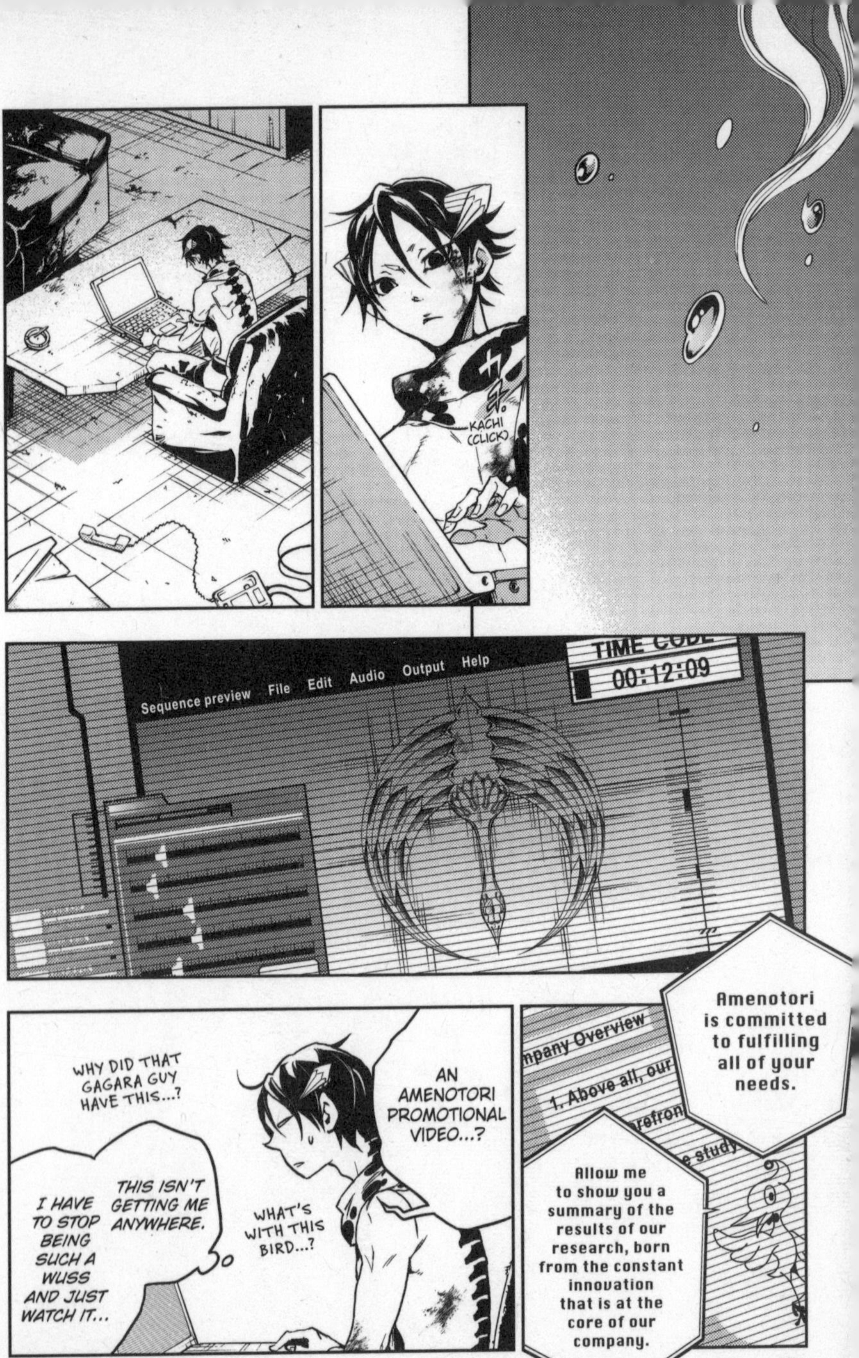
KACHI (CLICK)
Sequence preview File Edit Audio Output Help
TIME CODE
00:12:09
Amenotori is committed to fulfilling all of your needs.
1. Above all, our
Allow me to show you a summary of the results of our research, born from the constant innovation that is at the core of our company.
AN AMENOTORI PROMOTIONAL VIDEO...?
WHY DID THAT GAGARA GUY HAVE THIS...?
WHAT'S WITH THIS BIRD...?
THIS ISN'T GETTING ME ANYWHERE.
I HAVE TO STOP BEING SUCH A WUSS AND JUST WATCH IT...

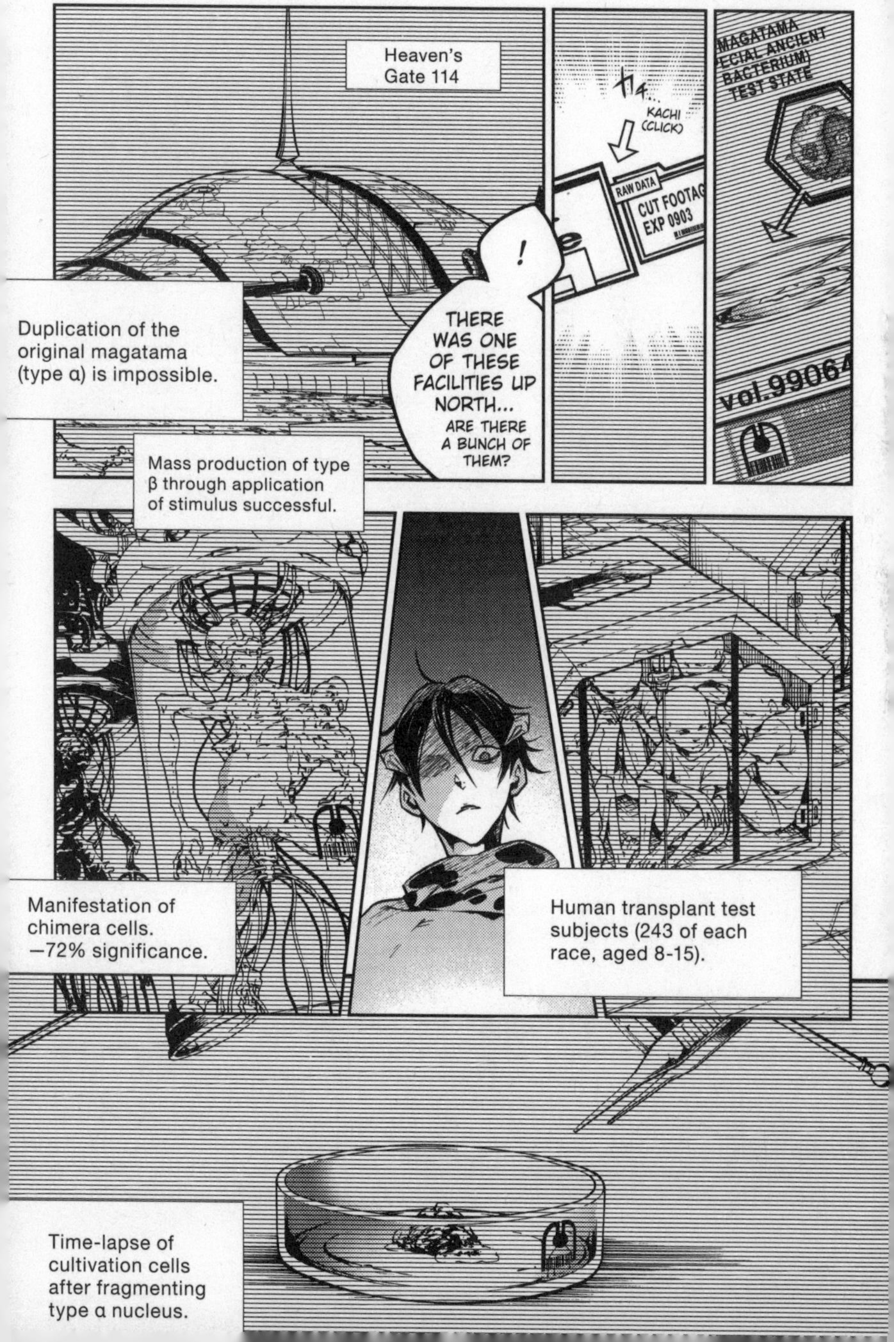
MAGATAMA
ECIAL ANCIENT
BACTERIUM)
TEST STATE
vol.99064
KACHI (CLICK)
RAW DATA
CUT FOOTAG
EXP 0903
!
THERE WAS ONE OF THESE FACILITIES UP NORTH...
ARE THERE A BUNCH OF THEM?
Heaven's Gate 114
Duplication of the original magatama (type α) is impossible.
Mass production of type β through application of stimulus successful.
Human transplant test subjects (243 of each race, aged 8-15).
Manifestation of chimera cells. —72% significance.
Time-lapse of cultivation cells after fragmenting type α nucleus.

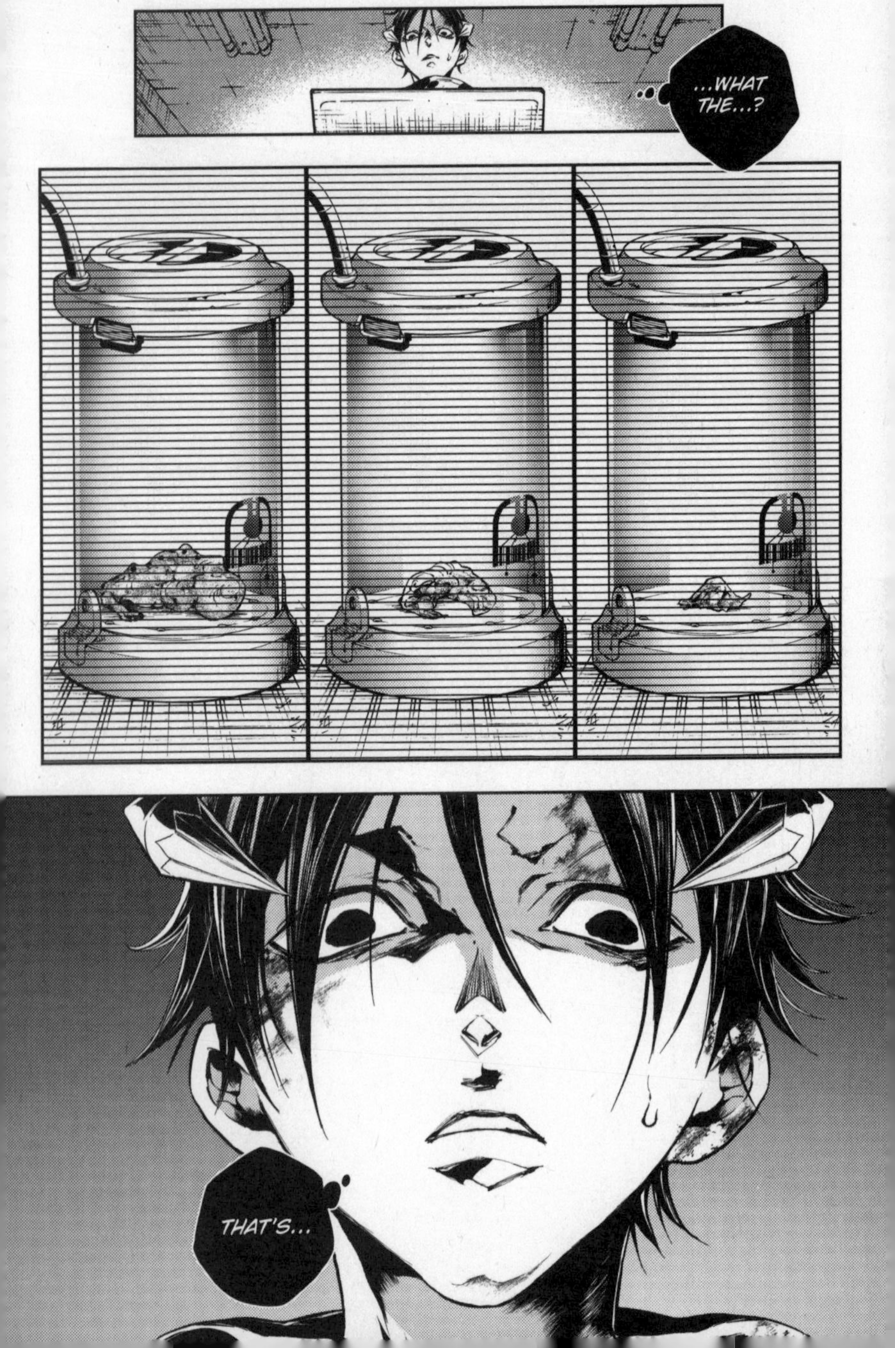
...WHAT THE...?
THAT'S...

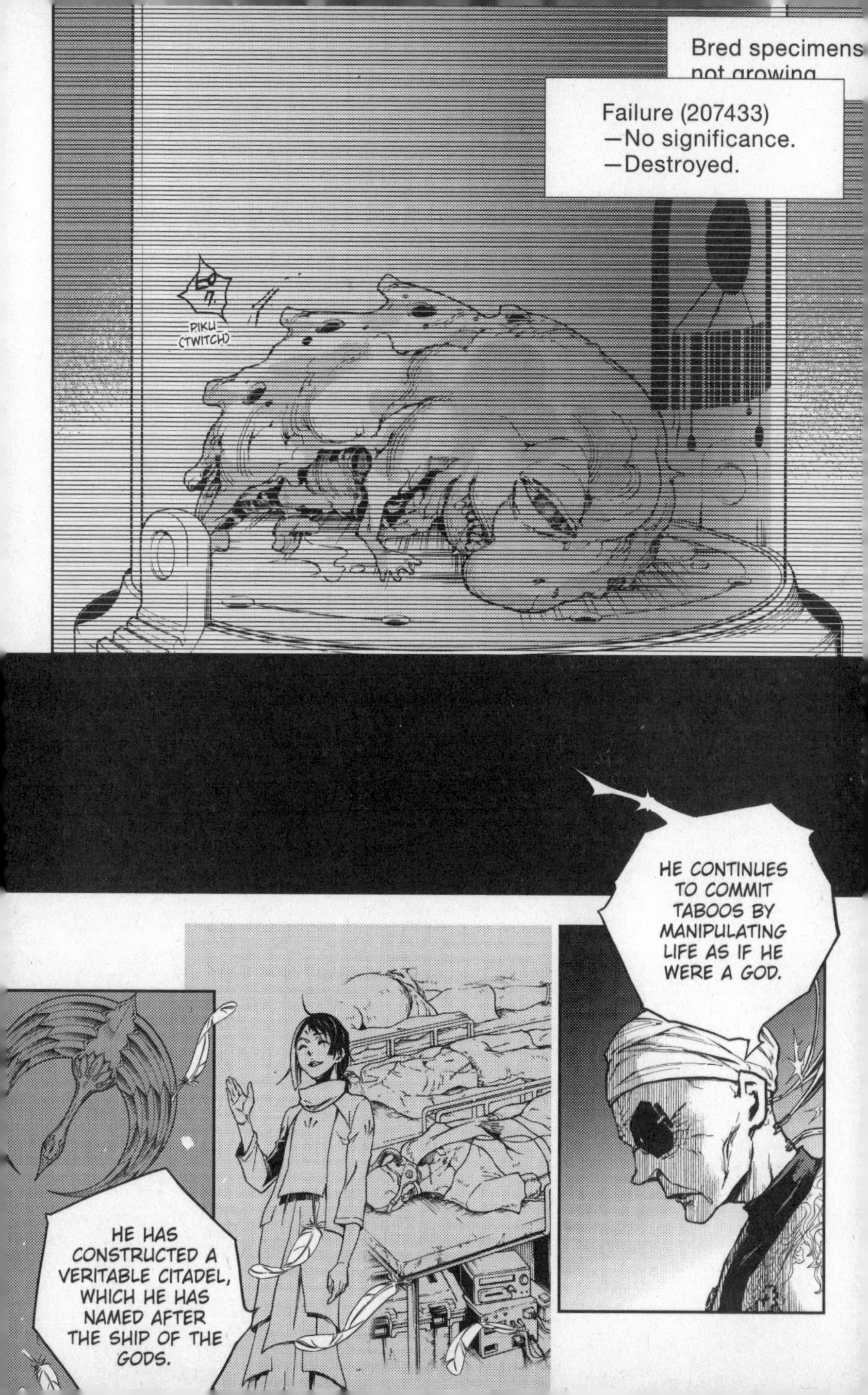

Bred specimens not growing
Failure (207433)
—No significance.
—Destroyed.
PIKU (TWITCH)
HE CONTINUES TO COMMIT TABOOS BY MANIPULATING LIFE AS IF HE WERE A GOD.
HE HAS CONSTRUCTED A VERITABLE CITADEL, WHICH HE HAS NAMED AFTER THE SHIP OF THE GODS.

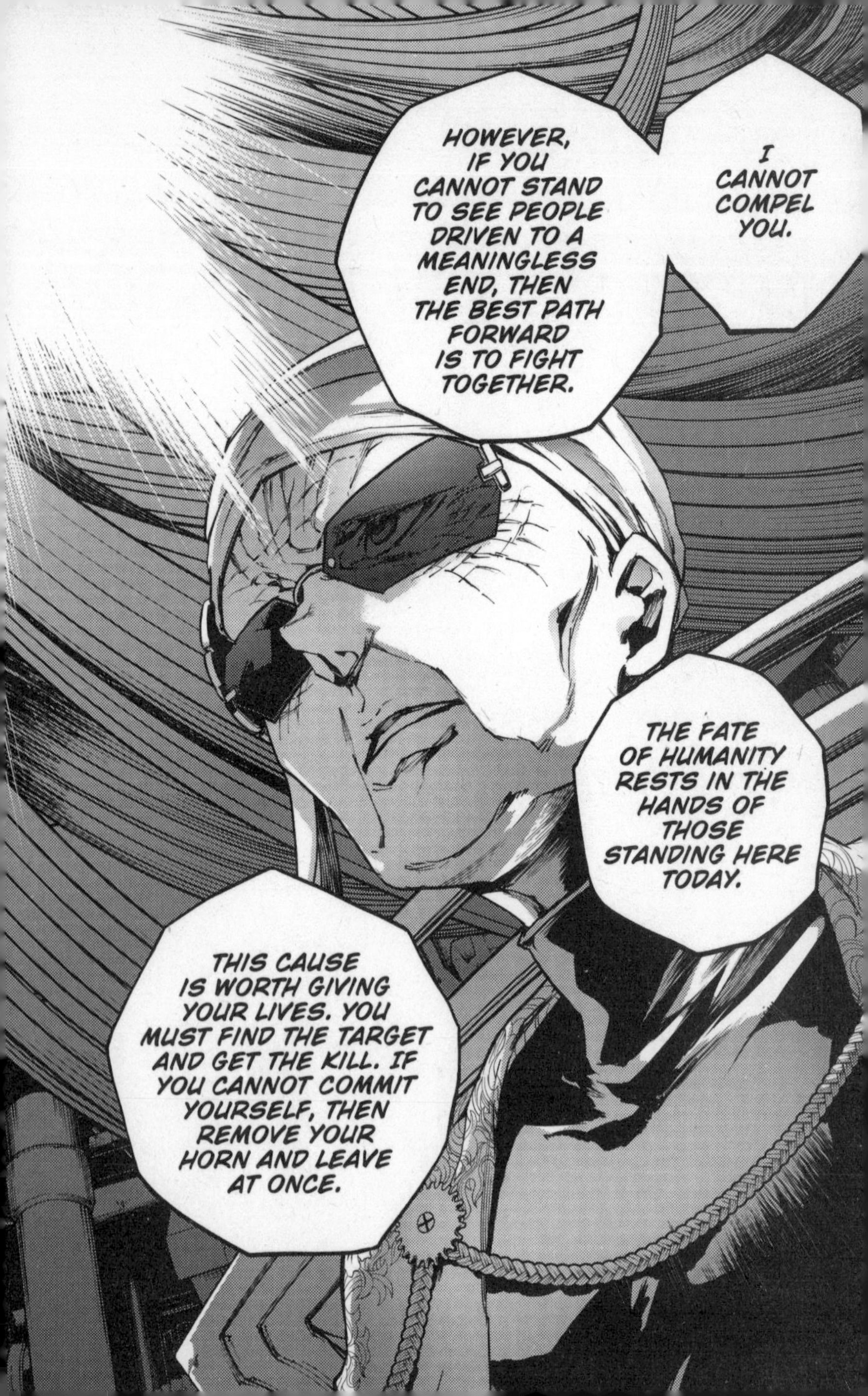
I CANNOT COMPEL YOU.
HOWEVER, IF YOU CANNOT STAND TO SEE PEOPLE DRIVEN TO A MEANINGLESS END, THEN THE BEST PATH FORWARD IS TO FIGHT TOGETHER.
THE FATE OF HUMANITY RESTS IN THE HANDS OF THOSE STANDING HERE TODAY.
THIS CAUSE IS WORTH GIVING YOUR LIVES. YOU MUST FIND THE TARGET AND GET THE KILL. IF YOU CANNOT COMMIT YOURSELF, THEN REMOVE YOUR HORN AND LEAVE AT ONCE.

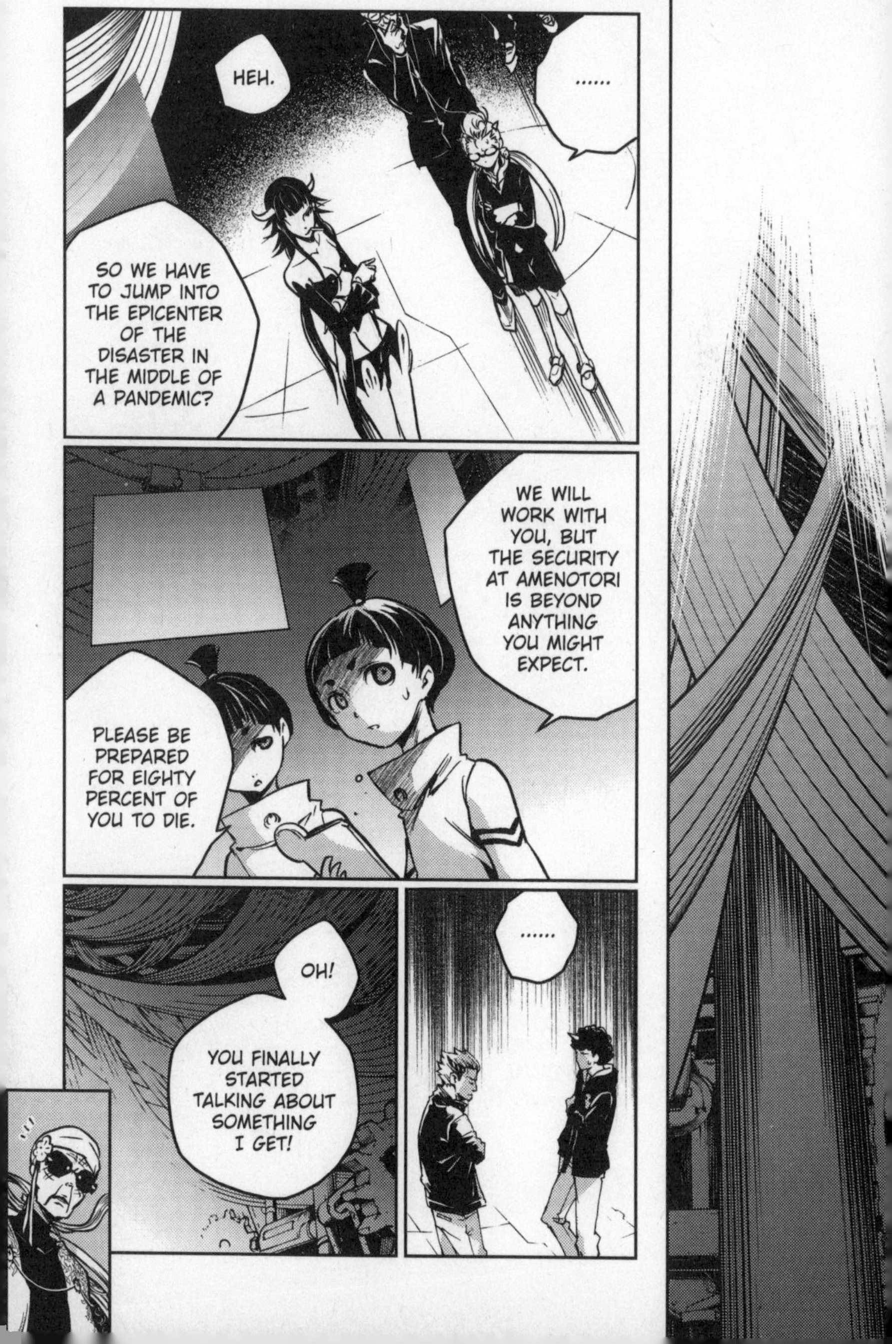
......
HEH.
SO WE HAVE TO JUMP INTO THE EPICENTER OF THE DISASTER IN THE MIDDLE OF A PANDEMIC?
WE WILL WORK WITH YOU, BUT THE SECURITY AT AMENOTORI IS BEYOND ANYTHING YOU MIGHT EXPECT.
PLEASE BE PREPARED FOR EIGHTY PERCENT OF YOU TO DIE.
......
OH!
YOU FINALLY STARTED TALKING ABOUT SOMETHING I GET!

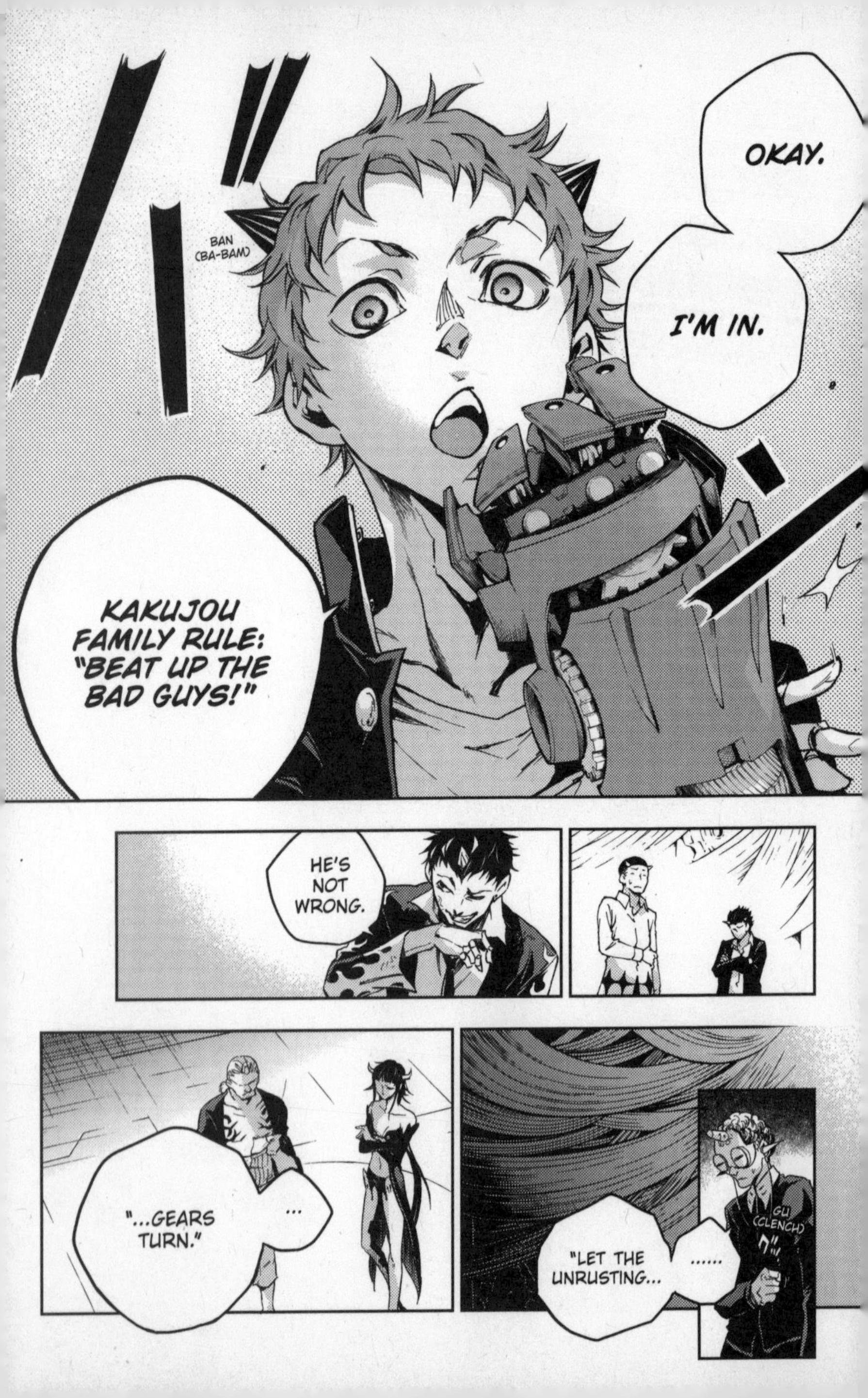
OKAY.
I'M IN.
BAN (BA-BAM)
KAKUJOU FAMILY RULE: "BEAT UP THE BAD GUYS!"
HE'S NOT WRONG.
GU (CLENCH)
......
"LET THE UNRUSTING...
...
"...GEARS TURN."

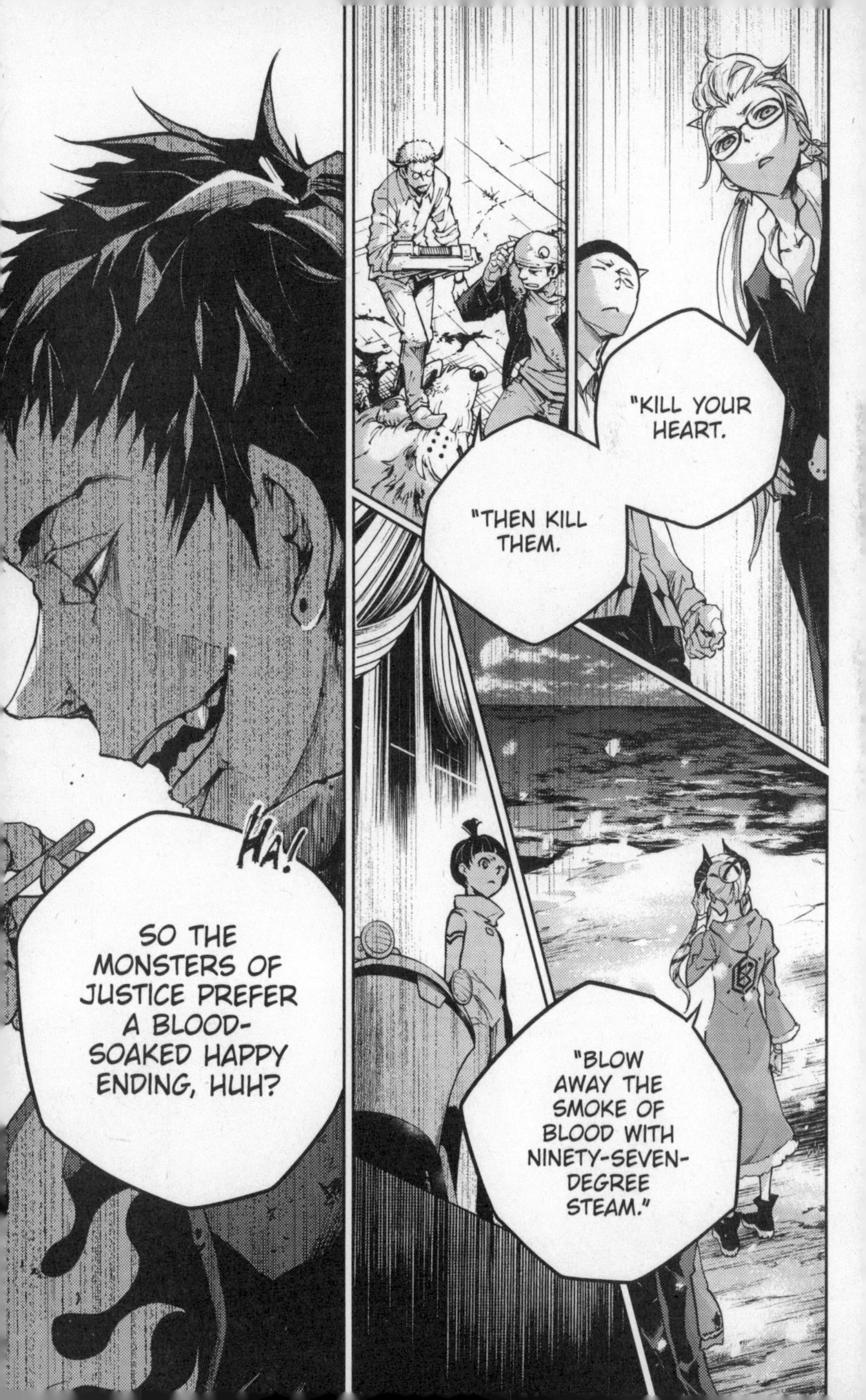
"KILL YOUR HEART.
"THEN KILL THEM.
"BLOW AWAY THE SMOKE OF BLOOD WITH NINETY-SEVEN-DEGREE STEAM."
HA!
SO THE MONSTERS OF JUSTICE PREFER A BLOOD-SOAKED HAPPY ENDING, HUH?

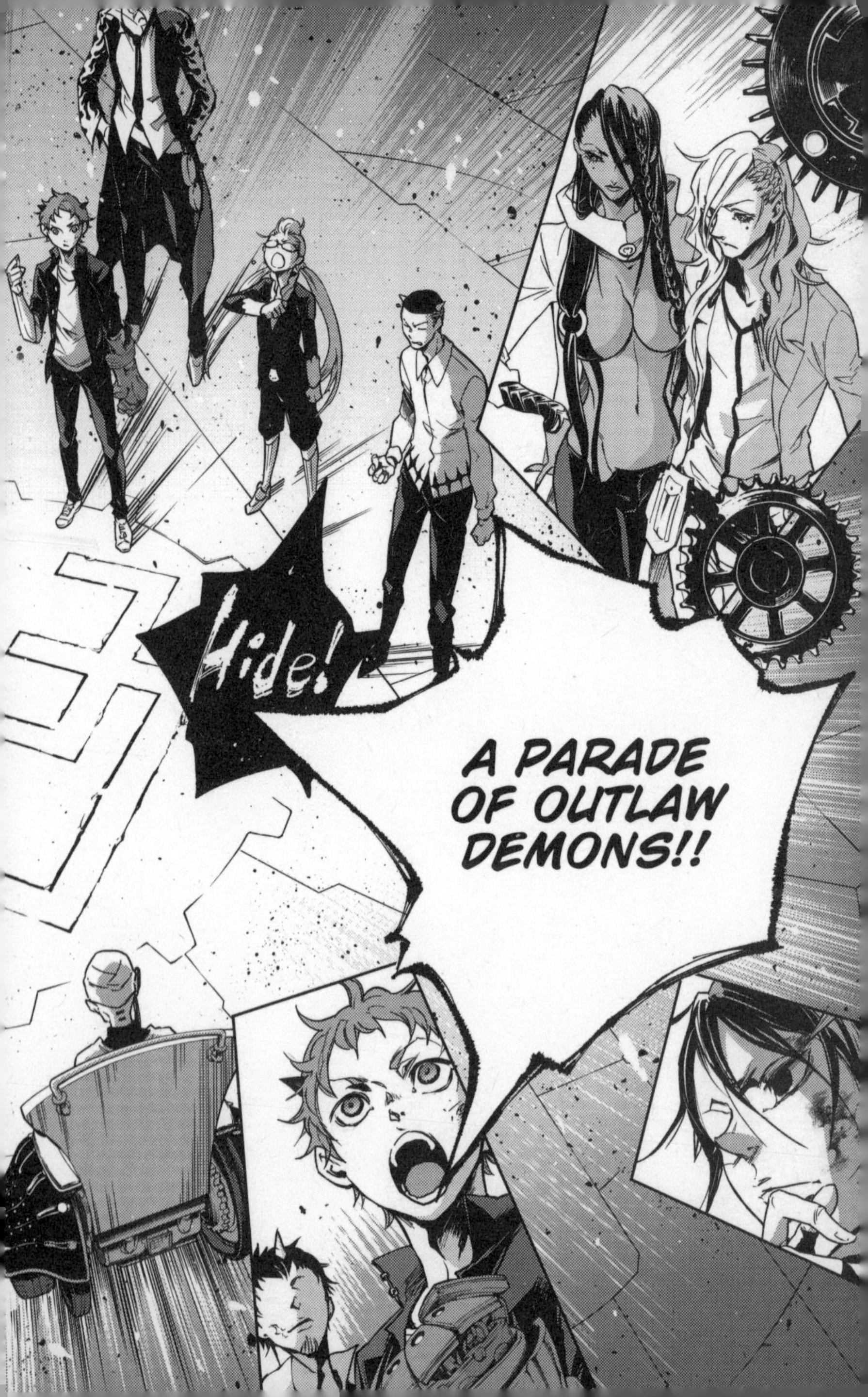
Hide!
A PARADE OF OUTLAW DEMONS!!

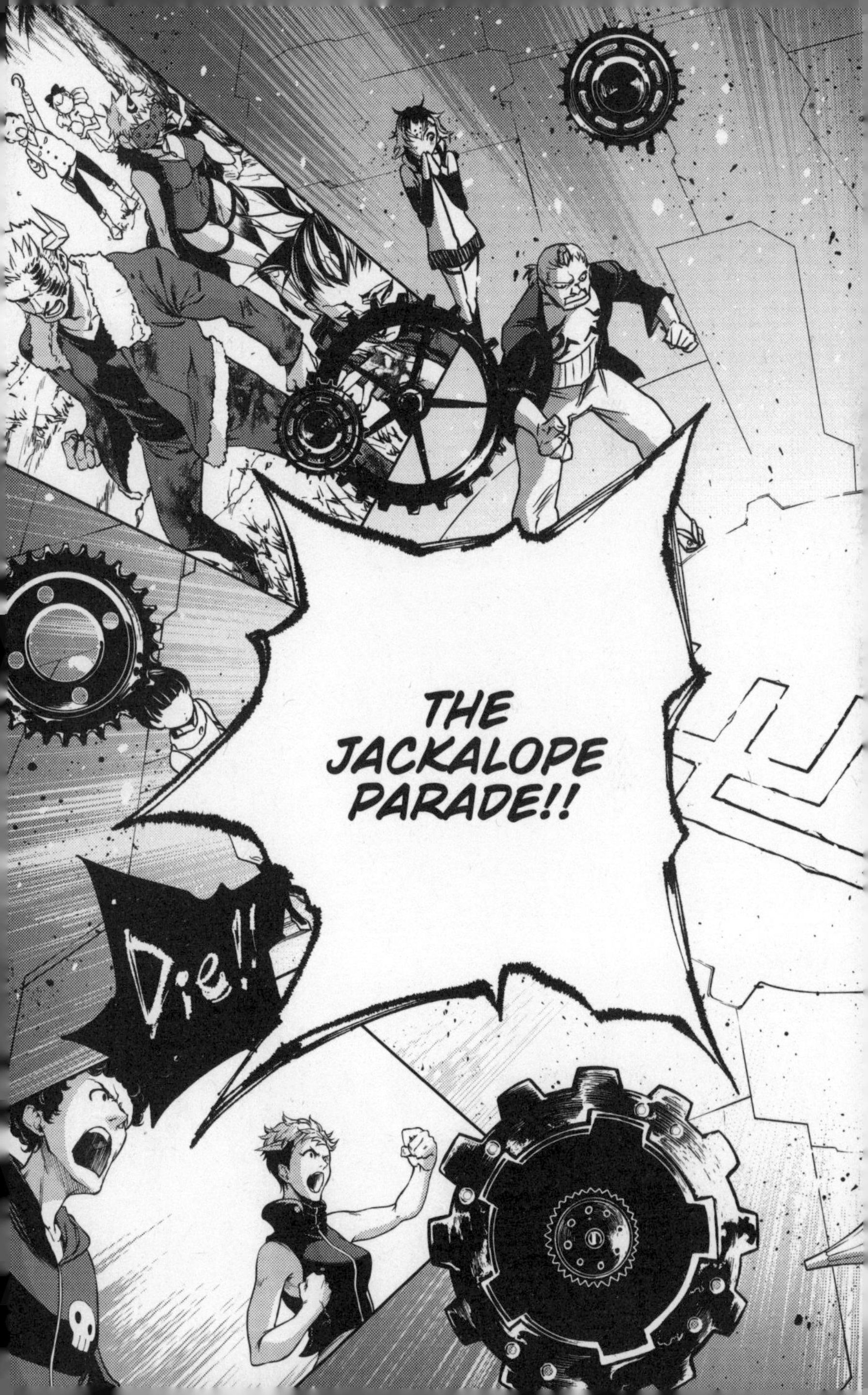
THE JACKALOPE PARADE!!
Die!!

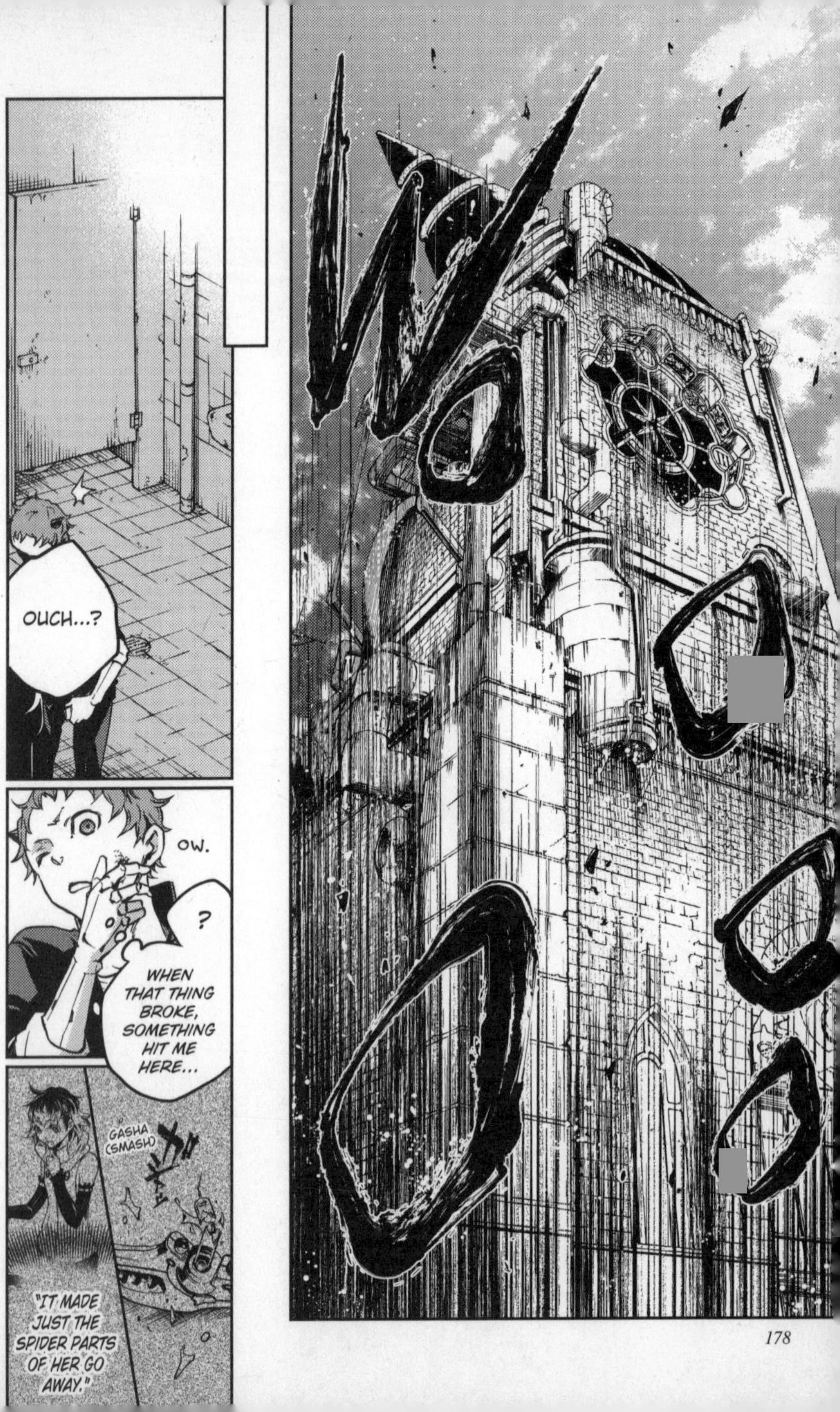
OUCH...?
OW.
?
WHEN THAT THING BROKE, SOMETHING HIT ME HERE...
GASHA (SMASH)
"IT MADE JUST THE SPIDER PARTS OF HER GO AWAY."

松建

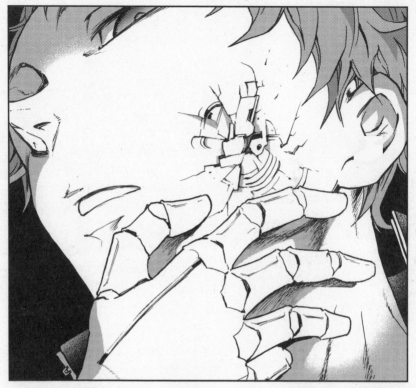

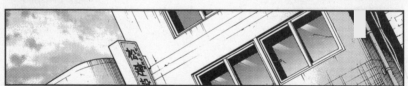

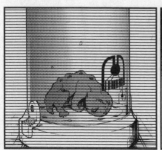

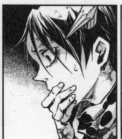

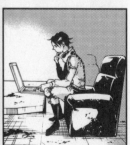

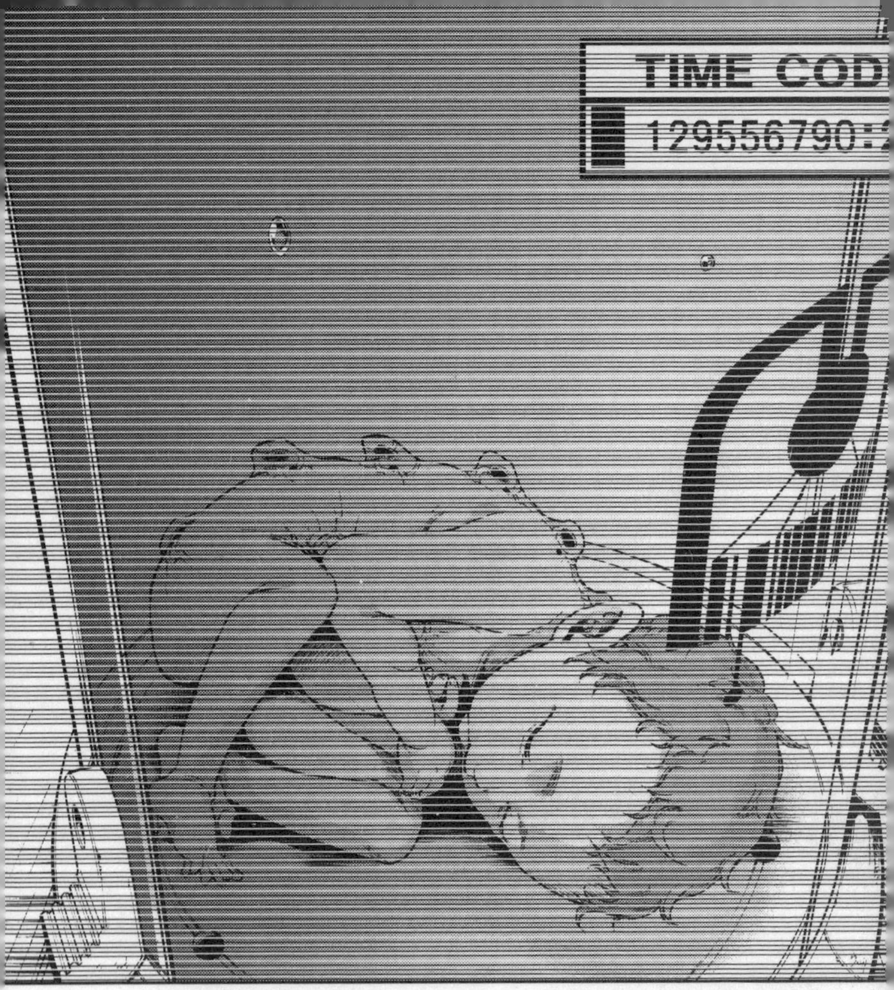
TIME COD
129556790:
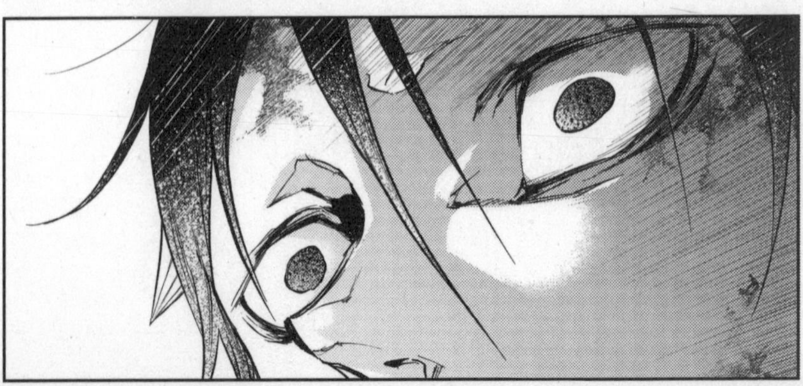

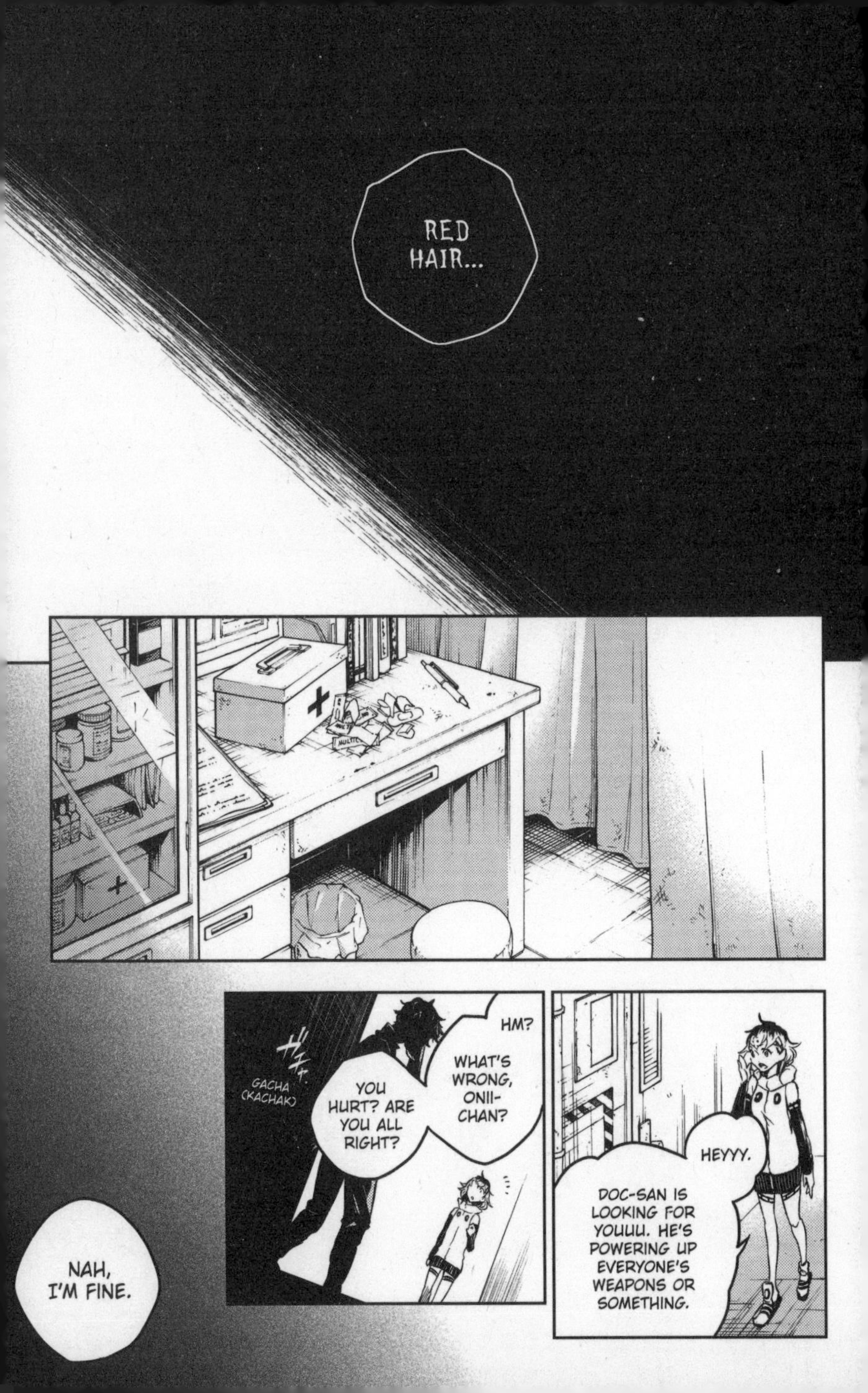
RED HAIR...
HEYYY.
DOC-SAN IS LOOKING FOR YOUUU. HE'S POWERING UP EVERYONE'S WEAPONS OR SOMETHING.
HM?
WHAT'S WRONG, ONII-CHAN?
YOU HURT? ARE YOU ALL RIGHT?
GACHA (KACHAK)
NAH, I'M FINE.

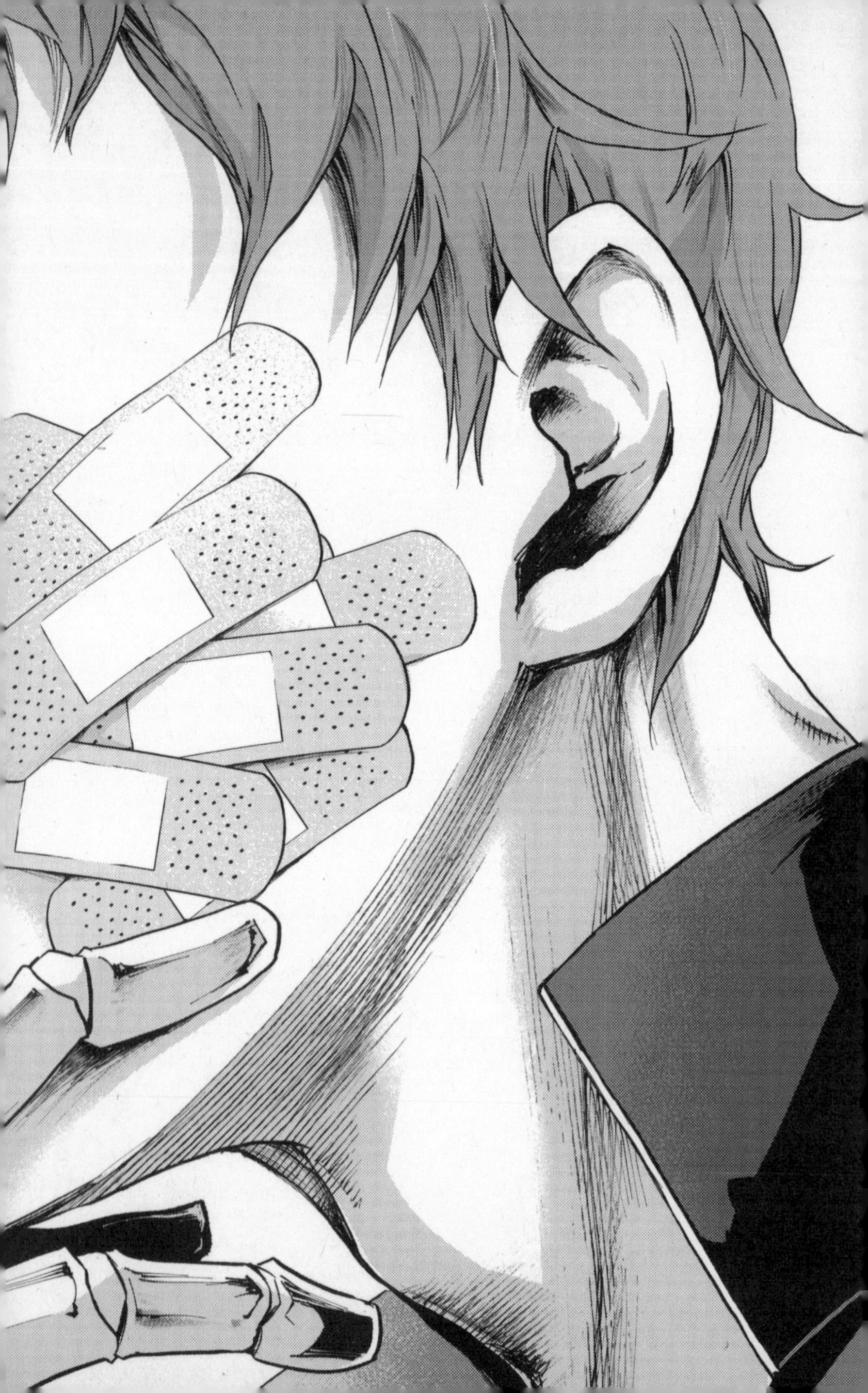

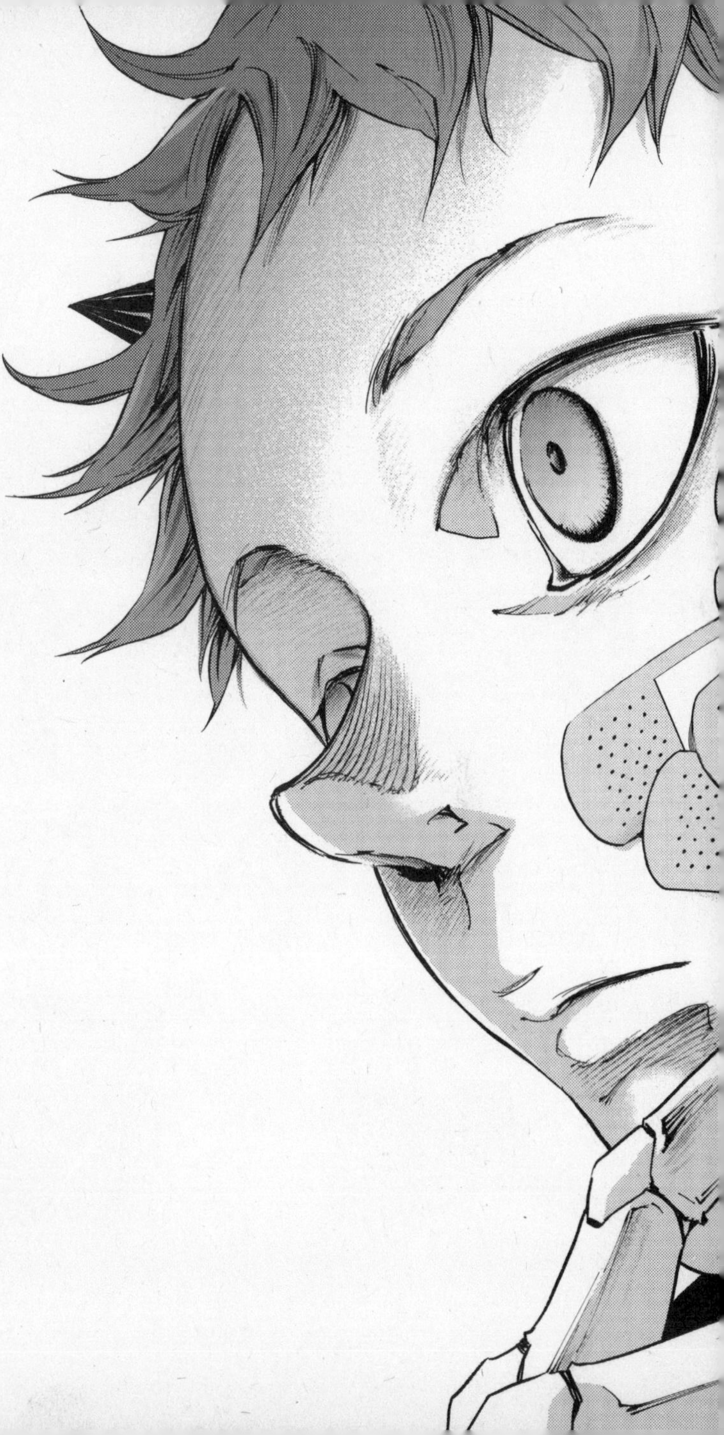

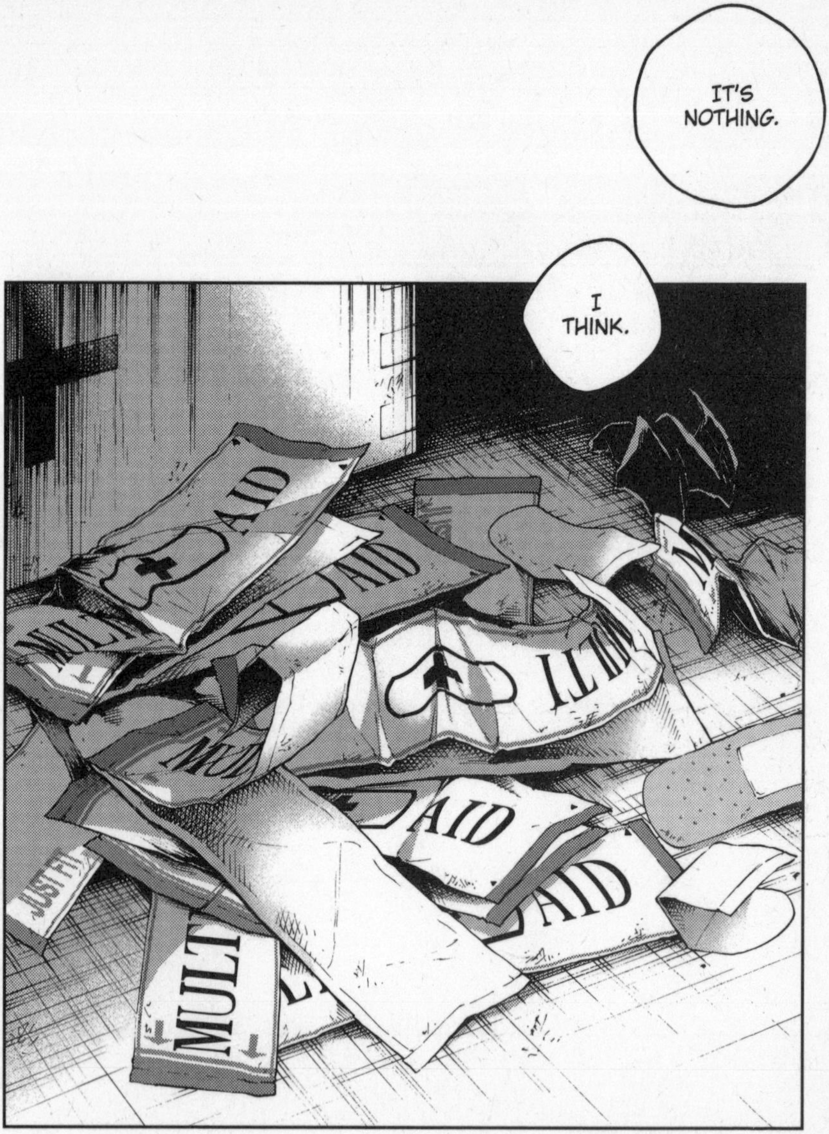
IT'S NOTHING.
I THINK.

SMOKIN' PARADE

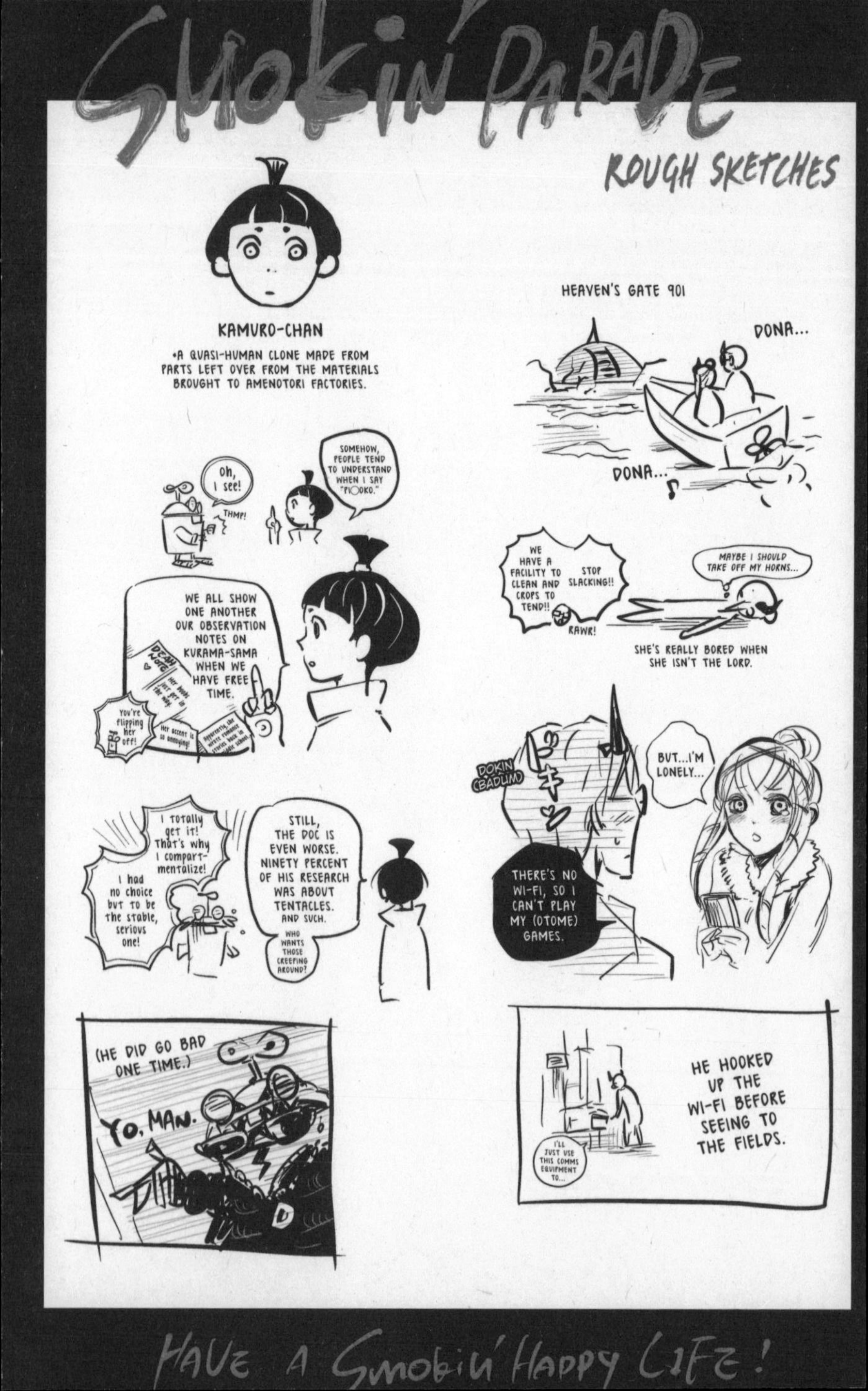
SMOKIN' PARADE
ROUGH SKETCHES
HEAVEN'S GATE 901
DONA...
DONA...
WE HAVE A FACILITY TO CLEAN AND CROPS TO TEND!!
STOP SLACKING!!
RAWR!
MAYBE I SHOULD TAKE OFF MY HORNS...
SHE'S REALLY BORED WHEN SHE ISN'T THE LORD.
BUT...I'M LONELY...
DOKIN (BADUM)
THERE'S NO WI-FI, SO I CAN'T PLAY MY (OTOME) GAMES.
HE HOOKED UP THE WI-FI BEFORE SEEING TO THE FIELDS.
I'LL JUST USE THIS COMMS EQUIPMENT TO...
KAMURO-CHAN
•A QUASI-HUMAN CLONE MADE FROM PARTS LEFT OVER FROM THE MATERIALS BROUGHT TO AMENOTORI FACTORIES.
SOMEHOW, PEOPLE TEND TO UNDERSTAND WHEN I SAY "PI◯OKO."
Oh, I see!
THMP!
WE ALL SHOW ONE ANOTHER OUR OBSERVATION NOTES ON KURAMA-SAMA WHEN WE HAVE FREE TIME.
DEATH NOTE
Her boobs just get in the way.
Apparently, she wrote romance stories back in
Her accent is so annoying!
You're flipping her off!
STILL, THE DOC IS EVEN WORSE. NINETY PERCENT OF HIS RESEARCH WAS ABOUT TENTACLES. AND SUCH.
WHO WANTS THOSE CREEPING AROUND?
I totally get it! That's why I compartmentalize!
I had no choice but to be the stable, serious one!
(HE DID GO BAD ONE TIME.)
YO, MAN.
HAVE A Smokin' Happy LIFE!

TRANSLATION NOTES

PAGES 62-63

The "divine boat" Kurama references is the *Ame-no-torifune* (literally "Heavenly Bird Boat"), which comes from Japanese mythology, referring both to an actual boat that the gods used to travel to the heavens and a divine incarnation of that boat. Amenotori takes its very name from this ship, indicating their willingness to "play god" in their research endeavors and perhaps lead humanity to a "higher" plane.

The "sinking ship" refers to the mud boat in the folktale "*Kachi Kachi Yama*." The boat, literally made from mud, dissolves in the water. The term can be used for an organization or plan that's doomed to fail quickly.

PAGE 186

"Dona Dona" is a Yiddish language song about a calf being sent to slaughter. It's been translated into multiple languages around the world, including Japanese and Russian.

Otome ("maiden") games are story-based video games targeted toward women, and usually take the form of visual novels and dating simulations.

Pinoko is a character from the manga *Black Jack*. Originally the sentient remains of a conjoined twin who was left inside her own sister as a tumor, the surgeon Black Jack removes Pinoko from her sister's body and constructs an artificial body for Pinoko. Pinoko winds up being a regular part of the manga as Black Jack's assistant and companion.

Our Last CRUSADE *New World*
OR THE RISE OF A

KIMI TO BOKU NO SAIGO NO SENJO,
ARUI WA SEKAI GA HAJIMARU SEISEN
©okama 2019 / HAKUSENSHA, Inc.
©2018 Kei Sazane · Ao Nekonabe / KADOKAWA
THE WAR ENDS THE WORLD / RAISES THE WORLD
©Kei Sazane, Ao Nekonabe 2017
/ KADOKAWA CORPORATION

LIGHT NOVEL

MANGA

LOVE IS A BATTLEFIELD

AVAILABLE NOW
WHEREVER BOOKS
ARE SOLD!

When a princess and a knight from rival nations
fall in love, will they find a way to end a war
or remain star-crossed lovers forever...?

For more information
visit www.yenpress.com

From the *New York Times* bestselling author of *Durarara!!* comes a light novel series full of mobsters, thieves, and immortals!

BACCANO!

VOLUMES 1-13 AVAILABLE NOW

WWW.YENPRESS.COM

"BACCANO! © RYOHGO NARITA   ILLUSTRATION: KATSUMI ENAMI
KADOKAWA CORPORATION ASCII MEDIA WORKS"

COMBATANTS WILL BE DISPATCHED!

Always bring a gun to a sword fight!

With world domination nearly in their grasp, the Supreme Leaders of the Kisaragi Corporation—an underground criminal group turned evil megacorp—have decided to try their hands at interstellar conquest. A quick dice roll nominates their chief operative, Combat Agent Six, to be the one to explore an alien planet... and the first thing he does when he gets there is change the sacred incantation for a holy ritual to the most embarrassing thing he can think of. But evil deeds are business as usual for Kisaragi operatives, so if Six wants a promotion and a raise, he'll have to work much harder than that! For starters, he'll have to do something about the other group of villains on the planet, who are calling themselves the "Demon Lord's Army" or whatever. After all, this world doesn't need two evil organizations!

AVAILABLE WHEREVER BOOKS ARE SOLD!

LIGHT NOVEL
VOLUMES 1–3

MANGA
VOLUMES 1–2

©Natsume Akatsuki, Kakao • Lanthanum 2017
KADOKAWA CORPORATION
©Masaaki Kiasa 2018 ©Natsume Akatsuki, Kakao • Lanthanum 2018
KADOKAWA CORPORATION

For more information
visit www.yenpress.com

YEN ON   Yen Press

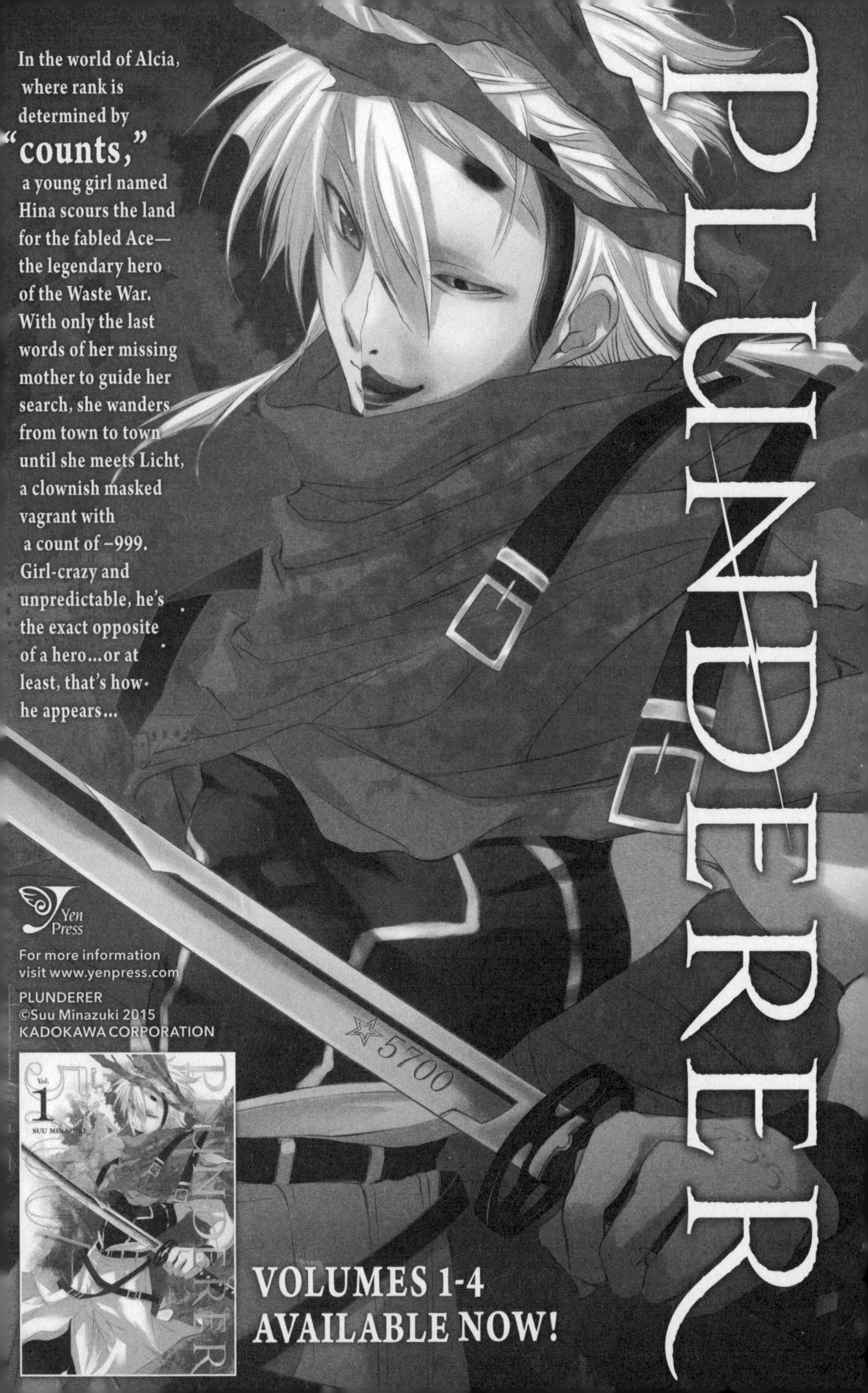
PLUNDERER
In the world of Alcia, where rank is determined by "counts," a young girl named Hina scours the land for the fabled Ace—the legendary hero of the Waste War. With only the last words of her missing mother to guide her search, she wanders from town to town until she meets Licht, a clownish masked vagrant with a count of −999. Girl-crazy and unpredictable, he's the exact opposite of a hero...or at least, that's how he appears...
5700
Yen Press
For more information visit www.yenpress.com
PLUNDERER
©Suu Minazuki 2015
KADOKAWA CORPORATION
VOLUMES 1-4
AVAILABLE NOW!
Vol. 1
SUU MINAZUKI
PLUNDERER

BUNGO STRAY DOGS

Volumes 1–15
available now

BUNGO STRAY DOGS 01
Story by KAFKA ASAGIRI   Art by SANGO HARUKAWA

If you've already seen the anime, it's time to read the manga!

Having been kicked out of the orphanage, Atsushi Nakajima rescues a strange man from a suicide attempt—Osamu Dazai. Turns out that Dazai is part of a detective agency staffed by individuals whose supernatural powers take on a literary bent!

BUNGO STRAY DOGS © Kafka Asagiri 2013
© Sango Harukawa 2013
KADOKAWA CORPORATION

www.yenpress.com

Yen Press

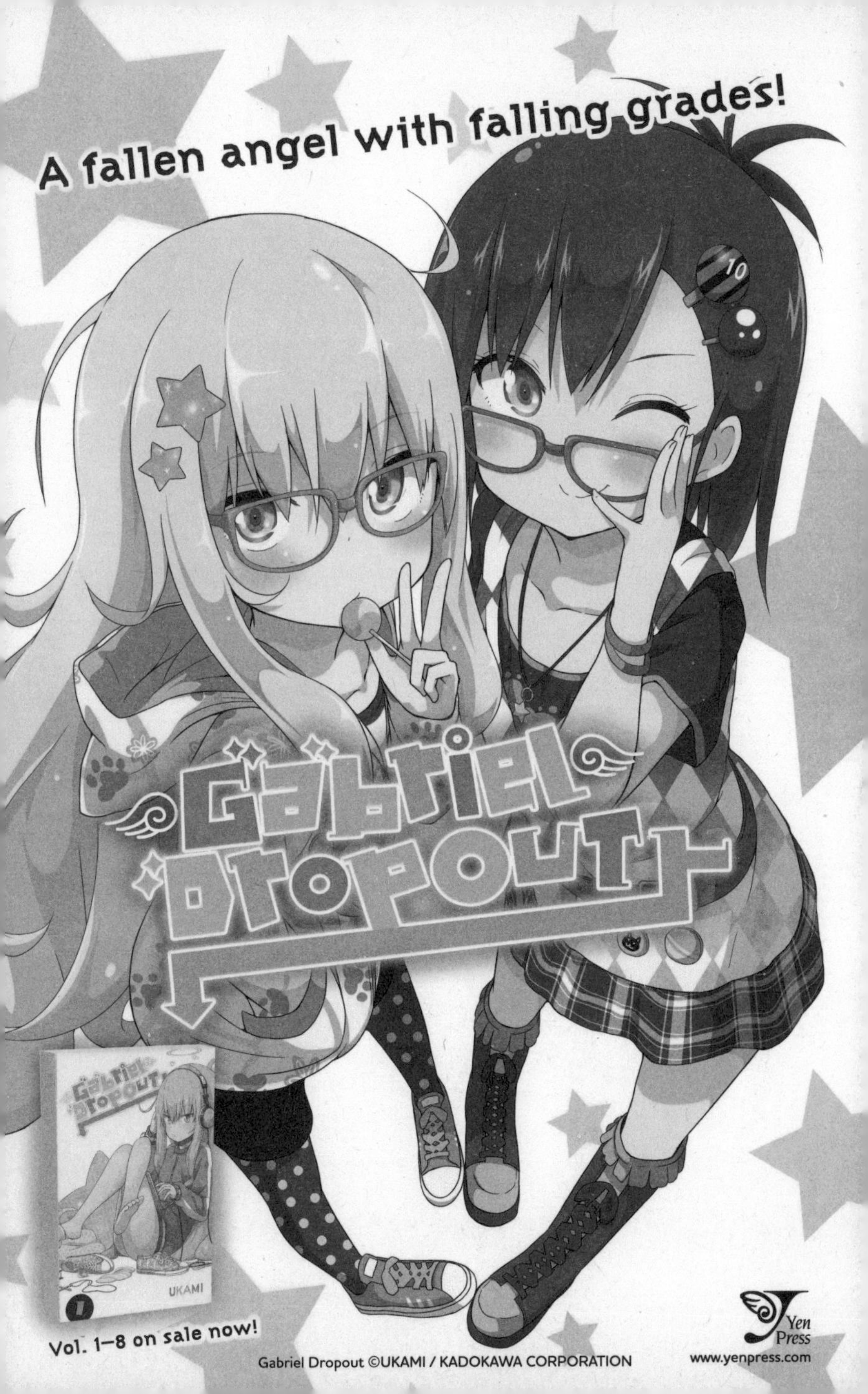
A fallen angel with falling grades!
Gabriel Dropout
Gabriel Dropout
UKAMI
Vol. 1–8 on sale now!
Gabriel Dropout ©UKAMI / KADOKAWA CORPORATION
Yen Press
www.yenpress.com

ENJOY EVERYTHING.

YOU SHOULD COME PLAY WITH YOTSUBA TOO!

Join Yotsuba as she delights in the things many of us take for granted in this Eisner-nominated series.

VOLUMES 1-14
AVAILABLE NOW!

Visit our website at www.yenpress.com.

Yotsuba&! © Kiyohiko Azuma / YOTUBA SUTAZIO

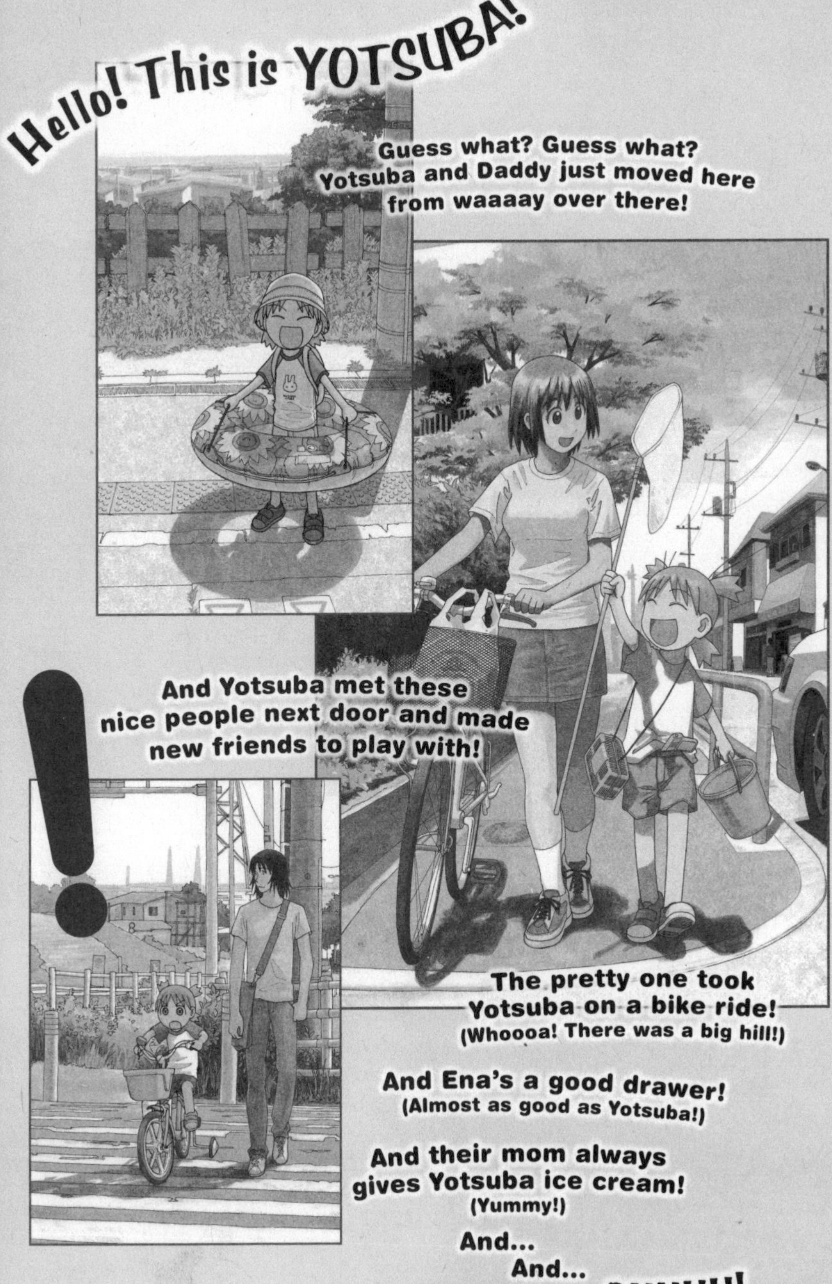
Hello! This is YOTSUBA!
Guess what? Guess what? Yotsuba and Daddy just moved here from waaaay over there!
And Yotsuba met these nice people next door and made new friends to play with!
!
The pretty one took Yotsuba on a bike ride!
(Whoooa! There was a big hill!)
And Ena's a good drawer!
(Almost as good as Yotsuba!)
And their mom always gives Yotsuba ice cream!
(Yummy!)
And...
And...
OHHHH!

SMOKIN' PARADE #08

By Jinsei Kataoka, Kazuma Kondou

Translation: Leighann Harvey
Lettering: Abigail Blackman

This book is a work of fiction. Names, characters, places, and incidents are the product of the author's imagination or are used fictitiously. Any resemblance to actual events, locales, or persons, living or dead, is coincidental.

SMOKIN' PARADE Volume 8
©Jinsei Kataoka 2020
©Kazuma Kondou 2020
First published in Japan in 2020 by KADOKAWA CORPORATION, Tokyo. English translation rights arranged with KADOKAWA CORPORATION, Tokyo through TUTTLE-MORI AGENCY, INC., Tokyo.

English translation © 2020 by Yen Press, LLC

Yen Press, LLC supports the right to free expression and the value of copyright. The purpose of copyright is to encourage writers and artists to produce the creative works that enrich our culture.

The scanning, uploading, and distribution of this book without permission is a theft of the author's intellectual property. If you would like permission to use material from the book (other than for review purposes), please contact the publisher. Thank you for your support of the author's rights.

Yen Press
150 West 30th Street, 19th Floor
New York, NY 10001

Visit us at yenpress.com
facebook.com/yenpress
twitter.com/yenpress
yenpress.tumblr.com
instagram.com/yenpress

First Yen Press Edition: August 2020

Yen Press is an imprint of Yen Press, LLC.
The Yen Press name and logo are trademarks of Yen Press, LLC.

The publisher is not responsible for websites (or their content) that are not owned by the publisher.

Library of Congress Control Number: 2016958477

ISBNs: 978-1-9753-1552-8 (paperback)
       978-1-9753-1553-5 (ebook)

10 9 8 7 6 5 4 3 2 1

WOR

Printed in the United States of America